Wild Turkeys in Texas

Perspectives on South Texas
Sponsored by Texas A&M University–Kingsville
Timothy E. Fulbright, General Editor

Wild Turkeys in Texas

Ecology and Management

William P. Kuvlesky Jr., Leonard A. Brennan, J. Alfonso Ortega-S., Damon L. Williford, Jason B. Hardin, Humberto L. Perotto-Baldivieso, Landon C. Fritz, Clayton D. Hilton, Fred C. Bryant, Steve A. Nelle, Brandon M. Mitchell, and Nova J. Silvy

Foreword by James Earl Kennamer

TEXAS A&M UNIVERSITY PRESS COLLEGE STATION

First edition

This paper meets the requirements of ANSI/NISO Z39.48–1992
(Permanence of Paper).
Binding materials have been chosen for durability.
Manufactured in China through Four Colour Print Group.

Library of Congress Cataloging-in-Publication Data

Names: Kuvlesky, William P. Jr., author. | Brennan, Leonard A. (Leonard Alfred), author. | Ortega-S., J. Alfonso, author. | Williford, Damon L., author.
Title: Wild turkeys in Texas : ecology and management / William P. Kuvlesky Jr., Leonard A. Brennan, J. Alfonso Ortega-S., Damon L. Williford, Jason B. Hardin, Humberto L. Perotto-Baldivieso, Landon C. Fritz, Clayton D. Hilton, Fred C. Bryant, Steve A. Nelle, Brandon M. Mitchell, Nova J. Silvy ; foreword by James Earl Kennamer.
Other titles: Perspectives on south Texas.
Description: First edition. | College Station : Texas A&M University Press, [2020] | Series: Perspectives on south Texas | Includes bibliographical references and index.
Identifiers: LCCN 2019052020 | ISBN 9781623498559 (hardcover) | ISBN 9781623498566 (ebook)
Subjects: LCSH: Wild turkey—Ecology—Texas. | Wild turkey—Habitat—Conservation—Texas. | Game bird management—Texas.
Classification: LCC QL696.G27 .K88 2020 | DDC 598.6/4509764—dc23
LC record available at https://lccn.loc.gov/2019052020

A list of titles in this series is available at the end of the book.

In Memory of James "Randy" Fugate (1950–2015)

Randy Fugate.

My wife always says it is better to go to funerals than to weddings. She is right, of course. She always is. I just wish it hadn't been Randy's. But, like everyone else who was there, I wouldn't have missed it for the world. Randy was a colleague and a friend, and a fine one at that.

You can tell much about a man by his funeral. And I couldn't help but take comfort that Randy would have loved the setting of his—a beautiful spring day in a fine South Texas town, with a church lot full of country pickups, many with Parks and Wildlife emblems, and many without.

Oh, Randy would have had a big time there, all right. He would have pulled up in a big wake of dust, in that familiar gray TPWD truck of his that hadn't seen a bath in a long while. His bosses would have winced and shaken their heads in unison at the sight, and Randy would have flashed that big toothy grin, telling his passenger that he was going to be in big trouble, going on and on about being put on probation, but knowing, not really. Randy never stayed in trouble very long.

As he pulled in, he would have picked out one of his unwitting game warden or biologist buddies and swerved at them, making them jump, once again laughing all the way with that great big grin of his. He would have gotten out and greeted everyone by name, talking about the country, the game, and the weather.

He would have spoken to all the ladies and asked about their children and families, but most of all, he would have just reveled in the presence of the people whose company he cherished and who cherished him—biologists and game wardens, ranchers and ranch hands, bird-watchers and bird dog men, camp cooks and cowboys, troopers and deputies, families and friends, one and all. He was one of us, and we were one with him.

James "Randy" Fugate was a gentle giant of a man, a welcome and favorite guest around the deer camps, ranch houses, and campfires of South Texas. His presence and ever-present good cheer lit up many a Brush Country locale and all those who were around him. Sadly, he is no longer in it.

Randy was employed as a wildlife biologist by the Texas Parks and Wildlife Department for 42 years. A native son of Cotulla, Randy started his wildlife career working on white-winged doves in the Rio Grande Valley. He and his beloved wife, June, later moved up to Falfurrias and the fabled ranch country, where he worked with the big ranches and their hunters and biologists, advising them on all things deer, dove, turkey, quail, water, waterfowl, and a whole lot more.

The nature of Randy's business was nature. And what a student and steward of it he was. Oh, don't get me wrong. Randy would play the country boy on you if he thought you'd let him get away with it. But behind that big, impish grin of his and that "aw shucks" demeanor was an artesian well of knowledge of birds and brush and butterflies and bobwhites, grass and grasslands, wetlands and waterfowl, deer, dove, and turkey. He especially loved the turkeys.

Entrusted with a key to nearly every ranch gate in South Texas, he knew just about everything there was to know about the Brush Country—its ranches and ranchmen, the ones who were friendly and the ones who weren't, its county roads and country towns, its deer camps and the best camp cooks and where to find the best fideo and the best barbacoa. He knew when mesquite leaves would come and when they'd go, when the hawks and cranes would migrate through and the bobwhites would begin to pair off and the turkey hens would go off to nest. It seemed he knew about everything one needed to know.

I first met Randy in 1993. I was so low on the TPWD totem pole that I didn't even have a title. Rest assured, Randy certainly didn't care about such things, then or ever. As far as he was concerned, I was the new spring chicken, the one he could con into opening his gates, conducting his spotlight counts, running his Hahn lines, tabulating his call counts, and clipping his vegetation plots. After about a year or so, Bob Cook, the wildlife division director at the time, broke the news to me that I really wasn't expected to open all his gates, fix his flat tires, conduct his surveys, or cook him dinner. Funny how Randy never mentioned that.

On the morning he died, Randy was headed to Austin. He was going to a Texas Parks and Wildlife Commission meeting to see his colleague Dana Wright be honored by the National Wild Turkey Federation with its most prestigious conservation award, the Joe Kurz Excellence in Wildlife Management Award. It is given each year to only one biologist across the entire country in recognition of his or her exemplary work and contributions to wild turkey conservation. More so than most, Randy knew something about just how meaningful that award was, because he was the only other biologist in Texas history to have received it.

In the 1980s, Randy led efforts to trap and transport turkeys to suitable habitats throughout South Texas, helping transform the region into one of the most thriving and populous areas for Rio Grande turkeys across the country. Throughout his career, graduate students and scientists alike turned to him for help securing study sites and for technical advice about where to find the birds and how to trap them. On the nearly two million acres of private lands in which Randy helped with wildlife management plans, landowners consulted him about how to enhance roosting, nesting, brooding, and foraging sites. If there was a "go-to" guy on turkeys in South Texas, Randy was at the top of the list.

Randy was a man of many gifts, uncommon humility, and a generosity of spirit and friendship as big as the state he called home. Randy wore a big hat, big boots, a big smile, and a big heart. He made our lives and our home ground a whole lot better because of the simple fact that he was in it. He'll now make the great campfires and turkey roosts in the sky a lot finer too.

Adios, our friend.

Carter Smith
Executive Director, Texas Parks and Wildlife Department
August 15, 2016

Contents

Foreword

The great state of Texas has always been at the forefront of US history, beginning with the Alamo. What a lot of people don't realize, though, is the involvement of Texas in wild turkey research and restocking from the beginning of restoration following World War II. Those actions changed the face of wildlife management in this country.

W. C. Glazener, a wonderful friend, wrote in 1947 in the *Texas Game and Fish* magazine about new homes for wild turkeys. He also published a paper in 1959 in the *Proceedings of the First National Wild Turkey Symposium*. His work regarding wild turkey research needs helped launch a nationwide effort to learn more about wild turkey biology and management. His contributions to the development of turkey law and restoration in Texas, plus the design of the drop-net trap, paved the way for others to expand that knowledge to other states. The first practical book on wild turkeys, *The Wild Turkey and Its Management*, was published by The Wildlife Society in 1967. Glazener was on the committee to craft the chapters. Naturally he wrote the chapter titled "Management of the Rio Grande Turkey."

The next and most recent book, *The Wild Turkey: Biology and Management*, published in 1992, was a National Wild Turkey Federation and USDA Forest Service publication. It was edited by Dr. James G. Dickson of the Southern Forest Experiment Station, based in Nacogdoches, Texas. The chapter on Rio Grande turkeys was authored by Sam Beasom, director of the Caesar Kleberg Wildlife Research Institute in Kingsville, Texas. His coauthor, Don Wilson, was the Upland Game Program leader with the Texas Parks and Wildlife Department.

These men set the standards for wild turkey research and management, but it didn't stop there. Texas played a major and leading role in not only restoring Eastern wild turkeys to millions of acres in Texas but also providing the funds through Target 2000 to buy thousands of acres of public lands in other states that people enjoy today.

Target 2000 was a partnership between Texas and other state wildlife agencies. The framework of Target 2000 included requests by the Texas Parks and Wildlife Department for Eastern wild turkeys from other states. The program later expanded to additional states, which Texas would in turn pay $500 for the trapping or replacement value of each bird. Many states, such as Georgia, Iowa, and South Carolina, used the dollars to buy land like that used for the Joe Kurz Wildlife Management Area. Kurz, who was Georgia's chief of game, was the catalyst for moving the turkeys. The very first transfer was from Thompson, Georgia, to Tyler, Texas. This opened the door for states to donate birds to Texas and became part of the Win/Win Partnership. This new procedure, coordinated by the National Wild Turkey Federation, allowed sportsmen to hunt turkeys on public lands in many states where that had once been only a dream.

When Bill Kuvlesky asked me to write this foreword, I was honored because this unique publication is what you would expect from the Great State of Texas. This book is a continuation of one of the biggest success stories in the research, restoration, and management of the wild turkey in North America.

James Earl Kennamer
Development Adviser, National Wild Turkey Federation
November 10, 2016

Preface

Texans have a long tradition of appreciating their wild turkeys. Most Texans who have the privilege of being outdoors early on a spring morning in wild turkey range enjoy hearing the "gobbles" of strutting wild turkey gobblers. Many appreciate the challenge associated with calling a wary gobbler into shotgun range. The citizens of Cuero, Texas, appreciate wild turkeys so much that "Gobblers" is the official mascot of the high school. Cuero also hosts an annual Turkey Festival every fall, highlighted by the "Great Gobbler Gallop," a race between Cuero's gobbler, named "Ruby Begonia," and a gobbler from Worthington, Minnesota, named "Paycheck." This event and Cuero's Turkey Festival are so popular that thousands of people from all over the state attend every year.

Texans appreciate that "everything is bigger in Texas" and therefore should be proud to know that the biggest wild turkey population in North America exists in Texas. Moreover, Texas is one of the few states that harbor three subspecies of wild turkeys: the Eastern, Rio Grande, and Merriam's wild turkeys. Consequently, we thought it strange that no one had ever written a book about wild turkeys in Texas. Numerous books on quail and deer in Texas have been published, but there has never been a book published devoted solely to Texas wild turkeys. In fact, only four books that we are aware of have ever been written about wild turkeys in North America. Most are devoted to Eastern wild turkeys, and the most recent was published almost 25 years ago. Therefore, we thought it was time to write a book devoted to wild turkeys in Texas.

The book is a scientific endeavor in that the content is derived from scientific studies of wild turkeys, although we have made a concerted to effort to make the content interesting to a broad audience. Our hope is that not only professional wildlife biologists but also students in university wildlife programs, high school students, private landowners, turkey hunters, birders, and other outdoor enthusiasts will find the book useful.

This book will provide a detailed, comprehensive overview of wild turkeys in Texas by professional wildlife scientists who have been involved in wild turkey research and management. We have not organized the book into three sections, one for each of the three wild turkey subspecies that occur in Texas, in order to avoid redundancy. Instead, the 14 chapters are organized in a logical manner that will enable readers to learn about the entirety of wild turkey ecology and management, or if they prefer, to focus on a specific subject that interests them.

Texans can take pride in the work that has been accomplished to restore, conserve, and manage wild turkey populations in Texas. Much has been done for wild turkeys, but more work remains to ensure their future in Texas. Our hope is that the material compiled in this book will continue to move wild turkey conservation and management forward.

Acknowledgments

First it is necessary to acknowledge Drs. Allen Rasmussen, former dean, and Shad Nelson, dean of the Dick and Mary Lewis Kleberg College of Agriculture and Natural Resources at Texas A&M University–Kingsville, because they encouraged William Kuvlesky to organize and lead the effort to write this book. Were it not for their encouragement and patience during workdays, it would have been much more challenging to lead the effort to write this book. Additionally, the flexible and productive work environment provided by Fred Bryant and Dave Hewitt, former director and current director, respectively, of the Caesar Kleberg Wildlife Research Institute, as well Scott Henke, chair of the Department of Rangeland and Wildlife Sciences at Texas A&M University–Kingsville, allowed a number of the coauthors to devote time to writing this book. The C. C. Winn Endowed Chair for Quail Research supported Leonard Brennan's efforts. Bart DuPont, wildlife manager of La Paloma Ranch, permitted Landon Fritz to devote time to writing this book. Furthermore, Clayton Wolf, director of the Wildlife Division of the Texas Parks and Wildlife Department, permitted Jason Hardin to devote work hours to writing portions of this book. Shyla Rabe of the Caesar Kleberg Wildlife Research Institute should also be recognized for her support in obtaining quality photos. Shannon Davies, former director of Texas A&M University Press, encouraged William Kuvlesky for years to write a book on wild turkeys in Texas and remained a constant source of encouragement throughout the writing and publishing process. In addition, Patricia Clabaugh, associate editor; Laurel Anderton, copyeditor; and Stacy Eisenstark, former acquisitions editor for natural conservation and agriculture, were extremely helpful throughout the editorial process. Their patience, advice, and help were instrumental in getting this book published. We thank the Texas Parks and Wildlife Department for providing financial support for publishing this book, as well as Timothy Fulbright, editor of the Perspectives on South Texas series, for securing financial support from Dr. Steven Tallant, president emeritus of Texas A&M University–Kingsville.

This book contains many excellent photographs thanks to the generosity of numerous people, and we want to recognize the photographers. Larry Ditto provided some wonderful photos of wild turkeys as well as other important wildlife species and their habitats. Tim Fulbright, Eric Grahmann, David Hewitt, Rick Machen, Jesse Oetgen, Kory Perlicheck, and Robert Sanders provided excellent photos of wild turkeys in Texas, their habitats, and specific plant species. Daniel Sullivan, a new PhD from the University of Georgia, very kindly sacrificed time while finishing his dissertation to wade through his many Eastern wild turkey photos to provide some photos of East Texas that we desperately needed. Chad Lehman and Scott Lerich, both wild turkey biologists for the South Dakota Game, Fish, and Parks Department and the National Wild Turkey Federation, respectively, provided much needed photos of Merriam's wild turkey habitats. Special thanks also go to Matt Lindler, vice president of communications for the National Wild Turkey Federation, and his staff members Frank Thurston and the late Guy Tillett, for the high-resolution photographs of wild turkeys they provided. Many of the figures were adapted and produced by Geospatial Technologies Laboratory, Caesar Kleberg Wildlife Research Institute. Finally, we would not have been able to obtain and use the photos of the Guadalupe Mountains in the book without the generous assistance of Elizabeth Jackson, chief of interpretation at Guadalupe Mountains National Park.

Thanks also go to the numerous private landowners who encouraged us to write this book about wild turkeys in Texas, recognizing that such a book was needed. We are especially grateful to Renato Ramirez, owner of El Veleno Ranch; Stuart Stedman, owner of Faith and Elizita Ranches; Lee Bass, owner of La Paloma and El Coyote Ranches; Charlie Hoffman, owner of Hoffman HC 30 Ranch; Henry Hammond, owner of El Gato del Monte Ranch; and the late Buddy Temple and his wife, Ellen, former owners of Temple Ranch, as well as their former manager Robert Sanders. We also want to recognize Dr. Steve DeMaso for giving the Caesar Kleberg Wildlife Research Institute its start in wild turkey research. Finally, we want to acknowledge the love and encouragement of our wives and significant others for supporting and encouraging us to write this book during the many evening hours and weekends we devoted to this endeavor.

Wild Turkeys in Texas

1

Introduction

I wish the bald eagle had not been chosen as the representative of our country; he is a bird of bad moral character; like those among men who live by sharking and robbing, he is generally poor, and often very lousy. The turkey is in comparison a much more respectable bird and withal a true original Native of America. . . . He is besides, though a little vain and silly, a Bird of Courage.

—BENJAMIN FRANKLIN (1784)

The wild turkey (*Meleagris gallopavo*) is an iconic game bird with a long history of association with humans throughout North and Central America, though most people associate wild turkeys with only the Thanksgiving holiday. Even fewer people understand the important ecological role wild turkeys play in the ecosystems they occupy. Many Texans probably do not know that wild turkeys even exist in Texas, and those who do probably do not realize that Texas supports the largest wild turkey population in the United States. Moreover, the majority of Texans also probably do not know that three subspecies of wild turkeys occur in Texas: the Eastern wild turkey (*Meleagris gallopavo silvestris*), the Rio Grande wild turkey (*M. g. intermedia*), and the Merriam's wild turkey (*M. g. merriami*). With the exception of wild turkey hunters and professional wildlife biologists, few Texans know much about the ecology and management of wild turkeys in Texas because most people think about turkeys only when they purchase them in grocery stores to eat at Thanksgiving.

About This Book

Considerable research has been completed on wild turkeys in Texas since the publication of James Dickson's book *The Wild Turkey: Biology and Management* over 25 years ago (1992). Although Dickson's book includes chapters on the three wild turkey subspecies that occur in Texas, only the chapter on Rio Grande wild turkeys focuses on Texas. Much of the book is devoted to Eastern wild turkeys simply because they are the most abundant subspecies in North America, occur in almost every state east of the Mississippi River, and consequently have been studied more thoroughly than other subspecies. Therefore, the purpose of this book is to synthesize the results of recent research on the three wild turkey subspecies that occur in Texas into a single source. This book provides the most current information about the ecology and management of wild turkeys in Texas to people interested in them, ranging from amateur naturalists to wild turkey hunters, university students of wildlife biology, high school students of agriculture and science, and professional wildlife biologists.

Composition of the Book

The most recently published book on wild turkeys is James Dickson's book, mentioned above, which covers the ecology and management of all wild turkey subspecies found in North America. It is a great source of information about wild turkeys for anyone interested in learning more about them, and it remains an important resource for both wild turkey biologists and wild turkey enthusiasts among the lay public. However, the book is over 25 years old, and the current population status of wild turkeys has changed over that time. Additionally, wild turkey science has progressed significantly since the book's publication. Therefore, new information about wild turkey biology and how to better manage turkey populations has been published. This is particularly true in Texas, where a substantial amount of research has been devoted to wild turkeys since 2000 that is relevant to all aspects of wild turkey ecology and management. Beyond this introductory chapter, this book is organized into 13 additional chapters covering the important aspects of wild turkey ecology and management that are relevant to Texas. A brief summary of each chapter follows.

Taxonomy and evolution

The taxonomy and evolution of wild turkeys have not been studied extensively, and little work has been done in Texas. Only one detailed genetic study has been published for wild turkeys in Texas, and it focused on Merriam's wild turkeys in the Davis Mountains to determine whether Merriam's wild turkeys translocated to the area were hybridizing with Rio Grande wild turkeys, which indeed they were. Therefore, we know almost nothing about the origin of wild turkeys in Texas or how each subspecies is related to one another. In order to better understand wild turkey ecology, it is important to understand more about their evolution and genetics. Therefore, chapter 2 begins with a discussion of the fossil history of wild turkeys. The six existing subspecies of wild turkeys that occur in the Americas are discussed, as well as their evolutionary history and phylogenetic relationships. Details about wild turkey population genetics and adaptive radiation are also provided. The chapter concludes with research recommendations that include resolving phylogenetic relationships, focusing more on historical demography, performing more studies on range-wide structures of adaptive genetic variation, and determining the effects of restocking and hunting on the genetic diversity of wild turkeys.

Life history

Chapter 3 provides details about wild turkey life history, including many characteristics specific to wild turkeys in general as well as some specific to each of the three subspecies in Texas. This chapter includes descriptions of the general appearance and physical characteristics of each subspecies, as well as its longevity and sensory capabilities. Additionally, the geographic distribution in Texas and movements for each subspecies are described. The seasons of the year relevant to each subspecies in Texas are defined, and common wild turkey predators are identified.

Restoration

Wild turkey population restoration has a long history in Texas. Most efforts have focused on restoring Rio Grande wild turkey populations, which has been enormously successful. Restoration of the Eastern subspecies has largely been the focus of recent restoration efforts in East Texas and has achieved success in some counties. Early attempts to restore Merriam's wild turkey populations in the mountains of West Texas occurred in the 1930s and again in the 1980s, but it appears that these efforts were unsuccessful. Recent research has focused on efforts to improve the restoration and conservation of Eastern wild turkey populations in East Texas, an effort that has been ongoing for over 30 years. Chapter 4 discusses the history of wild turkey restoration in Texas, including its successes and failures, as well as current efforts to restore wild turkey populations, particularly in East Texas.

Population ecology

Chapter 5 begins by addressing the question of why managers should understand wild turkey population ecology. It then proceeds to discuss the reproductive and demographic characteristics of each wild turkey subspecies, including nesting and renesting rates, nest success, clutch size, fertility and hatching success, and age- and sex-specific survival rates. Population trends for each subspecies are also provided, as are harvest rates and harvest management information. Emphasis is placed on what we do not know about wild turkey population ecology and the need for additional research.

Behavioral ecology

Chapter 6 discusses the behavior of wild turkeys, which is remarkably consistent across subspecies. Behavioral attributes such as locomotion, foraging, self-maintenance, reaction to threats, reproduction, behavioral development of young birds, social behaviors, and vocalizations are discussed. The chapter concludes with a brief discussion of how wild turkey behavior is related to management and population recovery.

Habitat requirements

Chapter 7 is devoted to the habitat requirements of the three wild turkey subspecies in Texas. It begins by identifying the specific ecological characteristics of the ecoregions of Texas occupied by wild turkeys. It then discusses the specific habitat needs of each subspecies, including requirements for roosting, nesting, brood rearing, foraging, and water. The landscape ecology of wild turkeys, such as the distribution and spatial structure of vegetation communities, is discussed. The home range of each subspecies is also detailed. A brief discussion about the utility of wild turkey habitat suitability models is included. The chapter concludes with a summary of wild turkey research needs in Texas.

Habitat management

Chapter 8 covers the management of habitats for the three wild turkey subspecies in Texas. It first discusses the importance of assessment to determine the status of wild turkey habitat, as well as habitat monitoring after improvements have been made. Specific management techniques are identified that can be used to manage turkey habitat. Providing water, managing grazing and brush, using prescribed burning and herbicides, and establishing food plots to improve wild turkey habitat are all discussed. In addition, a section on forest management for Eastern wild turkeys is provided. The chapter concludes by identifying future research needs.

Diseases and parasites

One area of wild turkey ecology that has not been studied extensively in Texas is the effect of diseases and parasites on wild turkeys. Most wild turkey disease research was conducted in a few counties throughout the state at least 35 years ago. Until recently, wild turkey disease fieldwork has been largely ignored. Therefore, chapter 9 reviews diseases that affect wild turkeys and includes information on wild turkey parasites. Viruses and bacteria, as well as the endoparasites and ectoparasites that wild turkeys are susceptible to, particularly in Texas, are reviewed. Novel diseases that could potentially impact wild turkey populations in Texas are also identified. Furthermore, potential impacts of diseases and parasites on wild turkey populations are discussed, as well as recommendations to effectively deal with disease outbreaks. Disease surveillance studies and other research recommendations are provided.

Wild turkey management

Chapter 10 is devoted to wild turkey management in Texas. It describes why wild turkey management is important for maintaining healthy, self-sustainable populations. The statewide wild turkey plan developed by the Texas Parks and Wildlife Department (TPWD) is then described, as is the agency's technical guidance program. A list of TPWD wildlife management areas where wild turkeys occur is included. Additionally, TPWD's statewide wild turkey survey is discussed. The rest of the chapter provides guidance on developing a wild turkey management plan, which will be helpful to private landowners who are interested in establishing or maintaining wild turkeys on their property. Estimating wild turkey abundance is highlighted because monitoring wild turkey trends is an important part of a management plan. Managing wild turkey habitat is then discussed, and specific management alternatives are identified for each of the three subspecies. Water development for wild turkeys is also briefly mentioned, as are other management considerations, such as supplemental feeding and the need to manage predators. Also included are recommendations for managing turkey hunting. The chapter concludes with suggestions about how landowners and other individuals interested in wild turkeys can obtain professional assistance in developing a wild turkey management plan.

Establishing and maintaining relationships with landowners

Anyone interested in wild turkeys in Texas, from hunters who want to pursue wild turkeys to professional wildlife biologists who want to manage wild turkey populations, will almost certainly have to work with private landowners, because private lands make up over 95% of the acreage of Texas. Consequently, knowing how to effectively work with private landowners is an essential skill for anyone interested in wild turkeys in Texas. Chapter 11 provides detailed suggestions about how to work effectively with private landowners to manage the natural resources on their property. It begins by detailing how to build relationships with private landowners and discusses the personal characteristics they appreciate. Finally, the importance of professionalism is featured, as well as the value of developing, maintaining, and improving technical expertise.

Conservation

Chapter 12 highlights wild turkey conservation. It begins by describing the near extirpation of wild turkeys in the United States and how it occurred, as well as how it was circumvented and wild turkey recovery was achieved. Three important facets of wild turkey conservation are identified: (1) habitat, (2) education, and (3) hunting. Conserving wild turkey habitat is of course essential because without required habitat conditions, wild turkey populations will decline and eventually disappear, as happened almost a century ago throughout the North American range of the species. Education is equally important because without it, citizens will not know about the history of wild turkey conservation or understand how vital providing adequate habitat and managing wild turkey harvests are to wild turkey conservation. The significance of hunting to wild turkey conservation is also described. Finally, wild turkey conservation today is summarized.

Research priorities

Chapter 13 is a compilation of the research priorities that emanate from most of the other chapters. These priorities, if accomplished, would fill in some of the gaps in our knowledge of wild turkey ecology and management in Texas and throughout the geographic ranges of each of the three subspecies highlighted in the book.

The future

Chapter 14 summarizes thoughts about the future of wild turkeys in Texas. It first considers the current status of the three subspecies on their geographic ranges in Texas. Specific challenges relative to moving wild turkey conservation, management, and research forward are then identified. In addition, the importance of involving public stakeholders in wild turkey conservation and management is discussed. This involves education, which is also identified as a primary focus for moving forward. The chapter concludes with our assessment of the future of wild turkeys in Texas.

Additional resources

Appendix 1 identifies additional resources that readers interested in wild turkeys can consult if they would like to learn more. Books, federal and state agency and extension bulletins, and several websites relevant to wild turkeys are listed.

Literature Cited

Dickson, J. G. 1992. The wild turkey: biology and management. Stackpole Books, Mechanicsburg, Pennsylvania, USA.

2

Taxonomy and Evolution

Nothing in biology makes sense except in the light of evolution

—THEODOSIUS DOBZHANSKY (1973)

Evolution and taxonomy are often viewed as esoteric subjects divorced from wildlife biology and management. The reality is that evolution and taxonomy intersect with wildlife biology and management on multiple levels. Evolution is the unifying theory of biology (Dobzhansky 1973, Futuyma 1998, Wolff 2000). Wildlife biologists and managers collect large amounts of data, but an evolutionary framework is necessary to discover the causes of the observed biological phenomena and patterns.

Taxonomic classifications may seem arbitrary, but modern taxonomy attempts to construct a classification system that conveys information about evolutionary relationships. The importance of taxonomy becomes apparent when one considers that species checklists and biodiversity inventories are still one of the basic tools of conservation (Mace 2004). There are an estimated 8.75 million extant species (Mora et al. 2011), of which 1.6–1.7 million have been named and described (May 2010). Unfortunately, our understanding of the evolutionary relationships of extant organisms is extremely limited, especially at the level of species and subspecies, and severely underestimates phylogenetic and taxonomic diversity (May 1988, 2010; Brito 2004). Subspecies are often used as proxies for management units and are assumed to be genetically distinct lineages that accurately reflect the geographic distribution of genetic diversity and adaptive variation within a species (Zink 2004). Most recognized subspecies, including those of the wild turkey, were described during the premolecular era (nineteenth and early twentieth centuries) based on morphology, behavior, and other phenotypic traits; however, many descriptions were based on small sample sizes (sometimes as few as one) and a limited number of characters (Zink 2004, Rising 2007, Pyron and Burbrink 2009). The decline of taxonomy as a major area of study in American and European universities has led to a backlog of ill-defined subspecies that will remain on the "taxonomic books" until someone takes the time to study them in detail (Winker 2010). Time, effort, money, and other resources may be wasted if conservation efforts are based on spurious or dubious taxonomy (Dubois 2003, Avise 2004, Zink 2004, Bortolus 2008).

The development and growth of molecular biology has produced numerous genetic tools that wildlife scientists can use to evaluate subspecies taxonomy. Improvements in molecular techniques eventually led to the establishment of phylogeography, the study of the principles and processes that influence geographic patterns of genetic variation (Avise 2000). As with wildlife science, phylogeography is a field in which multiple disciplines converge, including evolutionary biology, population genetics, phylogenetics, taxonomy, paleontology, biogeography, demography, and ecology (Avise 2000). Contemporary patterns of genetic variation in any species have been shaped largely by historical events such as past fragmentation, demographic growth and decline, and termination and renewal of gene flow among populations. A phylogeographic approach to genetic studies allows wildlife biologists to assess relationships among spatially structured populations, differentiate between historical and recent isolation and gene flow, and elucidate the historical causes of contemporary population structure and levels of genetic diversity (Avise 2000, 2004; DeYoung and Honeycutt 2005). Phylogeography has become the primary way that biologists study the historical biogeography of a species and assess whether described subspecies accurately reflect the intraspecific distribution of genetic diversity.

Fossil History

The fossil history of turkeys reaches as far back as the Miocene epoch of the Cenozoic era (23.03–5.33 million years ago, MYA). The oldest and smallest species of prehistoric turkey is *Rhegminornis calobates*, originally described by Alexander Wetmore (1943) based on the distal end of a right tarsometatarsus recovered from early Miocene deposits (ca. 18 MYA) in Florida. Although it was originally classified as a jacana, a detailed examination by Olson and Farrand (1974) led them to realize that *Rhegminornis* was actually an early small-bodied turkey. The second-oldest fossil, of the species *Proagriocharis kimballensis*, consisted of a coracoid and three tarsometatarsi recovered from the late Miocene (8.3–6.5 MYA) deposits of the Kimball Formation in Nebraska (Martin et al. 1970, Diffendal et al. 1996). The relationship of *Rhegminornis* and *Proagriocharis* to more recent species (*Meleagris*) of turkeys is not well understood; however, *Rhegminornis* and *Proagriocharis* appear to be closely related to each other (Steadman 1980). *Rhegminornis, Proagriocharis,* and *Meleagris* represent a gradual increase in body size from the early Miocene to the Pliocene and Pleistocene; however, this conclusion is complicated by older fragmentary turkey fossils from New Mexico, Florida, and Virginia that represent taxa larger than *Proagriocharis* and may be part of *Meleagris* (Steadman 1980). In light of this, Steadman (1980) suggested that *Rhegminornis* and *Proagriocharis* may represent a sibling lineage to the larger-bodied *Meleagris* (fig. 2.1).

The remaining fossil taxa of turkeys belong to *Meleagris* (Steadman 1980). The oldest fossils that can be confidently classified as *Meleagris* are 5.33–2.58 million years old, including *M. progenes* from Kansas, *M. leopoldi* from Texas, *M. anza* from southern California, and unnamed fossils from Florida; however, some scientists view these fossils as representatives of the same species because of strong skeletal similarities

Figure 2.1. Cladogram showing hypothesized evolutionary relationships among extinct and extant turkeys based on Steadman (1980), Rea (1980), and Stidham (2011) (figure by Damon Williford).

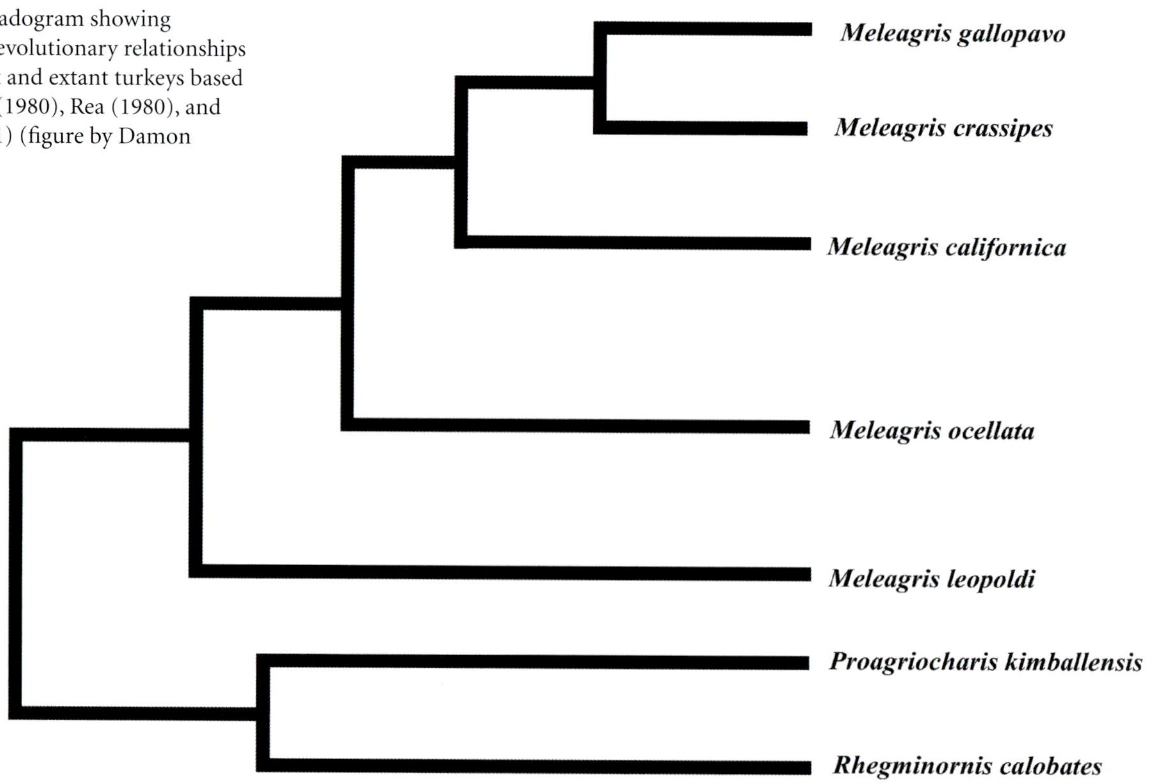

(Steadman 1980, Stidham 2011). All other fossils of *Meleagris* species are from late Pleistocene (126,000–11,700 years ago) deposits, including *M. californica* of California; *M. crassipes*, which was distributed from Arizona to Nuevo Léon, Mexico; and *M. gallopavo*, the extant wild turkey (Steadman 1980, Rea 1980). Fossils of *M. gallopavo* have been recovered from late Pleistocene and Holocene deposits from the eastern, central, and southwestern United States and from eastern and western Mexico. *Meleagris californica* and *M. gallopavo* share more osteological similarities with one another than either does with *M. ocellata* or *M. crassipes*, which supports earlier divergences for *M. ocellata* and *M. crassipes* (Bocheński and Campbell 2006). The relationship of *M. crassipes* to other members of *Meleagris* is uncertain (Steadman 1980).

Steadman (1980) proposed two possible explanations for the strong osteological similarity between *M. californica* and *M. gallopavo*: (1) both species were subject to similar selective pressures in the environments of their respective ranges, or (2) both species shared a common ancestor and the lineage leading to *M. californica* became isolated in California as western Arizona became more arid. Bocheński and Campbell (2006) argued that recent common ancestry was a more likely explanation because the historical range of *M. gallopavo* included swampy and humid forests in the southeastern United States as well as more arid woodlands in the American Southwest, yet the skeletons of all populations exhibit no qualitative differences. If its habitat requirements were similar to those of *M. gallopavo*, then *M. californica* may have been driven to extinction by the loss of woodlands (Bocheński and Campbell 2006) as southern California became increasingly arid following the end of the last glaciation 11,500 years ago (Heusser 1978, Heusser and Sirocko 1997, Mensing 2001, Koehler et al. 2005). Evidence of human-turkey interaction in California during the late Pleistocene is lacking, but *M. gallopavo* was heavily hunted by indigenous peoples in other parts of North America (Schorger 1966, Neumann 1989), which suggests that heavy exploitation by human hunters could have played a role in the extinction of *M. californica* (Bocheński and Campbell 2006). The only species of turkey in the American Southwest during the late Pleistocene and early Holocene was *M. crassipes*. Radiocarbon dates indicate that it was present in southwestern North America as early as 25,000 years ago and disappeared between 6,600 and 3,300 years ago. The extinction of *M. crassipes* may also have been due to the increased aridity in North America following the end of the last ice age 10,000 years ago (Rea 1980).

Fossils of the ocellated turkey (*M. ocellata*), the only other extant species of turkey, are relatively recent (11,000 years old or younger) and have been found in southern Mexico, Guatemala, and Belize. Steadman (1980) suggested that the lineage leading to *M. ocellata* may have become isolated in the Yucatán Peninsula because of elevated sea level during a Pleistocene interglacial. The ocellated turkey was placed in a separate genus, *Agriocharis*, throughout much of the twentieth century; however, Steadman argued that this was unwarranted based on the strong skeletal and life history similarities of ocellated and wild turkeys. Based on Steadman's findings, the American Ornithologists' Union relegated *Agriocharis* to a junior synonym and placed the ocellated turkey within *Meleagris* (Munroe et al. 1995).

Systematics

Although turkeys have been classified as a separate family, Meleagridae, phylogenetic studies based on molecular data have consistently recovered turkeys as a unique lineage embedded within the family Phasianidae, which also includes chickens, peafowl, grouse, and pheasants (Dimcheff et al. 2002, Crowe et al. 2006, Zhao et al. 2012, Wang et al. 2013). Therefore, most current classifications treat turkeys as a subfamily (Meleagrinae) of Phasianidae (American Ornithologists' Union 1988). Genetic data indicate that grouse and ptarmigan (Tetraoninae) are the closest relatives of turkeys, and that these two subfamilies probably diverged from their shared common ancestor 28 MYA (Dimcheff et al. 2002). Schorger (1966) provides a detailed history of the wild turkey's taxonomy and the etymology of the genus *Meleagris* as well as its discovery by Europeans (see also Crawford 1992).

Multiple subspecies of the wild turkey have been described, but only six are now considered valid (McRoberts et al. 2014). Schorger (1966), Aldrich (1967), and McRoberts et al. (2014) provide detailed accounts of the geographic distributions and physical traits of each subspecies. McRoberts et al. divided the

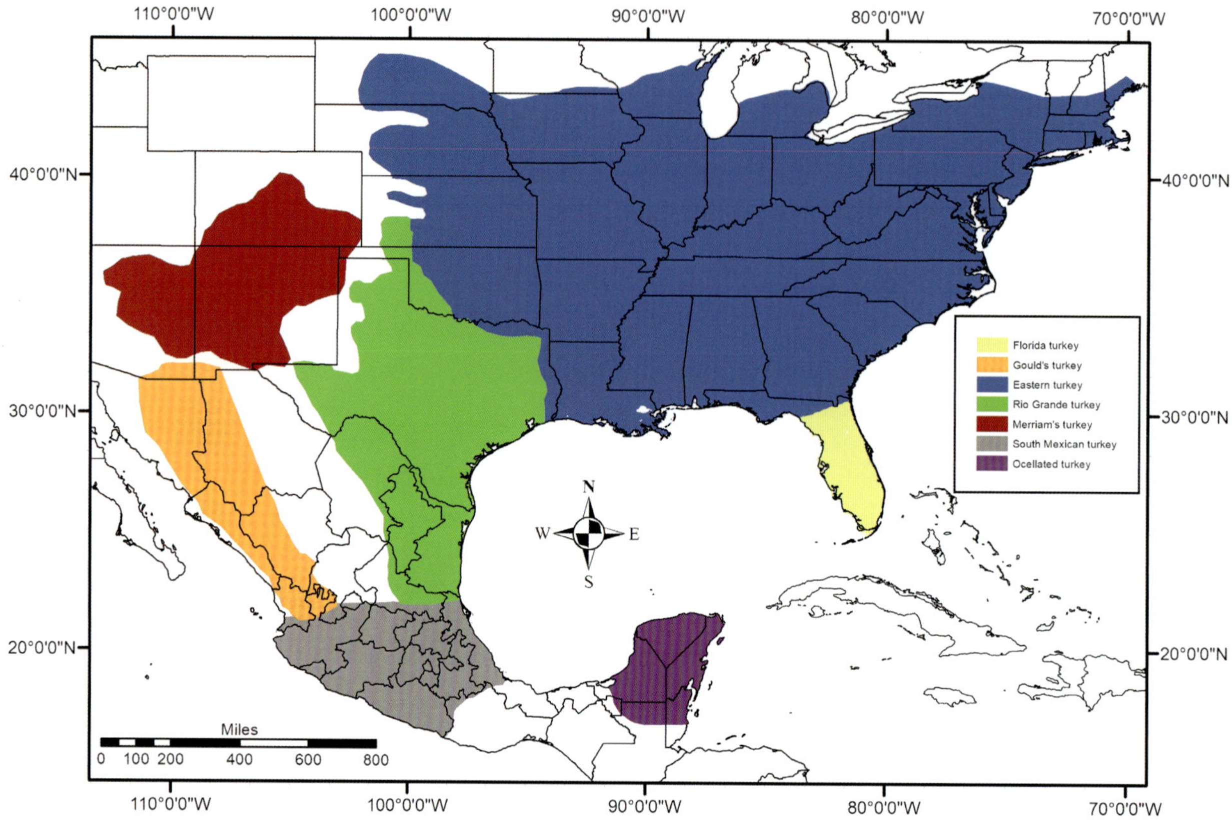

Figure 2.2. Historic geographic distributions of the subspecies of wild and ocellated turkeys based on Moore (1938), Ridgway and Friedmann (1946), Leopold (1959), Schorger (1966), and Mock et al. (2002) (figure by Damon Williford).

subspecies into an Eastern Group (subspecies east of the Mississippi River) and a Western Group (subspecies that naturally occur west of the Mississippi River) (fig. 2.2).

Eastern group

- Eastern turkey, *M. g. silvestris* Vieillot, 1817 (includes *M. g. fera* Vieillot, 1817; *M. g. americana* Hildreth, 1823; and *M. g. occidentalis* Allen, 1876). The historical distribution included much of the eastern United States (except Peninsular Florida).
- Florida turkey, *M. g. osceola* Scott, 1890 (includes *M. g. occidentalis* Bartram, 1791). Restricted to Peninsular Florida.

Western group

- Rio Grande turkey, *M. g. intermedia* Sennett, 1879 (includes *M. g. ellioti* Sennett, 1892). The historical distribution included southwestern Oklahoma, Texas, and northern Mexico (Tamaulipas, Nuevo Léon, San Luis Potosí, and Coahuila). Has been established in many areas outside its native range.
- Merriam's turkey, *M. g. merriami* Nelson, 1900. Formerly occurred in the Rocky Mountains of Colorado, Arizona, New Mexico, and West Texas. Rea (1980) and McKusick (1980) argued that Merriam's turkey may have evolved from ancient domestic stocks that became feral; however, this theory has been questioned by other scientists (Breitburg 1988, Senior and Pierce 1989, Munroe 1994, Newbold et al. 2012; see below for further discussion). Has been established in many areas outside this native range.
- Gould's turkey, *M. g. mexicana* Gould, 1856 (includes *M. g. onusta* Moore, 1938). Distributed through western Mexico from Chihuahua south through Durango to northern Jalisco and in scattered localities in the southwestern United States. Within the United States, Gould's turkey is found in parts of Arizona, including the Huachuca and Galiuro Mountains; riparian areas along Bonita Creek, the San Pedro River, and San Bernardino

Valley; and the Peloncillo Mountains in Arizona and New Mexico (Heffelfinger et al. 2000).

- South Mexican turkey, *M. g. gallopavo* Linnaeus, 1758 (includes *Gallopavo primus* Lesson, 1831). Formerly distributed throughout much of southern Mexico from Michoacán east to Veracruz and south to Oaxaca. Nearly extinct in the wild. The South Mexican turkey was the source for the modern domestic turkey (Crawford 1992, Speller et al. 2010, Aslam et al. 2012, Monteagudo et al. 2013). Domestic stocks of this subspecies were established at least by 180 AD in the Tehuacán Valley; however, analysis of DNA from bones recovered from an archaeological site in Petén, Guatemala, suggests that domesticated South Mexican turkeys may have been kept by the Maya as early as 300 BC (Thornton et al. 2012).

Assessment of subspecies distinctiveness based on morphological data has produced conflicting results. Plumage coloration of the wild turkey appears to be clinal, with a gradual transition from purplish bronze in northern populations to greenish or reddish gold in southern populations (Aldrich 1967). Plumage coloration also varies longitudinally in accordance with Gloger's rule, with the darkest plumages occurring in the humid eastern United States and the palest birds in northwestern Mexico and the southwestern United States (Aldrich 1967). Plumage variation within each of the six subspecies appears to be nearly as great as the variation among subspecies (Stangel et al. 1992). Stangel et al. (1992) found no statistically significant differences in body weight or beard length among wild turkey subspecies; however, spur length differed significantly among subspecies, with Eastern and Florida turkeys possessing the largest spurs and Merriam's and Gould's the smallest. The extensive geographic variation observed may indicate some level of local adaptation or sexual selection (Stangel et al. 1992).

Genetic evidence supporting the validity of wild turkey subspecies has also been mixed. To date, most studies using genetic data have relied on the mitochondrial control region, nuclear microsatellite DNA, or amplified fragment length polymorphisms (AFLPs) to assess the genetic distinctiveness of and evolutionary relationships among turkey subspecies (Szalanski et al. 2000, Mock et al. 2002, Latch 2004, Speller et al. 2010).

Unlike nuclear DNA, which is inherited from both parents, mitochondrial DNA (mtDNA) is strictly maternally inherited in animals. Uniparental inheritance means that, generally, recently diverged populations will achieve genetic distinctiveness in terms of mitochondrial lineages long before the same is achieved in nuclear DNA (Avise 2000, Hung et al. 2016). Because of its simpler inheritance, mtDNA is an excellent genetic marker for assessing historical phylogeographic structure within a species and inferring the demographic processes underlying that structure (Zink and Barrowclough 2008). If subspecies of the wild turkey represent long-standing, historically independent populations, then mtDNA should recover that phylogeographic structure. However, a minimum spanning tree, or haplotype network, constructed from wild turkey mitochondrial control region DNA sequences reveals a lack of phylogeographic structure congruent with subspecies taxonomy (fig. 2.3). Although each of the wild turkey subspecies possesses unique haplotypes (variants of the control region), most haplotypes are shared by two or more subspecies, and similar results have been reported by other studies (Szalanski et al. 2000, Mock et al. 2002, Latch 2004, Speller et al. 2010). The wild turkey haplotype network exhibits a starlike pattern, or "star phylogeny," in which a widespread ancestral haplotype sits at the center of the network and descendant haplotypes radiate out from it. Star phylogenies often indicate minimal long-term historical population structure and rapid population growth (Slatkin and Hudson 1991). Star phylogenies are a recurrent finding in North American phylogeographic studies because the distributions of species of warm-temperate animals and plants were severely reduced during the Last Glacial Maximum (26,500–19,000 years ago), but many of these species underwent rapid range expansions as the climate warmed during the Holocene (Avise 2000). Evidence of post-Pleistocene range expansion and population growth in the wild turkey is also provided by a unimodal mismatch distribution (fig. 2.4). An estimation of changes in female effective population size (number of females contributing to the genetic diversity of the next generation) based on the mitochondrial control region indicates that the wild turkey underwent a dramatic increase in effective population size beginning 20,000 years ago (fig. 2.5), which coincides with the end of the last Pleistocene glaciation (Clark et al. 2009). Pairwise

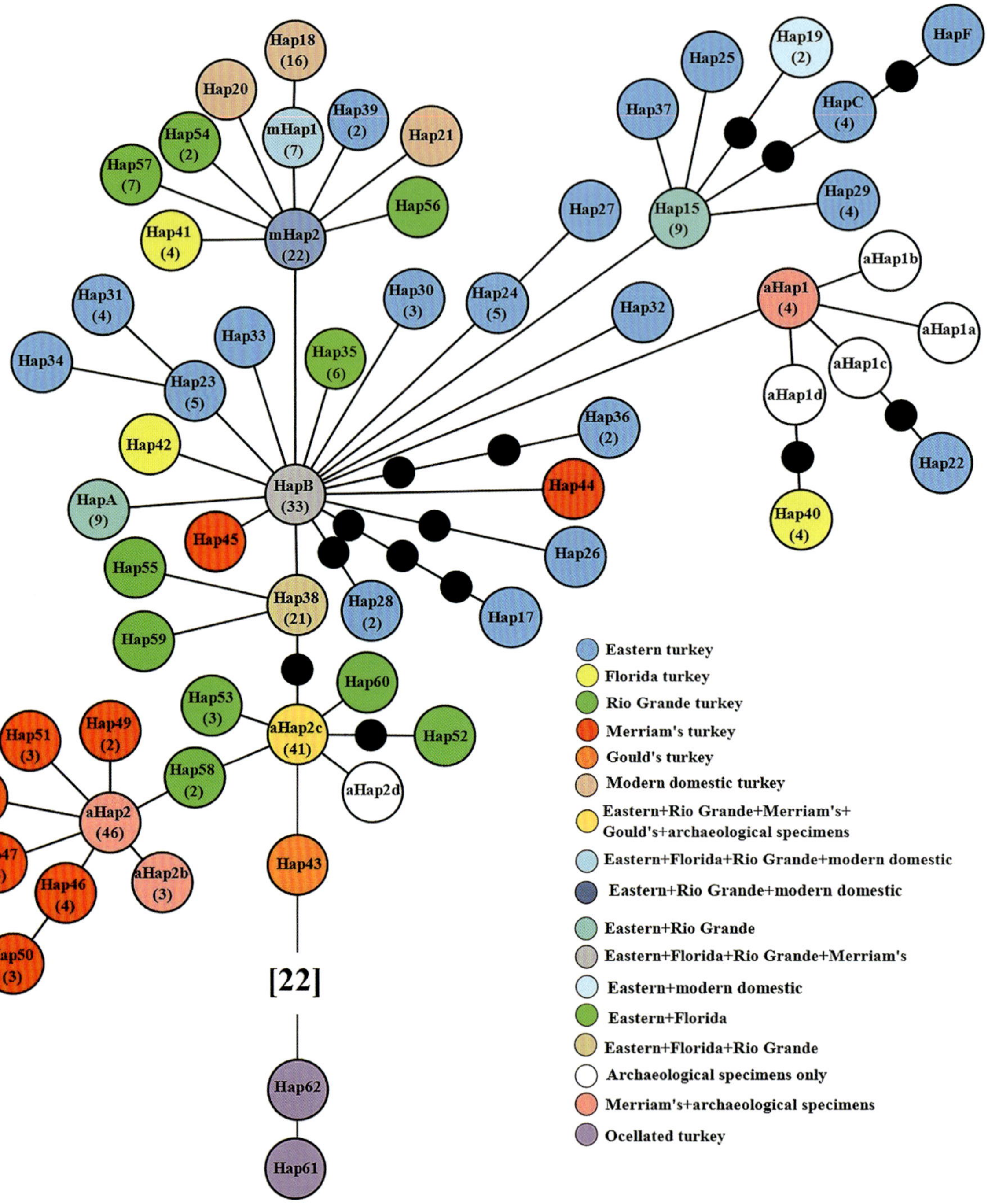

Figure 2.3. Minimum spanning tree of 53 mitochondrial control region haplotypes (412 base pairs) found among wild and ocellated turkeys. Large colored circles with labels represent unique haplotypes (see legend); numbers in parentheses represent the number of sequences identical to that haplotype; each line represents a single base substitution mutation; and small solid black circles represent inferred missing haplotypes. The color of each haplotype indicates which subspecies carried that haplotype (see legend). The white haplotypes represent those observed by Speller et al. (2010) in bones and coprolites from archaeological sites that were not identical to any sequences from modern populations. Note the lack of any kind of structure consistent with accepted subspecies taxonomy and the widespread sharing of haplotypes among subspecies. Individual control region sequences were originally from Szalanski et al. (2000), Mock et al. (2001, 2002), Petersen (2003), Guan et al. (2009), Speller et al. (2010), Reed (2011, unpublished), and Monteagudo et al. (2013). The minimum spanning tree was constructed based on pairwise distances using the computer programs Arlequin, version 3.5 (Excoffier and Lischer 2010), and HapStar, version 0.6 (Teacher and Griffiths 2011) (figure by Damon Williford).

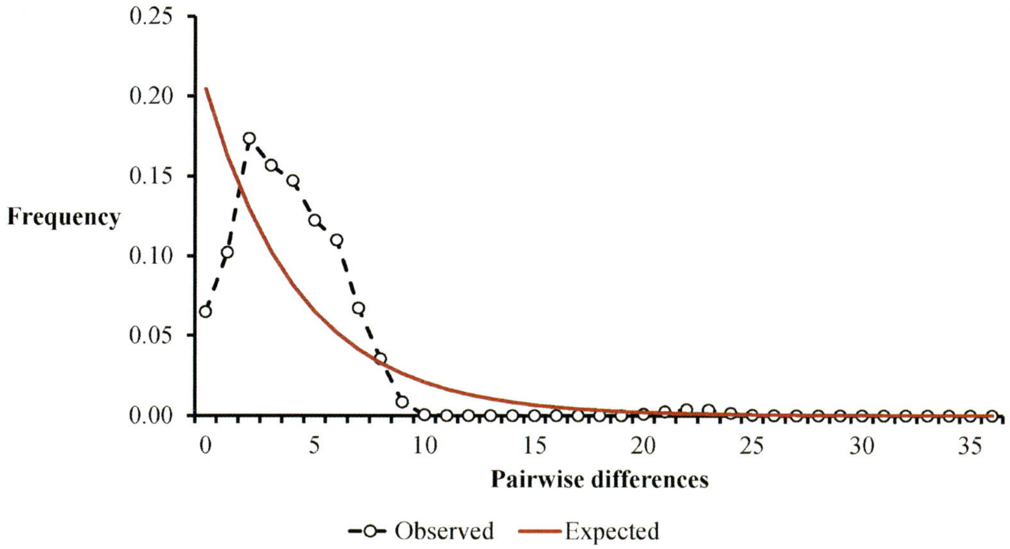

Figure 2.4. Distribution of pairwise nucleotide differences, or mismatch distributions, observed in the mitochondrial control region sequences of the wild turkey. The dotted line represents the observed mismatch distributions, and the solid line represents the expected distribution under the assumption of a constant population size. The x-axis is the number of pairwise differences (mismatches), and the y-axis is the frequency of differences. A unimodal mismatch distribution often indicates recent, sudden demographic growth, whereas bimodal or multimodal distributions indicate demographic equilibrium or decline (Rogers and Harpending 1992). The mismatch distribution was constructed using the computer program DnaSP, version 5.1 (Librado and Rozas 2009) (figure by Damon Williford).

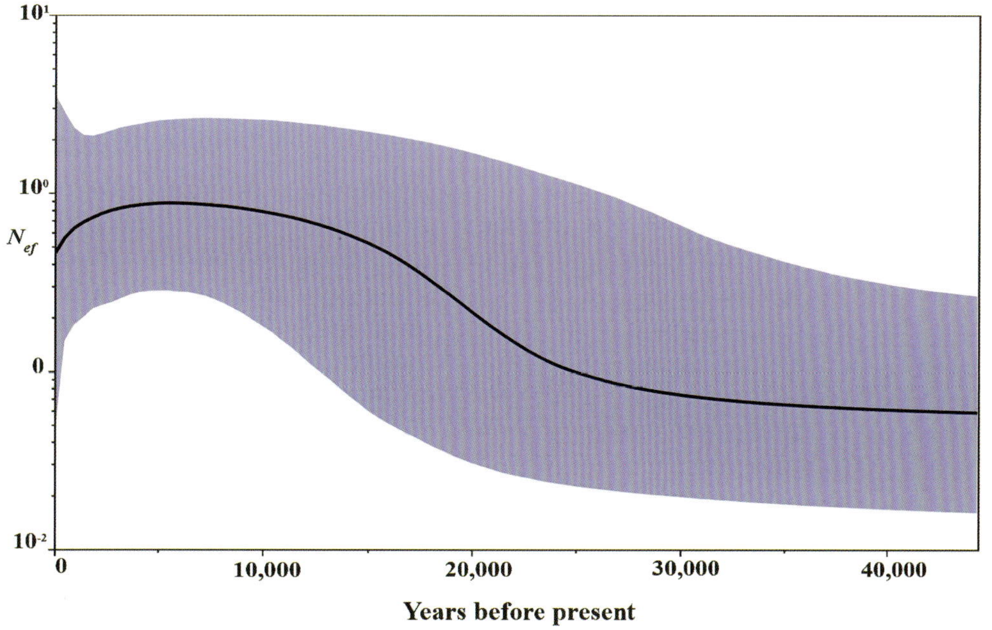

Figure 2.5. Bayesian skyline plot (Drummond et al. 2005) representing changes in the female effective population size (*Nef*) of the wild turkey over time, inferred from the analysis of mitochondrial control region sequences. The x-axis is the time in years before the present, and the y-axis is the female effective population size. The black line is the median estimate, and the shaded area represents the variance (Drummond et al. 2012). The skyline was constructed using the BEAST software package, version 1.8 (Drummond et al. 2012), based on the HKY model of nucleotide substitution (Hasegawa et al. 1985) with a gamma distribution, relaxed lognormal molecular clock (Drummond et al. 2006), and the mutation rate for the grouse mitochondrial control region of 0.0723% per site per million years (Drovetski 2003) (figure by Damon Williford).

Table 2.1. Sequence divergence (below diagonal) with standard error (above diagonal), based on the mitochondrial control region (*n* = 316,398 base pairs) among the ocellated turkey and wild turkey subspecies.

	Eastern	Florida	Rio Grande	Merriam's	Gould's	Domestic	Ocellated
Eastern		0.002	0.002	0.005	0.004	0.003	0.013
Florida	0.006		0.002	0.005	0.004	0.003	0.012
Rio Grande	0.007	0.006		0.004	0.003	0.003	0.012
Merriam's	0.014	0.013	0.012		0.003	0.006	0.013
Gould's	0.010	0.008	0.008	0.006		0.005	0.012
Domestic	0.009	0.008	0.009	0.019	0.014		0.013
Ocellated	0.061	0.058	0.058	0.061	0.055	0.062	

Note: Sequence divergences were computed based on the Kimura-2-parameter model (Kimura 1980), and standard error was estimated from 1,000 bootstrap replicates. The larger sequence divergences indicate greater genetic dissimilarity and lower levels of gene flow or longer periods of isolation. Sequence divergences were calculated using the computer program MEGA6 (Tamura et al. 2013).

Table 2.2. Matrix of the average pairwise unbiased genetic distances (below diagonal) with standard error (above diagonal) among wild turkey subspecies based on microsatellite data.

	Eastern	Florida	Rio Grande	Merriam's	Gould's
Eastern		0.019	0.038	0.058	0.065
Florida	0.171		0.044	0.048	0.065
Rio Grande	0.349	0.493		0.020	0.022
Merriam's	0.626	0.812	0.278		0.027
Gould's	0.441	0.441	0.327	0.337	

Note: Genetic distances are based on Nei (1978), and microsatellite data are from Mock et al. (2002). The larger sequence divergences indicate greater genetic dissimilarity and lower levels of gene flow or longer periods of isolation.

Table 2.3. Matrix of the average pairwise unbiased genetic distances (below diagonal) with standard error (above diagonal) among wild turkey subspecies based on AFLP data.

	Eastern	Florida	Rio Grande	Merriam's	Gould's
Eastern		0.002	0.003	0.002	0.004
Florida	0.031		0.004	0.003	0.004
Rio Grande	0.064	0.064		0.003	0.005
Merriam's	0.094	0.089	0.090		0.005
Gould's	0.145	0.143	0.121	0.132	

Note: Genetic distances are based on Nei (1978), and AFLP data are from Mock et al. (2002). The larger sequence divergences indicate greater genetic dissimilarity and lower levels of gene flow or longer periods of isolation.

sequence divergences among pairs of wild turkey subspecies were relatively small and ranged from 0.6% to 1.9% (table 2.1), which supports a relatively recent origin for all wild turkey subspecies. In contrast, pairwise comparisons involving the ocellated turkey ranged from 5.5% to 6.2%, indicating that ocellated and wild turkeys diverged from one another before any of the wild turkey subspecies evolved. Assuming that sequence divergence occurs at an average rate of 2% every million years (Wilson et al. 1985), it is probable that the various wild turkey subspecies diverged from one another between 950,000 and 300,000 years ago, whereas the ocellated and wild turkeys diverged from their common ancestor between 3.1 and 2.75 MYA.

In contrast to results based on mitochondrial DNA, Mock et al. (2002) were able to differentiate most wild turkey subspecies from one another using microsatellites and AFLPs. Pairwise genetic distances were largest for comparisons involving either Gould's or Merriam's, whereas the genetic distances between the Eastern and Florida subspecies were the smallest (Mock et al. 2002) (tables 2.2 and 2.3). Rio Grande, Merriam's, and Gould's turkeys were consistently recovered by Mock et al. (2002) as distinct clusters in additional analyses based on genetic distances; however, Florida and Eastern turkeys could not be differentiated from one another. Microsatellites and AFLPs are frequency-based approaches, the analysis of which involves averaging over several independent loci. Given sufficient sample sizes, any reduction in gene flow that allows for the divergence of allelic frequencies among populations can be detected with these methods; however, such a finding may not reflect long-standing historically independent populations (Zink and Barrowclough 2008, Zink 2010). In other words, the apparent distinctiveness of Merriam's, Gould's, and Rio Grande turkeys may be due to the relatively recent reductions in gene flow among regions during the last few hundred or thousand years, rather than the result of long-term isolation over millions of years. Although microsatellites and AFLPs can be used to distinguish two subspecies or other taxa, it is not possible to use these markers to determine when those taxa diverged from their common ancestor.

The evolutionary history and phylogenetic relationships among the six subspecies of wild turkeys are still unclear. Because of the differences in effective population sizes, modes of inheritance, and analytical procedures, different types of genetic markers may lead to very different interpretations of systematic relationships and evolutionary history (Galla and Johnson 2015). Mitochondrial DNA sequence data suggest that the wild turkey may have occupied only a fraction of its historical range during the last ice age, but it underwent rapid population growth and expanded its geographic distribution as the climate warmed and favorable habitat became more widespread. Similar genetic patterns have been observed in many other warm-temperate North American species of animals and plants, suggesting that the Pleistocene distributions of many species were greatly restricted and that most of the present geographic range has been colonized relatively recently (Avise 2004, Soltis et al. 2006). Morphological differences among wild turkey subspecies may have evolved rapidly once gene flow ceased among ancestral populations. The genes underlying morphological traits such as plumage coloration are under the influence of natural and sexual selection and thus evolve more rapidly than mitochondrial genes (Greenberg et al. 1998, Zink et al. 1991, Oyler-McCance et al. 2010, Pérez-Emán et al. 2010). Alternatively, the plumage differences of wild turkey subspecies may have evolved during an earlier period of isolation that was not long enough for the completion of lineage sorting (i.e., evolution of distinct lineages that do not share mitochondrial haplotypes). If isolation lasted long enough for the completion of lineage sorting, the phylogenetic signal may have been erased by hybridization and introgression when contact was renewed among formerly isolated subspecies after the last ice age. Admixture and hybridization resulting from wild turkey reintroduction programs during the twentieth century may also have contributed to the loss of the phylogenetic signal (Leberg et al. 1994, Avise 2004). This seems less likely, however, because it was possible to detect the historical phylogeographic structure of white-tailed deer (*Odocoileus virginianus*), another species that has been the subject of intensive restoration projects (Ellsworth et al. 1994). The lack of evidence for phylogeographic structure in the control region of the wild turkey could have been caused by selective sweeps and genetic hitchhiking, which produce patterns of genetic variation that resemble those caused by population growth (Ballard and Whitlock 2004). A selective sweep occurs when an advantageous mutation rapidly replaces older variants in a population, resulting in reduced genetic variation (Smith and Haigh 1974, Kaplan et al. 1989). Because all mitochondrial genes are linked in a single genome, certain haplotypes of the control region may become very common because of the coincidental association of that locus with a protein-coding gene that is under selection (Smith and Haigh 1974).

Finally, the lack of resolution among turkey subspecies based on mtDNA may be because most previous studies have used small pieces of the control region, which may not provide a sufficient phylogenetic signal to recover historical differentiation among wild turkey subspecies. Because the control region evolves rapidly, it is subject to homoplasy, the evolution of DNA sequences that are identical by state as a result of mutation rather than identical by descent (Estoup et al. 2002, Phillips et al. 2009). Homoplasy can create patterns that mimic demographic expansions and long-distance dispersal (Flanders et al. 2009, Phillips et al. 2009). Protein-coding genes evolve more slowly because of selection against deleterious mutations and are thus more likely to preserve phylogenetic signals. Based on a short segment of cytochrome *b*, Latch (2004) showed that eastern subspecies (Eastern and Florida turkeys) were weakly differentiated from western subspecies (Gould's and Merriam's turkeys). Repeating the work of Mock et al. (2002) with multiple mitochondrial protein-coding genes would provide a test of whether the control region data accurately reflect the biogeographic and demographic history of the wild turkey and help assess the validity of and relationships among its six subspecies.

One aspect of subspecies taxonomy that genetic data have been able to resolve is the question of whether Merriam's turkey is a naturally occurring population in the American Southwest or the descendant of ancient domestic stock that became feral. McKusick (1980, 1986) identified two distinct domestic subspecies of wild turkeys based on the analysis of skeletal remains from archaeological sites in the southwestern United States: the small Indian domestic turkey (*M. g. tularosa*; originally described by Schorger 1970) and the large Indian domestic turkey. McKusick argued that contemporary populations of Merriam's turkeys were the descendants of large Indian domestic turkeys based on the (former) absence of turkey fossils within the historical range of the Merriam's subspecies prior to 500 AD, the co-occurrence of turkey remains with evidence of agriculture, and the lack of shared morphological characters between Merriam's and the geographically closest subspecies (Rio Grande, Gould's, and South Mexican turkeys). An alternative hypothesis for the origin of *M. g. merriami*, developed by David E. Brown, postulated that Merriam's turkey evolved from either the Gould's or Rio Grande subspecies as populations expanded northward in conjunction with the spread of pine-oak forests and woodlands after the end of the Last Glacial Maximum (Shaw and Mollohan 1992).

McKusick's delineation of two breeds of domestic turkeys has been criticized for not taking into account phenotypic plasticity and environmental effects (Breitburg 1988, Senior and Pierce 1989, Munroe 1994). Recently, the bones of early Holocene (9,500–9,000 years ago) turkeys were recovered from the North Creek Shelter in southern Utah and provided evidence of a native population of wild turkeys in the American Southwest prior to the earliest use of domestic turkeys by the Mogollon culture (ca. 300 BC; Newbold et al. 2012). A close relationship between Merriam's, Rio Grande, and Gould's turkeys is supported by mtDNA, microsatellites, and AFLPs (Mock et al. 2002, Speller et al. 2010) (fig. 2.3). Analysis of mitochondrial DNA from turkey bones and coprolites from archaeological sites revealed that two distinct lineages of ancient domestic turkeys had formerly existed in the American Southwest (Speller et al. 2010). One lineage (haplogroup H1 of Speller et al., represented in fig. 2.3 by haplotypes aHap1, aHap1a, aHap1b, Hap1c, and Hap1d) was closely related to contemporary Eastern, Florida, and Rio Grande turkeys. The second lineage (haplogroup H2, represented in fig. 2.3 by haplotypes aHap2, aHap2b, aHap2c, and aHap2d) was closely related to modern Gould's and Merriam's turkeys. Speller et al. also recovered South Mexican turkeys and modern commercial breeds as a separate lineage. The discovery of two genetic lineages among archaeological turkey remains that were not closely related to the South Mexican turkey or modern commercial breeds indicates that pre-Columbian cultures of the American Southwest exploited two distinct turkey populations. Speller et al. found that most H1 haplotypes were unique to archaeological remains, except for haplotype aHap1, which occurred in a small number of modern Merriam's turkeys, whereas the H2 haplotypes were either identical or closely related to mtDNA sequences from modern Merriam's or Gould's turkeys. The presence of distinct genetic lineages among archaeological turkey remains suggests that (1) pre-Columbian peoples in the American Southwest exploited native wild turkeys as well as domestic turkey stock that was introduced into the region from elsewhere; and (2) there were two or more centers of turkey domestication in North America, including the American Southwest (Nott 2010, Speller et al. 2010, Thornton and Emery 2017, Lipe et al. 2016). Speller et al. argued that the occurrence of shared haplotypes among contemporary populations and archaeological remains indicates some level of introgression between ancient domestic and wild populations in the past. This is underscored by the sharing of haplotypes among modern commercial breeds and contemporary Eastern, Florida, and Rio Grande turkeys.

Population Genetics and Adaptive Variation

Most population genetics research on wild turkeys has focused on characterizing local population structure (Leberg 1991, Stangel et al. 1992, Rhodes et al. 1995, Harmon and van den Bussche 2000, Latch and Rhodes 2006) or assessing the effects of restocking efforts (Boone and Rhodes 1996, Mock et al. 2004, Latch and Rhodes 2005, Latch et al. 2006a, b). Early electrophoretic studies of wild turkeys produced conflicting estimates of genetic structure at the local level. Substantial genetic differentiation was observed among flocks of Eastern turkeys in South Carolina (Boone and Rhodes 1996, Latch 2004) and Rio Grande turkeys in Kansas (Rhodes et al. 1995), whereas no genetic structure was detected among wild turkey flocks in other parts of the eastern United States (Leberg 1991, Stangel et al. 1992) or in Oklahoma (Harmon and van den Bussche 2000). Latch and Rhodes (2006) used microsatellites and mitochondrial control region data to investigate the effect of season and sampling scheme on estimates of local population structure in wild turkeys in southwestern Indiana. They found that females sampled in winter exhibited low but statistically significant values of F_{ST} (correlation of randomly chosen alleles within the same subpopulation relative to the total population; Holsinger and Weir 2009) for both genetic markers, whereas the F_{ST} values for males collected during the spring were not statistically different from zero. It seems likely that differences in sampling scheme and time of sample collection largely explain the conflicting results in studies of local population structure in wild turkeys (Latch and Rhodes 2006, Latch et al. 2007). Boone and Rhodes (1996) and Rhodes et al. (1995) used samples from both sexes trapped during the winter, Leberg (1991) used samples from males harvested by hunters during the spring hunting season, and Harmon and van den Bussche (2000) used samples from both sexes collected during the spring. Stangel et al. (1992) did not mention whether their samples were collected during winter or spring. Winter flocks contain large numbers of closely related females and their offspring, but in spring these large aggregations break up into smaller bands of related males and small female breeding harems of males (McRoberts et al. 2014). This seasonal social reorganization alters the weak population structure that existed among winter flocks, resulting in admixed groups in spring (Latch and Rhodes 2006).

The study by Latch and Rhodes (2006) remains the only one to assess the relationship between season and local population structure in wild turkeys. Additional work needs to be devoted to assessing the relationship between season, social organization, and local population structure in wild turkeys, as well as developing standardized methods of conducting such studies. Latch and Rhodes suggested that F_{IS} (the correlation of alleles within individuals relative to the subpopulation in which they occur; Holsinger and Weir 2009) may be a more informative statistic than F_{ST}. Admixed populations should exhibit positive values of F_{IS} because of a deficiency of heterozygotes, and Latch and Rhodes noted that all spring-collected samples exhibited positive values of F_{IS}. Latch and Rhodes also found that the population Bayesian clustering approach implemented in the computer program STRUCTURE (Pritchard et al. 2000) failed to detect population structure in either winter or spring samples, probably because of weak genetic differentiation. STRUCTURE, however, has undergone further development since 2006, and its ability to detect weak population structure in admixed populations has improved (Porras-Hurtado et al. 2013). Another option for future studies of local population structure in wild turkeys may be to use Bayesian clustering programs that incorporate spatial data (François and Durand 2010).

Only a handful of population genetics studies of turkeys have been conducted at the landscape scale, but those few have revealed substantial population structure (Leberg 1991, Mock et al. 2002, Seidel et al. 2013, Davis 2016). Microsatellite and AFLP data analyzed by Mock et al. (2002) indicated significant genetic differentiation among most wild turkey subspecies. Despite weak within-region genetic structure, Eastern turkeys from Connecticut, Kentucky, Tennessee, and Arkansas were well differentiated (Leberg 1991). On smaller spatial scales, Seidel et al. (2013) and Davis (2016) each detected three distinct genetic clusters in eastern Texas and Mississippi, respectively. Leberg (1991) hypothesized that habitat fragmentation caused by European settlement may have increased regional genetic differentiation within the historical range of the wild turkey. In addition to habitat fragmentation, the contemporary regional genetic structure of wild turkeys has also likely been shaped by restocking programs, which created admixed and hybridized populations of genetically distinct lineages (Leberg et al. 1994, Mock et al. 2004, Latch and Rhodes 2005, Seidel et al. 2013, Davis 2016). Of 294 wild turkeys sampled from eastern Texas, Seidel et al. (2013) found that 33% were genetically similar to turkeys from the Midwest, fewer than 5% were genetically similar to turkeys in the southeastern United States, and 63% were admixed birds derived from native Texas populations and other sources. Wild turkeys in Kansas retain much of the historical population structure, with Eastern turkeys in eastern Kansas and Rio Grande turkeys in western Kansas (Latch et al. 2006a). Latch et al. (2006a) also detected hybridization between Eastern and Rio Grande turkeys in eastern Kansas but were unable to determine whether this was a natural or human-mediated hybrid zone. Hybridization between Rio Grande and Merriam's turkeys is frequent in extreme southwestern Kansas, possibly because of the immigration of Merriam's turkeys from Colorado or New Mexico (Latch et al. 2006a). Latch et al. (2006b) detected hybridization in the Davis Mountains of Texas between native Rio Grande turkeys and a population of Merriam's turkeys that had been established in 1983. Of the 27 Merriam's turkeys sampled, nearly two-thirds were either F_1 hybrids or genetically identical to Rio Grande turkeys despite a distance of 20–30 km separating the populations of the two subspecies in the Davis Mountains (Latch et al. 2006b). In contrast, Mock et al. (2001) detected no hybridization among Merriam's and reintroduced Gould's turkeys in the Huachuca Mountains.

Assessments of genetic diversity in wild turkeys have generally focused on comparing natural populations to those founded through translocations. Genetic diversity is often lower in populations established through translocations than in natural populations because the founding individuals of translocated populations were not representative of the source population's gene pool (i.e., founder effect; Mayr 1999, Hedrick et al. 2001). The founder effect can be magnified if (1) the founding population is exceptionally small, (2) the translocation is derived from a single source, and (3) genetic diversity in the source population is low (Mock et al. 2004, Stephen et al. 2005, Wright et al. 2014). The genetic diversity of a translocated population may further decline because of low reproductive success, successive population bottlenecks, and lack of gene flow and immigration (Mock et al. 2004, Stephen et al. 2005, Wright et al. 2014). A population of Gould's turkey reestablished in the Huachuca Mountains between 1983 and 1987 exhibited lower genetic diversity than populations of Gould's turkey in Mexico or nearby populations of Merriam's turkeys (Mock et al. 2001). Similarly, isolated populations of Merriam's turkeys in Colorado and Arizona established through translocations during the 1950s displayed lower genetic diversity than the source populations (Mock et al. 2004). Merriam's turkeys on the Kaibab Plateau in Arizona exhibited higher genetic diversity than other translocated populations in Mount Trumbull, Arizona, and the Spanish Peaks area in Colorado. Mock et al. (2004) hypothesized that the higher genetic diversity displayed on the Kaibab Plateau was due to larger population size and greater availability of suitable habitat.

The main concern regarding founder effects and hybridization caused by translocations is their effects on the genetic variation that underlies adaptive traits. Fitness and the ability to adapt to environmental change are correlated with genetic diversity, and small, isolated populations generally have lower genetic diversity than larger populations (Frankham 1995,

2005). A small number of founders in a translocated population may suffer additional losses of genetic diversity because the effects of inbreeding and genetic drift lead to lowered disease resistance and adaptability to environmental changes (Lacy 1987, Roelke et al. 1993, Hitchings and Beebee 1998, Reed and Frankham 2003, Spielman et al. 2004). Translocations that lead to admixture among genetically distinct populations may result in outbreeding depression, reduced fitness of offspring, or later generations because of the erosion of local adaptive genetic variation (Svärdson 1970, Rhymer and Simberloff 1996, Avise 2004, Edmands 2007). Founder effects can be minimized by acquiring transplants from multiple source populations and releasing translocated animals into areas that support large expanses of ideal habitat. For example, the use of multiple source populations and a greater amount of contiguous habitat in southern Indiana resulted in higher levels of gene flow among reestablished populations of wild turkeys (Latch and Rhodes 2005). In contrast, reintroduced turkey populations in northern Indiana exhibited greater genetic similarity to the source populations because of the use of fewer source populations and greater habitat fragmentation (Latch and Rhodes 2005). The best way to prevent outbreeding depression in restocking programs is to avoid mixing populations that are genetically distinct and adapted to different environments. Leberg et al. (1994) and Latch et al. (2006a, 2007) have argued that turkeys should not be translocated without assessing the genetic ancestry of the source populations and of populations surrounding the area targeted for restocking. However, much of the restocking of wild turkeys took place prior to the molecular era, so restocking programs often used multiple source populations, and turkeys of unknown ancestry were used to establish populations outside the native range (Latch et al. 2006a). Genetic markers that are unaffected or only weakly affected by natural selection, such as microsatellites and mtDNA, are known as neutral markers. Neutral markers are useful for inferring demographic history but provide only an indirect understanding of how adaptive genetic variation is apportioned among populations. Currently, we have no understanding of how restocking affected adaptive genetic variation in wild turkeys because most genetic studies of this species have employed neutral markers.

Most research on adaptive genetic variation in turkeys has consisted of gene-phenotype association studies, including genetic control of the circadian clock (Adikari 2012), effects of aging (Adikari et al. 2013), growth and meat quality and yield (Aslam et al. 2011), eggshell structure (Mann and Mann 2013), plumage variation (Vidal et al. 2010, Corso et al. 2017), susceptibility and resistance to aflatoxin B_1 (Rawal et al. 2009, Kim et al. 2013, Monson et al. 2014, 2015, 2016), pathogen resistance (Ramasamy et al. 2012), and round heart disease (Reed et al. 2007, Mendoza et al. 2008). Although much of the above research has been conducted on domestic turkeys, these studies have identified genes underlying traits that may be under selection in wild populations. Immunity and disease resistance is one area where several studies have compared wild and domestic turkeys. Kim et al. (2013) found that Eastern and Rio Grande turkeys and the Royal Palm heritage breed were more resistant to aflatoxin B_1 than the Nicholas commercial-line breed. Intense selection for other traits in the commercial line may have inadvertently resulted in the loss of aflatoxin-protective alleles (Kim et al. 2013). Embryos of Eastern wild turkeys are also more resistant to aflatoxin B_1 than the embryos of domestic stocks up to day 4 of development; however, exposure to aflatoxin B_1 at day 5 resulted in reduced growth of Eastern turkey embryos because of detrimental effects on the mitochondria of liver cells (Monson et al. 2016). Eastern, Rio Grande, and Merriam's turkeys exhibit higher diversity in the B-locus of major histocompatibility complex (MHC) diversity than domestic breeds (Chaves et al. 2011). Restocked wild turkeys in southern Wisconsin exhibited higher MHC diversity as a consequence of being established from several maternal lineages (Bauer et al. 2013).

Conclusions

Despite several decades of genetic research on the wild turkey, questions regarding the validity of and relationships among its six subspecies remain unresolved. Fully assessing the relationships and distinctiveness of the six subspecies will require replicating the work of Mock et al. (2002) using additional genetic markers. Future phylogeographic studies of the wild turkey should utilize several mitochondrial protein-coding genes because this approach would provide a test of phylogeographic inferences based on the noncoding control region. Alternatively, future mitochondrial phylogeographic studies of the wild turkey could utilize whole mitochondrial genomes, which are now relatively easy and inexpensive to obtain from multiple individuals (do Amaral et al. 2015, Nunez and Oleksiak 2016). A mitochondrial approach should be coupled with markers from the nuclear genome. Recent advances in DNA sequencing technology have made it possible for wildlife biologists to conduct genome-wide studies in wild populations of animals and plants (Davey and Blaxter 2010, Ekblom and Galindo 2011, Andrews et al. 2016). Rather than sequencing whole nuclear genomes, genomic research on wild populations often utilizes single nucleotide polymorphisms (SNPs), short segments of DNA that differ by a single nucleotide base. SNPs are abundant in the genomes of most organisms and provide a wellspring of information about neutral and adaptive genetic variation. Recently developed techniques such as restriction site–associated DNA sequencing have reduced the difficulty and cost of obtaining a panel of 20,000 or more SNPs (Davey and Blaxter 2010). Rather than generating a completely new panel of SNPs, future genomic studies of wild turkeys could use a high-density SNP chip, the Axiom Turkey Genotyping Array, which has been developed by the US Department of Agriculture and two private companies, Aviagen and Hendrix Genetics (Aslam et al. 2012). In many ways, the wild turkey is the ideal wild species for genomic research because studies of domestic turkeys have identified the genes underlying traits that may be under selection in the wild, and the genome of the domestic turkey has been sequenced and annotated (Dalloul et al. 2010). The existence of a sequenced, annotated genome is a major advantage when attempting to determine the location of candidate loci that may be under selection, which could prove useful in future genetic studies of wild turkeys. A range-wide SNP-based study of the wild turkey would provide another means of assessing its phylogeographic structure, testing its morphology-based subspecies taxonomy, and identifying genes involved in local adaptation. A genomic approach may also be useful for investigating the genetic effects of restocking, dispersal and gene flow, mating success and parentage, effects of habitat fragmentation, and temporal changes in genetic diversity and population structure.

Literature Cited

Adikari, A. M. J. B. 2012. DNA sequence and haplotype variation analyses of circadian clock genes and their effects on phenotypes in the turkey, *Meleagris gallopavo*. Dissertation, Virginia Polytechnic Institute and State University, Blacksburg, USA.

Adikari, A. M. J. B., W. A. D. Nayananjalie, J. Xu, and E. J. Smith. 2013. Haplotype structure and variation of the telomerase reverse transcriptase (*tur*TERT) gene in turkeys (*Meleagris gallopavo*). Rajarata University Journal 1:10–14.

Aldrich, J. W. 1967. Taxonomy, distribution and present status. Pages 17–44 *in* O. H. Hewitt, editor. The wild turkey and its management. The Wildlife Society, Washington, DC, USA.

American Ornithologists' Union. 1988. Check-list of North American birds. Seventh edition. American Ornithologists' Union, Washington, DC, USA.

Andrews, K. R., J. M. Good, M. R. Miller, G. Luikart, and P. A. Hohenlohe. 2016. Harnessing the power of RADseq for ecological and evolutionary genomics. Nature Reviews Genetics 17:81–92.

Aslam, M. L., J. W. M. Bastiaansen, R. P. M. A. Crooijmans, A. Vereijken, and M. A. M. Groenen. 2011. Whole genome QTL mapping for growth, meat quality and breast meat yield traits in turkey. BMC Genetics 12:61.

Aslam, M. L., J. W. M. Bastiaansen, M. G. Elferink, H. J. Megens, R. P. M. A. Crooijmans, L. A. Blomberg, R. C. Fleischer, C. P. Van Tassell, T. S. Sonstegard, S. G. Schroeder, M. A. M. Groenen, and J. A. Long. 2012. Whole genome SNP discovery and analysis of genetic diversity in turkey (*Meleagris gallopavo*). BMC Genomics 13:391.

Avise, J. C. 2000. Phylogeography. Harvard University Press, Cambridge, Massachusetts, USA.

Avise, J. C. 2004. Molecular markers, natural history, and evolution. Second edition. Sinauer Associates, Sunderland, Massachusetts, USA.

Ballard, J. W. O., and M. C. Whitlock. 2004. The incomplete natural history of mitochondria. Molecular Ecology 13:729–744.

Bauer, M. M., M. M. Miller, W. E. Briles, and K. M. Reed. 2013. Genetic variation at the MHC in a population of introduced wild turkeys. Animal Biotechnology 24:210–228.

Bocheński, Z. M., and K. E. Campbell Jr. 2006. The extinct California turkey, *Meleagris californica*, from Rancho La Brea: comparative osteology and systematics. Natural

History Museum of Los Angeles County Contributions in Science 509:1–92.

Boone, M. D., and O. E. Rhodes Jr. 1996. Genetic structure among subpopulations of the Eastern wild turkey (*Meleagris gallopavo silvestris*). American Midland Naturalist 135:168–171.

Bortolus, A. 2008. Error cascades in the biological sciences: the unwanted consequences of using bad taxonomy in ecology. Ambio 37:114–118.

Breitburg, E. 1988. Prehistoric New World turkey domestication: origins, development, and consequences. Dissertation, Southern Illinois University, Carbondale, USA.

Brito, D. 2004. Lack of adequate taxonomic knowledge may hinder endemic mammal conservation in the Brazilian Atlantic Forest. Biodiversity and Conservation 13:2135–2144.

Chaves, L. D., G. M. Faile, J. A. Hendrickson, K. E. Mock, and K. M. Reed. 2011. A locus-wide approach to assessing variation in the avian MHC: the *B*-locus of the wild turkey. Heredity 107:40–49.

Clark, P. U., A. S. Dyke, J. D. Shakun, A. E. Carlson, J. Clark, B. Wohlfarth, J. X. Mitrovica, S. W. Hostetler, and A. M. McCabe. 2009. The Last Glacial Maximum. Science 325:710–714.

Corso, J., D. Hepp, M. C. Ledur, J. O. Peixoto, N. J. R. Fagundes, and T. R. O. Freitas. 2017. Genetic variation of the bronze locus (*MC1R*) in turkeys from southern Brazil. Genetics and Molecular Biology 40:104–108.

Crawford, R. D. 1992. Introduction to Europe and diffusion of domesticated turkeys from the Americas. Archivos de zootecnia 41:307–314.

Crowe, T. M., R. C. K. Bowie, P. Bloomer, T. G. Mandiwana, T. A. J. Hedderson, E. Randi, S. L. Pereira, and J. Wakeling. 2006. Phylogenetics, biogeography and classification of, and character evolution in, gamebirds (Aves: Galliformes): effects of character exclusion, data partitioning and missing data. Cladistics 22:495–532.

Dalloul, R. A., J. A. Long, A. V. Zimin, L. Aslam, K. Beal, L. Blomberg, P. Bouffard, et al. 2010. Multi-platform next-generation sequencing of the domestic turkey (*Meleagris gallopavo*): genome assembly and analysis. PLoS Biology 8(9):e1000475.

Davey, J. W., and M. L. Blaxter. 2010. RADSeq: next-generation population genetics. Briefings in Functional Genomics 9:416–423.

Davis, A. M. 2016. Landscape ecology of Eastern wild turkeys in Mississippi. Thesis, Mississippi State University, Starkville, USA.

DeYoung, R. W., and R. L. Honeycutt. 2005. The molecular toolbox: genetic techniques in wildlife ecology and management. Journal of Wildlife Management 69:1362–1384.

Diffendal, R., Jr., R. K. Pabian, and J. R. Thomasson. 1996. Geologic history of Ash Hollow State Historical Park, Nebraska. Institute of Agriculture and Natural Resources Educational Circular 5a. University of Nebraska–Lincoln, USA.

Dimcheff, D. E., S. V. Drovetski, and D. P. Mindell. 2002. Phylogeny of Tetraoninae and other galliform birds using mitochondrial 12S and ND2 genes. Molecular Phylogenetics and Evolution 24:203–215.

do Amaral, F. R., L. G. Neves, M. F. R. Resende Jr., F. Mobili, C. Y. Miyaki, K. C. M. Pellegrino, and C. Biondo. 2015. Ultraconserved elements sequencing as a low-cost source of complete mitochondrial genomes and microsatellite markers in non-model amniotes. PLoS ONE 10(9):e0138446.

Dobzhansky, T. 1973. Nothing in biology makes sense except in the light of evolution. American Biology Teacher 35:125–129.

Drovetski, S. V. 2003. Plio-Pleistocene climatic oscillations, Holarctic biogeography and speciation in an avian subfamily. Journal of Biogeography 30:1173–1181.

Drummond, A. J., A. Rambaut, B. Shapiro, and O. G. Pybus. 2005. Bayesian coalescent inferences of past population dynamics from molecular sequences. Molecular Biology and Evolution 22:1185–1192.

Drummond, A. J., S. J. W. Ho, M. J. Phillips, and A. Rambaut. 2006. Phylogenetics and dating with confidence. PLoS Biology 4(5):e88.

Drummond, A. J., M. A. Suchard, D. Xie, and A. Rambaut. 2012. Bayesian phylogenetics with BEAUti and the BEAST 1.7. Molecular Biology and Evolution 29:1969–1973.

Dubois, A. 2003. The relationships between taxonomy and conservation biology in the century of extinctions. C. R. Biologies 326:S9–S21.

Edmands, S. 2007. Between a rock and a hard place: evaluating the relative risks of inbreeding and outbreeding for conservation and management. Molecular Ecology 16:463–475.

Ekblom, R., and J. Galindo. 2011. Applications of next-generation sequencing in molecular ecology of non-model organisms. Heredity 107:1–15.

Ellsworth, D. L., R. L. Honeycutt, N. J. Silvy, J. W. Bickham, and W. D. Klimstra. 1994. Historical biogeography and contemporary patterns of mitochondrial DNA variation in white-tailed deer from the southeastern United States. Evolution 48:122–136.

Estoup, A., P. Jarne, and J.-M. Cornuet. 2002. Homoplasy and mutation model at microsatellite loci and their consequences for population genetics analysis. Molecular Ecology 11:1591–1604.

Excoffier, L., and H. E. Lischer. 2010. Arlequin suite ver 3.5: a new series of programs to perform population genetics analyses under Linux and Windows. Molecular Ecology Resources 10:564–567.

Flanders, J., G. Jones, P. Benda, C. Dietz, S. Zhang, G. Li, M. Sharifi, and S. J. Rossiter. 2009. Phylogeography of the greater horseshoe bat, *Rhinolophus ferrumequinum*: contrasting results from mitochondrial and microsatellite data. Molecular Ecology 18:306–318.

François, O., and E. Durand. 2010. Spatially explicit Bayesian clustering models in population genetics. Molecular Ecology Resources 10:773–784.

Frankham, R. 1995. Conservation genetics. Annual Review of Genetics 29:305–327.

Frankham, R. 2005. Genetics and extinction. Biological Conservation 126:131–140.

Frankham, R. 2008. Genetic adaptation to captivity in species conservation programs. Molecular Ecology 17:325–333.

Futuyma, D. J. 1998. Evolutionary biology. Third edition. Sinauer Associates, Sunderland, Massachusetts, USA.

Galla, S. J., and J. A. Johnson. 2015. Differential introgression and effective size of marker type influence phylogenetic inference of a recently divergent avian group (Phasianidae: *Tympanuchus*). Molecular Phylogenetics and Evolution 84:1–13.

Greenberg, R., P. J. Cordero, S. Droege, and R. C. Fleischer. 1998. Morphological adaptation with no mitochondrial DNA differentiation in the coastal plain swamp sparrow. Auk 115:706–712.

Guan, X., P. Silva, K. B. Gyenai, J. Xu, T. Geng, Z. Tu, D. C. Samuels, and E. J. Smith. 2009. The mitochondrial genome sequence and molecular phylogeny of the turkey, *Meleagris gallopavo*. Animal Genetics 40:134–141.

Harmon, S. A., and R. A. van den Bussche. 2000. Genetic attributes of a declining population of reintroduced Eastern wild turkeys (*Meleagris gallopavo silvestris*). Southwestern Naturalist 45:258–266.

Harris, S. E., J. Munshi-South, C. Obergfell, and R. O'Neill. 2013. Signature of rapid evolution in urban and rural transcriptomes of white-footed mice (*Peromyscus leucopus*) in the New York Metropolitan Area. PLoS ONE 8(8):e74938.

Hasegawa, M., H. Kishino, and T. Yano. 1985. Dating the human-ape splitting by a molecular clock of mitochondrial DNA. Journal of Molecular Evolution 22:160–174.

Hedrick, P. W., G. A. Gutierrez-Espeleta, and R. N. Lee. 2001. Founder effect in an island population of bighorn sheep. Molecular Ecology 10:851–857.

Heffelfinger, J., B. Wakeling, J. Millican, S. Stone, T. Skinner, M. Fredlake, and M. Adkins. 2000. Southeastern Arizona wild turkey management plan. Arizona Game and Fish Department, Phoenix, USA.

Heusser, L. 1978. Pollen in Santa Barbara Basin, California: a 12,000-yr record. Geological Society of America Bulletin 89:673–678.

Heusser, L. E., and F. Sirocko. 1997. Millennial pulsing of environmental change in southern California from the past 24 k.y.: a record of Indo-Pacific ENSO events. Geology 25:243–246.

Hitchings, S. P., and T. J. C. Beebee. 1998. Loss of genetic diversity and fitness in common toad (*Bufo bufo*) populations isolated by inimical habitat. Journal of Evolutionary Biology 11:269–283.

Holsinger, K. E., and B. S. Weir. 2009. Genetics in geographically structured populations: defining, estimating and interpreting F_{ST}. Nature Reviews 10:639–650.

Hung, C.-M., S. V. Drovetski, and R. M. Zink. 2016. Matching loci surveyed to questions asked in phylogeography. Proceedings of the Royal Society of London B 283:2012340.

Kaplan, N. L., R. R. Hudson, and C. H. Langley. 1989. The "hitchhiking effect" revisited. Genetics 123:887–899.

Kim, J. E., B. R. Bunderson, A. Croasdell, K. M. Reed, and R. A. Coulombe Jr. 2013. Alpha-class glutathione S-transferase in wild turkeys (*Meleagris gallopavo*): characterization and role in resistance to the carcinogenic mycotoxin aflatoxin B_1. PLoS ONE 8(4):e60662.

Kimura, M. 1980. A simple method for estimating evolutionary rate of base substitutions through comparative studies of nucleotide sequences. Journal of Molecular Evolution 16:111–120.

Koehler, P. A., R. S. Anderson, and W. G. Spaulding. 2005. Development of vegetation in the central Mojave Desert of California during the late Quaternary. Palaeogeography, Palaeoclimatology, Palaeoecology 215:297–311.

Lacy, R. C. 1987. Loss of genetic diversity from managed populations: interacting effects of drift, mutation, immigration, selection, and population subdivision. Conservation Biology 1:143–158.

Latch, E. K. 2004. Population genetics of reintroduced wild turkeys: insights into hybridization, gene flow, and social structure. Dissertation, Purdue University, West Lafayette, Indiana, USA.

Latch, E. K., and O. E. Rhodes Jr. 2005. The effects of gene flow and population isolation on the genetic structure of reintroduced wild turkey populations: are genetic signatures of source populations retained? Conservation Genetics 6:981–997.

Latch, E. K., and O. E. Rhodes Jr. 2006. Evidence for bias in estimates of local genetic structure due to sampling scheme. Animal Conservation 9:308–315.

Latch, E. K., E. J. Smith, and O. E. Rhodes Jr. 2002. Isolation and characterization of microsatellite loci in wild and domestic turkeys (*Meleagris gallopavo*). Molecular Ecology Resources 2:176–178.

Latch, E. K., R. D. Applegate, and O. E. Rhodes Jr. 2006a. Genetic composition of wild turkeys in Kansas following decades of translocations. Journal of Wildlife Management 70:1698–1703.

Latch, E. K., L. A. Harveson, J. S. King, M. D. Hobson, and O. E. Rhodes Jr. 2006b. Assessing hybridization in wildlife populations using molecular markers: a case study in wild turkeys. Journal of Wildlife Management 70:485–492.

Latch, E. K., K. E. Mock, and O. E. Rhodes Jr. 2007. The use of molecular markers in wild turkey management. Proceedings of the National Turkey Symposium 9:33–44.

Leberg, P. L. 1991. Influence of fragmentation and bottlenecks on genetic divergence of wild turkey populations. Conservation Biology 5:522–530.

Leberg, P. L., P. W. Stangel, H. O. Hillestad, R. L. Marchinton, and M. H. Smith. 1994. Genetic structure of reintroduced wild turkey and white-tailed deer populations. Journal of Wildlife Management 58:698–711.

Leopold, A. S. 1959. Wildlife of Mexico. University of California Press, Berkeley, USA.

Librado, P., and J. Rozas. 2009. DnaSP v5: a software for comprehensive analysis of DNA polymorphism data. Bioinformatics 25:1451–1452.

Lipe, W. D., R. K. Bocinsky, B. S. Chisholm, R. Lyle, D. M. Dove, R. G. Matson, E. Jarvis, K. Judd, and B. M. Kemp. 2016. Cultural and genetic contexts for early turkey domestication in the northern Southwest. American Antiquity 81:97–113.

Mace, G. M. 2004. The role of taxonomy in species conservation. Philosophical Transactions of the Royal Society of London B 359:711–719.

Mann, K., and M. Mann. 2013. The proteome of the calcified layer organic matrix of turkey (*Meleagris gallopavo*) eggshell. Proteome Science 11:40.

Martin, L. D., J. Tate, and J. Tate Jr. 1970. A new turkey from the Pliocene of Nebraska. Wilson Bulletin 82:214–218.

May, R. M. 1988. How many species are there on Earth? Science 241:1441–1449.

May, R. M. 2010. Tropical arthropod species, more or less? Science 329:41–42.

Mayr, E. 1999. Systematics and the origin of species from the viewpoint of a zoologist. Harvard University Press, Cambridge, Massachusetts, USA.

McKusick, C. R. 1980. Three groups of turkeys from southwestern archaeological sites. Natural History Museum of Los Angeles County Contributions in Science 330:225–235.

McKusick, C. R. 1986. Southwest Indian turkeys—prehistory and comparative osteology. Southwest Bird Laboratory, Globe, Arizona, USA.

McRoberts, J. T., M. C. Wallace, and S. W. Eaton. 2014. Wild turkey (*Meleagris gallopavo*). Account 22 *in* A. Poole, editor. The birds of North America online. Cornell Laboratory of Ornithology, Ithaca, New York, USA. http://bna.birds.cornell.edu/bna/species/022.

Mendoza, K. M., W. Chiang, G. M. Strasburg, and K. M. Reed. 2008. Characterization of a cardiac complementary deoxyribonucleic acid library from the turkey (*Meleagris gallopavo*). Poultry Science 87:1165–1170.

Mensing, S. A. 2001. Late-glacial and early Holocene vegetation and climate change near Owens Lake, eastern California. Quaternary Research 55:57–65.

Mock, K. E., T. C. Theimer, B. F. Wakeling, O. E. Rhodes Jr., D. L. Greenberg, and P. Keim. 2001. Verifying the origins of a reintroduced population of Gould's wild turkey. Journal of Wildlife Management 65:871–879.

Mock, K. E., T. C. Theimer, O. E. Rhodes Jr., D. L. Greenberg, and P. Keim. 2002. Genetic variation across the historical range of the wild turkey (*Meleagris gallopavo*). Molecular Ecology 11:643–657.

Mock, K. E., E. K. Latch, and O. E. Rhodes Jr. 2004. Assessing losses of genetic diversity due to translocation: long-term case histories in Merriam's turkey (*Meleagris gallopavo merriami*). Conservation Genetics 5:631–645.

Monson, M. S., R. E. Settlage, K. W. McMahon, K. M. Mendoza, S. Rawal, H. S. El-Nezami, R. A. Coulombe, and K. M. Reed. 2014. Response of the hepatic transcriptome to aflatoxin B_1 in domestic turkey (*Meleagris gallopavo*). PLoS ONE 9(6):e100930.

Monson, M. S., R. E. Settlage, K. M. Mendoza, S. Rawal, H. S. El-Nezami, R. A. Coulombe, and K. M. Reed. 2015. Modulation of the spleen transcriptome in domestic turkey (*Meleagris gallopavo*) in response to aflatoxin B_1 and probiotics. Immunogenetics 67:163–178.

Monson, M. S., C. J. Cardona, R. A. Coulombe, and K. M. Reed. 2016. Hepatic transcriptome response of domesticated and wild turkey embryos to aflatoxin B_1. Toxins 8:16.

Monteagudo, L. V., R. Avellanet, R. Azon, and M. T. Tejedor. 2013. Mitochondrial DNA analysis in two heritage European breeds confirms Mesoamerican origin and low genetic variability of domestic turkey. Animal Genetics 44:786.

Moore, R. T. 1938. A new race of wild turkey. Auk 55:112–115.

Mora, C., D. P. Tittensor, S. Adl, A. G. B. Simpson, and B. Worm. 2011. How many species are there on Earth and in the oceans? PLoS Biology 9(8):e1001127.

Munroe, B. L., Jr., R. C. Banks, J. W. Fitzpatrick, T. R. Howell, N. K. Johnson, H. Ouellet, J. V. Remsen, and R. W. Storer. 1995. Fortieth supplement to the American Ornithologists' Union Check-List of North American Birds. Auk 112:819–830.

Munroe, N. D. 1994. An investigation of Anasazi turkey production in southwestern Colorado. Thesis, Simon Fraser University, Vancouver, British Columbia, Canada.

Nei, M. 1978. Estimation of average heterozygosity and genetic distance from small numbers of individuals. Genetics 89:583–590.

Neumann, T. W. 1989. Human-wildlife competition and prehistoric subsistence: the case of the eastern United States. Journal of Middle Atlantic Archaeology 5:29–57.

Newbold, B. A., J. C. Janetski, M. L. Bodily, and D. T. Yoder. 2012. Early Holocene turkey (*Meleagris gallopavo*) remains from southern Utah: implications for the origins of the Puebloan domestic turkeys. Kiva 78:37–60.

Nott, B. M. 2010. Documenting domestication: molecular and palynological analysis of ancient turkey coprolites from the American Southwest. Thesis, Washington State University, Pullman, USA.

Nunez, J. C. B., and M. F. Oleksiak. 2016. A cost-effective approach to sequence hundreds of complete mitochondrial genomes. PLoS ONE 11(8):e0160958.

Olson, S. L., and J. Farrand Jr. 1974. *Rhegminornis* restudied: a tiny Miocene turkey. Wilson Bulletin 86:114–120.

Oyler-McCance, S. J., J. St. John, and T. W. Quinn. 2010. Rapid evolution in lekking grouse: Implications for taxonomic definitions. Ornithological Monographs 67:114–122.

Pérez-Emán, J. L., R. L. Mumme, and P. G. Jabło ski. 2010. Phylogeography and adaptive plumage evolution in Central American subspecies of the slate-throated redstart (*Myioborus miniatus*). Ornithological Monographs 67:90–102.

Petersen, J. L. 2003. MtDNA investigation of river mediated gene flow in the Illinois population of Eastern wild turkey, *Meleagris gallopavo silvestris*. Thesis, Western Illinois University, Macomb, USA.

Phillips, C. D., R. G. Trujillo, T. S. Gelatt, M. J. Smolen, C. W. Matson, R. L. Honeycutt, J. C. Patton, and J. W. Bickham. 2009. Assessing substitution patterns, rates and homoplasy at HVRI of Steller sea lions, *Eumetopias jubatus*. Molecular Ecology 18:3379–3393.

Porras-Hurtado, L., Y. Ruiz, C. Santos, C. Phillips, A. Carracedo, and M. V. Lareu. 2013. An overview of STRUCTURE: applications, parameter settings, and supporting software. Frontiers in Genetics 4:98.

Pritchard, J. K., M. Stephens, and P. Donnelly. 2000. Inference of population structure using multilocus genotype data. Genetics 155:945–959.

Pyron, P. A., and F. T. Burbrink. 2009. Systematics of the common kingsnake (*Lampropeltis getula*; Serpentes: Colubridae) and the burden of heritage in taxonomy. Zootaxa 2241:22–32.

Ramasamy, K. T., M. R. Reddy, P. C. Verma, and S. Murugesan. 2012. Expression analysis of turkey (*Meleagris gallopavo*) toll-like receptors and molecular characterization of avian specific TLR15. Molecular Biology Reports 39:8539–8549.

Rawal, S., K. M. Mendoza, K. M. Reed, and R. A. Coulombe Jr. 2009. Structure, genetic mapping, and function of the cytochrome P450 3A37 gene in the turkey (*Meleagris gallopavo*). Cytogenetic and Genome Research 125:67–73.

Rea, A. M. 1980. Late Pleistocene and Holocene turkeys in the Southwest. Natural History Museum of Los Angeles County Contributions in Science 330:209–224.

Reed, D. H., and R. Frankham. 2003. Correlation between fitness and genetic diversity. Conservation Biology 17:230–237.

Reed, K. M., K. M. Mendoza, G. R. Hu, L. R. Sullivan, M. W. Grace, L. D. Chaves, and D. L. Kooyman. 2007. Genomic analysis of genetic markers associated with inherited cardiomyopathy (round heart disease) in the turkey (*Meleagris gallopavo*). Animal Genetics 38:211–217.

Rhodes, O. E., Jr., D. J. Buford, M. S. Miller, and R. S. Lutz. 1995. Genetic structure of reintroduced Rio Grande wild turkeys in Kansas. Journal of Wildlife Management 59:771–775.

Rhymer, J. M., and D. Simberloff. 1996. Extinction by hybridization and introgression. Annual Review in Ecology and Systematics 27:83–109.

Ridgway, R., and H. Friedmann.1946. The birds of North and Middle America. Bulletin of the United States National Museum, Number 50, Part 10. United States National Museum, Washington, DC, USA.

Rising, J. D. 2007. Named subspecies and their significance in contemporary ornithology. Ornithological Monographs 63:45–54.

Roelke, M. E., J. S. Martenson, and S. J. O'Brien. 1993. The consequences of demographic reduction and genetic depletion in the endangered Florida panther. Current Biology 3:340–350.

Rogers, A. R., and H. Harpending. 1992. Population growth makes waves in the distribution of pairwise genetic differences. Molecular Biology and Evolution 9:552 569.

Schorger, A. W. 1966. The wild turkey: its history and domestication. University of Oklahoma Press, Norman, USA.

Schorger, A. W. 1970. A new subspecies of *Meleagris gallopavo*. Auk 87:168–170.

Seidel, S. A., C. E. Comer, W. C. Conway, R. W. DeYoung, J. B. Hardin, and G. E. Calkins. 2013. Influence of translocations on Eastern wild turkey population genetics in Texas. Journal of Wildlife Management 77:1221–1231.

Senior, L. M., and L. J. Pierce. 1989. Turkeys and domestication in the Southwest: implications from Homol'ovi III. Kiva 54:245–259.

Shaw, H. G., and C. Mollohan. 1992. Merriam's turkey. Pages 331–349 *in* J. G. Dickson, editor. The wild turkey: biology and management. Stackpole Books, Mechanicsburg, Pennsylvania, USA.

Slatkin, M., and R. R. Hudson. 1991. Pairwise comparisons of mitochondrial DNA sequences in stable and exponentially growing populations. Genetics 129:555–562.

Smith, J. M., and J. Haigh. 1974. The hitch-hiking effect of a favourable gene. Genetic Research 23:23–35.

Soltis, D. E., A. B. Morris, J. S. McLachlan, P. S. Manos, and P. S. Soltis. 2006. Comparative phylogeography of unglaciated eastern North America. Molecular Ecology 15:4261–4293.

Speller, C. F., B. M. Kemp, S. D. Wyatt, C. Monroe, W. D. Lipe, U. M. Arndt, and D. Y. Yang. 2010. Ancient mitochondrial DNA analysis reveals complexity of indigenous North American turkey domestication. Proceedings of the National Academy of Science of the USA 107:2807–2812.

Spielman, D., B. W. Brook, D. A. Briscoe, and R. Frankham. 2004. Does inbreeding and loss of genetic diversity decrease disease resistance? Conservation Genetics 5:439–448.

Stangel, P. W., P. L. Leberg, and J. I. Smith. 1992. Systematics and population genetics. Pages 18–28 *in* J. G. Dickson, editor. The wild turkey: biology and management. Stackpole Books, Mechanicsburg, Pennsylvania, USA.

Steadman, D. W. 1980. A review of the osteology and paleontology of turkeys (Aves: Meleagridinae). Natural History Museum of Los Angeles County Contributions in Science 330:131–207.

Stephen, C. L., D. G. Whittaker, D. Gillis, L. L. Cox, and O. E. Rhodes Jr. 2005. Genetic consequences of reintroductions: an example from Oregon pronghorn antelope (*Antilocapra americana*). Journal of Wildlife Management 69:1463–1474.

Stidham, T. A. 2011. The carpometacarpus of the Pliocene turkey *Meleagris leopoldi* (Galliformes: Phasianidae) and the problem of morphological variability in turkeys. PaleoBios 30:13–17.

Svärdson, G. 1970. Significance of introgression in coregonid evolution. Pages 33–59 *in* C. C. Lindsey and C. S. Woods, editors. Biology of coregonid Fishes. University of Manitoba Press, Winnipeg, Canada.

Szalanski, A. L., K. E. Church, D. W. Oates, R. Bischof, and T. O. Powers. 2000. Mitochondrial-DNA variation within and among wild turkey (*Meleagris gallopavo*) subspecies. Transactions of the Nebraska Academy of Sciences 26:47–53.

Tamura, K., G. Stecher, D. Peterson, A. Filipski, and S. Kumar. 2013. MEGA6: molecular evolutionary genetics analysis version 6.0. Molecular Biology and Evolution 30:2725–2729.

Teacher, A. G. F., and D. J. Griffiths. 2011. HapStar: automated haplotype network layout and visualization. Molecular Ecology Resources 11:151–153.

Thornton, E. K., and K. F. Emery. 2017. The uncertain origins of Mesoamerican turkey domestication. Journal of Archaeological Method and Theory 24:328–351.

Thornton, E. K., K. F. Emery, D. W. Steadman, C. Speller, R. Matheny, and D. Yang. 2012. Earliest Mexican turkeys (*Meleagris gallopavo*) in the Maya region: implications for pre-Hispanic animal trade and the timing of turkey domestication. PLoS ONE 7(8):e42630.

Vidal, O., J. Viñas, and C. Pla. 2010. Variability of the melanocortin 1 receptor (MC1R) gene explains the segregation of the bronze locus in turkey (*Meleagris gallopavo*). Poultry Science 89:1599–1602.

Wang, N., R. T. Kimball, E. L. Braun, B. Liang, and Z. Zhang. 2013. Assessing phylogenetic relationships among Galliformes: a multigene phylogeny with expanded taxon sampling in Phasianidae. PLoS ONE 8(5):e64312.

Wetmore, A. 1943. Fossil birds from the Tertiary deposits of Florida. Proceedings of the New England Zoological Club 22:59–68.

Wilson, A. C., R. L. Cann, S. M. Carr, M. George, U. B. Gyllensten, K. M. Helm-Bychowski, R. G. Higuchi, S. R. Palumbi, E. M. Prager, R. D. Sage, and M. Stoneking. 1985. Mitochondrial DNA and two perspectives on evolutionary genetics. Biological Journal of the Linnean Society 26:375–400.

Winker, K. 2010. Subspecies represent geographically partitioned variation, a gold mine of evolutionary biology, and a challenge for conservation. Ornithological Monographs 67:6–23.

Wolff, J. O. 2000. Reassessing research approaches in the wildlife sciences. Wildlife Society Bulletin 28:744–750.

Wright, D. J., L. G. Spurgin, N. J. Collar, J. Komdeur, T. Burke, and D. S. Richardson. 2014. The impact of translocations on neutral and functional genetic diversity within and among populations of the Seychelles warbler. Molecular Ecology 23:2165–2177.

Zhao, S., Y. Ma, G. Wang, H. Li, X. Liu, J. Yu, B. Yue, and F. Zou. 2012. Molecular phylogeny of major lineage of the avian family Phasianidae inferred from complete mitochondrial genome sequences. Journal of Natural History 46:757–767.

Zink, R. M. 2004. The role of subspecies in obscuring avian biological diversity and misleading conservation policy. Proceedings of the Royal Society of London B 271:561–564.

Zink, R. M. 2010. Drawbacks with the use of microsatellites in phylogeography: the song sparrow *Melospiza melodia* as a case study. Journal of Avian Biology 41:1–7.

Zink, R. M., and G. F. Barrowclough. 2008. Mitochondrial DNA under siege in avian phylogeography. Molecular Ecology 17:2107–2121.

Zink, R. M., W. L. Rootes, and D. L. Dittmann. 1991. Mitochondrial DNA variation, population structure, and evolution of the common grackle (*Quiscalus quiscula*). Condor 93:318–329.

3

Life History

The last word in ignorance is the man who says of an animal or a plant: what good is it?

—ALDO LEOPOLD (1949)

Numerous definitions exist for the term "life history" as it is applied to a living organism. Thompson and Post (2016) provide one of the simplest by defining an organism's life history as the sequence of events related to survival and reproduction that occur from birth through death. Like all species of game birds, wild turkeys have evolved unique physical and behavioral attributes, such as gobbling during the breeding season and roosting in trees, that enable them to survive, reproduce, and maintain sustainable populations in the geographic regions they occupy. Therefore, the seasonal behaviors and habitat requirements of wild turkeys in Texas reflect the adaptations they have evolved to exploit specific characteristics of their environment, thereby permitting wild turkey populations to sustain themselves from year to year.

The life history of wild turkeys is unique for each of the three subspecies in Texas and to some extent reflects their distribution in the state because they occupy different environments. This chapter will provide a summary of the life history characteristics unique to each subspecies as well as those that all subspecies generally share. In addition, the chapter will briefly discuss the relationship of turkeys with the native people and contemporary residents of Texas, as well as the history of wild turkey management in Texas.

Physical Characteristics

Size and weight

The wild turkey is the largest upland game bird in Texas. According to Stangel et al. (1992), the Merriam's subspecies is the largest, followed by the Eastern and Rio Grande subspecies. Pelham and Dickson (1992) state that mature males and females are 101 cm (40 in) and 76 cm (30 in) tall, respectively, regardless of subspecies. Cathey et al. (2008) give the same measurements for both sexes of the mature Eastern and Rio Grande subspecies. According to records maintained by the National Wild Turkey Federation (NWTF), the Eastern wild turkey is the heaviest subspecies, at 17.1 kg (37.6 lb), followed by the Merriam's at 17.0 kg (37.6 lb), and the Rio Grande at 16.9 kg (37.2 lb). However, sizes of wild turkeys can vary substantially depending on where the turkeys occur within their geographic range. Size, particularly weight, can also vary depending on seasonal and annual climatic conditions, as well as the availability of required food resources (Ligon 1946). For example, during drought in Texas when food resources are scarce, turkey weights may be lighter than during years of good rainfall when food is more abundant. Additionally, wild turkeys that inhabit areas where supplemental feed is provided for deer may maintain heavier weights than birds that are not presented with such opportunities. So Rio Grande wild turkeys inhabiting a ranch with excellent habitat conditions and supplemental food will likely be heavier than birds that inhabit a poorly managed ranch 48.km (30 miles) away where supplemental food is not available. Generally, weights of the adult Eastern and Rio Grande subspecies in Texas appear very similar, ranging from 7.7 to 9.5 kg (17 to 21 lb) for males and 3.6 to 5.0 kg (8 to 11 lb) for females (Cathey et al. 2008). Weights for the Merriam's subspecies in Texas are not available, although the weights provided by Schorger (1966) from Arizona, Colorado, New Mexico, and Wyoming and by Brown (1989) from Arizona indicate that the ranges of adult weights for both sexes are similar to the weights of the Eastern and Rio Grande subspecies. Ligon (1946) provided a weight range for mature Merriam's wild turkey males of 8.2–15. 9 kg (18–35 lb).

Wild turkey poults weigh about 45 g (1.6 oz) when they hatch (Pelham and Dickson 1992, McRoberts et al. 2014). Poults grow rapidly, gaining about 0.5 kg (1.1 lb)/month, and at about five to six months, a juvenile male weighs 4.1–5.0 kg (9–11 lb), whereas a juvenile female weighs about 3.6 kg (8 lb). Thereafter, growth continues, but at a slower rate until the bird's second fall, when it begins to attain adult weight.

General appearance, plumage, and distinguishing characteristics

The most prominent physical characteristic that distinguishes wild turkeys from other Texas game birds, apart from size, is the appearance of the head and neck. The head and much of the neck of wild turkeys has few feathers, although females have more feathers on their necks than males (Pelham and Dickson 1992). For most of the year, the color of bare skin on the head, neck, and throat of adult wild turkeys is blue gray, and the wattles and caruncles are often pink (McRoberts et al. 2014). The skin on the head and neck of young wild turkeys is gray, and young males gradually achieve the blue-gray color of adults as they mature (McRoberts et al. 2014). The skin of mature males changes to more brilliant and vibrant reds and blues as the spring breeding season begins. Leopold (1943) stated that the skin on the head and neck, as well as the frontal caruncle and neck wattle, is blue, while the caruncles on the lower part of the neck are bright red. Furthermore, Mosby and Handley (1943) indicated that the heads of mature males in breeding condition are brilliant red, with a "skull cap" that is often white. During February–June, the head and neck of mature males become scarlet, while the crown of the head becomes white and the skin surrounding the eyes and in front of the ear apertures becomes cobalt blue (McRoberts et al. 2014). Mature males can change the colors of the head and neck very rapidly during the breeding season; the blues and reds of the head and neck brighten almost instantaneously when birds are strutting and aroused (Schorger 1966). The throat wattles of mature males are more prominent and brightly colored than those of young males or females. No substantial differences appear to exist between subspecies in the skin color of the neck and head, although Ligon (1946) indicated that the head and neck of Merriam's wild turkey females and yearling males during winter are blackish, whereas the head and neck of the Eastern and Rio Grande subspecies are uniformly blue.

The plumage coloration of wild turkeys in Texas varies according to subspecies. Eastern wild turkeys (fig. 3.1) are generally darker than the Rio Grande (fig 3.2) and Merriam's (fig. 3.3) subspecies. Stangel et al. (1992) provided good, brief descriptions of the plumages of all three subspecies, as follows. The feathers on the bodies of Eastern wild turkeys are purplish to coppery bronze, while those of Rio Grande wild turkeys are coppery to greenish gold, and those of the Merriam's subspecies are purplish bronze. The rump feathers are coppery to greenish gold in the Eastern subspecies, greenish gold to bluish black in the Rio Grande subspecies, and bluish black in the Merriam's subspecies. The upper tips of the retrices, or tail feathers, are cinnamon to dark chestnut on Eastern wild turkeys, cinnamon to buff colored on Rio Grande wild turkeys, and buff to pinkish white on Merriam's wild turkeys. The tips of the tail feathers form a band when the tail is spread out, and the color of this band is generally the easiest way to differentiate subspecies. The plumage of females is duller than that of males (Cathey et al. 2008) (fig 3.4). Females can also be distinguished from males by the feathers on the breast, which on females are brown with buff tips (fig 3.5), and on males are uniformly dark brown (fig. 3.6) (Schorger 1966).

Poults are covered with yellow down with brown markings during their first two weeks of life (Schorger 1966) (fig. 3.7). They also possess several primary feathers on their wings when they emerge from the egg (Williams 1981), and these flight feathers grow so quickly that by the age of 8 to 12 days a poult can fly up to the branches of a small shrub or tree to roost at night (Pelham and Dickson 1992). Down replacement on poults occurs when brown body, wing, and tail feathers appear toward 3 to 4 weeks of age (McRoberts et al. 2014). By the tenth week of life, poults have replaced down with juvenal feathers except for remnants of down on the neck and head, which are

Figure 3.1. Eastern wild turkey mature male in full strut and gobbling. The purplish to coppery bronze body plumage is darker than that of the Rio Grande and Merriam's wild turkeys, and the tips of the tail feathers form a cinnamon to dark chestnut band that is lighter than the tail feather band of the other two subspecies (photo by Frank Thurston, National Wild Turkey Federation).

Figure 3.2. Three mature Rio Grande wild turkey males in breeding condition. Body plumage is coppery to greenish gold, and the tips of the tail feathers are cinnamon to buff colored, making the tail feather band lighter than that of the Eastern wild turkey but darker than that of the Merriam's wild turkey (photo by Larry Ditto).

Figure 3.3. A mature Merriam's wild turkey male in full strut. Body plumage is purplish bronze, and the tips of the tail feathers are buff to pinkish white, making the tail feather band lighter than that of the Eastern and Rio Grande wild turkeys (photo by Guy Tillett, National Wild Turkey Federation).

Figure 3.4. Merriam's wild turkey hen. Plumage is generally duller than that of males (photo by Larry Ditto).

Figure 3.5. Rio Grande wild turkey female showing the breast feathers. Female wild turkeys have buff tips on the breast feathers, which differentiates them from males (photo by Larry Ditto).

Figure 3.6. Rio Grande wild turkey males showing the breast feathers. Male breast feathers are uniformly dark brown, which differentiates them from females (photo by Larry Ditto).

Figure 3.7. Two Merriam's wild turkey poults approximately two weeks old. Poults are covered with yellow down with brown markings and have pin feathers on their wings (photo by Chad Lehman).

replaced with juvenal feathers at about ten weeks of age (Leopold 1943). Young wild turkeys undergo three molts and attain four different plumages during their first winter, but the colored feathers of adults begin to appear when birds are about three months old (Pelham and Dickson 1992). McRoberts et al. (2014) detail these four successive molts, which typically begin earlier in southern regions of the wild turkey's geographic range. In order of occurrence, they include (1) the prejuvenal molt (May–June); (2) the preformative molt (June–October); (3) the auxiliary preformative molt (August–September); and (4) the second and definitive prebasic molt (March–October).

Geographic Distribution

Wild turkeys currently occur in 223 of the 254 counties of Texas, but the Eastern, Rio Grande, and Merriam's subspecies are restricted to specific parts of the state (fig. 3.8). Additionally, Eastern/Rio Grande and Rio Grande/Merriam's hybrids occur in a few counties. The current distribution of wild turkeys in Texas is a measure of how successful efforts have been to restore wild turkey populations during the past 70 years, because in 1945 wild turkeys were restricted primarily to the western Edwards Plateau, smaller areas of East and South Texas, and very small pockets of the Rolling Plains, Cross Timbers, Coastal Prairies, and Post Oak Savanna (fig. 3.9).

The historic geographic range of Eastern wild turkeys in Texas was about 12.1 million ha (30 million acres) and included almost all East Texas counties where forests, or Piney Woods, were the major vegetation type and where rainfall averaged at least 102 cm (40 inches) annually. Beyond the 102 cm rainfall boundary, vegetation communities transitioned from Piney Woods to the more semiarid Post Oak Savanna, which is unsuitable habitat for Eastern wild turkeys. Eastern wild turkeys currently inhabit about 40 counties in East Texas. The Rio Grande wild turkey is the most abundant subspecies in Texas and has the widest distribution. It inhabits about the middle two-thirds of the state, including portions of the western and eastern Panhandle, and south on rangelands to the Rio Grande and east to the Gulf Coast and the 102 cm (40 in) rainfall boundary that figuratively separates the Rio Grande and Eastern subspecies ranges. Rio Grande wild turkeys also occur in the Trans-Pecos and are expanding their range by continuing to colonize several counties in this region of the state. The Merriam's subspecies probably inhabited select mountain ranges in

Figure 3.8. The current geographic distribution of wild turkeys in Texas (figure by Texas Parks and Wildlife Department).

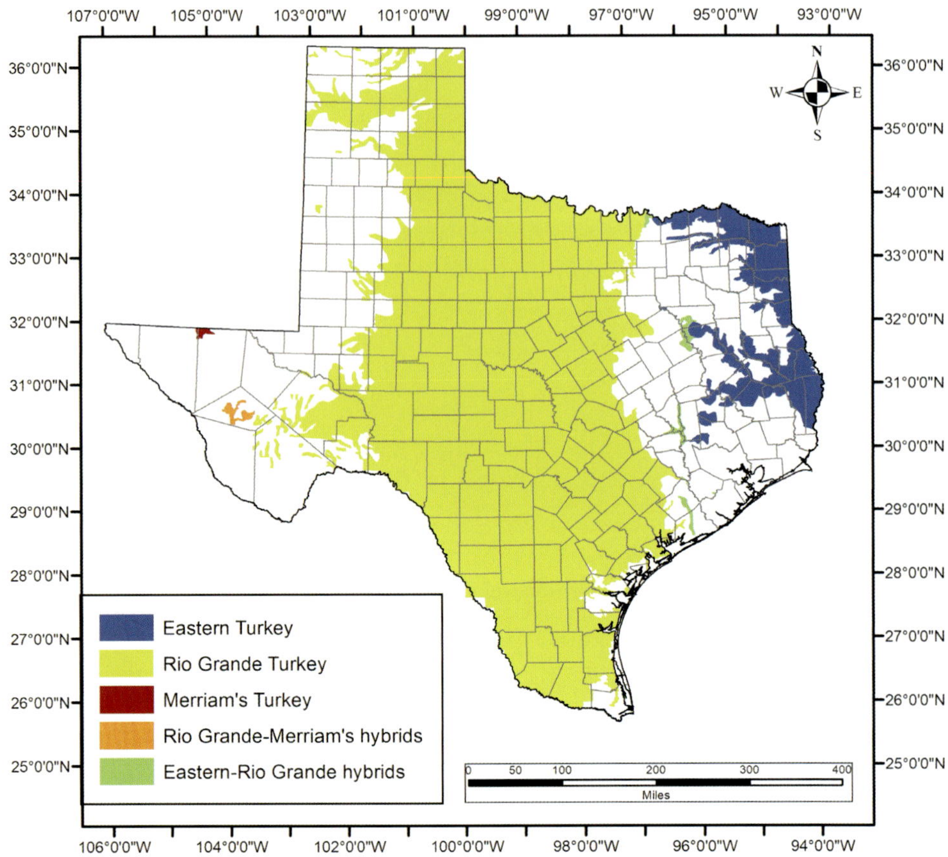

Figure 3.9. The geographic distribution of wild turkeys in Texas in 1945 (figure by Texas Parks and Wildlife Department).

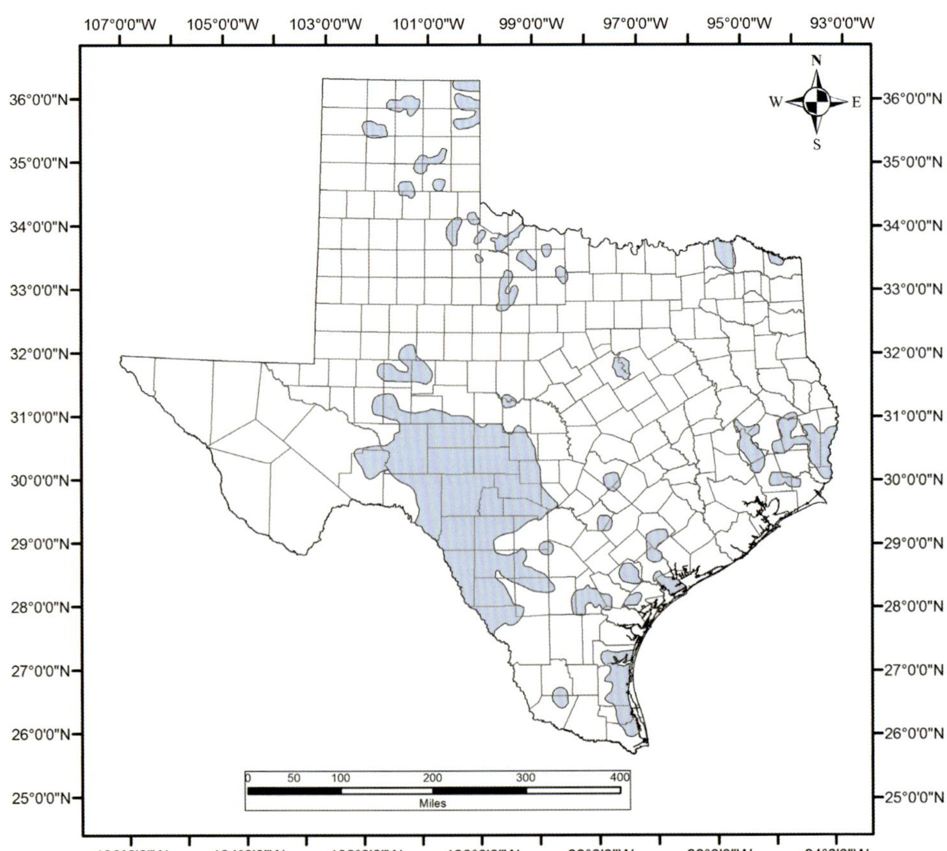

the Trans-Pecos, such as the Guadalupe, Franklin, and Davis Mountains, and possibly riparian areas along the Canadian River as far as Carson County (Schorger 1966, Shaw and Mollohan 1992). It is likely that the only remaining populations occur in the Guadalupe Mountains, and perhaps a few individuals in the Davis Mountains.

Longevity

The longevity of wild turkeys varies considerably, depending a great deal on habitat quality and quantity, the diversity and abundance of predator populations, weather, and the intensity of hunter harvests. Blankenship (1992) stated that wild turkey longevity increases substantially for birds that survive their first two weeks of life, as young poult mortality can be as high as 70%. Mosby and Handley (1943) believed that the average longevity of presumably Eastern wild turkeys was 5 years, but they cited field reports of turkeys living for up to 10–12 years. However, a band return from a mature Eastern wild turkey male in Massachusetts established conclusively that the bird was at least 15 years old at the time of its death (Cardoza 1995). Lewis (1967) provided an account of a Rio Grande wild turkey male in Texas that survived for over 14 years. R. Howard (personal communication) indicated that he saw a patagial-tagged female in South Texas that was at least 8 years old. Ligon (1946) reported that a Merriam's wild turkey lived for 9.5 years in New Mexico and believed that 10 years was the maximum age of Merriam's wild turkeys. Wild turkeys are intelligent birds that learn quickly from negative experiences, so it is not surprising that some birds can survive in the wild for a decade or more. Nevertheless, Mosby and Handley (1943) suggested that most wild turkeys live 4 to 5 years, and Cardoza (1995) believed that most turkeys do not survive longer than 6 years.

Movements

Wild turkeys can move significant distances, usually in their search for resources necessary for survival, but are generally not thought of as migratory (Schorger 1966). Merriam's wild turkeys that inhabit the mountains of Arizona, New Mexico, Colorado, and Utah move from lower-elevation winter ranges to higher-elevation summer ranges where breeding, nesting, and brooding occur, but this is movement up and down mountains (Brown 1989, Shaw and Mollohan 1992) rather than the long, annual hemispheric migrations exhibited by waterfowl and songbirds. However, Phillips et al. (2007) recently reported that Rio Grande wild turkeys in the Texas Panhandle exhibited migratory behavior by moving between spring and summer ranges. However, they also indicated that many long movements (10–13 km; 6-8 mi) were made by dispersing young females. Long movements are not unusual. Schorger (1966) provides numerous accounts of wild turkey movements for the three subspecies in Texas. Rio Grande wild turkeys in South Texas were reported to move 29–32 km (18–20 mi) from an area where they wintered to nesting and brooding habitat (Walker 1951). Movements of Rio Grande wild turkeys in Kerr County from winter roost sites to nesting and brooding areas did not exceed 8 km (5 mi), but in Menard and Kimble counties these movements were up to 29 km (18 mi) (Walker 1951). Eastern wild turkeys are also capable of moving substantial distances. Eaton et al. (1976) reported that a female banded as a poult was recovered 48 km (30 mi) from the area where it was initially captured. Wunz (1973) found that wild turkeys dispersed up to 16 km (10 mi) from Pennsylvania to New York. However, Wright and Vangilder (2007) indicated that once home ranges were established, the dispersal distances of male adult and juvenile Eastern wild turkeys were 2,773 m (3,302 yd) and 2,094 m (2,290 yd), respectively. Similarly, Godwin et al. (1994) found that mature and juvenile males did not move more than 2,500 m (2,734 yd) on their study area in Mississippi. Merriam's wild turkeys evidently move even greater distances than Rio Grande or Eastern wild turkeys. Ligon (1946) stated that the wintering and nesting habitats of Merriam's wild turkeys can be 40 to 60 km (25 to 40 mi) apart. Moreover, Schorger (1966) believed that Merriam's wild turkey populations on mountains in the Southwest were colonized by birds that emigrated across grasslands or deserts from neighboring mountain ranges. He provided accounts suggesting that birds moved 16–48 km (10–30 mi) between mountain ranges (Spicer 1957, Knopp 1959). However, birds established on mountain ranges seem to typically move shorter distances; Hoffman (1986) indicated that in Colorado males moved approximately

3.2 km (2 mi) from wintering to breeding grounds, while females moved an average of 9.7 km (6 mi).

The movements of nesting females and females with broods are more restricted. Lehman et al. (2005) reported that movements of females declined abruptly when they transitioned from prelaying behavior to incubation. Eastern, Rio Grande, and Merriam's wild turkey females moved less than 364 m (400 yd), 115 m (126 yd), and 331 m (362 yd), respectively. Eastern wild turkey females with month-old poults restricted daily movements to 137–457 m (150–500 yd) in East Texas (Alldredge et al. 2014), while females with poults several weeks old in the South Texas Coastal Prairie moved 3.2–4.8 km (2–3 mi) from nest sites on grasslands to large oak (*Quercus virginiana*) mottes that served as more secure roosts (Guarneros-Altamirano 2008).

Sensory Capabilities

Vision

Anyone who has hunted or otherwise spent time observing wild turkeys has learned that wild turkeys have excellent vision. They can easily detect the slightest movement of an object within a field of 360 degrees (Schorger 1966). Pelham and Dickson (1992) provided a concise summary of wild turkey vision. They indicated that the monotypic vision of wild turkeys, and the position of the eyes on the head, allow them to assimilate objects in their field of view very quickly and from a 360-degree perspective. Because turkeys are diurnal, they do not have many rod cells in the retinas of their eye, which is a characteristic of nocturnal birds such as owls (*Bubo virginianus*). Instead, the retina is composed predominantly of cone cells, which are associated with diurnal activity. The bright colors of male heads and necks during the breeding season, and their ability to change these colors rapidly, evolved in order to make males noticeable to females, indicating that wild turkeys are clearly capable of distinguishing colors.

Hearing, taste, and smell

Wild turkeys also have acute hearing. Although they do not have an external structure such as an ear to concentrate sounds, they can distinguish lower-frequency sounds better than humans can (Pelham and Dickson 1992). Wild turkeys do not possess taste buds, so they have a poorly developed sense of taste. However, avoidance of medicated baits suggests that they learn to distinguish altered food, indicating some ability to taste food (Pelham and Dickson 1992). Schorger (1966) indicated that there is little evidence that wild turkeys have a well-developed sense of smell, but he did provide accounts from hunters who claimed that wild turkeys were able to smell them.

Seasons Relevant to Wild Turkeys

As with all wild animals, the annual life cycle of wild turkeys is influenced by the seasons of the year. Therefore, their behavior, food, and cover needs change on a seasonal basis. The annual life cycle of the wild turkey can be partitioned into five seasons: (1) breeding, (2) nesting, (3) brooding/poult rearing, (4) forming winter flocks, and (5) dispersing in spring (Cathey et al. 2008, Locke et al. 2008). One of the most important seasons is the breeding season, because breeding ensures that turkey populations perpetuate themselves on an annual basis. Because of their extensive latitudinal range in Texas, the breeding season for Rio Grande wild turkeys extends from February to May (Cathey et al. 2008). In the Piney Woods, breeding for the Eastern subspecies generally occurs between March and June (Alldredge et al. 2014). No information is available for the breeding season of Merriam's wild turkeys in Texas, but Hoffman et al. (1993) indicated that breeding can occur from February to June. Merriam's wild turkeys in the Guadalupe Mountains probably follow a similar pattern.

Breeding

Breeding activity is stimulated largely by the increasing day length of spring but is also influenced by temperature; unseasonably warm weather in early spring can initiate early breeding, while colder temperatures can delay it (Healy 1992). The elevation of male sex hormones occurs in response to increased day length, stimulating gobbling and strutting among males (Healy 1992), which heralds the beginning of the breeding season. Males generally become sexually receptive before females, who follow in perhaps a week or two (McRoberts et al. 2014), but Smith (1977) indicated that females sometimes become receptive as early as February. Because early spring temperatures influence the onset of breeding, the initiation of breeding depends on not only latitude but also annual variations in spring temperatures. Therefore, Rio Grande wild turkeys in South Texas sometimes begin breeding in February (Glazener 1944, Smith 1977, Dominquez 2006), whereas wild turkeys in the Rolling Plains may not start breeding until March (Hohensee and Wallace 2001) or April (Huffman 2005) (fig. 3.10). Similarly, initiation of breeding varies annually within a specific area or region depending on vagaries of annual temperature and precipitation. For example, in a four-year study in South Texas (Dominquez 2006) that encompassed a wet/dry cycle, wild turkeys initiated breeding in February one year when the winter was mild and wet, yet did not initiate breeding until March in another year when drought persisted over the previous winter.

Figure 3.10. Two breeding Rio Grande wild turkeys in South Texas (photo by Larry Ditto).

Nesting

Nesting among Rio Grande wild turkeys extends from about the first of March (Schorger 1966) during warm, wet years until August throughout their range in Texas (Cathey et al. 2008). In South Texas, nesting has been documented from April to June (Bailey and Rinell 1967) and from April to August (Beasom 1973). Cook (1972) indicated that nesting in the Edwards Plateau occurred between February and August. On the Rolling Plains, Hohensee and Wallace (2001) reported nesting from March to August, whereas Huffman (2005) stated that females nested between April and July. Eastern wild turkeys in the Piney Woods begin nesting in late March and early April (Alldredge et al. 2014), and as with the Rio Grande subspecies, this extends into the summer. Cook (1945) and Miller et al. (1998) reported wild turkey nesting in Mississippi between March and July. In neighboring Louisiana, Oberholser (1938) and Kopman (1921) also found that Eastern wild turkeys began nesting in early April. Information is not available for Merriam's wild turkey nesting seasons in Texas, but they are probably similar to those of populations elsewhere within the geographic range of the subspecies. Ligon (1927) found that nesting in New Mexico began in April and ended in May, though Ligon (1946) believed that egg laying started about mid-May. Brown (1989) also indicated that nesting in Arizona occurred between April and May. Rumble and Hodorff (1993) reported that Merriam's wild turkey females in South Dakota nested from mid-April to the end of June. Renesting is common for females of all subspecies that have failed in their first attempts to nest, and renesting probably represents most of the nesting attempts that occur during July and August.

Brooding and poult rearing

Poults begin to hatch in Texas during the latter part of April through June in most years, and then brooding activity occurs throughout the summer months (Watts 1969, Lockwood and Sutcliffe 1985, Cathey et al. 2008, Alldredge et al. 2014). Newly hatched poults leave the nest 24 hours after hatching (Cathey et al. 2008) and are considered precocial because they are mobile and active almost as soon as they leave the nest. Females are attentive to their broods, constantly communicating with them as they forage throughout the day. Poults grow very rapidly, gaining almost 0.45 kg (1 lb) per month on a diet composed almost entirely of invertebrates for their first few weeks of life. Poults develop sufficiently in two weeks to be capable of making short flights and using the branches of shrubs and small trees for roosts. Females with broods spend most of the day during the brood's first two months moving through openings dominated by grasses and forbs and foraging for insects. Poults begin to consume more plant material when they reach two months of age, and plants begin to dominate their diets soon thereafter.

Winter flock formation

Toward the end of summer when poults are almost the size of adults, females and their broods begin to congregate into the large flocks of fall and winter. These flocks are composed of females and their young of the year, and they remain together throughout the winter until the breeding season begins again the next spring. Mature males and jakes form smaller groups that generally remain together throughout the winter. Since food is often not as diverse and abundant during winter, wild turkey flocks spend considerable time during the day foraging. Vegetation communities that supply wild turkeys with required plant foods are important during winter, but of equal importance is adequate roosting habitat. Roosts are essential habitat features, and a congregation of suitable roost structures is often required to accommodate large winter flocks.

Spring dispersal

Rising temperatures, warmer weather, and increasing day length herald the approach of spring and a new wild turkey breeding season. Winter flocks begin to dissolve as females enter breeding condition. The dissolution of winter flocks results in wild turkey dispersal from their winter home ranges. Wild turkey movement is probably greatest immediately prior to or at the beginning of the breeding season. Wild turkeys become more mobile as they search for breeding opportunities or move away from familiar areas to establish new home ranges. Juvenile females are particularly mobile during late winter and early spring as they leave their winter flocks and disperse into areas they have never frequented to establish new home ranges. Phillips et al. (2007) and Reyes-Ramirez et al. (2012) reported that during late winter and early spring, juvenile females dispersed substantially greater distances than adult females or males in the Texas Panhandle and South Texas, respectively. Phillips et al. (2007) concluded that these dispersing young females largely ensure that new habitats or unoccupied habitats are filled every year. Increased movements during spring dispersal also help promote genetic diversity within turkey populations by increasing the probability that unrelated individuals have an opportunity to breed with one another.

Predators

A number of mammals, birds, and reptiles prey on wild turkeys in Texas. Poults are particularly vulnerable to predation during their first two weeks of life, as are females while they are nesting and males while they are strutting during the breeding season (Reagan and Morgan 1980, Miller and Leopold 1992, Alldredge et al. 2014). Swank et al. (1985) and Ransom et al. (1987) reported that about one-third of the radioed wild turkeys they studied were killed by predators on their East Texas and South Texas study areas, respectively. Alldredge et al. (2014) indicated that over half of the wild turkey nests produced in a year in East Texas were destroyed by predators. They provided a list of wild turkey predators that included snakes, four bird species, and nine mammal species. They indicated that nests are depredated most commonly by American crows (*Corvus brachyrhynchos*) (fig. 3.11) and raccoons (*Procyon lotor*) (fig. 3.12), followed by great horned owls (*Bubo virginianus*) (fig. 3.13), blue jays (*Cyanocitta cristata*), snakes, bobcats (*Lynx rufus*) (fig. 3.14), coyotes (*Canis latrans*) (fig. 3.15), feral pigs (*Sus scrofa*), gray foxes (*Urocyon cinereoargenteus*) (fig. 3.16), armadillos (*Dasypus novemcinctus*), opossums (*Didelphis virginiana*), and striped skunks (*Mephitis mephitis*) (fig. 3.17). Poults and young juveniles are often killed by great horned owls and red-tailed hawks (*Buteo jamaicensis*), as well as bobcats, coyotes, gray foxes, and raccoons, while great-horned owls, bobcats, and coyotes are threats to adults (Schorger 1966). Melville (2012) also found that American crows and raccoons were responsible for most depredation events that occurred in his study of predation on artificial wild turkey nests in East Texas. Numerous additional studies of predation effects on Eastern wild turkey populations (Speake 1980, Speake et al. 1985, Seiss 1989, Palmer 1990) support the observations of Alldredge et al. (2014) and Melville (2012).

Figure 3.11. American crows are important avian nest predators that prey on wild turkey eggs (photo by Larry Ditto).

Figure 3.12. Raccoons prey on wild turkey eggs, poults, and occasionally young juveniles (photo by Larry Ditto).

Figure 3.13. Great horned owls prey on wild turkey poults, juveniles, and occasionally vulnerable adults such as incubating hens (photo by Larry Ditto).

Figure 3.14. Bobcats depredate wild turkey nests, as well as poults, juveniles, and adults (photo by Larry Ditto).

Figure 3.15. Coyotes depredate wild turkey nests, as well as poults, juveniles, and adults (photo by Larry Ditto).

Figure 3.16. Gray foxes prey on wild turkey eggs, poults, and juveniles (photo by Larry Ditto).

Figure 3.17. The striped skunk is an important wild turkey nest predator that generally focuses on eggs (photo by Larry Ditto).

Rio Grande wild turkeys are also vulnerable to many of the same predators that prey on Eastern wild turkeys. Cook (1972) reported that over 60% of the wild turkey nests he monitored were destroyed by predators, including skunks, raccoons, bobcats, crows, and snakes. In a more recent Edwards Plateau study, Willsey (2004) believed that coyotes could have been contributing to a wild turkey decline in his study area. Furthermore, another Hill Country study revealed that raccoons and gray foxes depredated the most wild turkey nests, followed by feral hogs, common ravens (*Corvus corax*), striped skunks, bobcats, armadillos, and a Texas rat snake (*Elaphe obsoleta lindheimeri*) (Dreibelbis et al. 2008). In South Texas, Glazener (1967) reported that coyotes, bobcats, and raccoons were common predators. Similarly, Ransom et al. (1987) observed coyotes stalking strutting wild turkey males on the Welder Wildlife Refuge in South Texas. He also attributed most nest losses to raccoons, while bobcats and coyotes were responsible for most adult female mortalities. In the Texas Panhandle, Ballard et al. (2003) and Holdstock et al. (2007) found that coyotes and bobcats were frequent predators of wild turkeys.

Rumble et al. (2003) determined that the highest percentage of mortality for Merriam's wild turkeys in Arizona, Montana, and South Dakota was attributable to predation. Merriam's wild turkeys have some of the same predators as the Eastern and Rio Grande subspecies. Berdan (2010) found that birds, followed by mammals, were the most frequent predators of wild turkeys in the northern Black Hills of South Dakota. Coyotes, bobcats, mountain lions (*Felis concolor*), golden eagles (*Aquila chrysaetos*), and great horned owls were identified as important Merriam's wild turkey predators in various parts of their geographic range (MacDonald and Janzen 1967, Schemnitz et al. 1985). Rumble and Hodorff (1993) reported that coyotes, red foxes (*Vulpes vulpes*), and raptors were primarily responsible for mortality events during Merriam's wild turkey nest initiation and incubation in South Dakota. Lehman et al. (2007) found that coyotes, and to a lesser extent bobcats, were the principal predators associated with wild turkey nest destruction in South Dakota. They also documented a great horned owl killing an incubating female.

Predation probably has a limited impact on wild turkey populations that inhabit landscapes with sufficient resources to meet the seasonal requirements of the predator community. Under most circumstances, predation is a natural event that has served to regulate wild turkey populations for as long as wild turkeys have inhabited North America. Native Americans hunted wild turkeys, but they probably did not impact populations, except perhaps around villages. European colonization of wild turkey habitat had a far greater impact on wild turkey populations than predators or Native American hunters ever did. Eastern and Rio Grande wild turkey populations were almost extirpated in Texas during the late 1800s and early 1900s because of unregulated hunting (Alldredge et al. 2014, Cathey et al. 2008), just a few decades after the large influx of Anglo settlers arrived in Texas. Fortunately, timely legislation instituting hunting seasons and strict bag limits, as well as intensive restoration efforts, has allowed wild turkey populations in Texas to recover (Lehmann 1957). Hughes et al. (2007) believed that humans are the major predators of wild turkeys. This may apply to portions of Texas, depending on hunting intensity on individual properties or specific localities in the state. But Cathey et al. (2008) indicated that the results of recent research in the Hill Country and Rolling Plains revealed that hunter harvests represent a very minor portion of annual wild turkey mortality, and the same probably applies to South Texas as well, where fewer hunters pursue wild turkeys. Alldredge et al. (2014) also indicated that hunting is not causing population declines among Eastern wild turkeys in the Piney Woods.

Literature Cited

Alldredge, B. E., J. B. Hardin, J. Whiteside, J. L. Isabelle, S. Parsons, W. C. Conway, and J. C. Cathey. 2014. Eastern wild turkeys in Texas: biology and management. Texas AgriLife Extension publication WF-011. Texas A&M University, College Station, USA.

Bailey, R. W., and K. T. Rinell. 1967. Events in the turkey year. Pages 73–91 *in* O. H. Hewitt, editor. The wild turkey and its management. The Wildlife Society, Washington, DC, USA, 73–91.

Ballard, W. B, M. C. Wallace, J. H. Brunjes, R. Philips, D. Holdstock, G. Hall, R. Houchin, et al. 2003. Changes in land use patterns and their effects on Rio Grande wild turkeys in the Rolling Plains of Texas and southwest Kansas. Annual report submitted to the Texas Parks and Wildlife Department. Texas Tech University, Lubbock, USA.

Beasom, S. L. 1973. Ecological factors affecting wild turkey reproductive success in South Texas. Dissertation, Texas A&M University, College Station, USA.

Beasom, S. L., and D. Wilson. 1992. Rio Grande turkey. Pages 306–330 *in* J. G. Dickson, editor. The wild turkey: biology and management. Stackpole Books, Mechanicsburg, Pennsylvania, USA.

Berdan, T. C. 2010. Survival of male Merriam's wild turkeys in the northern Black Hills of South Dakota. Dissertation, South Dakota State University, Brookings, USA.

Blankenship, L. H. 1992. Physiology. Pages 84–100 *in* J. G. Dickson, editor. The wild turkey: biology and management. Stackpole Books, Mechanicsburg, Pennsylvania, USA.

Boeker, E. L., and V. E. Scott. 1969. Roost tree characteristics for Merriam's turkey. Journal of Wildlife Management 36:121–124.

Brown, D. E. 1989. Arizona game birds. University of Arizona Press, Tucson, USA.

Cardoza, J. E. 1995. A possible longevity record for the wild turkey (record de longevidad para individuo silvestre de *Meleagris gallopavo*). Journal of Field Ornithology 66:267–269.

Cathey, J. C., K. Melton, J. Dreibelbis, B. Cavney, S. L. Locke, S. J. DeMaso, T. W. Schwertner, and B. Collier. 2007. Rio Grande wild turkey in Texas: biology and management. Texas AgriLife Extension Report B-6198. Texas A&M University, College Station, USA.

Chamberlain, M. J., B. D. Leopold, and L. W. Burger. 2000. Characteristics of roost sites of adult wild turkey females. Journal of Wildlife Management 64:1025–1032.

Cook, F. A. 1945. Game birds of Mississippi. Mississippi Game and Fish Commission, Jackson, USA.

Cook, R. L. 1972. A study of nesting turkeys in the Edwards Plateau of Texas. Proceedings of the Annual Conference of the Southeastern Association of Game and Fish Commissioners 26:236–244.

Dominquez, M. 2006. The impact of overwinter nutrition on Rio Grande wild turkey productivity in South Texas. Thesis, Texas A&M University–Kingsville, Kingsville, USA.

Dreibelbis, J. Z., K. B. Melton, R. Aguirre, B. A. Collier, J. Hardin, N. J. Silvy, and M. J. Peterson. 2008. Predation of Rio Grande wild turkey nests on the Edwards Plateau, Texas. Wilson Journal of Ornithology 120:906–910.

Eaton, S. W., F. M. Evans, J. W. Glidden, and B. D. Penrod. 1976. Annual range of wild turkeys in southwestern New York. New York Fish and Game Journal 23:20–33.

Glazener, W. C. 1944. Management of the wild turkey in lower South Texas. US Fish and Wildlife Service, Pittman-Robertson Quarterly Report 4:121–122.

Glazener, W. C. 1967. Management of the Rio Grande wild turkey. Pages 453–492 *in* O. H. Hewitt, editor. The wild turkey and its management. The Wildlife Society, Washington, DC, USA.

Godwin, K. D., G. A. Hurst, and B. D. Leopold. 1994. Movements of wild turkey gobblers in central Mississippi. Proceedings of the Annual Conference of Fish and Wildlife Agencies 48:117–122.

Guarneros-Altamirano, R. 2008. Rio Grande wild turkey poult ecology in South Texas. Thesis, Texas A&M University–Kingsville, Kingsville, USA.

Healy, W. M. 1992. Behavior. Pages 46–65 *in* J. G. Dickson, editor. The wild turkey: biology and management. Stackpole Books, Mechanicsburg, Pennsylvania, USA.

Hoffman, R. W. 1986. Chronology of breeding and nesting activities of wild turkey in relation to timing of spring hunting seasons. Colorado Division of Wildlife, Federal Aid Report. Project 01–03–045 (W-37-R).

Hoffman, R. W., H. G. Shaw, M. A. Rumble, B. F. Wakeling, C. M. Mollohan, S. D. Schemnitz, R. Engel-Wilson, and D. A. Hengle. 1993. Management guidelines for Merriam's wild turkey. Colorado Division of Wildlife Report 18. Denver, USA.

Hohensee, S. D., and M. C. Wallace. 2001. Nesting and survival of Rio Grande turkeys in north central Texas. Proceedings of the National Wild Turkey Symposium 8:85–91.

Holdstock, D. P., M. C. Wallace, W. B. Ballard, J. H. Brunjes, R. S. Phillips, B. L. Spears, S. J. DeMaso, J. D. Jernigan, R. D. Applegate, and P. S. Gibson. 2007. Male Rio Grande wild turkey habitat characteristics in the Texas Panhandle and southwestern Kansas. Proceedings of the National Wild Turkey Symposium 9:217–229.

Huffman, R. T. 2005. The effect of precipitation and cover on Rio Grande wild turkey nesting ecology in the Texas Panhandle and southwestern Kansas. Thesis, Texas Tech University, Lubbock, USA.

Hughes, T. W., J. L. Tapley, J. E. Kennamer, and C. P. Lehman. 2007. The impacts of predation on wild turkeys. Proceedings of the National Wild Turkey Symposium 9:117–126.

Kennamer, J. E., M. Kennamer, and R. Brenneman. 1992. History. Pages 6–17 *in* J. G. Dickson, editor. The wild turkey: biology and management. Stackpole Books, Mechanicsburg, Pennsylvania, USA.

Knopp, T. B. 1959. Factors affecting the abundance and distribution of Merriam's turkeys (*Meleagris gallopavo merriami*) in southeastern Arizona. Thesis, University of Arizona, Tucson, USA.

Kopman, H. H. 1921. Wildlife resources of Louisiana. Louisiana Department of Conservation Bulletin 10. Baton Rouge, USA.

Latch, E. K., L. A. Harveson, J. S. King, M. D. Hobson, and O. E. Rhodes Jr. 2006. Assessing hybridization in wildlife populations using molecular markers: a case study in wild turkeys. Journal of Wildlife Management 70:485–492.

Lehman, C. P., L. D. Flake, M. A. Rumble, R. D. Shields, and D. J. Thompson. 2005. Pre-incubation movements of female wild turkeys relative to nest initiation in South Dakota. Wildlife Society Bulletin 33:1062–1070.

Lehman, C. P., L. D. Flake, and M. A. Rumble. 2007. Survival and cause-specific mortality of Merriam's turkeys in the southern Black Hills. Proceedings of the National Wild Turkey Symposium 9:295–301.

Lehman, C. P., M. A. Rumble, L. D. Flake, and D. J. Thompson. 2008. Merriam's turkey nest survival and factors affecting nest predation by mammals. Journal of Wildlife Management 72(8):1765–1774.

Lehmann, V. W. 1957. Conservation and management of game. Pages 761–766 (appendix) *in* Tom Lea, "The King Ranch," volume 2. Little, Brown, Boston, Massachusetts, USA.

Leopold, A. S. 1943. The moults of young wild and domestic turkeys. Condor 45:133–145.

Lewis, J. C. 1967. Physical characteristics and physiology. Pages 45–72 *in* O. H. Hewitt, editor. The wild turkey and its management. Tom Lea, "The King Ranch," volume 2. The Wildlife Society, Washington, DC, USA.

Ligon, J. S. 1927. Wildlife of New Mexico. New Mexico Department of Game and Fish. Santa Fe, USA.

Ligon, J. S. 1946. History and management of Merriam's wild turkey. New Mexico Game and Fish Commission. Santa Fe, USA.

Locke, S., J. C. Cathey, B. Collier, and J. Hardin. 2008. Rio Grande wild turkey life history and management calendar. AgriLife Extension, Texas A&M System. http://oaktrust.library.tamu.edu/bitstream/handle/1969.1/87532/pdf_2567.pdf?sequence=1&isAllowed=y.

Lockwood, D. R., and D. H. Sutcliffe. 1985. Distribution and reproduction of Merriam's wild turkey in New Mexico. Proceedings of the National Wild Turkey Symposium 5:309–316.

Lopez, R. R., W. E. Grant, N. J. Silvy, M. J. Peterson, C. K. Feuerbacher, and M. S. Corson. 2000. Restoration of the wild turkey in East Texas: Simulation of alternative restocking strategies. Ecological Modelling 132:275–285.

MacDonald, D., and R. A. Jansen. 1967. Management of Merriam's turkey. Pages 493–534 *in* O. H. Hewitt, editor. The wild turkey and its management. The Wildlife Society, Washington, DC, USA.

Mackey, D. L., and R. J. Jonas. 1982. Seasonal habitat use and food habits of Merriam's turkeys in southcentral Washington. Proceedings of the Western Wild Turkey Workshop 1:99–110.

McRoberts, J. T., M. C. Wallace, and S. W. Eaton. 2014. Wild turkey (*Meleagris gallopavo*). Account 22 *in* A. Poole, editor. The birds of North America online. Cornell Laboratory of Ornithology, Ithaca, New York, USA. http://bna.birds.cornell.edu/bna/species/022.

Melville, H. I. 2012. The impacts of three common mesopredators on the reintroduced population of Eastern wild turkeys in Texas. Dissertation, Texas A&M University, College Station, USA.

Miller, D. A., B. D. Leopold, and G. A. Hurst. 1998. Reproductive characteristics of a wild turkey population in central Mississippi. Journal of Wildlife Management 3:903–910.

Miller, J. E., and B. D. Leopold. 1992. Population influences: predators. Pages 119–128 *in* J. G. Dickson, editor. The wild turkey: biology and management. Stackpole Books, Mechanicsburg, Pennsylvania, USA.

Mosby, H. S., and C. O. Handley. 1943. The wild turkey in Virginia: its status, life history and management. Pittman-Robertson Projects. Virginia Division of Game, Commission of Game and Inland Fisheries, Richmond, USA.

National Audubon Society. 2015. Wild turkey results: Texas. http://netapp.audubon.org/CBCObservation/Historical/ResultsBySpecies.aspx?1.

Oberholser, H. C. 1938. The bird life of Louisiana. Louisiana Department of Conservation Bulletin 28. Baton Rouge, USA.

Palmer, W. E. 1990. Relationships of wild turkey hens to forested habitat in east-central Mississippi. Thesis, Mississippi State University, Starkville, USA.

Pelham, P. H., and J. G. Dickson. 1992. Physical characteristics. Pages 32–45 *in* J. G. Dickson, editor. The wild turkey: biology and management. Stackpole Books, Mechanicsburg, Pennsylvania, USA.

Petersen, L. E., and A. H. Richardson. 1973. Merriam's wild turkey in the Black Hills of South Dakota. Pages 3–9 *in* C. G. Sanderson and H. C. Schultz, editors. Wild turkey management: current problems and programs. University of Missouri Chapter of The Wildlife Society and University of Missouri Press, Columbia, USA.

Phillips, R. S., M. C. Wallace, B. L. Spears, J. H. Brunjes, W. B. Ballard, D. P. Holdstock, M. S. Miller, and S. J. DeMaso. 2007. Movement, fidelity and dispersal of Rio Grande wild turkeys in the Texas Panhandle. Proceedings of the National Wild Turkey Symposium 9:149–157.

Ransom, D., Jr., O. J. Rongstad, and D. H. Rusch. 1987. Nesting ecology of Rio Grande turkeys. Journal of Wildlife Management 51:435–439.

Reagan, J. M., and K. D. Morgan. 1980. Reproductive potential of Rio Grande turkey hens in the Edwards Plateau of Texas. Proceedings of the National Wild Turkey Symposium 4:136–144.

Reyes-Ramirez, E., M. C. Clayton, C. W. Lawson, S. M. Burns, R. Guarneros-Altimirano, S. J. DeMaso, W. P. Kuvlesky Jr., D. G. Hewitt, J. A. Ortega-Santos, and T. A. Campbell. 2012. Home ranges of female Rio Grande turkeys (*Meleagris gallopavo intermedia*) in southern Texas. Southwestern Naturalist 57:198–201.

Rumble, M. A. 1990. The ecology of Merriam's turkey (*Meleagris gallopavo merriami*) in the Black Hills, South Dakota. Dissertation, University of Wyoming, Laramie, USA.

Rumble, M. A., and S. H. Anderson. 1996. Feeding ecology of Merriam's turkeys (*Meleagris gallopavo merriami*) in the Black Hills, South Dakota. American Midland Naturalist 136:157–171.

Rumble, M. A., and R. A. Hodorff. 1993. Nesting ecology of Merriam's turkeys in the Black Hills, South Dakota. Journal of Wildlife Management 57:789–801.

Rumble, M. A., B. F. Wakeling, and L. D. Flake. 2003. Factors affecting survival and recruitment in female Merriam's turkeys. Intermountain Journal of Sciences 9:26–37.

Schemnitz, S. D., D. L. Goerndt, and K. H. Jones. 1985. Habitat needs and management of Merriam's wild turkey in southcentral New Mexico. Proceedings of the National Wild Turkey Symposium 5:199–231.

Schorger, A. W. 1966. The wild turkey: its history and domestication. University of Oklahoma Press, Norman, USA.

Seiss, R. S. 1989. Reproductive parameters and survival rates of wild turkey hens in east-central Mississippi. Thesis, Mississippi State University, Starkville, USA.

Shaw, H. G., and C. Mollohan. 1992. Merriam's turkey. Pages 331–349 *in* J. G. Dickson, editor. The wild turkey: biology and management. Stackpole Books, Mechanicsburg, Pennsylvania, USA.

Smith, D. M. 1977. The social organization of Rio Grande wild turkeys in a declining population. Dissertation, Utah State University, Logan, USA.

Speake, D. W. 1980. Predation on wild turkeys in Alabama. Proceedings of the National Wild Turkey Symposium 4:86–101.

Speake, D. W., R. Metzler, and J. McGlincy. 1985. Mortality of wild turkey poults in northern Alabama. Journal of Wildlife Management 49:472–474.

Spicer, R. L. 1957. Emigration in Merriam's wild turkey. Proceedings of the Annual Conference of the Western Association of State Game and Fish Commissioners 37:230–233.

Stangel, P. W., P. L. Leberg, and J. I. Smith. 1992. Systematics and population genetics. Pages 18–28 *in* J. G. Dickson, editor. The wild turkey: biology and management. Stackpole Books, Mechanicsburg, Pennsylvania, USA.

Swank, W. G., D. J. Martin, J. J. Campo, and C. R. Hopkins. 1985. Mortality and survival of wild trapped Eastern wild turkeys in Texas. Proceedings of the National Wild Turkey Symposium 5:113–120.

Thompson, J. N., and E. Post. 2016. Population ecology. Encyclopedia Britannica. http://www.britannica.com/science/population-ecology#ref588043.

Walker, E. A. 1951. Land use and wild turkeys. Texas Game and Fish 9:12–16.

Watts, C. R. 1969. The social organization of wild turkeys on the Welder Wildlife Refuge, Texas. Dissertation, Utah State University, Logan, USA.

Williams, L. E. 1981. The book of the wild turkey. Winchester Press, Tulsa, USA.

Willsey, B. J. 2004. Survival and mammalian predation of Rio Grande turkeys on the Edwards Plateau, Texas. Dissertation, Texas A&M University, College Station, USA.

Wright, G. A., and L. D. Vangilder. 2007. Survival and dispersal of Eastern wild turkey males in western Kentucky. Proceedings of the National Wild Turkey Symposium 9:367–373.

Wunz, G. A. 1973. Evaluation of game-farm and wild-trapped turkeys in Pennsylvania. Pages 199–209 *in* G. C. Sanderson and H. C. Schultz, editors. Wild turkey management: current problems and programs. Missouri Chapter of The Wildlife Society and University of Missouri Press, Columbia, USA.

4

Restoration

Few problems are less recognized, but more important than, the accelerating disappearance of the earth's biological resources. In pushing other species to extinction, humanity is busy sawing off the limb on which it is perched.

—PAUL R. EHRLICH

A century ago, the wild turkey was on the verge of extinction in North America because of habitat destruction and market hunting by humans. Wild turkey restoration in Texas has been occurring for over a century. Texans have a reputation for being independent souls who take great pride in their state, and many possess a good understanding of the state's ecological diversity. Conservation and restoration of wild turkeys in Texas depends on private landowners, since 99% of the land area is privately owned. The Texas Game, Fish, and Oyster Commission, the forerunner of Texas Parks and Wildlife Department (TPWD), was responsible for many statewide wild turkey restoration activities about 70 years ago, and TPWD continues to play an important role in wild turkey restoration because of its legislative mandated authority over the management of fish and wildlife in Texas, the leadership role it plays, and the guidance TPWD biologists provide to private landowners.

This chapter provides a brief review of wild turkey and human interactions, the history of restoration efforts, including failures and successes, and information on the status of restoration efforts to date. Because wild turkey restoration requires assessment of habitat quantity and quality relative to seasonal requirements, a brief summary of these activities is included. Furthermore, a review of how new populations are established will be provided. Wild turkey restoration is a multifaceted endeavor that requires the cooperative efforts of numerous groups, which will be discussed briefly at the end of the chapter.

History of Wild Turkeys and Texans

Native Americans and wild turkeys

The exact number of wild turkeys in Texas prior to European exploration and settlement is unknown, although Beasom and Wilson (1992) estimated that upward of three million birds occurred from Kansas south to the Rio Grande. Therefore, wild turkeys were abundant enough in certain regions of Texas to have been part of human culture long before the first Spaniards entered the Southwest. For example, Schorger's (1966) thorough review of the relationship between turkeys and the Native Americans of the Southwest indicates that turkeys were an important source of food, as evidenced by the remains of turkeys found in many archaeological sites throughout the Southwest. In fact, Schorger mentioned the speculation that Merriam's wild turkeys descended from the turkeys domesticated by pre-Columbian inhabitants of Arizona and New Mexico. Numerous historical accounts detail the relationship between wild turkeys and Native American tribes in Texas. For example, the Coahuiltecans who inhabited the Rio Grande Valley for thousands of years hunted turkeys with bows and arrows (Campbell 1983, Salinas 1990, Lovett et al. 2014). Additionally, Sjoberg (1953) indicated that Lipan Apaches sought wild turkeys for food but evidently preferred to consume larger wild mammals. Similarly, Smith (2006) reported that wild turkeys were the only birds the Lipan Apaches would eat, and that some tribes considered turkey eggs a delicacy. Smith also noted that Lipan Apaches and Comanches used wild turkey feathers on arrows, turkey spurs as arrowheads, and turkey bones to make spoons and awls as well as assorted beads and decorations. Although most tribes probably did not make a purposeful effort to conserve wild turkey populations, it is also very unlikely that they overharvested populations. There is general agreement in the wild turkey literature that the demise of the wild turkey in North America started with the arrival of Europeans, who destroyed habitat and gradually extirpated populations via unregulated hunting throughout the year (Kennamer et al. 1992). Therefore, it is unlikely that Native American consumptive use of wild turkeys had a detrimental impact on wild turkey populations in Texas.

Wild turkeys also had cultural value to some Native American tribes. For example, the Caddo tribe of East Texas incorporated wild turkeys into its cultural traditions. Carter (2015) described the "Turkey Dance" held by the Caddo tribe. No one is certain of the origins of this dance, but tradition holds that a hunter in the woods heard beautiful songs one day and upon investigation observed a group of turkey females dancing around a male. He fixed the dance in his memory and then hurried back to his people to describe it to them. From that day forth, the Turkey Dance that the hunter described was performed with songs composed to record Caddo history. The Caddo Turkey Dance has prevailed over many generations and continues today using the original songs developed years ago, although new songs are occasionally added. The dance is initiated by women, who encourage young men to join, and it may last for several hours or until the sun goes down, because it must end at dusk when wild turkeys roost. Carter (2015) indicated the Caddo Turkey Dance was one of two dances that represent the heart of the Caddo culture because of its significance in preserving their language and thoughts, and the spirits of past and present tribal members. Wild turkeys have been an important part of Caddo culture for as long as current tribal elders can remember. Despite this cultural value, tribal members were unable to preserve wild turkeys in East Texas because they eventually lost control of their ancestral lands.

European colonists and wild turkeys

Anglo settlers started harvesting turkeys soon after they arrived in Texas, with little thought toward conservation. Imagine a settler witnessing hundreds of wild turkeys assembling to roost in the evenings in large trees along a Texas river, and concluding that a bird so abundant could never disappear. Such was probably the attitude of most early Texas colonists when they encountered turkeys. Consequently, unregulated harvests of native wildlife, primarily by market hunting, occurred for years until wild turkey populations were almost extirpated from their geographic range in Texas.

Schorger (1966) provided numerous historic accounts of settler encounters with Rio Grande wild turkeys as well as how the birds were utilized. For instance, Bracht (1849) reported observing a flock of 400–500 birds in Bexar County, and Cook (1907) described thousands of wild turkeys roosting every night along the Salt Fork of the Brazos River. Similarly, Elgin (1938) noted that as a young man in 1872, he saw "great droves" of wild turkeys in groups of 20–30 and up to several hundred filling a 4–5 ha (10–12 ac) opening along the upper Brazos River. These early Texans took full advantage of the abundant turkeys they witnessed and often harvested as many as they wanted. In Mason County, Bingham (1878) reported that 91–136 kg (200–300 lb) of turkey meat was harvested every night, and Strong (1926) stated that he saw army officers in the late 1800s fill two wagons with wild turkeys they had harvested during two nights in Jack County. Wilhelm (1882) reported visiting a plaza in San Antonio where he saw a wagonload of wild turkeys for sale and was assured by the vendor that 50–60 birds could be harvested every night along the Frio River. He was so disturbed by what he witnessed that he thought this type of hunting should be discontinued.

The demise of the Eastern wild turkey followed a pattern similar to that experienced by the Rio Grande subspecies. Like their counterparts living among Rio Grande wild turkeys, the settlers of East Texas believed that an inexhaustible supply of wild turkeys existed in the Piney Woods. Newman (1945) indicated that overhunting was the primary reason for the decline of wild turkeys in East Texas. He stated that wild turkeys provided delicious meat and great sport for anyone who wanted to harvest one. The most popular method of hunting wild turkeys involved calling birds during the spring breeding season when turkeys were particularly vulnerable. Additionally, Newman stated that several types of ingenious traps were used to capture groups of birds. One unique hunting method that often yielded multiple birds in one attempt involved digging a narrow trench, baiting the bottom of it, and then shooting all the turkeys that were attracted to it. Little or no consideration was given to the age or sex of birds harvested. Newman believed that by 1883, overhunting was responsible for the extirpation of wild turkeys in the more densely populated counties of East Texas. He also indicated that the timber industry overharvested hardwoods over large areas of East Texas during the early 1900s, removing a significant amount of mast that represented essential turkey food. Consequently, habitat destruction along with unregulated harvest contributed to the near extirpation of wild turkeys from East Texas.

Merriam's wild turkey populations were probably restricted primarily to some of the mountain ranges of West Texas, principally the Davis and Guadalupe Mountains, although Schorger (1966) speculated that they inhabited the western Canadian River breaks in the Panhandle. Why Merriam's wild turkeys disappeared from everywhere except the Guadalupe Mountains is unknown, although it is possible that overhunting and habitat destruction were reasons for their almost complete extirpation from West Texas.

The Beginnings of Restoration

The earliest efforts to preserve wild turkeys and other wildlife occurred in the late 1800s when the Texas state legislature made an effort to curtail extensive market hunting (Suarez 2002). However, many early legislative measures were ineffective, and turkey population trends continued to decline during the first half of the twentieth century. Fortunately, some far-sighted individuals recognized that wild turkey populations were in trouble in Texas and decided to remedy the situation. Numerous people were likely responsible for initiating conservation measures that benefited wild turkeys. Many of these pioneering conservationists were landowners who not only had a passion for wildlife but also possessed important political connections and were perceptive enough politically to get some of the first wildlife conservation legislation implemented in Texas.

One of the most influential of these pioneering conservationists relative to initiating the restoration of wild turkeys in Texas was Caesar Kleberg. Lehmann (1957) provides a very good account of Kleberg's passion for wildlife, particularly wild turkeys, as well as his accomplishments in wildlife conservation. Kleberg was a member of the King Ranch family and was charged with managing the Norias Division of the ranch, located about halfway between Kingsville and the Lower Rio Grande Valley in Kenedy County. He was a pioneer of wildlife conservation in Texas, implementing game conservation measures on the King Ranch 10 years before Aldo Leopold published his book *Game Management* in 1933. The Texas legislature recognized him as "the father of wildlife conservation in Texas" in 2009 (Mattei 2010). Because of his love of wild turkeys and his concern for their decline, Kleberg almost single-handedly restored wild turkeys to the King Ranch by implementing hunting rules and management techniques that restored wild turkey populations on the portion of the ranch that he managed. Moreover, he prevailed on the heirs of the ranch to implement these measures on all ranch property, which totaled over 404,686 ha (1,000,000 ac). By the late 1920s, wild turkeys were abundant enough that surplus birds could be used to restock areas where wild turkey populations had disappeared. In the 1950s and 1960s, the King Ranch was the single largest contributor of wild turkeys for restoration in other areas of the state. This contribution of wild turkey stock has helped make Texas one of the top states for overall turkey density in the world. Furthermore, Kleberg's connections with important politicians in Austin, along with his political skills, contributed to the passage of much of the early wildlife conservation legislation that initiated the restoration of wild turkey populations in Texas. The passage of legislation that essentially started wild turkey restoration in Texas was largely the result of the dedicated efforts of influential conservation-minded landowners.

The state legislature enacted meaningful legislation in 1919 that instituted a reasonable annual bag limit of three wild turkey males per season (Suarez 2002). Such legislative measures, coupled with the efforts of conservation-minded landowners like Caesar Kleberg, resulted in the employment of game wardens in the 1920s who were charged with protecting the remaining wild turkey populations in Texas, along with other wildlife (Suarez 2002). However, though these hunting regulations were well intentioned, wild turkey populations had reached a level at which birds were restricted to a small portion of their original historic range in the state (fig. 3.9). By 1939, the Eastern subspecies was all but extirpated, with an estimated 125 birds remaining in Texas, and the populations of the Rio Grande subspecies could sustain hunting pressure in only a few locations in the Edwards Plateau and South Texas (Goodrum 1939). Clearly, aggressive efforts beyond legislation were needed to restore wild turkey populations in Texas.

Restoration of the Rio Grande Wild Turkey

Between 1920 and 2003, TPWD trapped and restored over 33,000 Rio Grande wild turkeys across Texas (Suarez 2002). Restoration started slowly and had limited success in the 1920s because of funding limitations and ineffective trapping techniques (Goodrum 1939). However, passage of the Federal Aid in Wildlife Restoration Act of 1937, also known as the Pittman-Robertson Act (PR), provided a significant boost to wild turkey restoration. These federal funds substantially increased the amount of money directed toward wild turkey restoration and management. This increased funding permitted employment of more professional wildlife staff to concentrate on wild turkeys. Increased funding and advances in capture methodology allowed for wild turkey translocations to historic parts of the wild turkey's range in Texas. This effort was aggressively pursued for almost 50 years and continues today for the Eastern subspecies. Additionally, a substantial amount of research was directed toward wild turkeys during this period, resulting in new information about wild turkey biology that furthered restoration and management of wild turkeys in Texas. Today, Rio Grande wild turkey populations have been restored to most of their historic range (fig. 3.8). Moreover, Texas supports the highest density of Rio Grande wild turkeys in the world, and some of the highest densities of any turkey subspecies in the nation (Eriksen et al. 2016). The Rio Grande wild turkey program has been so successful that only islands of suitable habitat remain unoccupied. Consequently, restoration of Rio Grande wild turkey populations is not deemed necessary and has been largely suspended, except for efforts to restore populations to portions of a few counties in South Texas and portions of the Trinity River watershed south of Dallas.

Restoration of the Merriam's Wild Turkey

Beyond two documented efforts by TPWD to restore Merriam's wild turkeys to the Guadalupe Mountains in 1955 and to the Davis Mountains in 1983, virtually nothing has been done to restore Merriam's wild turkey populations in Texas. The last estimate of the number of Merriam's wild turkeys in the Guadalupe Mountains was 75 birds in 1981 (National Park Service, Guadalupe Mountains National Park, unpublished data). In 1983, New Mexico Game and Fish biologists captured and transported 43 Merriam's wild turkeys from New Mexico and provided them to TPWD biologists for a restocking effort at The Nature Conservancy's Davis Mountains Preserve in Texas (Latch et al. 2006), and by the early 2000s, the estimated size of this population was 165 birds (King 2003). Unfortunately, genetic analyses conducted on this population indicated that an estimated two-thirds of these birds were Merriam's/Rio Grande hybrids (Latch et al. 2006). It will likely continue to be a challenge to restore Merriam's wild turkeys to the Davis Mountains because of the ongoing threat of hybridization with Rio Grande wild turkeys, which, as indicated in chapter 3, are present in and around the Davis Mountains. The Franklin Mountains are thought to represent historic range of Merriam's wild turkeys, so restoring them there may be possible if adequate habitat exists. However, perhaps the best opportunity to restore populations is in Guadalupe Mountains National Park, where some Merriam's wild turkeys still exist and where habitat is available. Translocating birds from nearby states such as New Mexico could bolster the existing population if habitat restoration occurs. However, this is a decision that the National Park Service and TPWD will have to make.

Restoration of the Eastern Wild Turkey

Restoration using Rio Grande wild turkeys

Because of the extirpation of Eastern wild turkeys from Texas and limited access to wild stock of the Eastern subspecies, early restorations in East Texas consisted of releasing wild-trapped Rio Grande turkeys into select areas in the Piney Woods of East Texas. This practice began in the 1920s with the release of limited numbers of Rio Grande turkeys (Goodrum 1939, Newman 1945). In 1939, the Game, Fish, and Oyster Commission instituted a deer and turkey restoration project utilizing PR funding with an objective of restoring wild turkeys to "all regions of the state suited to them" (Goodrum 1939). Through that project alone, 253 Rio Grande wild turkeys were trapped and released onto a 280,000-acre restoration site in Polk and Tyler Counties. Early reports suggested the measures were successful, with large numbers of broods observed (Goodrum 1939). From the 1940s through the 1970s, over 2,000 Rio Grande wild turkeys were released into 27 counties in East Texas (Boyd and Oglesby 1975). Rio Grande wild turkeys were released in numbers ranging from 50 to 150 birds per site. At least two release sites reported sustainable Rio Grande turkey populations for up to 10 years following stocking (Boyd and Oglesby 1975). In Freestone County, a remnant population of 15 to 30 Rio Grande wild turkeys stocked in 1949–1950 persisted into the 1970s (Boyd and Oglesby 1975, US Fish and Wildlife Service 1978b). The practice of releasing wild-trapped Rio Grande turkeys into the eastern third of Texas continued into the 1980s. By that time, these releases focused more on the Post Oak Savanna and Blackland Prairie regions than on the Piney Woods (US Fish and Wildlife Service 1982). Rio Grande wild turkeys are still being restocked within the Trinity River watershed.

As recently as 2009, Rio Grande wild turkey and Rio Grande/Eastern hybrid genetics were found in the Piney Woods of East Texas (Siedel 2010). It is unknown whether the occurrence of Rio Grande/Eastern wild turkey hybrids and turkeys with pure Rio Grande genetics are the result of these historic Rio Grande stocking efforts that occurred through the 1970s, or of more recent illegal releases of pen-raised Rio Grande turkeys into the wild by private individuals (Siedel 2010).

Restoration using game-farm stock

The practice of releasing wild-trapped Rio Grande turkeys into the Piney Woods of East Texas continued through the 1970s. During this same period, TPWD also actively developed state-run turkey propagation facilities in an effort to increase the numbers of Eastern and Rio Grande/Eastern hybrid turkeys into East Texas. Texas was not alone in the effort to restore wild turkeys to their historic range by mass-producing turkeys for release (Kennamer et al. 1992). At one time, many states across the United States made the same mistake. The release of pen-raised and game-farm Eastern wild turkeys in Texas began in the 1940s (Boyd and Oglesby 1975). By the 1950s, numerous state fish and game agencies were closing their game-farm operations to focus available funding on wild-trapped turkeys (Dichneite 1973, Hardy 1959). Unfortunately, Texas continued to propagate and release game-farm turkeys until the end of the 1970s. The hesitation to discontinue the game-farm approach and move exclusively to wild-trapped Eastern turkeys set the Texas Eastern wild turkey restoration program back at least 20 years (Kennamer et al. 1992). Thousands of game-farm Eastern and Rio Grande/Eastern hybrids were released from the Red River Valley in northeast Texas to the Texas coast (US Fish and Wildlife Service 1980).

There has long been a theory that a "hybridization zone" between the Rio Grande and Eastern subspecies once occurred naturally in Texas prior to European settlement (Newman 1945, Aldrich 1967). This zone of hybridization was believed to extend along the Red River Valley south into the Post Oak Savanna region and to the Gulf Coast. TPWD outlined a "hybridization zone" from the 95th meridian west to the 97th meridian in the late 1970s. TPWD had a long history of stocking both game-farm and wild-trapped Eastern wild turkeys with Rio Grande wild turkeys. In the 1970s, game-farm personnel actively developed Rio Grande/Eastern hybrid turkeys for release throughout East Texas.

In an effort to increase wild behavior and survival of game-farm stock, for a short period TPWD personnel placed game-farm Eastern turkey poults with wild-trapped Rio Grande females. These wild-trapped Rio Grande females were dosed with prolactin to induce broodiness and promote adoption of the game-farm poults. The females along with their adopted poults were then released into the wild at six weeks of age. This activity was not productive, as staff observed very low poult survival (US Fish and Wildlife Service 1978a).

Another method to establish turkey populations using game-farm turkeys included a soft-release program. Holding pens, known as "quiet release pens," were constructed at established release sites. Game-farm females and their broods were placed into the pens overnight. The following morning, hidden personnel remotely opened the door to the quiet release pen. This practice would continue throughout the summer, with new brood flocks released at one-week intervals (US Fish and Wildlife Service 1978a, b).

By the 1980s the practice of releasing game-farm turkeys in Texas was abandoned. By the mid-1980s TPWD would no longer release wild turkeys into areas known to harbor released pen-raised turkeys (US Fish and Wildlife Service 1990). For decades biologists have understood that game-farm and pen-raised turkeys are at a significant disadvantage despite any genetic wildness they may have (Kennamer et al. 1992). Communication between wild turkey poults and females occurs while poults are still in the egg. Poults imprint on the female in the minutes following hatching. They learn quickly and leave the nest within a few hours of hatching in response to female vocalizations, entering a dangerous world where they serve as prey for most predatory species. Poults must quickly learn from and respond to wild female vocalizations that warn them about predators, encourage social behavior with other turkeys, and help them survive (Kennamer et al. 1992). This process cannot be replicated in a pen.

Today it is illegal to release game-farm turkeys into the wild in Texas (title 5, subtitle B, chapter 64 of TPWD code). However, although releasing game-farm or pen-raised turkeys into the wild is neither legal nor biologically sound, this activity is still practiced by often well-meaning but uninformed landowners who see "Wild Turkeys" advertised on websites and in magazines (Kennamer et al. 1992). Concerns today with the release of pen-raised turkeys include predators developing a search image for these less-than-wild birds, as well as the potential to introduce diseases and parasites to wild populations.

Restoration using translocated Eastern wild turkeys

Boyd and Oglesby (1975) detailed restoration efforts in East Texas from 1959 to 1975. They indicated that the first efforts to restore Eastern wild turkeys using wild birds captured from Eastern states and translocated to Texas occurred in 1959 and continued through 1974. Texas received 99 Eastern wild turkeys from Florida, Georgia, and South Carolina between 1959 and 1964. Although Boyd and Oglesby described the turkeys as "Eastern wild turkeys," they used the Latin name *Meleagris gallopavo osceola* (the Florida subspecies), which leaves the exact subspecies released in question, but presumably they were the Eastern subspecies.

Those original wild turkeys from Florida, Georgia, and South Carolina were released at four sites in the Piney Woods. The largest and most successful release site was along the lower Neches River and encompassed portions of Jasper, Tyler, and Hardin Counties. This site received only Florida Eastern turkey stock and was later supplemented with Rio Grande wild turkeys between 1959 and 1962. The other three sites included Alabama Creek in Trinity County along the Neches River, Nelson Creek in Walker County, and Caney-Russell Creek in Tyler County. Alabama Creek was the sole release site for birds from South Carolina and Georgia (29 birds). Nelson Creek and Caney-Russell Creek received birds from Florida exclusively (Boyd and Oglesby 1975).

From 1966 until 1971, TPWD personnel utilized Texas brood stock trapped at the lower Neches River restoration site as brood stock for new restorations. Considering that a little over 30% of the birds originally stocked into the lower Neches River were Rio Grande wild turkeys, it is likely that the restorations that took place between 1966 and 1971 consisted of hybrid Rio Grande/Eastern wild turkeys. From 1966 to 1973, TPWD trapped 103 wild turkeys from the lower Neches River and placed them into five sites. Stocking densities ranged from 9 birds released at the Angelina-Neches site in Jasper County in 1973 to 28 birds at the Red Oak site in Robertson County. In 1971 and again in 1973, two sites along the Neches River in Cherokee County were stocked with a combination of Rio Grande wild turkeys, game-farm turkeys, and turkeys trapped from the lower Neches River site. In 1973, staff once again obtained brood stock from Florida and released 7 Florida birds and 2 lower Neches River birds along the Neches River in Jasper County (Angelina-Neches). In 1974 the turkey population at the lower Neches site crashed, as observations went from 281 birds in 1969 to only 31 birds in 1974. Boyd and Oglesby (1975) attributed this decline to blackhead disease and not to the removal of 103 wild turkeys over an eight-year period. A stocking in 1974 at an Arcadia release site in Shelby County consisted of 7 wild-trapped birds from the Caney-Russell Creek release site in Tyler County (originally stocked in 1964 with 25 Eastern wild turkeys from Florida), as well as 56 pen-reared turkeys from TPWD's own M&R Station Game Farm in Tyler (Boyd and Oglesby 1975).

Efforts to move turkeys in the state were unproductive in the late 1970s and early 1980s, with only small numbers of turkeys trapped and relocated to new restoration sites. In the late 1970s and portions of the 1980s, TPWD initiated wildlife trades with other states in order to obtain wild turkey stock. In 1979, Texas traded pheasants to Louisiana at a rate of five pheasants per wild turkey. In 1987, TPWD exchanged otters for Eastern wild turkeys in Missouri. These agreements allowed TPWD to supplement state trapping efforts. However, the numbers received from other states were low throughout the early 1980s (US Fish and Wildlife Service 1981).

Over the next few years Texas continued to receive small numbers of turkeys from various states, including Louisiana, Mississippi, and Oklahoma (US Fish and Wildlife Service 1981). Texas also continued to trap and translocate small numbers from in-state trap sites (US Fish and Wildlife Service 1983). However, in 1988 the Eastern wild turkey restoration program increased significantly. TPWD formed a partnership with the National Wild Turkey Federation (NWTF) and many other state agencies to obtain large numbers of wild turkeys. That year, 396 Eastern wild turkeys were relocated to Texas from out of state and released onto 21 sites in 13 counties (US Fish and Wildlife Service 1988). Another 442 Eastern wild turkeys were released in East Texas in 1989 (US Fish and Wildlife Service 1990).

Therefore, 1988 can be thought of as the beginning of the most ambitious era in Eastern wild turkey restoration in Texas history. Today this era of restoration is known by TPWD and NWTF biologists as the "block stocking era." Block stocking refers to the method TPWD biologists used to develop county-wide turkey populations. The goal of block stocking was to release flocks of turkeys, typically 15 to 20 birds, at multiple sites across a county. The idea was that flocks would become established, reproduce, and over time establish a county-wide turkey population.

In the late 1990s, realizing that wild turkey populations in many of the block-stocked sites were not growing or were even declining, TPWD began to supplement previous release sites by releasing additional birds in the years following the original release (Whiting et al. 2005). By 2003, TPWD had released over 7,000 Eastern wild turkeys at over 320 locations in 54 counties across the eastern third of Texas (Whiting et al. 2005). Release sites expanded from the Red River to the Texas coast and from Milam County to the Louisiana border. The block-stocking era ended in 2003, and success was mixed. Today, Texas has an open turkey season in 12 of the original 54 counties that received block stocking between 1987 and 2003. Grayson County in North Texas is the only county with an Eastern wild turkey season today that never had translocated Eastern turkeys. The Red River area in northeast Texas experienced the most positive response to the block-stocking efforts, followed by successes in other counties of the Piney Woods of southeast Texas. However, sustainable wild turkey populations were not established in most of the counties, if any, that were stocked with translocated wild turkeys in the central portion of the Post Oak Savanna during the block-stocking era.

As a consequence of aggressive restocking efforts over almost three decades, Eastern wild turkey hunting opportunities have been available in East Texas since the early 1980s in select counties. In 1995, Texas began regulating harvest of Eastern turkeys at the county level and requiring mandatory harvest reporting in Red River County. By 2005, 43 East Texas counties had an open Eastern wild turkey season. Harvests peaked in 2005 and then began a precipitous decline for the next few years. In response to declining harvests, TPWD initiated new research projects and adjusted wild turkey harvest regulations. In 2012 TPWD delayed the opening day of the season to mid-April and closed the season in 15 counties. TPWD again closed the Eastern turkey season in 11 additional counties in 2016, and in 2018 it delayed the opening day until late April and shortened the season to three weeks. Today, Texas has an open Eastern turkey season in only 13 counties. Clearly, the goal of restoring sufficient numbers of wild turkeys throughout East Texas to sustain hunting has been only partially realized. Therefore, wild turkey biologists sought a new approach to improve restoration efforts.

A twenty-first-century approach to Eastern wild turkey restoration in Texas

Research during the latter part of the block-stocking era identified flaws in Eastern wild turkey stocking methodology. Several researchers also questioned the ability of Eastern wild turkey stock from the Midwest to adapt to the Piney Woods and Post Oak Savanna of East Texas. Therefore, in 2007 TPWD spearheaded an ambitious research project with Stephen F. Austin State University (SFA) to examine a number of potential explanations for the poor establishment of Eastern wild turkeys despite years of effort.

Lopez et al. (2000) indicated that supplemental stocking efforts are not as effective as the initial stockings. They also noted that releasing an even ratio of juvenile and adult turkeys and releasing 20 males and 50 females, or "super stocking," increased the long-term potential for successful restoration. Finally, and possibly most importantly, Lopez et al. (2000) suggested that under the usual scenario of low survival and low productivity, one-year post-release super stocking had the greatest potential to successfully restore wild turkey populations in East Texas.

A criticism of the block-stocking era of Eastern turkey restoration in Texas was the lack of quality habitat at release sites. Early habitat evaluation procedures placed less value on habitat structure, nesting cover, and brood-rearing habitat (Lopez et al. 1998) than on species richness of trees and shrubs, property size, and landowner guarantees of habitat management. Lopez et al. (1998) found nesting and brood-rearing cover to be a limiting factor of restoration sites in the Post Oak Savanna region. Therefore, they recommended that adequate nesting and brooding cover be present on any future release sites in East Texas to increase the probability of successful wild turkey restoration.

In 2007, TPWD funded research by SFA to empirically test the Lopez super stocking model. The results of this research strongly suggested that restoration of the Eastern wild turkey was feasible using super stocking in East Texas if suitable habitat was present within large landscapes and if a large number of turkeys (at least 75 birds) were released during a single year rather than over multiple years (Isabelle et al. 2016).

Another research project initiated at SFA in 2008 evaluated the success of wild turkey restoration in East Texas by examining the current genetic composition of wild turkeys harvested there. Siedel (2010) collected genetic material from harvested wild turkeys to determine their genetic lineage and reported three distinct genetic clusters: north Texas, southeast Texas, and an area around Polk and Trinity Counties. There was also a clear influence from past translocations. Although some researchers question the ability of midwestern turkeys to adapt to Texas, genetic data suggest that Eastern wild turkey populations in Texas today represent similar percentages of the original stockings from the Midwest and Southeast (Siedel 2010). Probably of greater importance is the wildness of those turkeys used for restoration and the avoidance of "nuisance" or "suburb" birds adapted to significant human activity.

Following the completion of SFA's evaluation of the super stocking model, TPWD began development of a new Habitat Suitability Index (HSI) to better evaluate proposed release sites. This new HSI was developed in response to previous concerns about past Eastern wild turkey release site evaluations (Lopez et al. 1998). It was broken into two phases. The first phase consists of Geographic Information System (GIS) analysis of proposed release sites. Key variables evaluated in the GIS analysis of proposed release sites include a minimum contiguous landscape of 4,047 ha (10,000 ac) (Isabelle 2010), interspersion of open habitat types in predominantly forested landscapes (Glennon and Porter 1999), and a lack of fragmenting features (e.g., state and interstate highways, expansive open areas, dense human populations, reservoirs) on the landscape that may prevent population dispersal (Fleming and Porter 2005).

Those proposed release sites meeting the prerequisites outlined in the GIS evaluation of TPWD's new HSI are then scrutinized on the ground by a team of wildlife biologists. The on-the-ground evaluations occur only in May and June. Evaluating the potential of a site to support wild turkeys during this time is critical because it represents the period of greatest reproductive effort. Sites are critiqued for both forest habitat and brood range. Forest measurements include the percentage of usable habitat, the percentage of forest with herbaceous understory, and the percentage of woody understory less than 1 m (3 ft) in height (Schroeder 1985, Lopez et al. 1998). Open habitat measurements are also made to assess potential brooding cover. Vegetative height, percentage of bare ground, and species composition are key measurements for available open habitat. Staff also examine the proposed release sites for signs of active habitat management such as previous prescribed fire activity.

TPWD began evaluating potential release sites in 2013. The first super stockings took place in the winter of 2014. TPWD staff released close to 1,000 wild turkeys in East Texas between 2014 and 2019 using this super stocking approach. TPWD also continues to fund research to improve habitat evaluation criteria.

To be more proactive and to expand beyond the scale of the individual release site, TPWD staff constructed a landscape-scale HSI for wild turkeys in East Texas to serve as a decision support tool for future restoration activities (Estrella et al. 2015). Habitat suitability was based on four criteria: (1) edge habitat, (2) human disturbance, (3) land use/land cover, and (4) riparian corridors. The model created habitat values at a 10 m (30 ft) resolution to designate habitat "Hot Spots" across East Texas (fig. 4.1). TPWD staff utilized this hot spot map to develop priority landscapes (fig. 4.2) for future restoration efforts (Estrella et al. 2015).

In 2016 TPWD completed a Biologist Ranking Index (BRI) for East Texas. This BRI will be incorporated into future focal landscape analyses. GPS tracking of

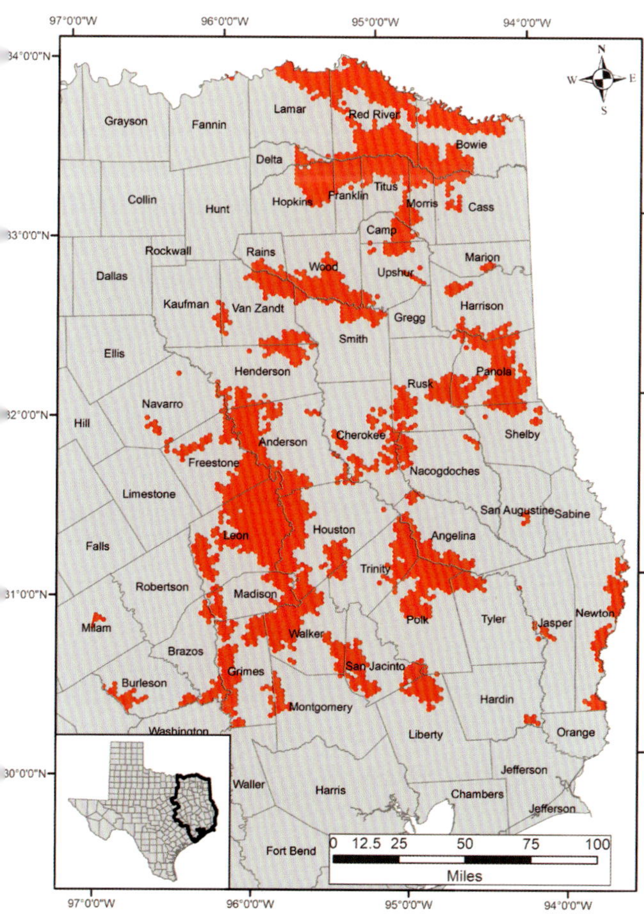

Figure 4.1. Results of Eastern wild turkey landscape analysis identifying potential hot spots of suitable habitat in which to focus wild turkey management activities (figure by Jason Hardin).

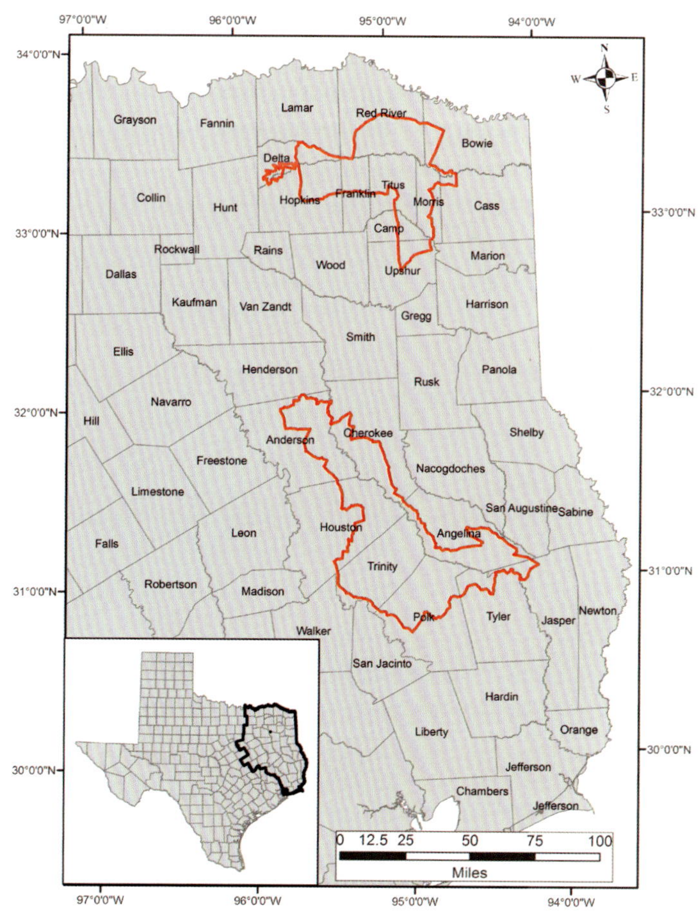

Figure 4.2. Focal landscapes generated by TPWD Eastern wild turkey model (figure by Jason Hardin).

wild turkeys has allowed researchers to examine wild turkey demographics in ways not possible prior to 2009. As new data become available, it will be critical for TPWD to adjust how it evaluates forested landscapes for wild turkeys. A better understanding of the best wild turkey subspecies to potentially restore in the Post Oak Savanna and Blackland Prairie in East Texas is needed. At a landscape scale, the ways in which the shape, size, and distribution of openings and burns in forested landscapes define habitat quality are not well understood and therefore need to be examined. As new peer-reviewed findings become available, TPWD will adjust models accordingly to provide the highest probability of successful restoration of the wild turkey in East Texas.

Restoration and Hybrids

Biologists have also grappled with the exact line of demarcation between the Rio Grande and the Eastern wild turkey. In 1975, Boyd and Oglesby suggested a line running northwest to south, from the Red River in Wichita County to the Gulf Coast in Brazoria County, as the demarcation zone between Rio Grande and Eastern wild turkeys (fig. 4.3). In 1978, TPWD identified an area from the 95th meridian west to the 97th meridian as the "Rio Grande/Eastern" hybrid zone. Lopez et al. (2000) described the historic range of the Eastern wild turkey as including the northern and eastern edges of the Post Oak Savanna, all of the Piney Woods, and portions of the eastern Coastal Prairie in Texas (fig. 4.4). Others have suggested that the Eastern subspecies may have ranged as far west as Hardeman County along the Red River. Unfortunately, no historic specimens exist today that would allow biologists to estimate just how far east the Rio Grande turkey might have occurred and to what extent a hybridization zone occurred in Texas. Even so, the suggestion of a hybridization zone may have some validity.

The idea of a hybridization zone between the Eastern wild turkey range to the east and the Rio Grande wild turkey zone to the west, suggested by Newman in 1945 and Aldrich in 1967, has been realized in Grayson and Fannin Counties in North Texas and to a greater extent in Oklahoma, Kansas, and Nebraska, as seen in the National Wild Turkey Federation (2017) wild turkey range map (fig. 4.5) (Gonzales et al. 1996, Lafon and Schemnitz 1996, Eriksen et al. 2016). In 1975, Boyd and Oglesby estimated the wild

Figure 4.3. Demarcation boundary between Rio Grande and Eastern wild turkeys (Boyd and Oglesby 1975) (figure by Jason Hardin).

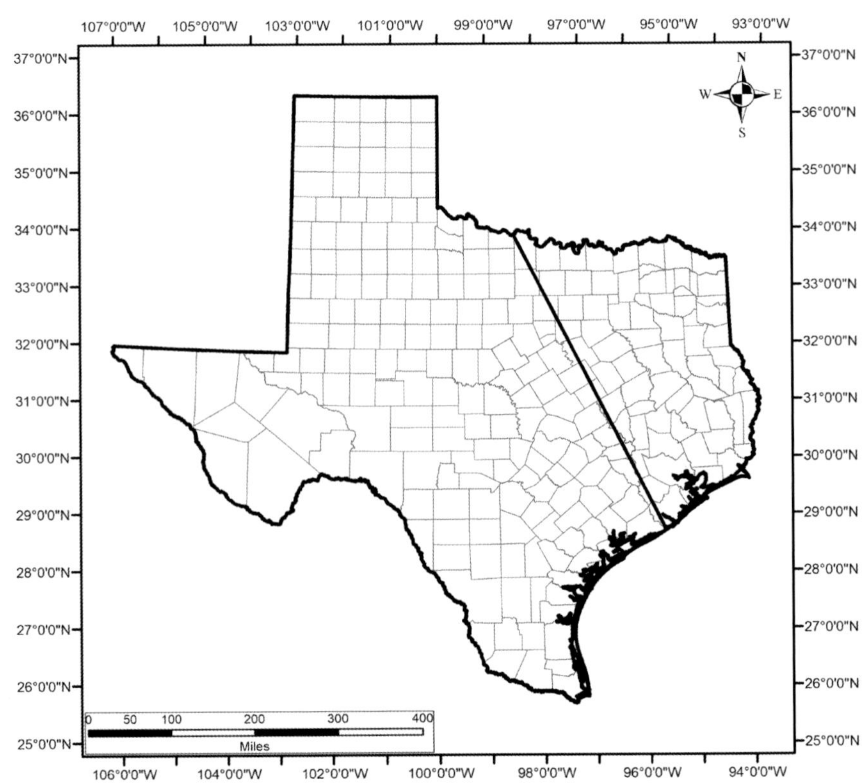

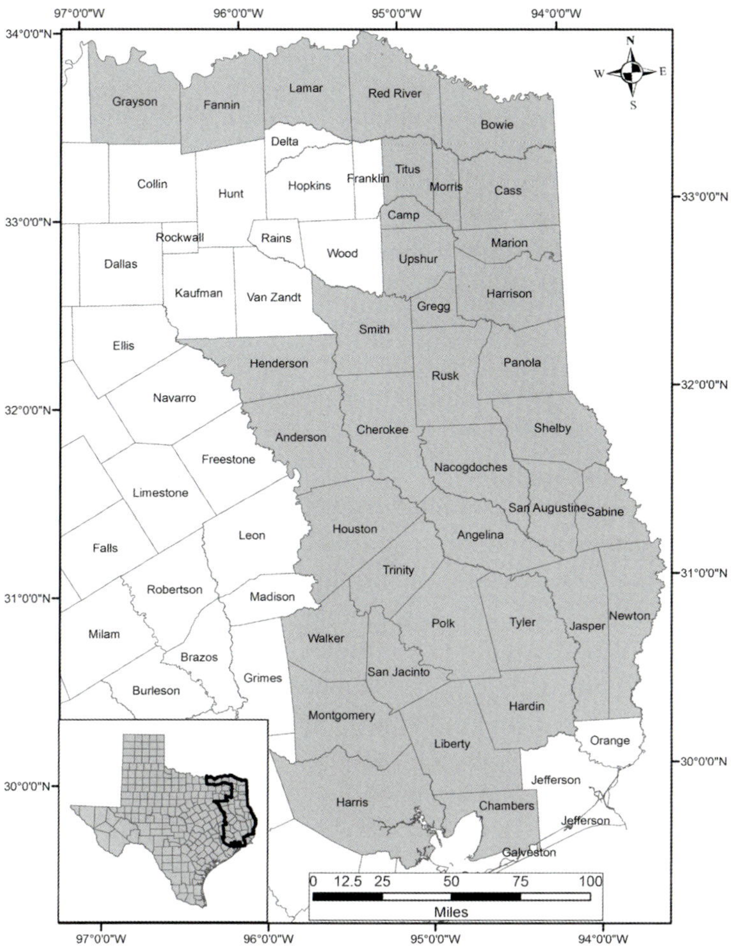

Figure 4.4. Historic range of the Eastern wild turkey (Lopez 2000) (figure by Jason Hardin).

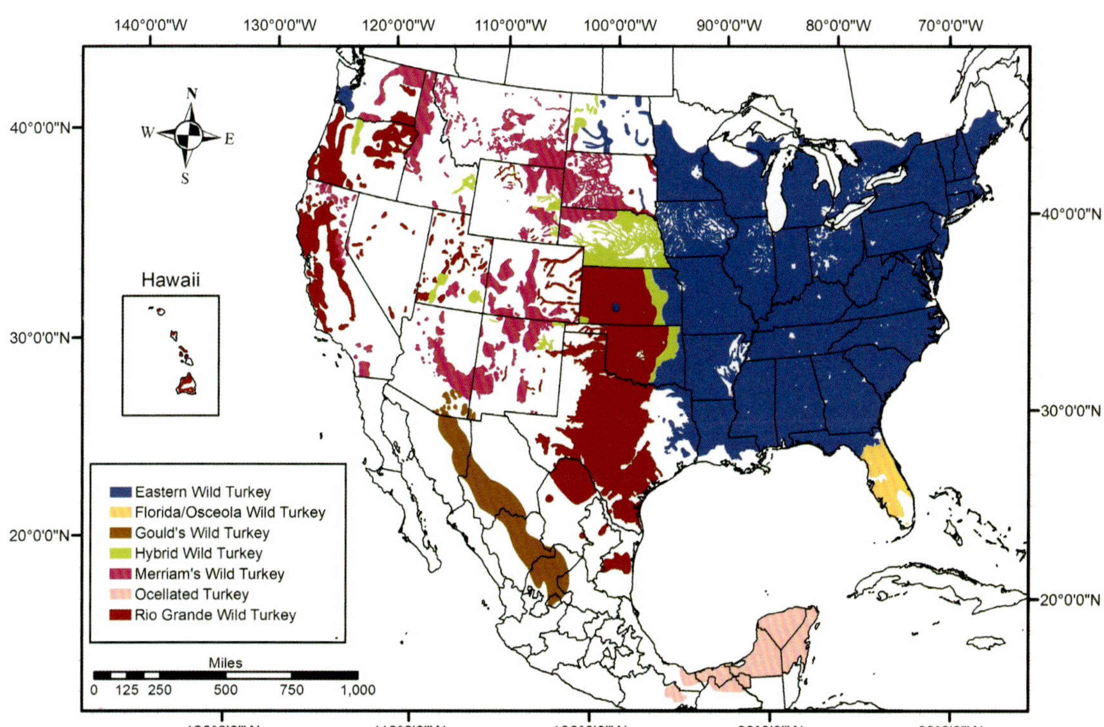

Figure 4.5. Estimated distribution of wild turkeys by subspecies and of ocellated turkeys (*Meleagris ocellata*) in 2014. US data are from survey data submitted by state wildlife agencies. (Gonzales et al. 1996, Lafon and Schemnitz 1996) (figure by National Wild Turkey Federation).

turkey population in East Texas at 1,000 Eastern and Eastern/Rio Grande hybrids. Siedel (2010) genetically identified a population with naturally occurring hybridization along the Red River Valley in northeast Texas. Siedel's findings suggest several things: (1) Rio Grandes (46.7%), Easterns (33.3%), and hybrids (19%) make up the population of wild turkeys in Grayson County; (2) Rio Grandes do not appear to exist east of Grayson County; and (3) although the majority of the turkey population east of Grayson County is made up of the Eastern subspecies, a small percentage of wild turkeys in Fannin and Lamar Counties are hybrids. Today, sustainable populations of pure Eastern wild turkeys are located along the 95th meridian in East Texas, and sustainable populations of pure Rio Grande wild turkeys are found along the 97th meridian. Unfortunately, a large area of the state just south of Dallas, within the Oaks and Prairies Bird Conservation Region (BCR 21) between the 95th and 97th meridians, remains unoccupied (fig. 4.6).

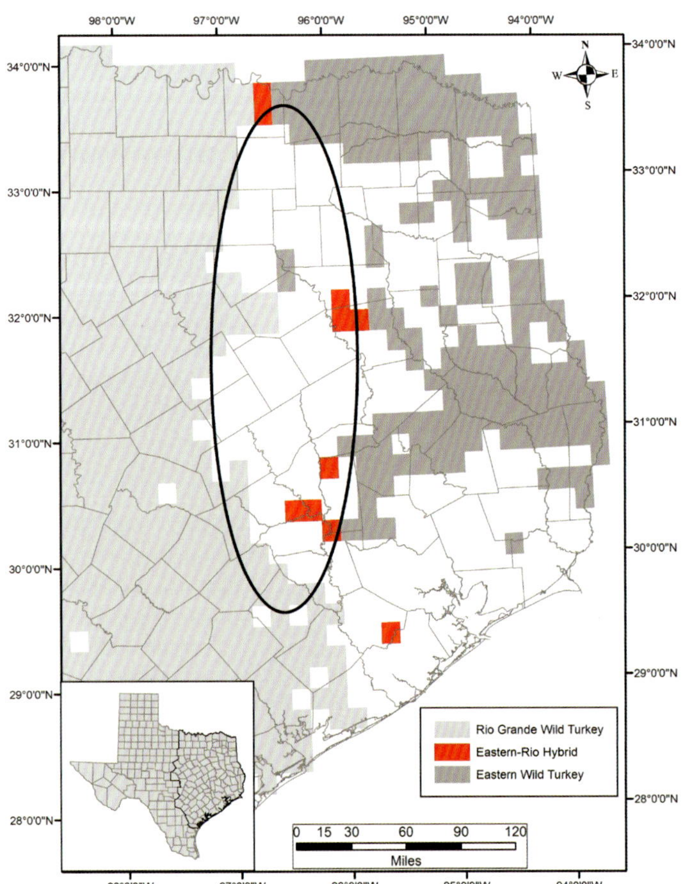

Figure 4.6. Circle indicates area of primarily unoccupied wild turkey habitat from the 95th to the 97th meridians in Texas (figure by Jason Hardin).

This returns us to the question of what the appropriate subspecies is for the landscape south of Dallas along the Trinity River watershed and the 96th meridian (BCR 21). Despite decades of restoration efforts utilizing wild-trapped Rio Grande wild turkeys, game-farm Eastern and Rio Grande/Eastern hybrids, and more recently wild-trapped Eastern wild turkeys in the hybridization zone, the area remains largely unoccupied. Is the next step in restoration the promotion of a hybrid turkey zone in which wild-trapped Rio Grande and Eastern subspecies are released into the same landscape at the same time? Or is the habitat simply not suitable for wild turkeys? Is it wrong to promote hybridization between subspecies? Some biologists argue for the value of pure-strain wild turkeys, which currently occupy most of the wild turkey range in Texas. But do landowners and hunters in this area (fig. 4.6) of the state care about a wild turkey population's questionable genetics? These and other questions remain to be answered for this last large void in turkey distribution in Texas.

Cooperation Generates Success

Successfully restoring a species generally requires the cooperation of numerous entities. The restoration of wild turkeys in Texas is a good model of cooperation, because without a cooperative effort, the restoration may not have been successful. Rio Grande wild turkeys now inhabit most of their historic range in Texas thanks to the dedicated cooperative efforts of TPWD personnel and private landowners who not only wanted turkeys on their property but were also generous enough to permit TPWD personnel to remove wild turkeys for restocking purposes. In addition, nongovernment organizations (NGOs) like the NWTF have used and continue to use their credibility and influence with a number of state wildlife agencies to facilitate the translocation of Eastern wild turkeys from other states to East Texas. The NWTF also continues to contribute the expertise of its biologists to assist in the continuing efforts to restore wild turkeys to East Texas. Other NGOs, private timber industry companies, and foundations have also played a significant role in Eastern wild turkey restoration by providing release sites on their properties and facilitating restoration efforts whenever possible. Research conducted by scientists and graduate students from several universities in Texas has also been instrumental in determining how best to restore wild turkeys to East Texas. Hundreds of wild turkey advocates have volunteered their free time over the years to restoring wild turkeys to the state of Texas. Finally, Texas hunters, through their purchase of hunting licenses and hunting equipment, actually foot most of the costs associated with restoration activities. Clearly, the successful restoration of wild turkeys in Texas has been a genuine cooperative effort, and although restoration of the Eastern subspecies is ongoing, continued cooperative efforts among private landowners, state and federal agencies, NGOs, university scientists, hunters, and the many citizen volunteers who are involved should continue to yield success.

Literature Cited

Aldrich, J. W. 1967. Taxonomy, distribution and present status. Pages 45–72 *in* O. H. Hewitt, editor. The wild turkey and its management. The Wildlife Society, Washington, DC, USA.

Beasom, S. L., and D. Wilson. 1992. Rio Grande turkey. Pages 306–330 *in* J. G. Dickson, editor. The wild turkey: biology and management. Stackpole Books, Mechanicsburg, Pennsylvania, USA.

Bingham, H. L. 1878. A thousand wild turkeys. Forest and Stream 11:410–411.

Boyd, C. E., and R. D. Oglesby. 1975. Status of wild turkey restoration in East Texas. Proceedings of the National Wild Turkey Symposium 3:1–21.

Bracht, V. 1849. Texas im Jahre. Elberfeld.

Campbell, T. N. 1983. Coahuiltecans and their neighbors. Handbook of North American Indians of the Southwest. Smithsonian Institution, Washington, DC, USA.

Carter, C. E. 2015. Caddo voices. Texas beyond history. University of Texas College of Liberal Arts. http://www.texasbeyondhistory.net/tejas/voices/credits.html.

Cook, J. R. 1907. The border and the buffalo. Crane and Company, Topeka, Kansas, USA.

Dichneite, D. F. 1973. Restoration of the Eastern wild turkey in Missouri. Proceedings of the National Wild Turkey Symposium 2:19–24.

Elgin, J. 1938. Christmas dinner on Upper Brazos in 1872. West Texas Historical Association Year Book 14:83–91.

Eriksen, R. E., T. A. Brown, K. B. Scott, T. W. Hughes, M. D. Akridge, and C. S. Penner. 2016. Status and distribution of wild turkey in the United States: 2014 status. Proceedings of the National Wild Turkey Symposium 11:7–18.

Estrella, J. A., J. Hardin, and D. O'Donnell. 2015. Using GIS to develop priority areas of the restoration of Eastern wild turkey in Texas. Abstract. Meeting of the Texas Chapter of The Wildlife Society, Corpus Christi.

Fleming, K. K., and W. F. Porter. 2005. Effects of landscape features and fragmentation on wild turkey dispersal. Proceedings of the National Wild Turkey Symposium 9:175–183.

Glennon, M. J., and W. F. Porter. 1999. Using satellite imagery to assess landscape-scale habitat for wild turkeys. Wildlife Society Bulletin 27:646–653.

Gonzales, M. J., H. B. Quigley, and C. I. Taylor. 1996. Habitat use, reproductive behavior and survival of ocellated turkeys in Tikal National Park, Guatemala. Proceedings of the National Wild Turkey Symposium 7:193–199.

Goodrum, P. D. 1939. Annual report of the Game, Fish, and Oyster Commission—Game Management. Pittman-Robertson Report. Texas Game, Fish, and Oyster Commission, Austin, USA.

Hardy, F. C. 1959. Results of stocking wild-trapped and game farm turkeys in Kentucky. Proceedings of the National Wild Turkey Symposium 1:61–65.

Isabelle, J. L. 2010. Survival, home range size, habitat selection, and reproduction ecology of the Eastern wild turkey in East Texas. Thesis, Stephen F. Austin State University, Nacogdoches, Texas, USA.

Isabelle, J. L., W. C. Conway, C. E. Comer, G. E. Calkins, and J. B. Hardin. 2016. Home range size and habitat selection of female wild turkeys translocated to East Texas. Proceedings of the National Wild Turkey Symposium 11:143–154.

Kennamer, J. E., M. Kennamer, and R. Brenneman. 1992. History. Pages 6–17 *in* J. G. Dickson, editor. The wild turkey: biology and management. Stackpole Books, Mechanicsburg, Pennsylvania, USA.

King, J. S. 2003. Status, ecology, and genetic identity of wild turkey in the Davis Mountains of Texas. Sul Ross State University, Alpine, Texas, USA.

Lafon, A., and S. D. Schemnitz. 1996. Distribution, habitat use, and limiting factors of Gould's turkey in Chihuahua, Mexico. Proceedings of the National Wild Turkey Symposium 7:185–191.

Latch, E. K., L. A. Harveson, J. S. King, M. D. Hobson, and O. E. Rhodes Jr. 2006. Assessing hybridization in wildlife populations using molecular markers: a case study in wild turkeys. Journal of Wildlife Management 70:485–492.

Lehmann, V. W. 1957. Game conservation and management. Pages 761–766 (appendix) *in* Tom Lea, "The King Ranch," volume 2. Little, Brown, Boston, Massachusetts, USA.

Leopold, B. D., and J. L. Cummins. 2016. Integrating science into the policy-making process. Proceedings of the National Wild Turkey Symposium 11:25–38.

Lopez, R. R., C. K. Feuerbacher, N. J. Silvy, M. A. Sternberg, and J. D. Burke. 1998. Survival and reproduction of

Eastern wild turkey relocated into the post oak savannah of Texas. Proceedings of the Annual Conference of the Southeastern Association of Fish and Wildlife Agencies 52:384–396.

Lopez, R. R., W. E. Grant, N. J. Silvy, M. J. Peterson, C. K. Feuerbacher, and M. S. Corson. 2000. Restoration of the wild turkey in East Texas: simulation of alternative restocking strategies. Ecological Modelling 132:275–285.

Lovett, B. L., J. L. Gonzalez, R. Bacha-Garza, and R. K. Skowronek. 2014. Native American peoples of South Texas. CHAPS, Community Historical Archaeology Project with Schools, University of Texas–Pan American, Edinburg, USA.

Mattei, E. 2010. King of conservation: Caesar Kleberg. Texas Parks and Wildlife Magazine (May).

National Wild Turkey Federation. 2017. Wild turkey distribution. http://www.nwtf.org/hunt/wild-turkey-basics/habitat.

Newman, C. C. 1945. Turkey restocking efforts in East Texas. Journal of Wildlife Management 9:279–289.

Salinas, M. 1990. Indians of the Rio Grande Delta: their role in the history of southern Texas and northeastern Mexico. University of Texas Press, Austin, USA.

Schroeder, R. L. 1985. Habitat suitability index models: Eastern wild turkey. US Fish and Wildlife Service Biological Report 82 (10.106).

Siedel, S. A. 2010. Genetic structure and diversity of the Eastern wild turkey (*Meleagris gallopavo silvestris*) in East Texas. Thesis, Stephen F. Austin State University, Nacogdoches, Texas, USA.

Sjoberg, A. F. 1953. Lipan Apache culture in historical perspective. Southwestern Journal of Anthropology, 9:76–98.

Smith, A. F. 2006. The fall and rise of the wild turkey. Pages 291–302 *in* Wild food: proceedings of the Oxford Symposium on Food and Cookery. Prospect Books, London, UK.

Strong, H. W. 1926. My frontier days and Indian fights on the Plains of Texas. Self-published, Dallas, Texas, USA.

Suarez, R. 2002. Texas turkey talk. Texas Parks and Wildlife Department Report PWD BK W7000–827 (5/02). Texas Parks and Wildlife Department, Austin, USA.

US Fish and Wildlife Service. 1975. Game trapping and transplanting. Federal Aid Report W-28-D. Region 2, Albuquerque, New Mexico, USA.

US Fish and Wildlife Service. 1978. Wildlife management coordination. Federal Aid Reports W-14-C-37 and 38. Region 2, Albuquerque, New Mexico, USA.

US Fish and Wildlife Service. 1980. Wildlife management coordination. Federal Aid Report W-14-C-39. Region 2, Albuquerque, New Mexico, USA.

US Fish and Wildlife Service, 1981. Wildlife management coordination. Federal Aid Report W-14-C-40. Region 2, Albuquerque, New Mexico, USA.

US Fish and Wildlife Service. 1982. Wildlife management coordination. Federal Aid Report W-14-C-41. Region 2, Albuquerque, New Mexico, USA.

US Fish and Wildlife Service. 1983. Wildlife management coordination. Federal Aid Report W-14-C-42. Region 2, Albuquerque, New Mexico, USA.

US Fish and Wildlife Service. 1988. Wildlife management coordination. Federal Aid Report W-14-C-47. Region 2, Albuquerque, New Mexico, USA.

US Fish and Wildlife Service. 1990. Wildlife management coordination. Federal Aid Report W-14-C-48. Region 2, Albuquerque, New Mexico, USA.

Whiting, R. M., B. P. Oswald, J. D. Kelly, and M. S. Fountain. 2005. Survival of supplementally stocked Eastern wild turkeys in East Texas. Proceedings of the National Wild Turkey Symposium 9:143–148.

Wilhelm. 1882. Turkeys in Texas. American Field 17:34.

5

Population Ecology

Populations are more abstract conceptual entities than cells or organisms and are somewhat more elusive, but they are nonetheless real.

—ERIC PIANKA (1978)

A population is a group of individuals of a species that occupy a particular place at a given time. Individuals within a group that is defined as a population usually interbreed. Defining a population is nearly always scale dependent, and at the organismal level it can be considered from spatial, demographic, and genetic perspectives (Wells and Richmond 1995). Often, wildlife scientists study a subset of a population of birds that corresponds to a delineated study area. A great deal of research on wild turkey populations has been conducted in this manner, using study areas such as wildlife management areas, national forests, and large private ranches.

Ecology is the study of the interrelationships of organisms and their environment. By extension, therefore, population ecology is scientific inquiry where the goal is to understand the factors that underlie and influence how populations change in space and over time.

Why Managers Should Understand Wild Turkey Population Ecology

The analysis of wild turkey populations has received significant attention during the past 50 years. The most recent comprehensive book on wild turkeys (Dickson 1992) contains at least five chapters—on diseases, parasites, predation, population dynamics, and population management—that address the factors that influence the population ecology of this species. Since 1992 a great deal of research has been published on wild turkey population ecology, especially for the Rio Grande subspecies in Texas and the Eastern subspecies elsewhere. Understanding wild turkey population ecology is critical for the effective management of their populations. Numerous factors work together to influence wild turkey population abundance and trends over time. Like any wildlife population, wild turkey populations are limited by both intrinsic and extrinsic factors. Reproductive potential, annual production, survival, and recruitment are influenced by the biological limitations of a species (intrinsic factors) as well as by habitat, weather, predators, and hunting (extrinsic factors). Effective population management involves understanding how these factors operate to regulate populations. Changes in the size of a wild turkey population are regulated by three processes: (1) birth or reproduction, (2) death or mortality, and (3) immigration or emigration. While these three factors seem relatively straightforward, McRoberts et al. (2014) noted that with respect to wild turkeys, it is "likely that multiple factors regulate populations simultaneously, and factors can be expected to vary spatially, temporally and among subspecies." The scientific literature on wild turkey population ecology certainly supports this point.

Reproduction and Demography among Subspecies

Vangilder (1992) organized the reproductive process of wild turkeys into five components: nesting rate, first-nest success, renesting rate, renest success, and female success (table 5.1). Early estimates of wild turkey nesting success ranged from about 35% to 40% (Schorger 1966). Vangilder (1992) considered these estimates were most likely biased because of factors such as the nests being located during different times after the clutches were laid, and failing to account for variation in egg exposure time using a Mayfield correction factor. The advent of radiotelemetry in wild turkey research in the late 1960s (Williams and Austin 1988) resulted in a considerable breakthrough for understanding wild turkey reproduction (Vangilder 1992). Radiotelemetry has allowed researchers to collect data on wild turkey reproductive ecology that would otherwise have been impossible to obtain (fig. 5.1).

Nesting rate

Nesting rates for the Eastern, Merriam's, and Rio Grande wild turkey subspecies, while somewhat variable, are usually quite high (table 5.2). The average wild turkey nesting rate is about 76% (range 23.4% to 100%) for adults. Average nesting rates for juvenile females (first-year breeding) are much lower (43.1% based on 10 studies, range 7.0% to 95%) than for adults (table 5.2). Because of differing methods, as well as losses of nests to predators before they are found by researchers, nesting rate estimates are almost certainly low (Vangilder 1992).

Renesting rate

The renesting rates for Eastern, Merriam's, and Rio Grande wild turkey subspecies are highly variable, ranging from 0 to 73.3% (table 5.3). Although only a few studies have reported renesting rates for juvenile females, estimates were considerably lower (0 to 33%) than for adults (table 5.3).

Nest success

The average success of first nests (approximately 33.5%; table 5.4) for Eastern, Merriam's, and Rio Grande wild turkeys ranged from 17% to 54%, thus indicating that the apparent nest success estimated by Schorger (1966) of about 35% was probably correct. However, the wide range in overall nesting success from multiyear studies (7% to 60%) indicates huge

Figure 5.1. A mature Eastern wild turkey gobbler with a GPS transmitter fitted between the wings (photo by Daniel Sullivan).

Table 5.1. Definitions of wild turkey reproductive parameters.

Nesting rate	Proportion of females that attempt to nest
First-nest success	Proportion of first nests from which at least one live poult hatches
Renesting rate	Proportion of females that were not successful on their first nesting attempt that attempt to renest
Renest success	Proportion of renest attempts from which at least one live poult hatches
Female success	Proportion of females that have a successful nest (hatch at least one live poult) in one of their nesting attempts

Source: Vangilder (1992).

Table 5.2. Nesting rates, in percentages, of females of three wild turkey subspecies.

	Adult		Juvenile	
Subspecies	**Mean**	**Range**	**Mean**	**Range**
Eastern[a]	87.5	79–96	-	-
Eastern[b]	49.0	-	-	-
Eastern[c]	100.0	-	100.0	-
Eastern-Merriam's[d]	96.0	-	88.0	-
Merriam's[e]	76.0	-	11.0	-
Merriam's[f]	97.0	-	73.0	-
Merriam's[g]	75.0	-	7.7	-
Merriam's[h]	100.0	-	30.8	-
Merriam's[i]	76.6	-	16.7	-
Rio Grande[j]	91.1	-	-	-
Rio Grande[k]	76.5	67–94	-	-
Rio Grande[l]	99.0	-	94.0	-
Rio Grande[m]	81.7	69–89	48.0	47–100
Rio Grande[n]	64.3	33–85	52.6	0–100
Rio Grande[o]	23.4	6–39	12.5	6–33
Rio Grande[p]	42.4	16–64	7.0	0–17
Rio Grande[q]	100.0	-	95.0	-

[a]Campo et al. (1984). Texas. First three nesting seasons after trap, transfer, and release.
[b]Isabelle et al. (2016). Texas. First two nesting seasons after trap, transfer, and release.
[c]Vangilder et al. (1987). Missouri. Four-year study.
[d]Porter et al. (1983). Minnesota. Two-year study.
[e]Schemnitz et al. (1985). New Mexico. Four-year study.
[f]Rumble and Hodorff (1993). South Dakota. Six-year study.
[g]Lockwood and Sutcliffe (1985). New Mexico. Five-year study.
[h]Lutz and Crawford (1987). Oregon. Two-year study.
[i]Flake and Day (1995). South Dakota. Two-year study.
[j]Conley et al. (2016). Texas. Two-year study.
[k]Melton et al. (2010). Texas. Three-year study.
[l]Keegan and Crawford (1993). Oregon. Three-year study.
[m]Collier et al. (2009). Texas. Seven-year study. Stable population.
[n]Collier et al. (2009). Texas. Seven-year study. Declining population.
[o]Randall et al. (2005). Texas. Three-year study. Stable population.
[p]Randall et al. (2005). Texas. Three-year study. Declining population.
[q]Schmutz and Braun (1989). Colorado. Two-year study.

Table 5.3. Renesting rates, in percentages, of females of three wild turkey subspecies.

	Adult		Juvenile	
Subspecies	Mean	Range	Mean	Range
Eastern[a]	47.4	0–100	-	-
Eastern[b]	14.0	-	33.0	-
Eastern[c]	44.8	14–75	-	-
Eastern-Merriam's[d]	57.1	-	33.3	-
Merriam's[e]	34.6	-	0.0	-
Merriam's[f]	0.0	-	0.0	-
Rio Grande[g]	49.0	20–74	-	-
Rio Grande[h]	73.3	-	-	-

[a]Campo et al. (1984). Texas. First three nesting seasons after trap, transfer, and release.
[b]Isabelle et al. (2016). Texas. First two nesting seasons after trap, transfer, and release.
[c]Vangilder et al. (1987). Missouri. Four-year study.
[d]Porter et al. (1983). Minnesota. Two-year study.
[e]Lockwood and Sutcliffe (1985). New Mexico. Five-year study.
[f]Lutz and Crawford (1987). Oregon. Two-year study.
[g]Melton et al. (2010). Texas. Three-year study.
[h]Keegan and Crawford (1993). Oregon. Three-year study.

Table 5.4. Nest success rates, in percentages, of females of three wild turkey subspecies.

	First nest		Renest	
Subspecies	Mean	Range	Mean	Range
Eastern[a]	44.6	40–46	44.4	0–50
Eastern[b]	38.0	21–48	-	-
Eastern[c]	30.7	14–47	30.0	0–60
Eastern-Merriam's[d]	62.0	-	72.7	-
Merriam's[e]	27.0	-	35.0	-
Merriam's[f]	43.6	-	-	-
Rio Grande[g]	38.7	-	-	-
Rio Grande[h]	14.5	7–19	-	-
Rio Grande[i]	54.0	48–60	30.0	-
Rio Grande[j]	17.0	-	-	-
Rio Grande[k]	2.0	-	-	
Rio Grande[l]	38.0	-	-	-

[a]Campo et al. (1984). Texas. First three nesting seasons after trap, transfer, and release.
[b]Isabelle et al. (2016). Texas. First two nesting seasons after trap, transfer, and release. Includes all nest attempts.
[c]Vangilder et al. (1987). Missouri. Four-year study.
[d]Porter et al. (1983). Minnesota. Two-year study.
[e]Rumble and Hodorff (1993). South Dakota. Six-year study.
[f]Flake and Day (1995). South Dakota. Two-year study.
[g]Conley et al. (2016). Texas. Two-year study.
[h]Melton et al. (2010). Texas. Three-year study.
[i]Keegan and Crawford (1993). Oregon. Three-year study.
[j]Locke et al. (2013). Edwards Plateau, Texas. Three-year study.
[k]Locke et al. (2013). Central Rio Grande Plains, Texas. Three-year study.
[l]Dreibelbis et al. (2008). Texas. Two-year study. Includes all nest attempts.

variation in this reproductive parameter among years. This wide amount of variation is typical for Rio Grande turkeys in South Texas because spring rainfall plays a significant role in their reproductive success.

As Vangilder (1992:146) noted: "Hen success is a function of first nest success, renesting rate and renest success." The overall average female success rate for adult Eastern, Merriam's, and Rio Grande wild turkeys is about 44% (table 5.5). Overall average juvenile female success is considerably lower (about 30.5%; table 5.5) than it is for adult females. Adult female success rates are about 10% higher than nest success rates and are probably a more realistic reproductive parameter with respect to wild turkey reproduction potential. Although apparent or even Mayfield-corrected nest success rates can be obtained by classical natural history observations, radiotelemetry has been essential for obtaining female success rates because it allows researchers to follow individual females across multiple nesting attempts during a nesting season.

Clutch size

Schorger (1966) summarized clutch sizes of Eastern, Merriam's, and Rio Grande wild turkeys from 14 states, and the average size was 11 eggs for Eastern, Rio Grande, and Merriam's wild turkeys. McRoberts et al. (2014) reported an average clutch size for Eastern and Merriam's wild turkeys of 11.8 eggs and 8.6 eggs for adults, respectively. Palmer et al. (1993) found that the average clutch size of Eastern wild

Table 5.5. Female success rates, in percentages, of three wild turkey subspecies.

	Adult		Juvenile	
Subspecies	**Mean**	**Range**	**Mean**	**Range**
Eastern[a]	51.8	45–70	-	-
Eastern[b]	35.0	-	50.0	-
Eastern[c]	40.0	10–65	30.0	0–100
Eastern-Merriam's[d]	64.0	-	61.0	-
Merriam's[e]	43.0	-	-	
Merriam's[f]	46.2	-	50.0	-
Merriam's[g]	75.0	-	25.0	-
Merriam's[h]	48.0	19–63	24.0	0–57
Rio Grande[i]	25.0	0–50	0.0	-
Rio Grande[j]	28.6	0–43	12.5	0–38
Rio Grande[k]	68.0	-	52.0	-
Rio Grande[l]	58.0	-	-	
Rio Grande[m]	27.0	0–93	-	-
Rio Grande[n]	17.7	1–70	-	-

[a]Campo et al. (1984). Texas. First three nesting seasons after trap, transfer, and release.
[b]Isabelle et al. (2016). Texas. First two nesting seasons after trap, transfer, and release.
[c]Vangilder et al. (1987). Missouri. Four-year study.
[d]Porter et al. (1983). Minnesota. Two-year study.
[e]Schemnitz et al. (1985). New Mexico. Four-year study.
[f]Lockwood and Sutcliffe (1985). New Mexico. Five-year study.
[g]Lutz and Crawford (1987). Oregon. Two-year study.
[h]Rumble and Hodorff (1993). South Dakota. Six-year study.
[i]Ransom et al. (1987). Texas. Two-year study.
[j]Reagan and Morgan (1980). Texas. Four-year study.
[k]Keegan and Crawford (1999). Oregon. Two-year study.
[l]Schmutz and Braun (1989). Colorado. Two-year study.
[m]Beasom and Pattee (1980). Santa Gertrudis Division, King Ranch, Texas. Ten-year study.
[n]Beasom and Pattee (1980). Encino Division, King Ranch, Texas. Ten-year study.

Table 5.6. Clutch sizes of females of three wild turkey subspecies.

	First nest			Renest		
Subspecies	**Mean**	**SE**	**N[a]**	**Mean**	**SE**	**N[a]**
Eastern[b]	10.7	0.27	69	8.5	0.34	28
Eastern[c]	10.3	-	-	10.3	-	-
Merriam's[d]	8.5	-	-	9.5	-	-
Merriam's[e]	9.2	-	-	9.2	-	-
Merriam's[f]	11.2	-	-	-	-	-
Rio Grande[g]	10.3	0.47	24	8.9	0.63	9
Rio Grande[h]	11.2	-	-	10.6	-	-
Rio Grande[i]	11.0	-	20	-	-	-

[a]Number of clutches.
[b]Vangilder et al. (1987). Missouri. Four-year study.
[c]Exum et al. (1987). Alabama.
[d]Lockwood and Sutcliffe (1985). New Mexico. Five-year study.
[e]Rumble and Hodorff (1993). South Dakota. Six-year study.
[f]Flake and Day (1995). South Dakota. Two-year study
[g]Reagan and Morgan (1980). Texas. Four-year study.
[h]Keegan and Crawford (1999). Oregon. Two-year study
[i]Schmutz and Braun (1989). Colorado. Two-year study.

Table 5.7. Fertility and hatching success for Merriam's and Rio Grande wild turkey females.

	Fertility[a]	Hatching success[b]	
Subspecies	**Mean**	**Mean**	**N[c]**
Eastern[d]	93	-	3
Eastern-Merriam's[e]	-	80	2
Merriam's[f]	66	-	3
Merriam's[g]	88	87	5
Merriam's[h]	-	86	6
Merriam's[i]	-	92	2
Rio Grande[j]	90	90	4
Rio Grande[k]	51	40	2
Rio Grande[l]	-	89	1

[a]Fertility = (number of eggs fertile / clutch size) × 100.
[b]Hatching success = (number eggs hatching / clutch size) × 100 for successful nests.
[c]N = number of years data were collected.
[d]Everett et al. (1980). Alabama.
[e]Porter et al. (1983). Minnesota. Two-year study.
[f]Schemnitz et al. (1985). New Mexico.
[g]Lockwood and Sutcliffe (1985). New Mexico.
[h]Rumble and Hodorff (1993). South Dakota.
[i]Flake and Day (1995). Two-year study.
[j]Cook (1972). Texas.
[k]Keegan and Crawford (1999). Oregon.
[l]Ransom et al. (1987). Texas.

turkey females in his study area in Mississippi was 9.1 eggs for first nests and 6.7 eggs for renests. Lutz and Crawford (1987) indicated that average clutch size for Merriam's wild turkey females in Oregon was 10.9 eggs. Flake and Day (1995) reported an average clutch size of 11.2 eggs for Merriam's wild turkey females in South Dakota. The clutch size for Rio Grande wild turkeys varies but generally ranges from 10 to 12 eggs. Cathey et al. (2007) and Collier et al. (2009) indicated that the average clutch size of Rio Grande females was about 11 eggs. Therefore, the average clutch size for the three wild turkey subspecies in Texas varies but generally ranges from 10 to 12 eggs. Except in one study of the Merriam's subspecies (Lockwood and Sutcliffe 1985), clutch size for first nests is typically larger than it is for renesting attempts (table 5.6), which is typical for most bird species. The three Rio Grande studies listed in table 5.6 seem to indicate that the clutch size for this subspecies is slightly larger than it is for Merriam's, but only by an average of about one egg.

Fertility and hatching success

In general, fertility and hatching success for Merriam's and Rio Grande wild turkeys are quite high (table 5.7). The average fertility rate is about 74%, and the average hatching success rate from five studies is 78% (table 5.7).

Poult survival rates

Unfortunately, very few studies have reported the survival rates of preflight wild turkey poults in Texas or elsewhere (fig. 5.2). Spears et al. (2007) found that preflight survival of Rio Grande wild turkey poults ranged from 12% to 52% at four sites in southwestern Kansas and the Texas Rolling Plains. Beasom (1970) estimated that poult mortality from 2 to 15 weeks posthatching at two South Texas sites was 22.9% in a study area dominated by mesquite (*Prosopis* spp.), and 12.1% in a study area dominated by live oak (*Quercus virginiana*).

Figure 5.2. A Rio Grande wild turkey hen with four-to-six-week-old poults (photo by Larry Ditto).

Annual survival rates

Because different studies report their data in different ways, it is difficult to compare survival rates across subspecies or within sex and age classes. In general, adult males seem to have slightly higher survival rates than females or juveniles, but not always (table 5.8). The data on annual survival rate in table 5.8 indicate a wide range in wild turkey survival rates (0.30 to 0.81) across the studies that have reported this information from Texas and other states.

Population Trends in Texas

McRoberts et al. (2014) noted that in 2009 the wild turkey population in Texas was estimated to be slightly less than half a million birds (approximately 460,000), although the method of enumeration was not clear.

The Texas Parks and Wildlife Department (TPWD) (2014) has collected data on wild turkey harvest from 1995 to 2014. These data include all three subspecies as well as Rio Grande/Merriam's hybrids (fig. 5.3). Wild turkey harvests were stable at about 62,000 birds between 1995 and 2005. After that, wild turkey harvests steadily declined statewide to a low of about 30,000 birds in 2013.

TPWD biologists have expended considerable effort to restore Eastern wild turkey populations to East Texas. Therefore, annual harvest records have been maintained for this subspecies because successful hunters are required to bring their harvested male to a TPWD check station. Eastern wild turkey hunting resumed in Texas in 1995 and has continued for over 20 years. Initially, fewer than 50 birds were harvested during the first two seasons, but then harvests increased substantially, to a high of almost 450 birds in

Table 5.8. Annual survival rates for wild turkeys.

Subspecies	Sex and age	Annual survival rate (range)	NI[a]
Eastern[b]	Males	0.710	14 (1979)
Eastern[b]	Females	0.580	24 (1979)
Eastern[b]	Females	0.600	25 (1980)
Eastern[c]	Males and females	0.676	74
Eastern[d]	Males	0.300	113[e]
Eastern[d]	Juvenile males	0.550	148[f]
Eastern[g]	Females	0.683 (0.50–0.81)	111[h]
Merriam's[i]	All ages	0.680 (0.33–0.760)	-
Rio Grande[j]	Juvenile and adult females	0.726	31
Rio Grande[k]	Adult females	0.710	40
Rio Grande[k]	Juvenile females	0.680	68
Rio Grande[l]	Juvenile males	0.597	115
Rio Grande[l]	Adult males	0.360	107
Rio Grande[m]	Males	0.621	-

[a]Number of marked individuals.
[b]Campo et al. (1984). Texas. First three nesting seasons after trap, transfer, and release.
[c]Swank et al. (1985). Texas. Two-year study.
[d]Byrne et al. (2014). Louisiana. 2002 through 2012.
[e]Total number of males captured and marked by Byrne et al. (2014).
[f]Total number of juvenile males captured and marked by Byrne et al. (2014).
[g]Palmer et al. (1993). Mississippi. 1987 through 1990.
[h]Total number of females captured and marked by Palmer et al. (1993).
[i]Flake and Day (1995). South Dakota. Two-year study.
[j]Ransom et al. (1987). Texas. Two-year study.
[k]Keegan and Crawford (1999). Oregon. Two-year study.
[l]Holdstock et al. (2006). Texas and Kansas. Two-year study.
[m]Miller (1993). Kansas. Two-year study.

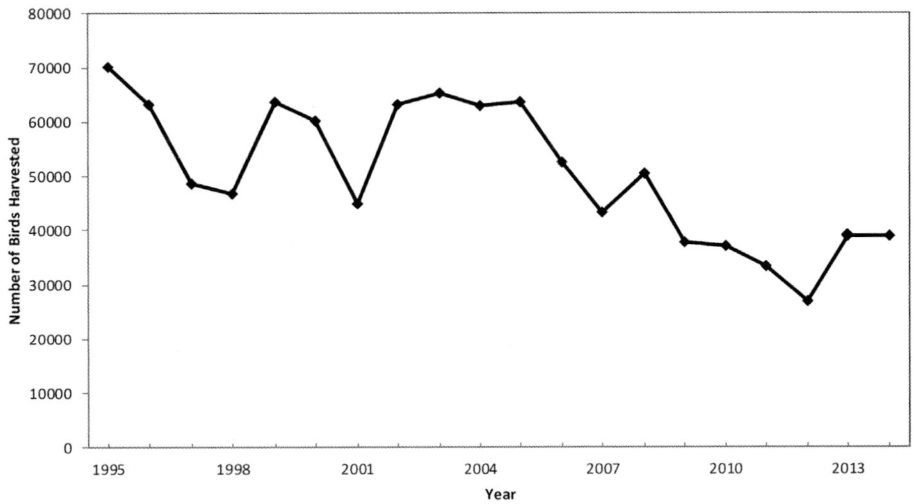

Figure 5.3. Wild turkey harvest in Texas, 1995–2015 (figure by Leonard Brennan).

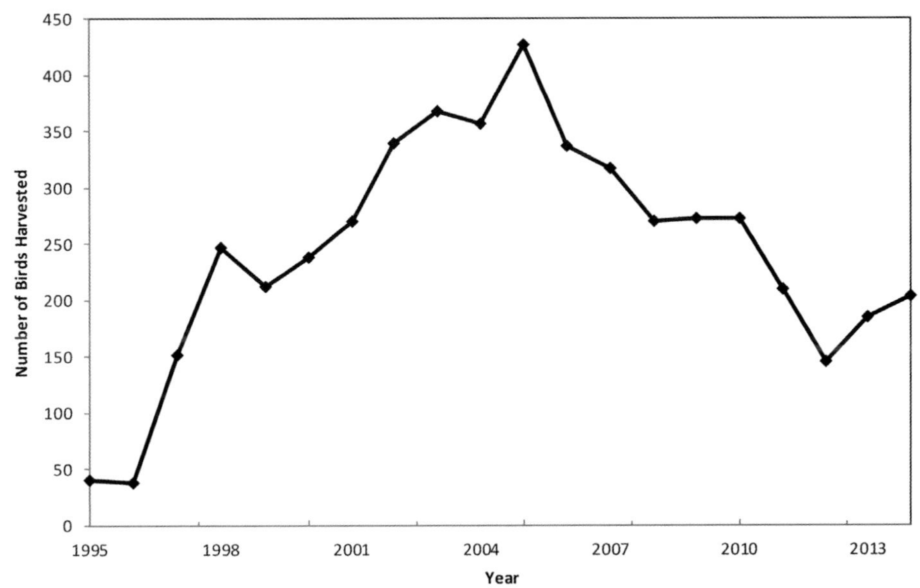

Figure 5.4. Eastern Wild Turkey harvest in Texas, 1995–2015 (figure by Leonard Brennan).

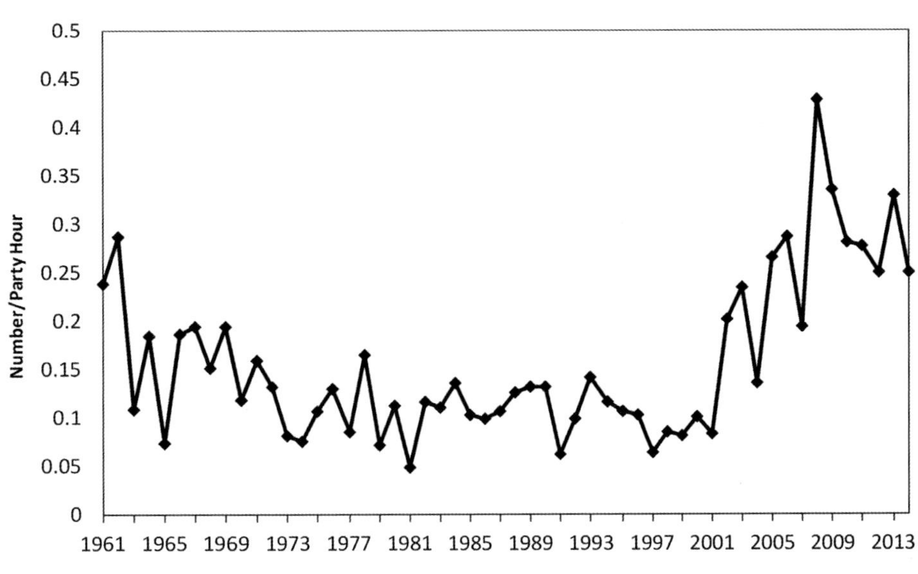

Figure 5.5. Wild turkey Christmas Bird Count, 1961–2013 (figure by Leonard Brennan).

2005 (fig. 5.4). Thereafter, Eastern wild turkey harvests steadily declined to about 200 for the 28 East Texas counties where hunting is permitted.

Wild turkey population trend data from the Christmas Bird Count, compiled annually by the National Audubon Society (2015), represent results for all three subspecies combined. The statewide population declined slightly between the mid-1970s and early 2000s and then began a significant increase that continued until 2009, when the statewide population again declined (fig. 5.5). Since most of these data reflect numbers for the Rio Grande subspecies, variation in abundance is likely attributable to variable rangeland conditions, which are often connected to variable annual rainfall.

Genetic Population Structure

Wild turkey population genetics are complicated and somewhat murky because of past population bottlenecks from drastic population reductions in the nineteenth and early twentieth centuries and widespread trap-and-transfer efforts aimed at population restoration (McRoberts et al. 2014). For example, Leberg (1991) attributed a large amount of genetic variation (89%) to differences among populations with different histories of manipulation. Such manipulations by humans have resulted in increased genetic differentiation related to population bottlenecks and fragmented geographic distributions. Additionally, Mock et al. (2004) found genetic evidence of population bottlenecks in three populations that were translocated between 42 and 53 years prior to their study. Latch et al. (2006) found that the genetic integrity of a population of the Merriam's subspecies introduced to the Davis Mountains in Texas was eroded by immigration from and hybridization with the Rio Grande subspecies from a nearby population. This occurred primarily from immigrant Rio Grande males mating with resident Merriam's females over a relatively short (19-year) period. This illustrates a case of the evolutionary integrity of a population of wild animals being impacted by rapid hybridization.

Ecology of a K-Selected Species

MacArthur and Wilson (1967) coined the terms *r*-selection and *K*-selection to denote two relatively different life history strategies of organisms. *R*-selected species are those that have rapid rates of reproduction (hence the "*r*") and mortality. These are classic boom-and-bust species such as the northern bobwhite (*Colinus virginianus*) that can respond rapidly to favorable environmental or habitat conditions. Such *r*-selected species are short-lived and have high annual population turnover. Conversely, *K*-selected species are regulated over the long term by the carrying capacity of the environment. These species are typically relatively long-lived, with low annual population turnover. Thus, compared to most species of galliforms, wild turkeys are easily considered a *K*-selected species. This life history strategy illustrates why wild turkeys will not attempt to nest in South Texas during the exceptionally dry spring months of a drought. They essentially hedge their bets that—unlike northern bobwhites—they will live long enough to make it to the next reproductive season, when conditions might improve. The 2012 wild turkey hunting season in South Texas reflected the *K*-selected nature of wild turkey life history. Nearly all the adult males in the population were either five years old (hatched during the rainy spring of 2007) or two years old (hatched during the rainy spring of 2010). There were no immature males in the South Texas wild turkey population that year, and none would be produced until the rainy spring of 2014 broke the drought.

Harvest Management

All 48 states in the conterminous United States have wild turkey hunting seasons. Annual survival among wild turkey age classes can be influenced by harvest mortality (McRoberts et al. 2014). For example, in Louisiana, annual survival of adult male wild turkeys in an area with a three-bird limit was 16%, and in an area with a two-bird limit it was nearly double, 31% (Chamberlain et al. 2012).

Although Texas has some of the most liberal wild turkey hunting seasons in the United States in both length and bag limits, harvest regulations for the Eastern subspecies are relatively strict, especially compared to the more liberal harvest regulations for the Rio Grande subspecies elsewhere in Texas. The relatively strict East Texas regulations have not seemed to help wild turkey population restoration efforts in that part of the state. Nevertheless, we can probably expect to see strict harvest regulations, including areas excluded from hunting because of population restoration efforts, for the foreseeable future in East Texas.

Fall either-sex hunting seasons run from November until early January in North Texas (123 counties) and from November to mid-January in 26 counties in South Texas. Four other South Texas counties have a fall season from November to late January. As explained earlier in this chapter, long-term population trend data show that wild turkey populations, especially those of the Rio Grande subspecies, are relatively stable in Texas and can evidently sustain annual losses to hunting. However, the potential impact of fall either-sex harvest remains equivocal with respect to wild turkey population ecology.

Priorities for Future Research

Although wild turkeys are a relatively well-studied game bird, there are still numerous priorities for future research on their ecology. For example, the optimal strategies for population restoration of the Eastern subspecies in East Texas are still not clear. The role that intensive pine (*Pinus* spp.) silviculture plays in limiting productive wild turkey habitat is not fully known, but it is most likely deleterious. Vast areas of tens of thousands of hectares of high-density pine plantations (about 2,000 trees/ha, or 800 trees/ac) where the forest understory is almost completely devoid of grasses and forbs are probably responsible for management challenges during past and ongoing restoration efforts.

Despite the relatively large number of wild turkey studies, there are few reliable density estimates of wild turkey populations. Thus, development of an accurate and precise technique to estimate wild turkey populations is needed.

Lack of suitable roost sites is a key factor limiting wild turkey population in some regions of South and West Texas. Therefore, there is a pressing need to determine where to locate constructed (anthropogenic) roosts on rangelands where natural roosting habitat is limited.

Wild turkey poult survival and mortality is a key gap in our understanding of the population ecology of this species. Thus, research on poult population ecology for Eastern and Rio Grande wild turkey populations, particularly in the Edwards Plateau, Rolling Plains, and South Texas, should be a priority.

Virtually no attention has been paid to the Merriam's subspecies in Texas. Biologists need to conduct research on the ecology of Merriam's wild turkey in Guadalupe Mountains National Park. This represents a unique opportunity to study a population not subjected to harvest by humans.

In South Texas, wild turkeys are highly sensitive to drought and shut down reproductive efforts during spring months with low rainfall. Thus, research on the impacts of climate change on wild turkey population dynamics should be a priority.

Literature Cited

Beasom, S. L. 1970. Turkey productivity in two vegetative communities in South Texas. Journal of Wildlife Management 34:166–175.

Beasom, S. L., and O. H. Pattee. 1980. The effect of selected climactic variables on wild turkey productivity. Proceedings of the National Wild Turkey Symposium 4:127–135.

Byrne, M. E., M. J. Chamberlain, J. G. Dickson, L. Savage, and N. J. Stafford III. 2014. Survival and recovery rates of male wild turkeys on private lands in north-central Louisiana. Journal of the Southeastern Association of Fish and Wildlife Agencies 1:110–114.

Campo, J. J., W. G. Swank., and C. R. Hopkins. 1984. Mortality and reproduction of stocked Eastern wild turkeys in East Texas. Proceedings of the Annual Conference of the Southeastern Association of Fish and Wildlife Agencies 38:78–86.

Cathey, J. C., K. Melton, J. Dreibelbis, B. Cavney, S. L. Locke, S. J. DeMaso, T. W. Schwertner, and B. Collier. 2007. Rio Grande wild turkey in Texas: biology and management. Texas AgriLife Extension Report B-6198. Texas A&M University, College Station, USA.

Chamberlain, M. J., B. A. Grisham, J. L. Norris, N. J. Stafford III, F. G. Kimmel, and M. W. Olinde. 2012. Effects of variable spring harvest regimes on annual survival and recovery rates of wild turkeys in southeast Louisiana. Journal of Wildlife Management 76:907–910.

Collier, B. A., K. B. Melton, J. B. Hardin, N. J. Silvy, and M. J. Peterson. 2009. Impact of reproductive effort on survival of Rio Grande wild turkey *Meleagris gallopavo intermedia* hens in Texas. Wildlife Biology 15:370–379.

Conley, M. D., J. G. Oetgen, J. Barrow, M. J. Chamberlain, K. L. Skow, and B. A Collier. 2016. Habitat selection, incubation, and incubation recess ranges of nesting female Rio Grande wild turkeys in Texas. Proceedings of the National Wild Turkey Symposium 11:117–126.

Cook, R. L. 1972. A study of nesting turkeys in the Edwards Plateau of Texas. Proceedings of the Annual Conference of the Southeastern Association of Fish and Game Commissioners 26:236–244.

Dickson, J. G., editor. 1992. The wild turkey: biology and management. Stackpole Books, Mechanicsburg, Pennsylvania, USA.

Dreibelbis, J. V., K. B. Melton, R. Aguirre, B. A. Collier, J. Hardin, N. J. Silvy, and M. J. Peterson. 2008. Predation of Rio Grande wild turkey nests on the Edwards Plateau, Texas. Wilson Journal of Ornithology 120:906–910.

Everett, D. D., D. W. Speake, and W. K. Maddox. 1980. Natality and mortality of a wild turkey population. Proceedings of the National Wild Turkey Symposium 4:117–126.

Exum, J. H., J. A. McGlincy, D. W. Speake, J. L. Buckner, and F. M. Stanley. 1987. Ecology of the Eastern wild turkey in an intensively managed pine forest in southern Alabama. Tall Timbers Research Station Bulletin 23. Tallahassee, Florida, USA.

Flake, L. D., and K. S. Day. 1995. Wild turkey reproduction in a prairie-woodland complex in South Dakota. Proceedings of the National Wild Turkey Symposium 7:153–158.

Holdstock, D. P., M. C. Wallace, W. B. Ballard, J. H. Brunjes, R. S. Phillips, B. L. Spears, S. J. DeMaso, J. D. Jernigan, R. D. Applegate, and P. S. Gipson. 2006. Male Rio Grande turkey survival and movements in the Texas Panhandle and southwestern Kansas. Journal of Wildlife Management 70:904–913.

Isabelle, J. L., W. C. Conway, C. E. Comer, G. E. Calkins, and J. B. Hardin. 2016. Reproductive ecology and nest-site selection of Eastern wild turkeys translocated to East Texas. Wildlife Society Bulletin 40:88–96.

Keegan, T. W., and J. A. Crawford. 1993. Renesting by Rio Grande wild turkeys after brood loss. Journal of Wildlife Management 57:801–804.

Keegan, T. W., and J. A. Crawford. 1999. Reproduction and survival of Rio Grande turkeys in Oregon. Journal of Wildlife Management 63:204–210.

Latch, E. K., L. A. Harveson, J. S. King, M. D. Hobson, and O. E. Rhodes Jr. 2006. Assessing hybridization in wildlife populations using molecular markers: a case study in wild turkeys. Journal of Wildlife Management 70:485–492.

Leberg, P. L. 1991. Influence of fragmentation and bottlenecks on genetic divergence of wild turkey populations. Conservation Biology 5:522–530.

Locke, S. L., J. Hardin, K. Skow, M. J. Peterson, N. J. Silvy, and B. A. Collier. 2013. Nest site fidelity and dispersal of Rio Grande wild turkey hens in Texas. Journal of Wildlife Management 77:207–211.

Lockwood, D. R., and D. H. Sutcliffe. 1985. Distribution, mortality, and reproduction of Merriam's turkey in New Mexico. Proceedings of the National Wild Turkey Symposium 5:301–316.

Lutz, R. S., and J. A. Crawford. 1987. Reproductive success and nesting habitat of Merriam's wild turkeys in Oregon. Journal of Wildlife Management 51:783–787.

MacArthur, R. A., and E. O. Wilson. 1967. The theory of island biogeography. Princeton University Press, Princeton, New Jersey, USA.

McRoberts, J. T., M. C. Wallace, and S. W. Eaton. 2014. Wild turkey (*Meleagris gallopavo*). Account 22 *in* A. Poole, editor. The birds of North America online. Cornell Laboratory of Ornithology, Ithaca, New York, USA. http://bna.birds.cornell.edu/bna/species/022.

Melton, K. B., J. Z. Dreibelbis, R. Aguirre, J. Hardin, N. J. Silvy, M. J. Peterson, and B. A. Collier. 2010. Reproductive parameters of Rio Grande wild turkeys on the Edwards Plateau, Texas. Proceedings of the National Wild Turkey Symposium 10:227–233.

Miller, M. S. 1993. Rio Grande wild turkey hen survival and habitat selection in south central Kansas. Thesis, Texas Tech University, Lubbock, USA.

Mock, K. E., E. K. Latch, and O. E. Rhodes Jr. 2004. Assessing losses of genetic diversity due to translocation: long-term case histories with Merriam's turkey (*Meleagris gallopavo merriami*). Conservation Genetics 5:631–645.

National Audubon Society. 2015. Audubon Christmas Bird Count. https://www.audubon.org/conservation/science/christmas-bird-count.

Palmer, W. E., G. A. Hurst, J. E. Stys, D. R. Smith, and J. D. Burk. 1993. Survival rates of wild turkey hens in loblolly pine plantations in Mississippi. Journal of Wildlife Management 57:783–789.

Pianka, E. R. 1978. Evolutionary ecology. Second edition. Harper and Row, New York, New York, USA.

Porter, W. F., G. C. Nelson, and K. Mattson. 1983. Effects of winter conditions on reproduction in a northern wild turkey population. Journal of Wildlife Management 47:281–290.

Randall, C. J., R. Aguirre, D. A. Jones, J. N. Schaap, B. J. Willsey, M. J. Peterson, and N. J. Silvy. 2005. Nesting ecology of Rio Grande wild turkeys in the Edwards Plateau of Texas. Proceedings of the National Wild Turkey Symposium 9:237–243.

Ransom, D., O. J. Rongstad, and D. H. Rusch. 1987. Nesting ecology of Rio Grande turkeys. Journal of Wildlife Management 51:435–439.

Reagan, J. M., and K. D. Morgan. 1980. Reproductive potential of Rio Grande wild turkeys in the Edwards Plateau of Texas. Proceedings of the National Wild Turkey Symposium 4:136–144.

Rumble, M. A., and R. A. Hodorff. 1993. Nesting ecology of Merriam's turkeys in the Black Hills, South Dakota. Journal of Wildlife Management 57:789–801.

Rumble, M. A., B. F. Wakeling, and L. D. Flake. 2003. Factors affecting survival and recruitment in female Merriam's turkeys. Intermountain Journal of Sciences 9:26–37.

Schemnitz, S. D., D. L. Goerndt, and K. R. Jones. 1985. Habitat needs and management of Merriam's turkey in southwestern New Mexico. Proceedings of the National Wild Turkey Symposium 5:199–231.

Schmutz, J. A., and C. E. Braun. 1989. Reproductive performance of Rio Grande wild turkeys. Condor 91:675–680.

Schorger, A. W. 1966. The wild turkey: its history and domestication. University of Oklahoma Press, Norman, USA.

Spears, B. L., W. B. Ballard, M. C. Wallace, R. S. Phillips, D. P. Holdstock, J. H. Brunges, R. D. Applegate, M. S. Miller, and P. S. Gipson. 2007. Survival of Rio Grande wild turkey chicks. Journal of Field Ornithology 76:12–20.

Swank, W. G., D. J. Martin, J. J. Campo, and C. R. Hopkins. 1985. Mortality and survival of wild trapped Eastern wild turkeys in Texas. Proceedings of the National Wild Turkey Symposium 5:113–120.

Texas Parks and Wildlife Department. 2014. Effect of variable harvest regimes on survival and recovery of Texas wild turkeys. Request for proposal. Austin, Texas, USA.

Wells, J. V., and M. E. Richmond. 1995. Populations, metapopulations, and species populations: what are they and who should care? Wildlife Society Bulletin 23:458–462.

Williams, L. E., Jr. and D. H. Austin. 1988. Studies of the wild turkey in Florida. Technical Bulletin Number 10. Florida Game and Freshwater Fish Commission, Gainesville, USA.

Vangilder, L. D. 1992. Population dynamics. Pages 144–164 *in* J. G. Dickson, editor. The wild turkey: biology and management. Stackpole Books, Mechanicsburg, Pennsylvania, USA.

Vangilder, L. D., E. W. Kurzejeski, V. L. Kimmel-Truitt, and J. B. Lewis. 1987. Reproductive parameters of wild turkey hens in north Missouri. Journal of Wildlife Management 51:535–540.

6

Behavioral Ecology

Wildness is strongly adaptive under natural conditions.

—A. S. LEOPOLD (1944)

In the most fundamental sense, behavior is movement. Wild turkeys, like any animal, exhibit a wide range of behaviors in relation to extrinsic factors such as environmental stimuli, and intrinsic factors such as hunger and the drive to reproduce. Wild turkeys have a unique social organization driven by their behaviors that is inextricably linked with their natural history. Leopold et al. (1981:5) considered natural history to be "all the habits and actions of a species that constitutes its normal way of living." Behavior is surely a large component of these "habits and actions." In their unique way of making a living, wild turkey females and males operate as two different entities during the months of the year when they exist in separate flocks. One concept that emerges from the vast scientific literature on wild turkeys is their largely consistent behaviors across subspecies. The basic courtship displays, social organization, and other aspects of wild turkey natural history do not seem to change much from east to west or north to south. What does change, however, is the timing of certain annual life cycle events such as initiation of breeding, dates of first eggs laid, first poults hatched, and so on. This makes sense for a bird that has several subspecies distributed across a large geographic area; a Rio Grande wild turkey in South Texas has an opportunity to nest much earlier than an Eastern wild turkey farther north in the Piney Woods, or a Merriam's wild turkey farther west where the winters are cooler and the environment is drier. Many publications cover the behavior of wild turkeys, beginning with Mosby and Handley (1943) and continuing through Williams (1981), Healy (1992), and McRoberts et al. (2014). The main intention of this chapter is to provide an overview of wild turkey behavior in an ecological and management context that uses as many examples as possible from Texas and nearby states.

Locomotion

The strong, muscular legs of wild turkeys evolved to permit them to spend most of their day on the ground. When undisturbed, they spend their day slowly walking throughout their home range in search of food and water. Most walking is done with the head up. However, wild turkeys are swift runners when alarmed and attempting to escape potential threats. Pelham and Dickson (1992) stated that they can achieve speeds of up to 19 km/hr (12 mi/hr), while other accounts indicate that turkeys can attain average speeds of 24–29 km/hr (15–18 mi/hr) when attempting to escape potential threats (Mosby and Handley 1943, McLaurin 1957). When the birds run, the head is often outstretched horizontally and level with the back.

Despite being large-bodied and heavy birds, wild turkeys are adept fliers (fig. 6.1). Hollow bones, as well as robust breast and wing musculature, allow wild turkeys to exhibit immediate and sustained flights of up to a mile (Schorger 1966, Pelham and Dickson 1992) and attain maximum speeds of 52–97 km/hr (32–60 mi/hr) (Rutledge 1941, Mosby and Handley 1943, Pelham and Dickson 1992). They initiate flight in a two-stage process, first by lowering the breast and

Figure 6.1. A Rio Grande wild turkey in flight (photo by Larry Ditto).

Figure 6.2. Rio Grande wild turkeys on a roost (photo by Larry Ditto).

crouching at the knee, and then by raising the breast, elongating the neck, opening the wings, and spreading the tail. The bird then takes a couple of short steps, followed by a couple of hops and a leap upward. The takeoff can be at a steep or shallow angle. Initial flight is usually a set of rapid wing beats followed with a glide that ends in landing on a perch or the ground. However, aside from flying up to roosts in the evenings (fig. 6.2), wild turkeys prefer to restrict mobility to ground activity because flight requires a significant expenditure of energy, so flight is generally utilized to escape perceived threats. Wild turkeys are capable of swimming, but according to McRoberts et al. (2014) they rarely engage in this activity. Nevertheless, Schorger (1966) provides numerous accounts indicating that wild turkeys are adept at swimming when forced to do so and can cross bodies of water up to a mile wide. He indicated that poults can also swim.

Foraging

Nearly all foraging by wild turkeys takes place on the ground (fig. 6.3). Occasionally, they will strip fruit from branches of shrubs and some trees. During the fall, winter, and spring, they aggressively scratch and dig the ground surface for mast and occasionally bulbs. The presence of sesamoid bones embedded in the tarsal (leg) muscles is thought to be an adaptation that strengthens their ability to scratch and dig (Doherty et al. 2010). Turkeys will strip seeds from grasses and sedges during spring, summer, and fall. Wild turkeys are highly opportunistic foragers. Their overall diet is highly diverse and varies widely among subspecies according to the available foods in the ecological region where each subspecies lives (McRoberts et al. 2014). They almost constantly explore objects on the ground, first by inspecting them and then by turning them over to examine them. Wild turkeys will readily eat small vertebrates such as lizards, along with a huge variety of plant materials.

Self-Maintenance

Wild turkeys exhibit a diverse set of self-maintenance behaviors such as stretching, dusting, and sunbathing (Hutto 1995, McRoberts et al. 2014). Roosting is a self-maintenance behavior that is critically important for avoiding nocturnal predators. Turkeys typically roost in trees of almost any species with relatively large lateral limbs (approximately the size of a baseball bat). Eastern wild turkeys typically roost in any trees wherever they end up at the end of the day. Compared to the Eastern subspecies, Rio Grande wild turkeys are more prone to use the same roost sites repeatedly

Figure 6.3. Rio Grande wild turkey gobblers foraging (photo by Larry Ditto).

because suitable roost sites are typically more limited in the rangeland habitats where this subspecies lives. The Merriam's subspecies also uses the same roost sites repeatedly, presumably for the same reason the Rio Grande subspecies does—because they are in short supply. Merriam's also tends to favor roost locations that have an eastern orientation (presumably for warmth early in the day during fall, winter, and spring) and are close to water (presumably so it can persist in arid areas) (Schemnitz et al. 1985).

Reactions to Threats

Wild turkey females typically signal potential danger to poults by making "putt" and "trill" vocalizations that alert them to seek cover or freeze until the female calls them out. While poults normally respond to danger by flushing and running, they will often react to snakes by mobbing them. They surround the snake and putt with great vigor until it moves away. Healy (1992) also noted that females and poults will sometimes react this way to mesomammals such as foxes, as well as larger raptors.

Reproduction

Increasing day length during late winter and early spring is the primary factor that stimulates reproduction by wild turkeys. The wild turkey breeding system is polygynous; one male often mates with many females during a breeding season. Typically beginning in late January in South Texas, and later farther north, males commonly exhibit a "strut" display (fig. 6.4) and "gobble" during the breeding season in order to attract females. Gobbles can be spontaneous and are followed by strut behaviors when one or more females come into a gobbling male's view. Groups of gobbling males often assemble in leks and exhibit strut displays as a group. Despite the intense competition among males for mates, and the establishment of dominance hierarchies—or pecking orders—among both males and females, territoriality, or the defense of boundaries in a given area, is poorly developed in wild turkeys (McRoberts et al. 2014).

Rio Grande wild turkey females become receptive to males during February in South Texas, and the other subspecies somewhat later. The female

Figure 6.4. Rio Grande wild turkey males in full strut (photo by Larry Ditto).

constructs the nest by making a shallow scrape on the ground surface. The first eggs are laid in March, with the first broods hatched in mid-April. Only females incubate. McRoberts et al. (2014) described the incubation sequence of wild turkey females as follows. Females, regardless of subspecies, lay an initial egg and deposit another perhaps every other day until the fifth egg is laid, after which females begin incubating eggs for lengthening periods. After a full clutch has been produced, females begin incubating on almost a 24-hour cycle. The incubation period for females is reported as 28 days throughout the literature (McRoberts et al. 2014.)

Females will often renest if the clutch is lost to predation and if environmental conditions are suitable, especially in the absence of drought. During periods of severe or extended drought in places such as South Texas, renesting typically does not occur during the latter part of the reproductive season; as a relatively long-lived bird, turkeys are apparently willing to wait until the next breeding season to try again.

Behavioral Development

Chicks are precocial and leave the nest soon after hatching. However, before even leaving the nest, each chick will become "imprinted" on the female (see below). Most wild turkey chicks can walk within 6 hours after hatching, but it takes 12–24 hours for them to become fully mobile. They alternate between periods of about 20–30 minutes of being brooded by the female and periods of about 5–10 minutes of walking for the next several days after hatching (fig. 6.5) (Healy 1992). Females feed the poults directly during the first few days of life. Females actively brood poults on the ground at night until they start to fly, about two weeks posthatching.

At about one week of age, poults will actively flee humans and other perceived threats. After roosting in trees begins, poults typically stay very close to the female, gradually increasing their distance from her as they grow. By the end of two months, broods are often roosting in more than one tree and are often intermingled with one or more other broods.

Only females care for young. Male poults stay with the female through their first fall; female poults typically stay with the female into early spring. Predator avoidance and other behaviors considered to be related to the "wildness" of wild turkeys are taught to the young poults by the female during the first summer and fall (Leopold 1944).

Social Behaviors

Wild turkeys are extremely gregarious. Social behaviors begin to develop almost immediately after

Figure 6.5. Female Eastern wild turkey with four-week-old poults (photo by Jason Hardin).

hatching when the members of a brood imprint on the female. Imprinting, a behavioral process whereby a newly hatched chick recognizes the female as its parent, is critical in the development of poults. It must happen within 24 hours of hatching and thus occurs quickly. Lorenz (1937) first recognized this process in a group of greylag geese (*Anser anser*) that imprinted on him as their parent immediately after they hatched. Imprinting is different from associative learning, or learning to survive by experience and perhaps an element of luck. Imprinting is essential for survival in many different species of precocial birds such as grouse, quail, turkeys, and ducks. Like Lorenz's geese, turkeys can imprint on people as well. Much information about wild turkey behavior has been gained from observations of birds that have imprinted on humans (Healy 1992, Hutto 1995). Wild turkeys raised in captivity usually do not imprint and as a consequence do not express parental behaviors when fully grown. This factor has had huge implications for population restoration, as noted later in this chapter.

As mentioned above, wild turkeys do not defend territories per se but rather exist in flocks of males and females where a strict dominance hierarchy or pecking order is established. The top or dominant individual is considered the alpha, and the lowest member of the group is considered the omega.

In a study conducted on the Welder Wildlife Refuge in South Texas, C. Robert Watts (1969) compiled some of the most extensive and detailed observations of wild turkey social organization. He found that Rio Grande turkeys at Welder aggregated during winter into flocks of adult and juvenile females, juvenile males (often called "jakes"), and mature males. Male flocks consisted of siblings that were raised as a brood, and they stayed together for life. Dominance hierarchy was determined by flocks of siblings that fought other flocks as units. The size of the sibling units was critical to establishing dominance because the larger groups usually prevailed. The pecking order was sorted out during late fall when the flocks of fully grown poults broke up into male and female groups. Although the study by Watts was based on the Rio Grande subspecies, Healy (1992:47) mentioned that this type of "social organization . . . is characteristic of all races." By "races," Healy obviously meant the various wild turkey subspecies.

Vocalizations

Wild turkeys are very social birds and possess an array of vocalizations for communication as well as other specific purposes. According to Williams (1984), wild turkeys have 28 distinct calls. McRoberts et al. (2014) provide a detailed description of wild turkey vocalizations. The most common one associated with wild turkeys is the "gobble" emitted by mature males during the breeding season (fig 6.6). Only the gobble call is given with what is considered a "fixed" intensity, meaning that it is expressed the same way each time. Gobbling evolved to attract females and repel competing males. Gobbling can occur spontaneously, and "shock gobbling" can be stimulated by sounds such as the slamming of a vehicle door, coyote howls, or crow and owl calls. Reflex gobbling occurs when one gobble initiates a response from numerous other males in an area. Shock and reflex gobbling are probably most prevalent during the peak of the breeding season, when subtle noises are sufficient to stimulate gobbling activity.

In addition to gobbling, both sexes share a number of vocalizations that are used for a variety of specific purposes (table 6.1). Different yelps, purrs, cackles, and other unique calls are used to threatened, provide alarms, assemble flocks, and express satisfaction. In contrast to gobbles, "alarm putts" can vary widely, and in general the louder the putt, the more dire the alarm. Evidently, turkeys can recognize the voices of other individual turkeys (Healy 1992).

Figure 6.6. Mature Rio Grande wild turkey male gobbling (photo by Larry Ditto).

Table 6.1. Common wild turkey vocalizations.

Vocalization	Sex and age	Purpose	Citation
Gobble	Males (adults)	Attract females and repel competing males.	Schleidt (1974)
Shock gobble	Males (adults)	Stimulated by loud noises; dog barking, coyote howl, owl call, car door slamming.	Schleidt (1974)
Plain yelp	Both sexes	Not understood.	Williams (1984)
Tree yelp	Both sexes	Given before flying to the ground.	Williams (1984)
Lost yelp	Both sexes (adults)	Reassemble the flock.	Williams (1984)
Assembly yelp	Female (adult)	Poults imprint on mother's voice.	Williams (1984)
Hatching yelp	Female (adult)	Given immediately after poults peep; bonding with poults while in the egg.	Williams (1984)
Plain cluck	Both sexes	Group communication?	Williams (1984)
Alarm putt	Both sexes and age classes	Given when predators detected.	Williams (1984)
Predator alarm	Both sexes and age classes	Warns flock of a nearby predator; high-pitched whistle from 14-week-old poults.	Williams (1984)
Cackle	Both sexes	Given when flying down from tree or negotiating obstacles while in flight.	Williams (1984)
Plain purr	Both sexes and age classes	Maintain proper spacing within flock while moving.	Williams (1984)
Rattle	Both sexes and age classes	Final warning before flight initiated.	Hale and Schein (1962), Williams (1984)
Feeding call	Both sexes and age classes	Given when consuming favored foods.	Hale and Schein (1962), Williams (1984)
Hissing call	Females (adults)	Assemble young poults.	Williams (1984)
Threat cooing	High-ranking male (adult)	Confirms dominance between males.	Hale and Schein (1962)
Peeping calls	Poults	Elicit yelps from females; occurs before and during hatching; when done while hatching, a response to stress.	Collias (1952)
Purr call	Poults	Most common call given by poults of any age. Contentment?	Healy et al. (1975)
Putt call	Poults	On 3rd day posthatch; response to a source of fear.	Healy et al. (1975)
Whistling	Poults	By 7th week posthatch; alerts female to solitary poult and encourages female to wait for brood assembly.	Williams (1984)

Sources: Collias (1952), Hale and Schein (1962), Schleidt (1974), Healy et al. (1975), Williams (1984), McRoberts et al. (2014).

Vocalizations begin before poults hatch. Healy (1992) stated that while poults are still in the egg they emit audible clicking and chipping vocalizations that serve to communicate with the female, who responds with soft clucking and increased attentiveness to her eggs. Hess (1972) indicated that prehatch communication between poults and female is critical to chick survival. Poults produce calls during hatching, which may be a response to the stress of the process (Collias 1952). After hatching, chicks emit a number of calls depending on their stage of development. Immediately after they hatch, poults often "purr," which, according to Healy et al. (1975), is the most common call during every stage of development. Healy et al. also noted that by the third day posthatch, poults emit a sharp putt, which they believed was a response to detection of a potential threat. Williams (1984) reported that by week 7, posthatch poults emit a series of high-pitched whistles after a brood has been disrupted by a predator, and he thought this call enables females to find solitary poults so that she can successfully assemble her brood. Williams indicated that this whistle eventually transforms into a "kee-kee-kee" call intermixed with yelps, and that as the poult develops, a yelping "keow-keow-keow" call becomes more common. Healy et al. (1975) stated that by the 11th week posthatch, poults of both sexes gobble when excited, though gobbling eventually stops among young females.

Relation of Behavior to Management and Population Recovery

Back in the 1930s when wild turkey populations in North America were at an all-time low, biologists considered the wild turkey to be a "specialist" species that required huge tracts of mature forest to exist. It was once thought that the only places wild turkeys would use for roosting were bottomland hardwood forests with open water beneath the trees. As it turned out, these factors were simply artifacts of where the remnant populations of wild turkeys persisted. Excessive harvest and large-scale forest removal for agriculture forced the birds into these types of refugia. Today, biologists have a completely different view of wild turkeys compared to that of 80 years ago. Trapping and transplanting efforts have been wildly successful thanks to the adaptable nature of this bird. Healy (1992) noted three social behaviors of wild turkeys that have facilitated their population restoration and recovery. The first is winter flocking, which typically concentrates birds in relatively small areas, allowing them to be trapped. Flocking also tends to hold birds together and thus allows them to form successful breeding units. The second behavior is dispersal of females for nesting. This allows birds to move into new areas, many of which are (or were) unoccupied. Moreover, juvenile wild turkey females tend to move two to three times as far as adult females when dispersing (Ellis and Lewis 1967), which makes colonization of unoccupied areas even more effective. Finally, the third behavior is flexibility in foraging patterns and willingness to exploit a diverse array of foods. This is another important factor that illustrates an important linkage between wild turkey behavior and management success. As noted earlier, the omnivorous ability of wild turkeys to eat just about any plant part with nutrition that is available, or any small animal they can capture, has allowed them to exist in places biologists never thought possible.

The concept of wildness in wild turkey behavior has also been a key element of restoration management success. The repeated and miserable failure of using pen-raised stock to restore wild turkey populations was most likely related to lack of imprinting (as noted above) and physiological changes that the birds endured as they were semidomesticated in game farms (Leopold 1944). The development of new technology, such as the cannon net, to easily and safely capture large numbers of wild turkeys in the wild and transfer them to new areas of unoccupied habitat confirmed Leopold's findings that using pen-raised stock for population restoration was a waste of valuable resources.

Literature Cited

Collias, N. E. 1952. The development of social behavior in birds. Auk 69:127–149.

Doherty, A. H., E. M. Lowder, R. D. Jacquet, and W. J. Landis. 2010. Murine metapodophalangeal sesamoid bones: morphology and potential means of mineralization underlying function. Anatomical Record 293:775–785.

Ellis, J. A., and J. B. Lewis. 1967. Mobility and annual range of wild turkeys in Missouri. Journal of Wildlife Management 31:568–581.

Hale, E. B., and M. W. Schein. 1962. The behavior of

turkeys. Pages 531–564 *in* E. S. E. Hafez, editor. The behavior of domestic animals. Bailliere, Tindal and Cox, London, UK.

Healy, W. M. 1992. Behavior. Pages 46–65 *in* J. G. Dickson, editor. The wild turkey: biology and management. Stackpole Books, Mechanicsburg, Pennsylvania, USA.

Healy, W. M., R. O. Kimmel, and E. J. Goetz. 1975. Behavior of human-imprinted and hen-reared wild turkey poults. Proceedings of the National Wild Turkey Symposium 3:97–107.

Hess, E. H. 1972. Imprinting in a natural laboratory. Scientific American 227(2):24–31.

Hutto, J. 1995. Illumination in the flatwoods. Lyons and Burford, New York, New York, USA.

Leopold, A. S. 1944. The nature of heritable wildness in turkeys. Condor 45:133–197.

Leopold, A. S., R. J. Gutiérrez, and M. T. Bronson. 1981. North American game birds and mammals. Charles Scribner's Sons, New York, New York, USA.

Lorenz, K. Z. 1937. The companion in the bird's world. Auk 54:245–273.

McLaurin, E. 1957. You gotta out-smart-em. Florida Wildlife 11:20–23.

McRoberts, J. T., M. C. Wallace, and S. W. Eaton. 2014. Wild turkey (*Meleagris gallopavo*). Account 22 *in* A. Poole, editor. The birds of North America online. Cornell Laboratory of Ornithology, Ithaca, New York, USA. http://bna.birds.cornell.edu/bna/species/022.

Mosby, H. S., and C. O. Handley. 1943. The wild turkey in Virginia: its status, life history and management. Pittman-Robertson Projects. Virginia Division of Game, Commission of Game and Inland Fisheries, Richmond, USA.

Pelham, P. H., and J. G. Dickson. 1992. Physical characteristics. Pages 32–45 *in* J. G. Dickson, editor. The wild turkey: biology and management. Stackpole Books, Mechanicsburg, Pennsylvania, USA.

Rutledge, A. H. 1941. Can the wild turkey survive? Fauna 3:93–95.

Schemnitz, S. D., D. L. Goerndt, and K. H. Jones. 1985. Habitat needs and management of Merriam's turkey in southwestern New Mexico. Proceedings of the National Wild Turkey Symposium 5:199–231.

Schleidt, W. M. 1974. How fixed is the fixed action pattern? Zeitschrift für Tierpsychologie 36:184–211.

Schorger, A. W. 1966. The wild turkey: its history and domestication. University of Oklahoma Press, Norman, USA.

Watts, C. R. 1969. The social organization of wild turkeys on the Welder Wildlife Refuge, Texas. Dissertation, Utah State University, Logan, USA.

Williams, L. E., Jr. 1981. The book of the wild turkey. Winchester Press, Tulsa, Oklahoma, USA.

Williams, L. E., Jr. 1984. The voice of and vocabulary of the wild turkey. Real Turkeys, Gainesville, Florida, USA.

7

Habitat Requirements

The final ingredient in applying habitat analysis and assessment is the wisdom of experienced biologists.

—WILLIAM F. PORTER (1992)

The concept of habitat in this chapter was proposed by Block and Brennan (1993) and Krausman and Morrison (2016). Habitat is organism specific and is defined as "a subset of physical environmental factors that a species requires for its survival and reproduction" (Block and Brennan 1993). The three subspecies of wild turkeys that inhabit Texas live in very different habitats, ranging from the Piney Woods ecoregion in the east to the Trans-Pecos in the west. However, a common element of the habitat structure used by turkeys across Texas is a combination of open herbaceous cover and trees (Porter 1992). Open areas with herbaceous cover provide food for adults and are particularly critical to poults when foraging for insects. Trees are used for roosting and loafing and provide escape cover and a food source. The objective of this chapter is to provide up-to-date information on habitat requirements for roosting, nesting, brood-rearing, foraging, and water needs for the three wild turkey subspecies of Texas. The final section of this chapter focuses on how home range analysis and landscape ecology can contribute to the quantification of habitat resources at multiple scales.

Wild Turkeys and the Ecoregions of Texas

Eastern wild turkeys are distributed mainly in the Piney Woods and Post Oak Savanna ecoregions of East Texas (Alldredge et al. 2014) (fig. 7.1). The Piney Woods ecoregion has a flat to gently rolling topography covered with pines and oaks (fig. 7.2). Soils are acidic, pale to dark gray sand and sandy loam, and rainfall averages 91.5–127.0 cm/year (36–50 in/year). The predominant tree species in this ecoregion include loblolly pine (*Pinus taeda*), longleaf pine (*P. palustris*), shortleaf pine (*P. echinata*), oak (*Quercus* spp.), southern magnolia (*Magnolia grandiflora*), elm (*Ulmus* spp.), hickory (*Carya* spp.), silver maple (*Acer saccharinum*), and sweetgum (*Liquidambar* spp.). Understory species are dominated by buttonbush (*Cephalanthus occidentalis*), American beautyberry (*Callicarpa americana*), yaupon (*Ilex vomitoria*), and flowering dogwood (*Cornus florida*).

The Post Oak Savanna ecoregion (fig. 7.1) is a transition zone between the tallgrass prairie communities to the west and the pine forests to the east. Topography in this ecoregion is gently rolling to hilly, covered with oak savanna and interspersed with patches of oak woodland. Soils are mainly acidic light-colored clay to sandy loam (bottomlands) or sandy loam to sand (uplands), with an average rainfall of 71.1–101.6 cm/year (28–40 in/year). Predominant grass species include little bluestem (*Schizachyrium scoparium*), Indiangrass (*Sorghastrum nutans*), brownseed paspalum (*Paspalum plicatulum*), and switchgrass (*Panicum virgatum*), interspersed with mottes of oak and hickory as well as eastern red cedar (*Juniperus virginiana*) and yaupon (Alldredge et al. 2014). Many grass species have unfortunately been replaced in large areas by cool-season pasture grasses such as coastal Bermuda grass (*Cynodon dactylon*) and

Figure 7.1. The ecoregions of Texas (Source: Texas Parks & Wildlife Department).

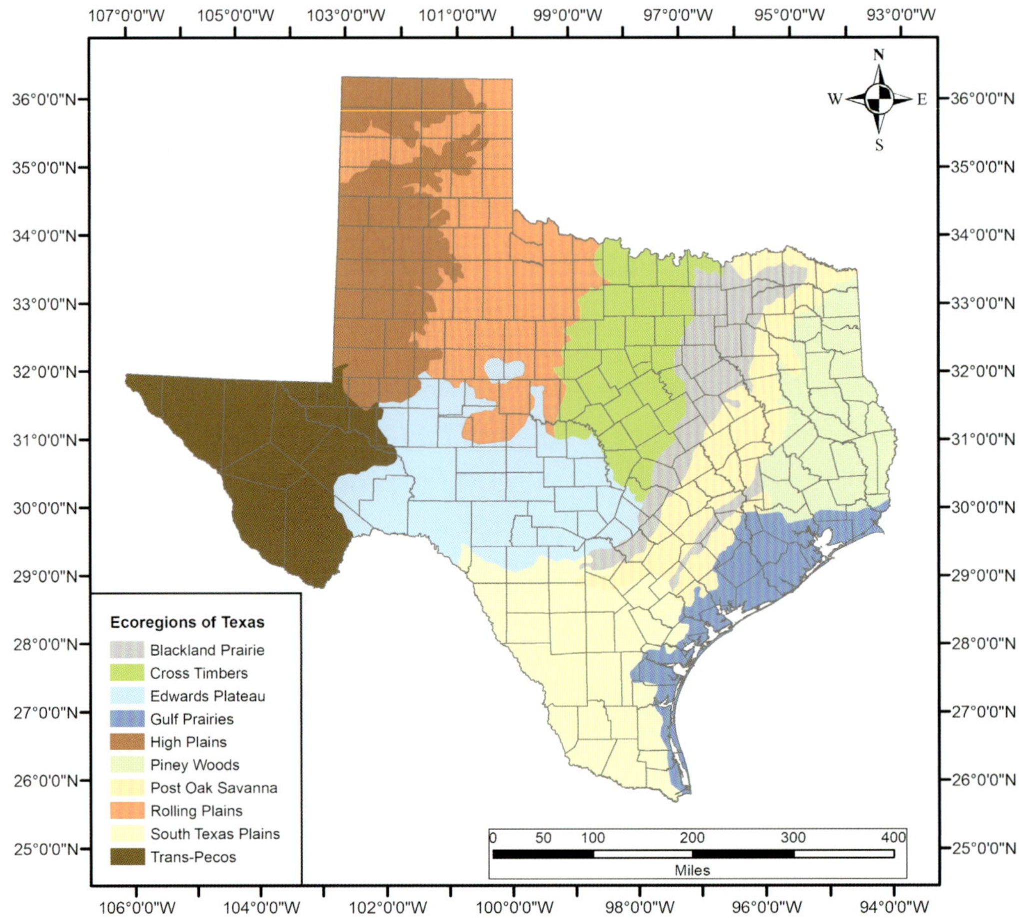

Figure 7.2. An aerial photo of Eastern wild turkey habitat in the Piney Woods of East Texas. The terrain is flat to gently rolling and is generally covered by oaks and pines (photo by Daniel Sullivan).

annual ryegrass (*Lolium multiflorum*), with potentially negative effects for grassland birds (Cooke 2007).

Rio Grande wild turkeys inhabit the Rolling Plains, Edwards Plateau, South Texas Plains, Cross Timbers, the southern portion of the Post Oak Savanna, and small portions of the Trans-Pecos ecoregions (fig. 7.1). Soils vary from neutral to lightly alkaline coarse sands along outwash terraces adjacent to streams, to tight clays and shales. Average annual precipitation ranges from 56.0 cm to 76.0 cm (22 to 30 in) (Texas A&M Forest Service 2014). Vegetation differs between the northern and southern portions of these ecoregions. The northern portion is characterized by black willow (*Salix nigra*), redberry juniper (*Juniperus pinchotii*), shin oak (*Quercus havardii*), and salt cedar (*Tamarix* spp.). Alternatively, the southern portion is dominated by pecan (*Carya illinoinensis*), persimmon (*Diospyros* spp.), netleaf hackberry (*Celtis laevigata* var. *reticulata*), live oak (*Quercus virginiana*), sugar hackberry (*Celtis laevigata*), Texas red oak (*Quercus buckleyi*), gum bumelia (*Sideroxylon lanuginosum*), and Ashe juniper (*Juniperus ashei*). Honey mesquite (*Prosopis glandulosa*), plains cottonwood (*Populus deltoides*), and western soapberry (*Sapindus saponaria*) are typical of both portions of the Rolling Plains ecoregion. Common shrubs include wild cherry (*Prunus avium*), plum (*Prunus* spp.), and sages (*Artemisia* spp.). Buffalograss (*Bouteloua dactyloides*), hairy grama (*Bouteloua hirsuta*), blue grama (*Bouteloua gracilis*), sideoats grama (*Bouteloua curtipendula*), big bluestem (*Andropogon gerardii*), Indiangrass, Canada wild rye (*Elymus canadensis*), and Texas bluegrass (*Poa arachnifera*) are common grasses in this ecoregion (Texas A&M Forest Service 2014).

The Edwards Plateau ecoregion (fig. 7.1) in Central Texas is composed of round, rolling hills (fig. 7.3). Soils are very shallow (less than 25 cm [10 in]) clays to clay loams with an underlying layer of solid limestone. Average annual precipitation ranges widely from 58.5 cm to 88.9 cm (23 to 35 in). Woody vegetation consists of pecan, Texas red oak, shin oak, post oak (*Quercus stellata*), live oak, Ashe juniper, and bald

Figure 7.3. The Edwards Plateau or Hill Country of Texas is composed of rolling round hills with shallow soils over an underlying layer of limestone (photo by Larry Ditto).

cypress (*Taxodium distichum*). Grasses include switchgrass, bluestem (*Andropogon* spp.), gramas (*Bouteloua* spp.), Indiangrass, curly mesquite (*Hilaria belangeri*), and buffalograss (Van Auken 1988, Perotto-Baldivieso et al. 2011).

The South Texas Plains ecoregion (fig. 7.1) has an almost flat topography. Dominant soils are acidic sands. Large rivers are usually associated with deep alluvial soils with a loamy to sandy texture (Texas A&M Forest Service 2014). Precipitation in this ecoregion follows a longitudinal gradient, with 58.5 cm (23 in) in the eastern portion and 48.3 cm (19 in) in the western portion. This region was once dominated by open grasslands with scattered trees and valley woodlands (fig. 7.4). Honey mesquite is the primary tree in the region. The flats and ridges are covered with honey mesquite, huisache (*Vachellia farnesiana*), blackbrush (*Coleogyne ramosissima*), guajillo (*Senegalia berlandieri*), cenizo (*Leucophyllum frutescens*), Texas mountain laurel (*Sophora secundiflora*), and Spanish dagger (*Yucca faxoniana*). Spiny hackberry (*Celtis ehrenbergiana*), bluewood (*Condalia hookeri*), Texas persimmon (*Diospyros texana*), lime prickly ash (*Zanthoxylum fagara*), guayacan (*Guaiacum angustifolium*), and kidneywood (*Eysenhardtia texana*) can be found in shallow arroyos and rocky draws (Texas A&M Forest Service 2014).

The Cross Timbers ecoregion (fig. 7.1) in North Texas is characterized by areas with high tree density and irregular plains and prairies (fig. 7.5) (Texas Parks and Wildlife Department 2016). Dominant soils are primarily sandy to loamy, with moderate, irregular rainfall (average 81.3 cm/year [32 in/year]). Landscapes change from savanna and woodland in the east and south to mixed-grass prairie in the west. Riparian areas are usually composed of pecan, bur oak (*Quercus macrocarpa*), American elm (*Ulmus americana*), slippery elm (*Ulmus rubra*), box elder (*Acer negundo*), cottonwood, sugar hackberry, and black willow. Conversely, upland species are post oak, blackjack oak (*Quercus marilandica*), cedar elm (*Ulmus crassifolia*), juniper, sugar hackberry, Texas red oak, and live oak (Texas A&M Forest Service 2014).

Merriam's wild turkeys inhabit the Guadalupe Mountains and possibly the Davis Mountains in the Trans-Pecos ecoregion of Texas (fig. 7.1) (Schorger 1966, Shaw and Mollohan 1992). They live on wooded mountain slopes with alkaline soils and rainfall averaging less than 30.4 cm/year (12 in/year) (fig. 7.6). These areas are dominated by juniper, oak,

Figure 7.4. The terrain of the South Texas Plains is flat and covered by thorny, woody vegetation dominated by mesquite (photo by Dave Hewitt).

Figure 7.5. The Cross Timbers ecoregion in North Texas is composed of irregular plains and prairies with high tree density (photo by Jesse Oetgen).

Figure 7.6. The higher elevations of the Guadalupe Mountains are dominated by oaks, juniper, pinyon pine, ponderosa pine, and Douglas fir (photo by Dave Hewitt).

pinyon pine (*Pinus edulis*), ponderosa pine (*Pinus ponderosa*), and Douglas-fir (*Pseudotsuga menziesii*). Some Chihuahuan desert vegetation can also be found on south- and west-facing slopes (Texas A&M Forest Service 2014). Merriam's wild turkeys winter in lower-elevation areas and move to higher ground during the breeding season, often traveling distances of over 64 km (40 mi) (Hoffman et al. 1993, Kennamer 2004).

While wild turkey habitat varies across Texas, turkeys always require roost sites, as well as cover and food resources for nesting and brood-rearing. A variety of year-round permanent food sources are also important for all three subspecies (Hughes and Lee 2015). Direct and indirect water sources (preformed and metabolic) are important to wild turkey survival and reproduction (Porter 1992). From a land-use and land-cover perspective, a combination of trees (15–35% woody vegetation cover) and open grassy areas are fundamental, as trees provide food, loafing, and escape cover as well as roost sites, and grasses offer food for adults and foraging habitat for poults (Perotto-Baldiviezo 2005). Grasslands can also be used as protective cover from predators during the nesting and brood-rearing periods (Alldredge et al. 2014).

Human disturbance can affect wild turkey habitat and decrease abundance across the landscape. For example, Perotto-Baldiviezo (2005) observed in the Edwards Plateau that the percentage of disturbed areas (12.4%) was higher where Rio Grande wild turkey populations had declined than in areas (3.7%) where populations were considered stable. Moreover, Kennamer (2004) reported that Merriam's wild turkeys can be particularly sensitive to disturbance such as infrastructure development; overgrazing or timber harvesting can affect population abundance.

Roosting

Eastern wild turkey

Roost sites are critical for Eastern wild turkeys, particularly during the winter months (Chamberlain et al. 2000). Eastern wild turkeys will use a variety of habitats for roosting, but they prefer areas dominated by conifers, with water nearby (Hurst and Dickson 1992). Selected roost sites will often be tall pine trees with several layers of horizontal branches (fig. 7.7) (Buser 2006). In addition, the overstory of large pine trees that serve as roosts provides thermal protection during the winter months (Chamberlain et al. 2000, Lehman et al. 2016). Roost sites tend to be mature stands near riparian areas (Streich et al. 2015). In the Piney Woods ecoregion, wild turkeys choose the largest trees that have dominant crowns (Buser 2006). Males tend to roost in areas with taller trees (average roost height = 15.4 m [50 ft]) than female wild turkeys (average roost height = 12.8 m [42 ft]). These heights do not depend on tree species but are based on tree architecture, because areas near the bottom of the tree crown and close to the tree trunk are preferred for roosting. The specific tree species also influences where Eastern wild turkeys roost in the tree (Buser 2006). During the winter in East Texas, wild turkeys roost closer to pine trunks (mean = 62 cm [2 ft]) than to hardwood trunks (mean = 76 cm [2.2 ft]), and the opposite is observed during warm seasons (Buser 2006). Understory canopy coverage around roost trees (9.8%) is lower than that of surrounding areas (11.3%). At small scales, roost sites are in open areas, but as scale increases, mean patch area and percentage of woody vegetation reveal that Eastern wild turkeys prefer areas that are not fragmented. More recently, Byrne et al. (2015) reported that roost site fidelity is not strong for Eastern wild turkeys because of the availability of roost sites across the landscape as well as suitable woody cover for movement and dispersal. Median distances between roost sites ranged from 0.73 km (0.5 mi) in April to 0.29 km (0.2 mi) in September. Alternatively, Gross et al. (2015) observed that 88% of the time, wild turkeys returned to previously used roost sites.

Rio Grande wild turkey

Roost site conservation is vital for managing Rio Grande wild turkey populations (Litton and Harwell 1995). Rio Grande wild turkeys prefer large trees with several horizontal limbs and a broad canopy (Haucke 1975). Roost trees preferred by wild turkeys in the Rolling Plains include live oak, sugar hackberry, pecan, and cottonwood (Cathey et al. 2007). In South Texas, common roost tree species include hackberry and mesquite (Haucke and Ables 1972). These regions of Texas are composed primarily of patches of large, tall trees, usually adjacent to clearings that often contain low-growing brush surrounding the roost patch and approaches to the roost (Haucke 1975).

Figure 7.7. Eastern wild turkey roosts are often tall pine trees with several layers of horizontal branches (photo by Jason Hardin).

Brushy areas may provide camouflage and refuge for winter roosts; however, in areas with high predator pressure, these areas could provide predator concealment before an attack. Rio Grande wild turkeys select the tallest trees available for roosting (fig. 7.8). In South Texas, Haucke (1975) reported that these trees (height = 13.2 m [43 ft]; diameter at breast height [DBH] = 0.6 m [2 ft]) were higher than average trees (height = 9.25 m [30.34 ft]; DBH = 0.34 m [1 ft]). Winter roost patches reached areas as big as 5.2 ha (12.8 ac), with a utilization area of 58%. In areas with a limited number of trees, roost sites had more trees (8–91 trees) than potential roosts, whereas in areas with greater roost site availability, the number of trees was not different from the number of potential roosts (Haucke 1975).

Rio Grande wild turkeys also use human-made features to roost, particularly if landscapes are composed of grasslands or brushlands with few tall trees for roosting. In South Texas, Haucke (1975) observed

Figure 7.8. Rio Grande wild turkeys use the tallest trees available for roosts. Live oaks provide very good roosts in South Texas (photo by Jason Hardin).

that wild turkeys used electrical transmission lines throughout the year. Other human-made features included camp houses, corrals, and windmills. These features may or may not be used depending on the abundance and availability of natural roosts, as well as the availability of cleared openings adjacent to roosts (Haucke 1975, Haucke and Ables 1972). In West Texas, wild turkeys were reported to use oil storage tanks and electric towers, as well as signal-pole and double electrical transmission line structures with heights ranging from 2.5 to 40 m (8 to 131 ft) (Kothman 1971, Kothman and Litton 1975).

Rio Grande wild turkey abundance in Texas has been linked to watercourses, as riparian areas provide many tall hardwood trees (Gore 1973, Litton 1977) (fig. 7.9). In the Rolling Plains ecoregion, wild turkeys are found within 1 km (0.6 mi) of riparian areas (Cathey et al. 2007). Similar distances from riparian areas were found across the Rio Grande wild turkey distribution in the United States (Wigal 1970, Keegan and Crawford 2000, Hennen and Lutz 2001). Also, winter roosts were found within 2.3 km (1.4 mi) of permanent water in South Texas (Haucke 1975). Winter roosting habitat is fundamental to Rio Grande wild turkeys, as it provides the "home base" for flocks during the winter and they spend about half their lives in or around these areas. Rio Grande wild turkeys are also a gregarious, nomadic species with distinct summer and winter roosts (Glazener 1967, Beasom and Wilson 1992). Observations in South Texas indicate that winter roost sites can support more than 500 turkeys on one roost.

Removal of roost sites can lead to a reduction in wild turkey populations (Cook 1972, Perotto-Baldivieso et al. 2011). Suitable roost sites as well as stands of woody species that provide food and cover

Figure 7.9. Tall hardwood trees that occur along creeks and rivers provide good roosting habitat for Rio Grande wild turkeys in Texas (photo by Kory Perlichek).

close to roosts are important along drainage systems. Perotto-Baldivieso et al. (2011) reported that low-frequency natural disturbances, such as the flooding associated with Tropical Storm Amelia, negatively impacted Rio Grande wild turkey habitat and led to long-term changes in wild turkey abundance. Perotto-Baldivieso et al. (2011) showed that the flooding reduced the suitability of roosting and feeding sites along the Medina River in the Edwards Plateau and that long-term impacts resulted from the incomplete recovery of the vegetation 17 years after the event.

Merriam's wild turkey

Merriam's wild turkeys prefer to roost in ponderosa pine trees (fig. 7.10) but will also use other large conifer species such as Douglas-fir, white fir (*Abies concolor*), and limber pine (*Pinus flexilis*), as well as cottonwoods, large oaks, and pinyon pines for roosting (Hoffman et al. 1993, Mollohan et al. 1995). A limiting factor in the distribution of Merriam's wild turkeys may be lack of available roost sites in West Texas, because turkeys invariably select mature trees and strongly prefer ponderosa pine. Preferred roost sites are composed of multistory stands with layered, open, horizontal branches separated by at least 60 cm (24 in). Areas with uneven canopy structures and clumped understories are preferred roost sites (Mollohan et al. 1995). In Arizona, winter roost sites had trees averaging 63 cm [24.8 in] DBH, and summer roost site trees averaged at least 41 cm [16.1 in] DBH. There was also strong selection for larger trees over more abundant and smaller trees. Similar trends were observed in Wyoming (Hengel and Anderson 1990) and South Dakota (Rumble 1992).

Roost sites are located on ridges or near the tops of slopes with an average of 5–13 trees per roost site.

Figure 7.10. Tall, mature ponderosa pine trees are preferred Merriam's wild turkey roosts (photo by Guadalupe Mountains National Park/Giraffescope).

In north-central Arizona, Mollohan et al. (1995) observed that summer roosts were in canyons or areas with steeper slopes (slope mean = 38.0% SD = 17.0%) than were feeding, loafing, or random sites (slope mean = 21.0% SD = 14.0%). If roost sites were in a canyon, more than half were in the upper third of the canyon wall. Trails turkeys used to access roost sites were important and were located along ridges offering vegetation and topographic cover. Mollohan et al. (1995) reported that 80% of roost sites had trails, and 87.5% had topographic cover. Subadult and adult Merriam's wild turkeys can travel up to 6.9 km (4.3 mi) and 2.8 km (1.7 mi), respectively, between roost sites (Hoffman 1991). Roost sites are also located near natural openings (Hoffman et al. 1993). Wakeling and Rogers (1995) found that daily activities occurred within 1.6 km (1 mi) of roost sites and suggested that food availability may drive roost site selection.

Winter roost sites can be used by several flocks of both sexes (more than 100 birds), while summer roosts will be utilized by smaller flocks composed mainly of females, females with poults, or males (Hoffman et al. 1993). While winter roosts are used repeatedly by the same flocks, summer roosts may be used by different flocks, as traditional use is not common unless roost site availability is limited. Site fidelity to roost sites is poor during the spring. Hoffman (1991) reported that adult and subadult males used previously used sites 19% and 29% of the time, respectively, in Colorado and New Mexico. Although roost site preferences typically differ between winter and summer, a small proportion of sites are used as year-long roosts (Mollohan et al. 1995). During brood-rearing, roosting is important because it reduces the danger from ground-dwelling predators (Kennamer 2004). Since turkey poults are capable of flight when they reach 10 days of age, they begin to roost in trees about two weeks after hatching (Hoffman et al. 1993).

Nesting

Eastern wild turkey

Females do not construct the traditional nest structures common to other ground-nesting birds like bobwhites. Nests are often a scraped-out depression on the ground, sometimes lined with twigs or blades of grass. Eastern wild turkeys commonly nest in newly burned forest stands (pine stands and mixed forests burned from three months to three years prior to nesting season) with vines, young trees, and shrub cover (fig. 7.11) (Alldredge et al. 2014, Streich et al. 2015). Yeldell et al. (2017) found that wild turkey nesting females in central Louisiana favored mature pines burned zero to five months prior to nesting and avoided areas burned two years prior. They also used pastures, rights-of-way, and clear-cuts

Figure 7.11. A prescribed burn in East Texas provides good Eastern wild turkey nesting habitat (photo by Robert Sanders).

Figure 7.12. Eastern wild turkey nest in a depression lined by pine needles (photo by Daniel Sullivan).

for nest sites. Wild turkeys tend to avoid dense forest canopy because ground cover is typically reduced (Lehman et al. 2008). Nests are typically shallow depressions on the ground (fig. 7.12) (Alldredge et al. 2014), but ground vegetation that provides suitable cover around the nest is fundamentally important across subspecies in North America (Byrne and Chamberlain 2013, Streich et al. 2015, Little et al. 2016a). This type of habitat provides dense screening cover and visual obstruction (50–66 cm tall [20–26 in]) to reduce predation risk (Alldredge et al. 2014, Little et al. 2016b). Streich et al. (2015) reported that areas with greater minimum vegetation height than random sites were selected for nesting in Georgia. In open grasslands, grasses and forbs are used as cover to conceal nests. In forested areas, vines, young trees, and shrubs provide the required cover for nesting. Small canopy breaks in forests provide nesting habitat, as debris and development of understory vegetation provide suitable cover from predators. Wild turkeys select nesting habitats with higher elevations in bottomland areas (Byrne and

Figure 7.13. Good Rio Grande wild turkey nesting habitat composed of properly grazed native herbaceous vegetation in South Texas (photo by Landon Fritz).

Chamberlain 2013). Typically, these are composed of 76.4% woody cover in nonflooded bottomland hardwood forest, with little fragmentation and low edge density (55.9 m/ha [197 ft/ac]), and are close to brood-rearing areas (Lazarus and Porter 1985, Byrne and Chamberlain 2013).

Rio Grande wild turkey

Nesting habitat is important because nesting cover is related to nesting success (Hohensee and Wallace 2001, Randel 2003). Females avoid heavily grazed pastures with reduced herbaceous cover (figs. 7.13–7.15). For example, Walker (1949) observed that in the Edwards Plateau of Texas, wild turkeys would nest near roadways because these areas provided better concealment than overgrazed pastures. Rio Grande wild turkeys typically construct nests between clumps of tall grasses and forbs or low-growing shrubs (figs. 7.16 and 7.17) (Beasom and Wilson 1992, Spears et al. 2007, Cathey et al. 2007). In addition, cover is more important for nesting females than nest construction itself. Therefore, female Rio Grande wild turkeys select nest sites with greater visual obstruction (51 cm [20 in]) and greater litter depth (4.5 cm [1.8 in]) than surrounding areas (visual obstruction = 16 cm [6.3 in]; litter depth = 1.4 cm [0.6 in]) (Schmutz et al. 1989; Randel 2003). Shade around the nest bowl is also an important factor affecting nest selection (Hohensee and Wallace 2001, Lehman et al. 2002). One of the most essential components of nesting habitat is proximity to water (Day et al. 1991). For example, in the Rolling Plains ecoregion, wild turkeys nested within 1 km (0.62 mi) of a water source (Mollohan et al. 1995, Cathey et al. 2007), and in the Edwards Plateau, nests were found within 0.4 km (0.25 mi) of permanent water (Beasom and Wilson 1992).

Figure 7.14. Kleingrass provides good wild turkey habitat in the Hill Country (photo by Kory Perlichek).

Figure 7.15. Downed tree limbs, shrubs, and good grass cover provide Rio Grande wild turkey nesting habitat in the Cross Timbers ecoregion of Texas (photo by Jesse Oetgen).

Figure 7.16. A Rio Grande wild turkey nest in South Texas constructed within tall clumps of ragweed (photo by Bill Kuvlesky).

Figure 7.17. A Rio Grande wild turkey nest in the Hill Country constructed in a stand of coastal Bermuda grass (photo by Kory Perlichek).

Figure 7.18. Merriam's wild turkey nesting habitat in the Guadalupe Mountains of Texas (photo by Guadalupe Mountains National Park/Giraffescope).

Merriam's wild turkey

Across the geographic range of Merriam's wild turkey, nest site characteristics are fairly similar. Nesting habitat for Merriam's wild turkey is composed of thinned stands of mixed conifers (New Mexico), ponderosa pine (Arizona and South Dakota), and white oak (*Quercus alba*) and Douglas-fir (Washington) (Lutz and Crawford 1987, Day et al. 1991) (fig. 7.18). When selective logging or thinning has been applied to a forest stand, the dense understory and slash provide excellent visual obstruction with reduced predation risk. For example, nests in Colorado were found in stands with clumped overstory canopy cover that ranged from 60% (Hoffman et al. 1993) to 95% (Mollohan et al. 1995). Merriam's wild turkeys select nest sites based on vegetation characteristics and surrounding land cover composition (Little et al. 2016b). Nest construction is not evident, and nests are rather shallow depressions excavated by females (Kennamer 2004). If an understory provides overhead concealment from avian predators as well as visual obstruction for nesting females, then twig and leaf arrangement is minimal.

The nest is located in areas that provide both cover and avenues for escape from predators (fig. 7.19). One side of the nest is open to provide access and escape, another side is against thickets, logs, rocks, or tree trunks that function as barriers, and the remainder is obscured by slash, branches, rocks, or herbaceous vegetation about 45 cm (18 in) in height (Hoffman et al. 1993). Mollohan et al. (1995) also found 39% of nests against a rock or cliff, 17% in or next to slash, and 14% on the uphill side of a tree. Additionally, dense horizontal cover (> 45% vegetative cover) surrounded nests out to about 200 cm (78.7 in) in Colorado. In Arizona, nest sites were found in areas with greater

Figure 7.19. A Merriam's wild turkey hen (head visible in approximate center of photo) on a nest constructed under a deadfall that provides good cover (photo by Chad Lehman).

canopy cover (14.4% vegetative cover) than random sites (7.5% vegetative cover), and this higher canopy cover was associated with high nest success (Mollohan et al. 1995). In addition, cliffs, rocks, and slash may also be found near nests (Hoffman et al. 1993). Merriam's wild turkey females tend to avoid gentle slopes (< 20%) and instead nest in areas with slopes greater than 30%, but if cover is adequate, aspect is not important (Hoffman et al. 1993, Mollohan et al. 1995). In Arizona, Mollohan et al. (1995) reported that nest sites were on slopes that averaged 53% and were higher than other slopes in similar sites used by wild turkeys. Most nest sites in Arizona (82%) were associated with canyons (Mollohan et al. 1995), and in the Rocky Mountains, Kennamer (2004) reported that wild turkeys moved to higher elevations to nest.

Brood-Rearing

Eastern wild turkey

Brood-rearing habitat for Eastern wild turkeys should provide abundant food resources for poults, especially invertebrates. These areas also need to provide ground cover of sufficient height (20–60 cm [8–24 in]) to protect the brood from predators (Alldredge et al. 2014). In East Texas, adequate ground cover for brood-rearing typically occurs in thinned or burned upland forest and in open areas such as prairies, pastures, and rights-of-way (fig. 7.20) (Alldredge et al. 2014). Forests subjected to prescribed fire typically provide abundant herbaceous vegetation soon after a burn, which makes good poult habitat because it is also insect habitat, and insects are a food staple for young poults (Streich et al. 2015). Broods tend to use open areas that range from 2 to 12 ha (5 to 30 ac) more than they use smaller openings of less than 0.4 ha (1 ac) (Alldredge et al. 2014). Closed canopy and flooded areas tend to be avoided during the brood-rearing season because of reduced ground cover or limited food resources (Byrne and Chamberlain 2013, Alldredge et al. 2014).

Rio Grande wild turkey

Ground-level vegetation structure is critical to the survival of Rio Grande wild turkey poults. The first 10 days are critical, as poults are not yet capable of flight and thus rely on escape cover provided by shrubs (Cathey et al. 2007). Broods feed in the morning in open herbaceous areas, loaf in woody cover until late afternoon, and then feed again until

Figure 7.20. A stand of mature pine managed for red-cockaded woodpeckers (*Picoides borealis*) via prescribed burning provides good brooding habitat for Eastern wild turkeys (photo by Robert Sanders).

Figure 7.21. Rio Grande wild turkey brooding habitat in South Texas is composed of a diversity of herbaceous vegetation close to woody escape cover (photo by Eric Grahmann).

dusk, when they move to roost sites (fig. 7.21) (Miller 1993). Poult foraging rates, herbaceous vegetation density, and invertebrate abundance are correlated (Healy 1985, Schmutz et al. 1989, Hennen 1999). Therefore, vegetation communities with abundant insects that provide poult escape cover yet are open enough for females to detect potential threats are important components of brood-rearing habitat (Randel 2003). From a landscape perspective, foraging habitat consists of open grassland with well-interspersed mottes of woody vegetation. Woody cover encroachment (> 60% woody cover) in the Edwards Plateau of Texas can have a negative impact on the amount and diversity of herbaceous vegetation (Perotto-Baldiviezo 2005). Conversely, open areas of herbaceous vegetation with few mottes of woody vegetation (< 15% woody cover) are not used by wild turkey broods (Quinton et al. 1980).

Merriam's wild turkey

Brood-rearing habitat of Merriam's wild turkey is similar to that of Eastern and Rio Grande wild turkeys. Open areas that provide foraging habitat and escape cover are essential. In Colorado, riparian zones, springs, seeps, and floodplains are all favored by females with broods (fig. 7.22) (Hoffman et al. 1993). Mollohan et al. (1995) identified ciénagas (moist-soil habitats) and parks as brood-rearing habitats because of abundant poult food resources and the presence of water. These areas usually have suitable forb, grass, and shrub cover that supports a high number of insects and therefore provides brood-rearing habitat (Hoffman et al. 1993). In addition, the proximity of open areas to escape cover provided by shrubs or other low-growing vegetation is important to broods (Hoffman et al. 1993). Loafing during brood-rearing tends to occur within 15–18 m (50–60 ft) of forests

Figure 7.22. Merriam's wild turkey brooding habitat often occurs in moist-soil habitats such as riparian areas and floodplains that support forb and grass communities as well as shrub escape cover (photo by Scott Lerich).

with open understory, dense overstory, and features that can be used as perches (rock outcrops, snags, logs, slash) (Hoffman et al. 1993).

Foraging

Eastern wild turkey

The Eastern wild turkey inhabits the forests of East Texas, so its diet is dominated by plants that are common in the Piney Woods, many of which provide important food (table 7.1). Alldredge et al. (2014) identified oaks (fig. 7.23), hickories, American beautyberry (fig. 7.24), dogwood, and plums as key food-bearing trees, while vines such as wild grape (*Vitis* spp.) and shrubs such as blackberry (*Rubus fruticosus*) are also critical. The large seeds of grasses and forbs such as beggar-weeds (*Desmodium* spp.), crabgrass (*Digitaria* spp.), paspalums, panic grasses (*Panicum* spp.), partridge pea (*Chamaecrista fasciculata*) (fig. 7.25), croton or doveweed (*Croton* spp.), wild beans (family Fabaceae), and ragweed (*Ambrosia psilostachya*) have been identified as important. Hurst and Dickson (1992) compiled a list of plants that represent the main food items for turkeys that inhabit the pine-oak forests of the southern United States. Hackberry fruit, pine nuts, and pecans were valuable foods supplied by woody species, and the fruits of French mulberry (American beautyberry), blueberry (*Vaccinium crassifolium*), and poison ivy (*Toxicodendron radicans*) were also valued. In addition, Hurst

Table 7.1. Common wild turkey foods of the Eastern, Rio Grande, and Merriam's subspecies.

Food class	Eastern wild turkey	Rio Grande wild turkey	Merriam's wild turkey
Mast/fruit	oak (acorns), hickory, American beautyberry, sassafras, plum, wild grape, dogwood, wild blackberry, hackberry, pecan, pine seeds, French mulberry, tree flowers, poison ivy, pepperweed	lime prickly ash, agarita, bumelia, broomweed, grape, ephedra, granjeno, hackberry, honey mesquite, juniper, littleleaf sumac, lotebush, oak (acorns), prickly pear, skunkbush, tasajillo, walnut, condalia, lantana, anaqua, persimmon	pinyon nuts, oak (acorns), juniper, wild strawberries, manzanita, rose haws, wild mulberry, prickly pear, red kinnikinnick, ponderosa pine nuts, raspberry, hawthorn, snowberry
Grasses/forbs	beggartick, crabgrass, paspalums, panic grass, partridge pea, croton, ragweed, wild beans, wood sorrel, wheat, corn, soybean, chufa, ryegrass	bristlegrass, beggartick, bladderpod, buffelgrass, catnip, noseburn, croton, euphorb, evening primrose, filaree, flatsedge, grama grasses, ground-cherry, groundsel, little barley, milk pea, milk vetch, palafoxia, panic grass, paspalum, pigeonberry, pinnate tansy mustard, plantago, rescuegrass, sand dropseed, sida, signal grass, silverleaf nightshade, smallflower corydalis, squirreltail grass, Texas cupgrass, Texas virgin's bower, tobosa, wild tridens, wild onion, wild tobacco, windmill grass, yellow wood sorrel	wild oats, brome, wheat, clover, sedges, currants, watercress, dandelion flowers, bluegrass
Nonvegetation	animal matter, beetles (Coleoptera), grasshoppers (Orthoptera), true bugs (Hemiptera), leafhoppers (Homoptera)	principally invertebrates, grasshoppers, snails	insects, snails

Sources: Eastern: Hurst and Dickson (1992), Alldredge et al. (2014).
Rio Grande: Beasom and Wilson (1992), Cathey et al. 2007.
Merriam's: Petersen and Richardson (1973), Scott and Boeker (1975), Rumble and Anderson (1996), Mackey and Jonas (1982), Schemnitz et al. (1985), Hoffman et al. (1993).

Figure 7.23. Acorns are important wild turkey foods throughout Texas (photo by Bill Kuvlesky).

Figure 7.24. The fruit of American beautyberry is an important Eastern wild turkey food (photo by Jason Hardin).

and Dickson indicated that wood sorrel (*Oxalis* spp.), ryegrass (*Lolium multiflorum*), and chufa (*Cyperus esculentus*) were important foods, as were crops such as corn (*Zea mays*) and soybeans (*Glycine max*). Invertebrates were also central food items, especially for rapidly growing poults. Hurst and Dickson reported that the diets of poults in the pine forests of Mississippi consisted of almost 80% insects during their first week after hatching, over 50% during their second week, and almost 40% their third week. Poults that foraged in fields consumed an even higher percentage of insects than they did in pine forests because insects were more abundant in fields. Preferred insects included beetles (Coleoptera), true bugs (Hemiptera), grasshoppers (Orthoptera) (fig. 7.26), and leafhoppers (Homoptera).

Seasonal food preferences for Eastern wild turkeys in southern forests depend on the availability of preferred foods. Hard mast (acorns, hickories, pecans), soft mast (blackberries, mulberries, poison ivy fruit, etc.), grass and forb seeds (paspalum, panic grasses, beggarweed, etc.), field crops, green forage (leaves and flowers of herbaceous plants), and animal matter (mainly invertebrates) are important food items throughout the year if they can be located.

Figure 7.25. The large seeds of partridge pea are an important Eastern and Rio Grande wild turkey food (photo by Eric Grahmann).

Eastern wild turkeys forage in areas with abundant ground cover or in woodlands that have been thinned or burned between three months and three years previously (Alldredge et al. 2014). During the fall, preferred areas are restored prairies, pastures, and utility rights-of-way with tall herbaceous vegetation where vegetation cover ranges from 30 to 60 cm (12 to 24 in) in height. This provides abundant sources of insects and grasses. During the winter, foraging areas are traditionally considered thinned or burned areas where mast can be found (Hurst and Dickson 1992). Creeks with hardwoods and wildlife openings with the above characteristics are preferred by Eastern wild turkeys. During the spring, open areas and male display areas are used. Overall, a variety of fire-maintained pine stands that are associated with open areas will be used by Eastern wild turkeys for foraging throughout the year (Hurst and Dickson 1992, Little et al. 2016a).

Figure 7.26. Grasshoppers are an important Eastern, Rio Grande, and Merriam's wild turkey food (photo by J. Alfonso Ortega-S.).

Rio Grande wild turkey

Although Rio Grande wild turkeys will consume some of the same food items as the Eastern subspecies, they have a much broader diet because their geographic range in Texas is larger than that of the Eastern wild turkey and thus includes more vegetation types (table 7.1). Beasom and Wilson (1992) indicated that seasonally important foods in South Texas include the seeds of grasses and flat sedge (*Cyperus* spp.) during spring and summer, and fruits and the seeds of woody plants from summer through fall. Forb seeds are consumed throughout the year but become especially important during fall and winter. Green forage, which is the leafy portions of grasses and forbs, is also consumed throughout the year, but like forb seeds, it becomes more important when other foods are less available. Beasom and Wilson (1992) also reported that animal matter (insects) provides wild turkey food throughout the year in South Texas. Snails in particular are a significant dietary item of females during egg laying.

Beasom and Wilson (1992) and Cathey et al. (2007) provided comprehensive lists of plants consumed by Rio Grande wild turkeys in Texas, including at least 15 woody species, 2 succulents (cacti), 2 subshrubs, several vines, and at least 48 species of grasses, forbs, and sedges (table 7.1). In South Texas, Beasom and Wilson (1992) reported that among mast-producing plants, acorns are widely regarded as turkey food, but because acorn production is often erratic, mast produced by

Figure 7.27. Mesquite beans are an important Rio Grande wild turkey food (photo by Eric Grahmann).

Figure 7.28. The fruit of granjeno is an important Rio Grande wild turkey food (photo by Larry Ditto).

Figure 7.29. The seeds of bristlegrass are an important Rio Grande wild turkey food (photo by Eric Grahmann).

sugar hackberry and honey mesquite (fig. 7.27) are more dependable because of their wider distribution and more regular mast crops. Other food-bearing plants listed were lime prickly ash, granjeno (*Celtis pallida*) (fig. 7.28), anacua (*Ehretia anacua*), bumelia (*Bumelia* spp.), persimmon, mustang grape (*Vitis mustangensis*), and bluewood. Beasom and Wilson (1992) stated that among grasses and grass-like species, turkeys favor plants that produce large seeds or have clustered seed heads that they can quickly remove from the plant, such as paspalums (*Paspalum* spp.), bristlegrasses (*Setaria* spp.) (fig. 7.29), windmill grasses (*Chloris* spp.), signal grasses (*Brachiaria* spp.), panic grasses, and flat sedges. Croton or doveweed (*Croton texensis*), ground cherry (*Physalis viscosa*), milk pea (*Galactia* spp.) wild tobacco (*Nicotiana repanda*), false dandelion (*Pyrrhopappus* spp.), indigo bush (*Amorpha fruticosa*), and euphorbias (*Euphorbia* spp.) were recognized as forbs that provide food for wild turkeys in South Texas.

In the central and northern portions of wild turkey range in Texas, Beasom and Wilson (1992) identified a variety of plants that are part of wild turkey diets. Texas cupgrass (*Eriochloa sericea*) and panicums are critical during spring and summer, while bristlegrass and white tridens (*Tridens albescens*) are essential foods during fall, as are rescue grass (*Bromus unioloides*) and little barley (*Hordeum pusillum*) during winter. Among woody species, the

Figure 7.30. The mast produced by skunkbush sumac is an important Rio Grande wild turkey food (photo by Tim Fulbright).

Figure 7.31. The seeds of silverleaf nightshade are an important Rio Grande wild turkey food (photo by Eric Grahmann).

seeds of honey mesquite and pecan are summer and fall foods. Tasajillo (*Cylindropuntia leptocaulis*) and bumelia are favored foods during fall, and skunkbush sumac (*Rhus trilobata*) (fig. 7.30) and prickly pear (*Opuntia* spp.) are vital winter foods. Forbs such as silverleaf nightshade (*Solanum elaeagnifolium*) (fig. 7.31), ground-cherry, wild onion (*Allium* spp.), and milk vetch (*Astragalus* spp.) are consumed from spring through fall. Greens provided by rescue grass, milk vetch, bladderpod (*Lesquerella* spp.), and filaree (*Erodium* spp.) constitute much of the winter diet. Other seasonally important parts of wild turkey diets in the Edwards Plateau in particular are acorns, sumac berries, hackberry seeds, juniper berries, elm seeds, grapes, prickly pear fruit, and blackberries, as well as the seeds of paspalum, dropseed (*Sporobolus* spp.), and grama (*Bouteloua* spp.) grasses (Walker 1941, Taylor 1943, Blakey 1944, Walker 1951). As in South Texas, animal matter in the form of insects and snails is also likely wild turkey food in the Edwards Plateau and Rolling Plains throughout the year.

Open areas, well interspersed with 15% to 35% woody vegetation patches, are critical foraging habitat for Rio Grande wild turkeys (Schorger 1966, Beasom and Wilson 1992). Habitat should have at least 50% open areas with well-interspersed mottes of trees and shrubs (fig. 7.32). These trees and shrubs provide the mast for wild turkey diets, while the open spaces provide the insects, grasses, and forbs frequently

Figure 7.32. Foraging habitat of Rio Grande wild turkeys in the Hill Country of Texas (photo by Kory Perlichek).

ingested by wild turkeys (Quinton et al. 1980, Randel 2003). Excessive woody cover (> 70%) can reduce the amount of open area and limit the quantities of insects, grasses, and forbs available to Rio Grande wild turkeys (Haucke 1975). Alternatively, a lack of woody patches (< 15% woody cover) in foraging areas can limit Rio Grande wild turkey escape routes, dispersal habitat, and overall use (Quinton et al. 1980, Randel 2003). Foraging areas within dispersal routes are critical to Rio Grande wild turkeys, as they have marked seasonal shifts in habitat use, with the largest portion of their movement occurring from their winter ranges to their reproductive areas in the spring (Thomas et al. 1966, Keegan and Crawford 2000).

Merriam's wild turkey

No information is available for Merriam's wild turkey food habits in Texas. However, the vegetation communities of the Guadalupe Mountains are similar to those inhabited by Merriam's wild turkeys elsewhere in portions of their historic range, so results of studies from these areas are provided. Merriam's wild turkeys have the same basic dietary requirements as the Eastern and Rio Grande subspecies. Most of their annual diet is composed of plant material in the form of hard and soft mast from trees, vines, and shrubs, grass and forb seeds, and foliage and invertebrates (table 7.1) (Petersen and Richardson 1973, Scott and Boeker 1975, Mackey and Jonas 1982, Schemnitz et al. 1985, Hoffman et al. 1993, Rumble and Anderson 1996). Rumble and Anderson (1996) found that wild turkeys in the Black Hills of South Dakota consumed 78 kinds of foods, the majority of which were plants, but 12 of these foods made up 96% of their diet. They reported that during winter in South Dakota, ponderosa pine seeds and kinnikinnick (*Arctostaphylos uva-ursi*) fruit (fig. 7.33) were food sources, as were Kentucky bluegrass (*Poa pratensis*) and corn. Scott and Boeker (1975) also noted that hard mast in the form of acorns, pinyon pine nuts, and juniper berries provided winter food in Arizona. Similarly, Shaw and Mollohan (1992) indicated that Merriam's wild turkeys consumed more mast during winter, as well as more grass seed heads, while insect and forb consumption declined. Schemnitz et al. (1985) reported that watercress (*Nasturtium officinale*) is often winter food for wild turkeys in New Mexico. From late winter through spring, Merriam's wild turkeys transition to more herbaceous foods such as grass and forb seeds and foliage (Shaw and Mollohan 1992, Rumble and Anderson 1996). Grasshoppers, snails, and other invertebrates, in addition to grasses and forbs, become valuable foods from late spring into summer.

Figure 7.33. The fruit of kinnikinnick is an important Merriam's wild turkey food (photo by Dave Hewitt).

Although Merriam's wild turkeys eat a variety of foods, they are selective feeders with a diet that fluctuates depending on precipitation across season, year, and region (Hoffman et al. 1993). Depending on availability, about 80% of Merriam's wild turkey diets consist of pine seeds, acorns, and other seeds. One of the most dependable food sources is grasses, but these may be very limited during winter months. One of the most important components of foraging habitat is cover (Mollohan et al. 1995). During years of good mast production, dense stands of ponderosa pine (fig. 7.34) and pinyon-juniper will provide sources of food. Open areas will be favored in years with limited mast production. During the brood-rearing season, females with poults select small canyons with woody cover (Mollohan et al. 1995). Forest openings ranging between 0.10 and 0.12 ha (0.25–0.34 ac) with gentle slopes (0–20%) are favored by most wild turkeys. Logging and fire provide these openings and a higher abundance of food. Mollohan et al. (1995) reported

Figure 7.34. The seeds of ponderosa pine cones provide an important food for Merriam's wild turkeys (photo by Scott Lerich).

that logged sites within five years after logging were preferred by turkeys, and logged areas more than 20 years old were avoided. Turkeys tend to prefer areas with higher species richness, dense overstory cover, and herbaceous cover about 0–0.45 m (0–18 in) high. During the winter, wild turkeys may move to riparian areas if snow cover is too deep or if food sources from coniferous stands and open areas are limited.

Water

Eastern wild turkey

As with any animal, water is a critical daily requirement of wild turkeys, but because they can move considerable distances daily, they generally have access to a water source. Schorger (1966) stated that turkeys drink at least twice a day, and this may be true periodically for the Rio Grande and Merriam's subspecies, which inhabit more arid areas of Texas. However, Alldredge et al. (2014) indicated that water is not a limiting factor for Eastern wild turkeys in the Piney Woods because of the abundant creeks and ponds, as well as plentiful moisture-laden food items. Indeed, if food items with high moisture content are abundant, wild turkeys may not require free water at all for considerable lengths of time. Exum et al. (1985) reported that females with broods in dry slash pine plantations in southern Alabama rarely approached within 100 m (110 yd) of available water and evidently did not use free water for weeks. They stated that poults and juveniles consumed the abundant berries that were available at the time of their study, but they also acknowledged that free water sources would clearly be important during droughts.

Rio Grande wild turkey

Beasom and Wilson (1992) indicated that water sources are important components of Rio Grande wild turkey habitat in Texas, but they suggested that turkeys are often associated with water because the tall trees they require as roosting habitat are generally near creeks and rivers. However, they did acknowledge that abundant sources of free water do benefit Rio Grande wild turkeys, and that reports exist of population increases and range expansions following the development of free water sources. For example, extensive construction of windmills and associated water troughs on the King Ranch during the early 1900s resulted in extensive turkey range expansion on the ranch. Lehmann (1957) indicated that wild turkeys were rare on the ranch in 1912 because of a lack of surface water but increased noticeably by 1920 after the development of windmills. Additionally, Ramsey (1958) and Glazener (1967) reported that Rio Grande wild turkey distribution increased in the Edwards Plateau and on the Welder Wildlife Refuge near Sinton, Texas, respectively, in response to the development of new water sources. As with Eastern wild turkeys, the preformed water of succulent food items such as fruits and insects can make birds less reliant on free water when these food items are readily available (Cathey et al. 2007). However, the broad distribution of wild turkeys in South Texas (Lehmann 1957, Glazener 1967) and the Edwards Plateau (Ramsey 1958) strongly suggests that a source of dependable drinking water is important on the drought-prone rangelands of Texas.

Merriam's wild turkey

Merriam's wild turkeys also inhabit semiarid habitats in the mountains of the Southwest, so water requirements there are similar to those of the Rio Grande wild turkey. Direct water sources are crucial to Merriam's wild turkeys, and sources that provide standing water during the warm season are essential. Wild turkeys can also obtain their water from dew and snow (Brown 1989, Hoffman et al. 1993). Scott and Boeker (1975) reported that few wild turkeys nest or roost more than 2.4 km (1.5 mi) from a water source. They also stated that Merriam's wild turkeys regularly visit springs, seeps, or stock tanks during early mornings or late afternoons. Schemnitz et al. (1985) also found that seeps and springs were habitat components for wild turkeys in New Mexico, particularly during winter and when food was scarce. Additionally, Hoffman et al. (1993) emphasized the importance of seeps, springs, creeks, puddles, and other impoundments as sources of free water for Merriam's wild turkeys. Like the Eastern and Rio Grande subspecies, Merriam's wild turkeys utilize succulent vegetation and invertebrates for preformed water, which supplements any available free water sources (Hoffman et al. 1993). Rumble and Anderson (1996) provided additional evidence that preformed water from green vegetation and fruit was a fundamental part of Merriam's wild turkey diets during dry winters in South Dakota, and that the diet of young poults consisted of more than 70%

invertebrates. Water sources are deemed so important to Merriam's wild turkeys that Hoffman et al. (1993) recommended providing a water source within every square mile of land that turkeys occupy.

Landscape Ecology

Landscape characteristics

Understanding the distribution and spatial structure of vegetation required to meet wild turkey habitat needs is valuable for effective habitat management. A discipline that can facilitate wild turkey habitat research and management is landscape ecology. "Landscape ecology emphasizes the interaction between spatial pattern and ecological process, that is, the causes and consequences of spatial heterogeneity across a range of scales" (Turner et al. 2001).

Landscape-level studies have addressed the relationship between the spatial structure of woody cover and Eastern wild turkey abundance. Thogmartin (1999) reported that woody vegetation patch size (mean = 6,912.6 ha, SE = 634.5 ha [mean = 17,081.4 ac, SE = 1,567.9 ac]) was positively related to nesting success in Arkansas. Furthermore, the amount of edge, topographic position, and patch type in mixed-pine and hardwood-forest patches can impact wild turkey nesting success (Thogmartin and Schaeffer 2000, Thogmartin 2001). In Mississippi, Miller et al. (1999) reported that habitat-use patterns are consistent for male and female wild turkeys across spatial scales. Moreover, in another Mississippi study, pine and hardwood patches were reported to be crucial features of wild turkey habitat, as were mature-tree stands that served as roosting habitat (Chamberlain et al. 2000). Roost sites are usually in drainage systems, which also serve as nest sites and dispersal corridors (Palmer and Hurst 1996, Miller et al. 2000). Similarly, Buser (2006) used class-level metrics such as mean patch area and percentage of woody cover to describe roost site landscape characteristics in East Texas.

Patches of large trees accompanied by low-growing brush on approaches to these patches and around them are often essential winter roosting habitats for Rio Grande wild turkeys. For example, woody patches near creeks, rivers, and intermittent or dry drainages are particularly important roost sites for Rio Grande wild turkeys in the Edwards Plateau and the Rolling Plains (e.g., Thomas et al. 1966, Gore 1973, Litton 1977). Perotto-Baldivieso et al. (2011) used landscape ecology principles to demonstrate the importance of roosting cover for Rio Grande wild turkeys along drainages in the Edwards Plateau of Texas (fig. 7.35).

Figure 7.35. The drainages of rivers and creeks in Edwards Plateau landscapes provide important roosting habitats for Rio Grande wild turkeys (photo by Kory Perlichek).

Their results showed that reductions in the amount, size, and complexity of woody vegetation patches along drainage networks could have a negative impact on wild turkey habitat use and connectivity. Using a similar approach, Dreibelbis (2008) identified vegetation structures used by nesting Rio Grande wild turkeys in the Edwards Plateau. Nesting areas in his study had less than 30% woody cover (fig. 7.36) (about one-third juniper and two-thirds oak), with small mean patch areas of less than 0.02 ha (0.05 ac), high patch density (> 5,000 patches/100 ha [2,024 patches/100 ac]), and high edge density (> 800 m/ha [1,062 ft/ac]). Additionally, open patches around nest sites were important for females.

In addition to the focal features of a landscape, scale and resolution are fundamental when evaluating wildlife habitat (Perotto-Baldivieso et al. 2009). Understanding the importance of scale in wild turkey studies is crucial to making habitat management decisions. For example, small spatial scale assessments are critical for Eastern wild turkeys, as this subspecies tends to use areas with high edge density and openings close to nest sites (Byrne and Chamberlain 2013). Similar results were reported by Little et al. (2016b), as wild turkey nest site selection at small scales depends on vegetation and its structure around the nest site, as well as vegetation configuration and predator densities at larger spatial scales. On the other hand, site selection at large scales will be influenced by fragmentation, which can increase risk of predation. In the Edwards Plateau, Schaap et al. (2005) reported that female Rio Grande wild turkeys had larger home ranges in landscapes with stable wild turkey populations than in landscapes with declining wild turkey populations. Perotto-Baldiviezo (2005) quantified the spatial structure of these Edwards Plateau sites and concluded that different home range size evaluations would produce different habitat suitability matrices,

Figure 7.36. An Edwards Plateau landscape with good nesting cover has less than 30% woody cover (photo by Rick Machen).

which could have a significant impact on habitat management decisions. In another Edwards Plateau study, Dreibelbis (2008) identified nest sites and the spatial structure of woody vegetation within a radius of 100 m (328 ft) and found that Rio Grande wild turkey females prefer areas with about 30% woody cover distributed in small, irregular patches within an open pasture matrix. Studies focused on Merriam's wild turkeys reported that nest site selection in South Dakota is a hierarchical process over multiple scales, where different habitat components are selected at different scales (Lehman et al. 2008). Finally, Conley et al. (2015) showed that incubation occurs at small scales of less than 3 ha (7.4 ac), which may influence nest site selection.

Home Ranges

The home ranges utilized by wild turkeys vary considerably according to season of the year, age, and sex and often depend on the availability of required food, water, and cover. Wigley et al. (1986) reported that the minimum size of Eastern wild turkey seasonal home ranges in the Ouachita Mountains of Arkansas averaged 1,295 ha (3,200 ac). Similarly, Campo and Dickson (1990) indicated that Eastern wild turkey home ranges in East Texas were about 404 ha (1,000 ac), although in poor habitat where resources were limited, home ranges could be as large as 1,214 ha (3,000 ac). Isabelle (2010) reported in a recent study in the Piney Woods that the average spring home ranges of Eastern wild turkeys on his study area were 1,146 ha (2,832 ac) and were reduced during summer, ranging from 628 to 1,118 ha (1,550 to 2,763 ac). Spring home ranges of transplanted birds were over twice as large (908 ha [2,245 ac]) as summer home ranges (443 ha [1,095 ac]). Female home ranges averaged 846 ha (2,091 ac), while male home ranges were 498 ha (1,231 ac), and those of transplanted birds were 901 ha (2,226 ac).

Rio Grande wild turkeys seem to have larger home ranges than wild turkeys in East Texas, which is probably a response to the need to move longer distances to locate required resources. For example, in the Texas Panhandle, Hall et al. (2006) reported that wild turkey home ranges ranged from 884 to 1,170 ha (2,184 to 2,891 ac) for adult females and from 601 to 1,330 ha (1,485 to 3,287 ac) for adult males. Juvenile female and male annual home ranges were larger, ranging from 1,846 to 3,092 ha (4,562 to 7,640 ac) and from 601 to 1,604 ha (1,485 to 3,959 ac), respectively. However, on their Kansas study area, annual home ranges for both sex and age cohorts were considerably larger. Adult female home ranges averaged 4,401 ha (10,875 ac), adult male home ranges averaged 4,260 ha (10,527 ac), juvenile female home ranges averaged 5,962 ha (14,732 ac), and juvenile male home ranges averaged 3,989 ha (9,857 ac). Evidently, the larger home ranges in Kansas reflected the greater movements required to secure adequate habitat in the fragmented Kansas landscape. In South Texas, Reyes-Ramirez et al. (2012) found that home ranges for Rio Grande wild turkeys were similar to those in the Texas Panhandle. Annual home ranges of adults ranged from 838 to 1,548 ha (2,071 to 3,825 ac) and were smaller than those of juveniles, which ranged from 1,124 to 5,667 ha (2,777 to 14,003 ac). Breeding and nesting home ranges of adult females were smaller, ranging from 263 to 616 ha (650 to 1,522 ac), and were larger than those of juvenile females, which ranged from 218 to 349 ha (537 to 862 ac). Like wild turkeys in Kansas, the subordinate juvenile wild turkeys in South Texas may have been forced to move greater distances to locate suitable roosting habitat, which was limited on the study area.

Since no scientific studies have been conducted on Merriam's wild turkeys in the Guadalupe Mountains, we presume that their home ranges may be similar to home ranges reported from other studies in the western United States. In ponderosa pine/Douglas-fir forests of Oregon, Lutz and Crawford (1989) reported that the average seasonal home range of the four age and sex classes they studied was 1,615 ha (3,991 ac). Holzer (1989) reported home ranges of 2,883 ha (7,124 ac) in Montana. In another Montana study, Thompson (1993) found that Merriam's wild turkey home ranges varied by age and sex and study area. The average spring/fall home range of adult males on one study site was 2,040 ha (5,041 ac), whereas for adult females it was 570 ha (1,409 ac). For subadult males the average spring/fall home range was 2,990 ha (7,380 ac), and 1,470 ha (3,632 ac) for subadult females. On the other study area the average spring/fall home range of adult males was 360 ha (890 ac), while adult female home range was 650 ha (1,606 ac). Subadult males had average spring/fall home ranges of 610 ha (1,507 ac), and subadult females had home ranges of 450 acres (1,112 ac). Hoffman (1991) reported that the average spring home range of adult male Merriam's wild turkeys in southern Colorado was 520 ha (1,285 ac), and for juvenile males 1,230 ha (3,039 ac). Clearly, the home range sizes for Merriam's wild turkeys reported in these studies vary considerably, and because the research was conducted in different states and likely in different vegetation communities of varying quality, turkey use of space was probably related to the availability of requisite habitats. Since Merriam's wild turkeys in the Guadalupe Mountains are on the southeastern fringe of the subspecies' geographic range, where habitats might be more limited, their home ranges may be similar to the larger home ranges in the studies reported here.

Habitat Suitability Models

Habitat suitability models have been utilized to evaluate habitat quality for wildlife (Schamberger et al. 1982, Brooks 1997, Kliskey et al. 1999, He et al. 2015). These models are designed to assess suitable areas using habitat characteristics considered essential to specific wildlife species (Schamberger and O'Neill 1986, Garcia and Armbruster 1997, Kliskey et al. 1999). Habitat suitability models are intended for use in conservation, planning, and management (Schamberger and O'Neill 1986, Brooks 1997, He at al. 2015). Geospatial technologies have added to the development of decision-making support tools based on habitat suitability models (Debeljak et al. 2001). Williamson and Koeln (1980) developed the first published habitat suitability models for wild turkeys using a computerized habitat evaluation system. Since then, habitat suitability models have been developed for Eastern wild turkeys using geographic information systems and landscape-level approaches (Schroeder 1985, Donovan et al. 1987, Fleming and Porter 2001), as well as for Merriam's wild turkeys (Rumble and Anderson 1995, Lehman et al. 2016). For Rio Grande wild turkeys in Texas, numerous studies have reported habitat characteristics (Walker 1949, 1950; Litton and Harwell 1995, Randel 2003, Schaap et al. 2005). However, there are only two habitat suitability models for Rio Grande wild turkeys: one for the western Cross Timbers region of Texas (Miller 2002) and one for the Edwards Plateau (Perotto-Baldiviezo 2005). The latter study is based on the principle that spatial characteristics such as the distribution and spatial structure of vegetation patches are important in defining habitat suitability. Mazerolle and Villard (1999) reported that landscape characteristics for birds could reliably predict species presence and abundance, and if scale was defined adequately, habitat suitability models could help conservation and management strategies.

Summary

While wild turkey habitat varies across Texas, wild turkeys always require roost sites as well as cover and food resources for nesting and brood-rearing. A variety of year-round permanent food sources is also important for all three subspecies (Hughes and Lee 2015). Direct and indirect water sources are central to wild turkey survival and reproduction (Porter 1992). A combination of trees (15–45% woody vegetation cover) and open grassy areas is fundamental, as trees provide food, loafing and escape cover, and roost sites, and grasses offer food for adults and foraging habitat for poults. Grasslands can also be used as protective cover from predators during the nesting and brood-rearing periods (Alldredge et al. 2014). Roost-site conservation is vital for managing wild turkey populations (Litton and Harwell 1995). The three wild turkey subspecies in Texas prefer large trees with several horizontal limbs and a broad canopy. Nesting habitat is important to nesting success (Hohensee and Wallace 2001, Randel 2003). Females avoid heavily grazed pastures with reduced herbaceous cover. When selective logging, thinning, or fire is applied to a forest stand, within three years the dense understory and slash provide excellent visual obstruction with reduced predation risk at nest sites for Eastern and Merriam's wild turkeys. Brood-rearing habitat for all three subspecies tends to provide abundant food resources for poults, especially invertebrates. Ground-level vegetation structure is critical to the survival of wild turkey poults. The first 10 to 14 days are especially important, as poults are not yet capable of flight and thus rely on escape cover provided by shrubs (Cathey et al. 2007).

All three subspecies have basically the same dietary requirements. Most of the annual diet is composed of plant material in the form of hard and soft mast from trees, vines, and shrubs; grass and forb seeds and foliage; and invertebrates (Petersen and Richardson 1973, Scott and Boeker 1975, Mackey and Jonas 1982, Schemnitz et al. 1985, Hoffman et al. 1993, Rumble and Anderson 1996). Forest openings ranging between 0.10 and 0.12 ha (0.25–0.34 ac) with gentle slopes (0–20%) are favored by most Eastern and Merriam's wild turkeys. Logging and fire provide these openings and a higher abundance of food than exists in areas that have not been managed with logging or fire. Open grasslands with well-interspersed woody vegetation are important for Rio Grande wild turkeys. Areas preferred by turkeys tend to have higher grass species richness and thus a high diversity of insects.

At the landscape level, these studies highlight the importance of scale when wild turkeys select sites for roosting or nesting. Vegetation structure, food availability, land cover composition and configuration, and predator densities all have an impact for management purposes. However, no published studies address wild turkey habitat from multiple temporal and spatial scales. While most studies implicitly use a temporal scale (e.g., nesting), we propose the use of combined spatial and temporal scales for the study of wild turkey habitat. Temporal scales can be defined by the relevant season of wild turkeys, while spatial scales can initially be defined by the use of home ranges at the individual level. Multiple-scale analysis needs to be conducted for wild turkey habitats to identify domains of scale in the scale continuum proposed by Wheatley (2010). Useful information can be provided by the home range data published for all three subspecies in Texas and the valuable information that has been generated in the last 75 years for Eastern and Rio Grande wild turkeys. There is an urgent need to assess habitat requirements and carry out landscape-level studies for Merriam's wild turkey populations in West Texas.

Literature Cited

Alldredge, B. E., J. B. Hardin, J. Whiteside, J. L. Isabelle, S. Parsons, W. C. Conway, and J. C. Cathey. 2014. Eastern wild turkeys in Texas: biology and management. Texas AgriLife Extension Publication WF-011. Texas A&M University, College Station, USA.

Bailey, R. W., and K. T. Rinell. 1967. Events in the turkey year. Pages 73–91 *in* O. H. Hewitt, editor. The wild turkey and its management. The Wildlife Society, Washington, DC, USA.

Beasom, S. L., and D. Wilson. 1992. Rio Grande turkey. Pages 306–330 *in* J. G. Dickson, editor. The wild turkey: biology and management. Stackpole Books, Mechanicsburg, Pennsylvania, USA.

Blakey, H. L. 1944. Welfare of the wild turkey closely associated with range management. Texas Agriculture Experiment Station Progress Report 894. Texas A&M University, College Station, USA.

Block, W. M., and L. A. Brennan. 1993. The habitat concept in ornithology: theory and application. Current Ornithology 11:35–91.

Brooks, R. P. 1997. Improving habitat suitability index models. Wildlife Society Bulletin 25:163–167.

Brown, D. E. 1989. Arizona game birds. University of Arizona Press, Tucson, USA.

Buser, P. E. 2006. Roost site selection of Eastern wild turkeys in intensely managed pine forests of East Texas. Thesis, Stephen F. Austin State University, Nacogdoches, Texas, USA.

Byrne, M. E., and M. J. Chamberlain. 2013. Nesting ecology of wild turkeys in a bottomland hardwood forest. American Midland Naturalist 170:95–110.

Byrne, M. E., B. A. Collier, and M. J. Chamberlain. 2015. Roosting behavior of male Eastern and Rio Grande wild turkeys. Proceedings of the National Wild Turkey Symposium 11:175–185.

Campo, J. J., and J. G. Dickson. 1990. The eastern wild turkey in Texas. Texas Parks and Wildlife Department Report PWD-8R-7100–137B-2/90. Texas Parks and Wildlife Department, Austin, USA.

Cathey, J. C., K. Melton, J. Dreibelbis, B. Cavney, S. L. Locke, S. J. DeMaso, T. W. Schwertner, and B. Collier. 2007. The Rio Grande wild turkey in Texas: biology and management. Texas AgriLife Extension Report B-6198. Texas A&M University, College Station, USA.

Chamberlain, M. J., B. D. Leopold, and B. L. Wes. 2000. Characteristics of roost sites of adult wild turkey females. Journal of Wildlife Management 64:1025–1032.

Conley, M. D., J. G. Oetgen, J. Barrow, M. J. Chamberlain, K. L. Skow, and B. A. Collier. 2015. Habitat selection, incubation, and incubation recess ranges of nesting female Rio Grande wild turkeys in Texas. Proceedings of the National Wild Turkey Symposium 11:117–126.

Cook, R. L. 1972. A study of nesting turkeys in the Edwards Plateau of Texas. Proceedings of the Annual Conference of the Southeastern Association of Game and Fish Commissioners 26:236–244.

Cooke, J. R. 2007. Quail regulations and the rule-making process in Texas. Pages 299–312 *in* L. A. Brennan, editor. Texas quails: ecology and management. Texas A&M University Press, College Station, USA.

Day, K. S., L. D. Flake, and W. L. Tucker. 1991. Characteristics of wild turkey nest sites in a mixed-grass prairie-oak-woodland mosaic in the northern Great Plains,

South Dakota. Canadian Journal of Zoology 69:2840–2845.

Debeljak, M., S. Džeroski, K. Jerina, A. Kobler, and M. Adamic. 2001. Habitat suitability modelling for red deer (*Cervus elaphus* L.) in south-central Slovenia with classification trees. Ecological Modelling 138:321–330.

Donovan, M. L., D. L. Rabe, and C. E. Olson. 1987. Use of geographic information systems to develop habitat suitability models. Wildlife Society Bulletin 15:574–579.

Dreibelbis, J. Z. 2008. Nesting ecology of Rio Grande wild turkeys in the Edwards Plateau of Texas. Thesis, Texas A&M University, College Station, USA.

Exum, J. H., J. A. McGlincy, D. W. Speake, J. L. Buckner, and F. M. Stanley. 1985. Evidence against dependence upon surface water by turkey hens and poults in southern Alabama. Proceedings of the National Wild Turkey Symposium 5:83–89.

Fleming, K. K., and W. F. Porter. 2001. A habitat suitability approach to evaluating landscape patterns for Eastern wild turkey. Proceedings of the National Wild Turkey Symposium 8:157–166.

Garcia, L. A., and M. Armbruster. 1997. A decision support system for evaluation of wildlife habitat. Ecological Modelling 102:287–300.

Glazener, W. C. 1967. Management of the Rio Grande wild turkey. Pages 453–492 *in* O. H. Hewitt, editor. The wild turkey and its management. The Wildlife Society, Washington, DC, USA.

Gore, H. G. 1973. Land-use practices and Rio Grande turkeys in Texas. Pages 253–263 *in* G. C. Sanderson and H. C. Schultz, editors. Wild turkey management: current problems and programs. University of Missouri Press, Columbia, USA.

Gross, J. T., A. R. Little, B. A. Collier, and M. J. Chamberlain. 2015. Space use, daily movements, and roosting behavior of male wild turkeys during spring in Louisiana and Texas. Journal of the Southeastern Association of Fish and Wildlife Agencies 2:229–234.

Hall, G. I., M. J. Butler, M. C. Wallace, W. B. Ballard, D. C. Ruthven III, R. L. Houchin, and R. D. Applegate. 2006. Rio Grande wild turkey home ranges in the southern Great Plains. Proceedings of the Southeastern Association of Fish and Wildlife Agencies 60:36–42.

Haucke, H. H. 1975. Winter roost characteristics of the Rio Grande wild turkey in South Texas. Proceedings of the National Wild Turkey Symposium 3:164–169.

Haucke, H. H., and E. D. Ables. 1972. Characteristics of wild turkey roosts on King Ranch. Texas Journal of Science 23:599–600.

He, K. S., B. A. Bradley, A. F. Cord, D. Rocchini, M. N. Tuanmu, S. Schmidtlein, W. Turner, M. Wegmann, and N. Pettorelli. 2015. Will remote sensing shape the next generation of species distribution models? Remote Sensing in Ecology and Conservation 1:4–18.

Healy, W. M. 1985. Turkey poult feeding activity, invertebrate abundance, and vegetation structure. Journal of Wildlife Management 49:466–472.

Hengel, D. A., and S. H. Anderson. 1990. Habitat use, diet, and reproduction of Merriam's turkeys near Laramie Peak, Wyoming. Final Report. Wyoming Cooperative Fish and Wildlife Research Unit, University of Wyoming, Laramie, USA.

Hennen, R. 1999. Reproductive ecology and survival of Rio Grande wild turkey hens in southcentral Kansas. Thesis, Texas Tech University, Lubbock, USA.

Hennen, R. S., and S. Lutz. 2001. Rio Grande wild turkey female survival in southcentral Kansas. Proceedings of the National Wild Turkey Symposium 8:117–122.

Hoffman, R. W. 1991. Spring movements, roosting activities, and home-range characteristics of male Merriam's wild turkey. Southwestern Naturalist 36:332–337.

Hoffman, R. W., H. G. Shaw, M. A. Rumble, B. F. Wakeling, C. M. Mollohan, S. D. Schemnitz, R. Engel-Wilson, and D. A. Hengel. 1993. Management guidelines for Merriam's wild turkeys. Colorado Division of Wildlife Report 18. Denver, USA.

Hohensee, S. D., and M. C. Wallace. 2001. Nesting and survival of Rio Grande turkeys in north central Texas. Proceedings of the National Wild Turkey Symposium 8:85–91.

Holzer, K. A. 1989. Ecology of the Merriam's wild turkey in the Helena National Forest. Thesis, Montana State University, Bozeman, USA.

Huffman, R. T. 2005. The effect of precipitation and cover on Rio Grande wild turkey nesting ecology in the Texas Panhandle and southwestern Kansas. Thesis, Texas Tech University, Lubbock, USA.

Hughes, T. W., and K. Lee. 2015. The role of recreational hunting in the recovery and conservation of the wild turkey (*Meleagris gallopavo* spp.) in North America. International Journal of Environmental Studies 72:797–809.

Hurst, G. A., and J. G. Dickson. 1992. Foods and feeding. Pages 66–83 *in* J. G. Dickson, editor. The wild turkey: biology and management. Stackpole Books, Mechanicsburg, Pennsylvania, USA.

Isabelle, J. L. 2010. Survival, home range size, habitat selection, and reproductive ecology of Eastern wild turkeys in East Texas. Thesis, Stephen F. Austin State University, Nacogdoches, Texas, USA.

Keegan, T. W., and J. A. Crawford. 2000. Seasonal habitat use and home ranges of Rio Grande turkeys in Oregon. Proceedings of the National Wild Turkey Symposium 8:109–116.

Kennamer, M. C. 2004. Merriam's wild turkey. National Wild Turkey Federation Bulletin no. 4. National Wild Turkey Federation, Edgefield, South Carolina, USA.

Kliskey, A. D., E. C. Lofroth, W. A. Thompson, S. Brown, and

H. Schreier. 1999. Simulating and evaluating alternative resource-use strategies using GIS-based habitat suitability indices. Landscape and Urban Planning 45:163–175.

Kothman, H. G. 1971. High rise roosts. EEI Bulletin 29:26–29.

Kothman, H. G., and G. W. Litton. 1975. Utilization of man-made roosts by turkey in West Texas. Proceedings of the National Wild Turkey Symposium 3:159–163.

Krausman, P. R., and M. L. Morrison. 2016. Another plea for standard terminology. Journal of Wildlife Management 80:1143–1144.

Lazarus, J. E., and W. F. Porter. 1985. Nest habitat selection by wild turkeys in Minnesota. Proceedings of the National Wild Turkey Symposium 5:67–81.

Lehman, C. P., L. D. Flake, and D. J. Thompson. 2002. Comparison of microhabitat conditions at nest sites between Eastern (*Meleagris gallopavo silvestris*) and Rio Grande wild turkey (*M. g. intermedia*) in northeastern South Dakota. American Midland Naturalist 149:192–200.

Lehman, C. P., M. A. Rumble, L. D. Flake, and D. J. Thompson. 2008. Merriam's turkey nest survival and factors affecting nest predation by mammals. Journal of Wildlife Management 72:1765–1774.

Lehman, C. P., M. A. Rumble, M. A. Battaglia, T. R. Mills, and L. A. Asherin. 2016. Influence of mountain pine beetle epidemic on winter habitat conditions for Merriam's turkeys: management implications for current and future condition. Proceedings of the National Wild Turkey Symposium 11:79–87.

Lehmann, V. W. 1957. Conservation and management of game. Pages 761–766 (appendix) *in* Tom Lea, "The King Ranch," volume 2. Little, Brown, Boston, Massachusetts, USA.

Little, A. R., M. J. Chamberlain, L. M. Conner, and R. J. Warren. 2016a. Habitat selection of wild turkeys in burned longleaf pine savannas. Journal of Wildlife Management 80:1280–1289.

Little, A. R., N. P. Nibbelink, M. J. Chamberlain, L. M. Conner, and R. J. Warren. 2016b. Eastern wild turkey nest site selection in two frequently burned pine savannas. Ecological Processes 5:1–10.

Litton, G. W. 1977. Food habits of the Rio Grande wild turkey in the Permian Basin of Texas. Texas Parks and Wildlife Department Report 18. Texas Parks and Wildlife Department, Austin, USA.

Litton, G. W., and F. Harwell. 1995. Rio Grande turkey habitat management. Texas Parks and Wildlife, Federal Aid Pittman-Robertson Project W-129-M. Texas Parks and Wildlife Department, Austin, USA.

Lutz, R. S., and J. A. Crawford. 1987. Reproductive success and nesting habitat of Merriam's wild turkeys in Oregon. Journal of Wildlife Management 51:783–787.

Lutz, R. S., and J. A. Crawford. 1989. Habitat use and selection and home ranges of Merriam's wild turkey in Oregon. Great Basin Naturalist 49:252–258.

Mackey, D. L., and R. J. Jonas. 1982. Seasonal habitat use and food habits of Merriam's turkeys in southcentral Washington. Proceedings of the Western Wild Turkey Workshop 1:99–110.

Mazerolle, M. J., and M. A. Villard. 1999. Patch characteristics and landscape context as predictors of species presence and abundance: a review. Ecoscience 6:117–124.

McRoberts, J. T., M. C. Wallace, and S. W. Eaton. 2014. Wild turkey (*Meleagris gallopavo*). Account 22 *in* A. Poole, editor. The birds of North America online. Cornell Laboratory of Ornithology, Ithaca, New York, USA. http://bna.birds.cornell.edu/bna/species/022.

Miller, C. J. 2002. Use of satellite imagery to model brood-rearing habitat for Rio Grande wild turkey populations occurring in the western Cross Timbers region of Texas. Thesis, University of North Texas, Denton, USA.

Miller, D. A., G. A. Hurst, and B. D. Leopold. 1999. Habitat use of Eastern wild turkey in central Mississippi. Journal of Wildlife Management 63:210–222.

Miller, D. A., B. D. Leopold, G. A. Hurst, and P. D. Gerard. 2000. Habitat selection models for Eastern wild turkey in central Mississippi. Journal of Wildlife Management 64:765–776.

Miller, M. S. 1993. Rio Grande wild turkey hen survival and habitat selection in south central Kansas. Thesis, Texas Tech University, Lubbock, USA.

Mollohan, C. M., D. R. Patton, and B. F. Wakeling. 1995. Habitat selection and use by Merriam's turkey in north-central Arizona: a final report. Arizona Game and Fish Department, Phoenix, USA.

Palmer, W. E., and G. A. Hurst. 1996. Drainage systems as minimum habitat management units for wild turkey hens. Proceedings of the National Wild Turkey Symposium 7:97–104.

Perotto-Baldivieso, H. L., E. Meléndez-Ackerman, M. A. García, P. Leimgruber, S. M. Cooper, A. Martínez, P. Calle, et al. 2009. Spatial distribution, connectivity, and the influence of scale: habitat availability for the endangered Mona Island rock iguana. Biodiversity and Conservation 18:905–917.

Perotto-Baldivieso, H. L., X. Ben Wu, M. J. Peterson, F. E. Smeins, N. J. Silvy, and T. Wayne Schwertner. 2011. Flooding-induced landscape changes along dendritic stream networks and implications for wildlife habitat. Landscape and Urban Planning 99:115–122.

Perotto-Baldiviezo, H. L. 2005. GIS-based multiple scale study of Rio Grande wild turkey habitat in the Edwards Plateau of Texas. Dissertation, Texas A&M University, College Station, USA.

Petersen, L. E., and A. H. Richardson. 1973. Merriam's wild turkey in the Black Hills of South Dakota. Pages 3–9 *in* C. G. Sanderson and H. C. Schultz, editors. Wild turkey management: current problems and programs. University of Missouri Press, Columbia, USA.

Porter, W. F. 1992. Habitat requirements. Pages 202–213 *in* J. G. Dickson, editor. The wild turkey: biology and management. Stackpole Books, Mechanicsburg, Pennsylvania, USA.

Quinton, D. A., A. K. Montei, and J. T. Flinders. 1980. Brush control and Rio Grande turkeys in north central Texas. Journal of Range Management 33:95–99.

Ramsey, R. R. 1958. Turkeys for tomorrow. Texas Game and Fish Magazine 16:16–17. Texas Parks and Wildlife Department, Austin, USA.

Randel, C. J., III. 2003. Influences of vegetation characteristics and invertebrate abundance on Rio Grande wild turkey populations, Edwards Plateau, Texas. Thesis, Texas A&M University, College Station, USA.

Reyes-Ramirez, E., M. C. Clayton, C. W. Lawson, S. M. Burns, R. Guarneros-Altimirano, S. J. DeMaso, W. P. Kuvlesky Jr., D. G. Hewitt, J. A. Ortega-Santos, and T. A. Campbell. 2012. Home ranges of female Rio Grande turkeys (*Meleagris gallopavo intermedia*) in southern Texas. Southwestern Naturalist 52:198–201.

Rumble, M. A. 1992. Roosting habitat of Merriam's turkeys in the Black Hills, South Dakota. Journal of Wildlife Management 56:750–759.

Rumble, M. A., and S. H. Anderson 1995. A test of the habitat suitability model for Merriam's wild turkeys. Proceedings of the National Wild Turkey Symposium 7:165–173.

Rumble, M. A., and S. H. Anderson. 1996. Feeding ecology of Merriam's turkeys (*Meleagris gallopavo merriami*) in the Black Hills, South Dakota. American Midland Naturalist 136:157–171.

Schaap, B. F., N. J. Silvy, M. J. Peterson, R. Aguirre, and H. L. Perotto-Baldivieso. 2005. Spatial distribution of female Rio Grande wild turkeys during the reproductive season. Proceedings of the National Wild Turkey Symposium 9:231–235.

Schamberger, M., A. H. Farmer, and J. W. Terrell. 1982. Habitat suitability index models: introduction. FWS/OBS-82/10. US Fish and Wildlife Service, Biological Services Program, Fort Collins, Colorado, USA.

Schamberger, M., and L. J. O'Neill. 1986. Concepts and constraints of habitat model testing. Pages 5–10 *in* J. Verner, M. L. Morrison, and C. J. Ralph, editors. Wildlife 2000: modeling habitat relationships of terrestrial vertebrates. University of Wisconsin Press, Madison, USA.

Schemnitz, S. D., D. L. Goerndt, and K. H. Jones. 1985. Habitat needs and management of Merriam's wild turkey in southcentral New Mexico. Proceedings of the National Wild Turkey Symposium 5:199–231.

Scott, V. E., and E. L. Boeker. 1975. Ecology of Merriam's wild turkey on the Fort Apache Indian Reservation. Proceedings of the National Wild Turkey Symposium 3:141–158.

Shaw, H. G., and C. Mollohan. 1992. Merriam's turkey. Pages 6–17 *in* J. G. Dickson, editor. The wild turkey: biology and management. Stackpole Books, Mechanicsburg, Pennsylvania, USA.

Schmutz, J. A., C. E. Braun, and W. F. Andelt. 1989. Nest habitat use of Rio Grande wild turkeys. Wilson Bulletin 101:591–598.

Schorger, A. W. 1966. The wild turkey: its history and domestication. University of Oklahoma Press, Norman, USA.

Schroeder, R. L. 1985. Habitat suitability index models: Eastern wild turkey. Biological Report 82 (10.106). US Fish and Wildlife Service, Washington, DC, USA.

Spears, B. L., M. C. Wallace, W. B. Ballard, R. S. Phillips, D. P. Holdstock, J. H. Brunjes, R. Applegate, M. S. Miller, and P. S. Gipson. 2007. Habitat use and survival of preflight wild turkey broods. Journal of Wildlife Management 71:69–81.

Streich, M. M., A. R. Little, M. J. Chamberlain, L. M. Conner, and R. J. Warren. 2015. Habitat characteristics of Eastern wild turkey nest and ground-roost sites in 2 longleaf pine forests. Journal of the Southeastern Association of Fish and Wildlife Agencies 2:164–170.

Taylor, W. P. 1943. The wild turkey in Texas. Proceedings and Transactions of the Texas Academy of Sciences 27:231–232.

Texas A&M Forest Service. 2014. Texas ecoregions. http://texastreeid.tamu.edu/content/texasEcoRegions/.

Texas Parks and Wildlife Department. 2016. Texas ecoregions. https://tpwd.texas.gov/education/hunter-education/online-course/wildlife-conservation/texas-ecoregions.

Thogmartin, W. E. 1999. Landscape attributes and nest-site selection in wild turkeys. Auk 116:912–923.

Thogmartin, W. E. 2001. Home-range size and habitat selection of female wild turkeys (*Meleagris gallopavo*) in Arkansas. American Midland Naturalist 145:247–260.

Thogmartin, W. E., and B. A. Schaeffer. 2000. Landscape attributes associated with mortality events of wild turkeys in Arkansas. Wildlife Society Bulletin 28:865–874.

Thomas, J. W., C. Van Hoozer, and R. G. Marburger. 1966. Wintering concentrations and seasonal shifts in range in the Rio Grande turkey. Journal of Wildlife Management 30:34–49.

Thompson, W. L. 1993. Ecology of Merriam's turkeys in relation to burned and logged areas in southeastern Montana. Dissertation, Montana State University, Bozeman, USA.

Turner, M. G., R. H. Gardner, and R. V. O'Neill. 2001. Landscape ecology in theory and practice. Springer, New York, New York, USA.

Van Auken, O. W. 1988. Woody vegetation of the southeastern escarpment and plateau. Pages 43–56 *in* B. B. Amos and F. R. Ghelbach, editors. Edwards Plateau vegetation. Baylor University Press, Waco, Texas, USA.

Wakeling, B. F., and T. D. Rogers. 1995. Winter habitat relationships of Merriam's turkeys along the Mogollon Rim, Arizona. Arizona Game and Fish Department Report 16. Arizona Game and Fish Department, Phoenix, USA.

Walker, E. A. 1941. The wild turkey and its management in the Edwards Plateau. Quarterly Progress Report, October–December. Texas Game, Fish and Oyster Commission, Austin, USA.

Walker, E. A. 1949. A study of factors influencing wild turkey populations in the central mineral region of Texas. Technical Report. Texas Game, Fish and Oyster Commission, Austin, USA.

Walker, E. A. 1950. A study of factors influencing wild turkey populations in the live oak–shin oak divide area of the Edwards Plateau. Technical Report. Texas Game, Fish and Oyster Commission, Austin, USA.

Walker, E. A. 1951. Land use and wild turkeys. Texas Game and Fish Magazine 9:12–16.

Wheatley, M. 2010. Domains of scale in forest-landscape metrics: Implications for species-habitat modeling. Acta Oecologica 36:259–267.

Wigal, D. D. 1970. Status of the introduced Rio Grande turkey in northeastern Iowa. Pages 35–43 *in* G. C. Sanderson and H. C. Schultz, editors. Wild turkey management: current problems and programs. University of Missouri Press, Columbia, USA.

Wigley, T. B., J. M. Sweeney, M. E. Garner, and M. A. Melchiors. 1986. Wild turkey home ranges in the Ouachita Mountains. Journal of Wildlife Management 50:540–544.

Williamson, J. F., and G. T. Koeln. 1980. A computerized wild turkey habitat evaluation system. Proceedings of the National Wild Turkey Symposium 4:233–239.

Yeldell, N. A., B. S. Cohen, A. R. Little, B. A. Collier, and M. J. Chamberlain. 2017. Nest site selection and nest survival of Eastern wild turkeys in a pyric landscape. Journal of Wildlife Management 81:1073–1083.

8

Habitat Management

We do not inherit land from our ancestors, we borrow it from our children.

—CHIEF SEATTLE

Wild turkeys can be found in every state of the United States except Alaska (Natural Resources Conservation Service 1999); therefore, habitat management for the wild turkey must be tailored to fit the needs of specific ecological sites. The main objective of any habitat management program is to fulfill the needs of wildlife species. As indicated in chapter 7, any wild animal requires water, food, and appropriate seasonal cover to fulfill its annual needs. Habitat management ensures that these three essential components are provided in sufficient quantity to maintain a self-sustaining wildlife population. Therefore, if wild turkeys are a management priority, it is the responsibility of the wildlife manager to provide sufficient food, water, and seasonal cover to fulfill the needs of the wild turkey population in that location. Knowing the habitat requirements of wild turkeys is of course important. However, some habitat components have strong interactions with other habitat characteristics such as roost sites and water availability, which often determine the way animals utilize the habitat and thus affect habitat selection and use. Therefore, before effective wild turkey habitat management can be implemented, the first priority must be assessing the habitat to determine what improvements, if any, are needed and then determining how to monitor these improvements.

Habitat Assessment and Monitoring

Baseline information on soils, vegetation communities, and water is imperative before a habitat management program can be developed. Identification of limiting factors for the target species is important in making decisions. It is possible to develop a long list of habitat management practices managers may use to improve habitat for wild turkeys, but it is the manager's responsibility to decide which practices should be applied to optimize habitat conservation, the biological performance of the species, and economic returns. There is no point in improving food availability when roost sites or water availability is a primary limiting factor. Recognizing required habitat components that are present and sufficient, as well as those that are limiting or absent, is essential before initiating habitat management. Habitat requirements for wild turkeys are discussed in chapter 7. Habitat management for wild turkeys involves proper cattle grazing and the use of prescribed fire, mechanical practices, and herbicides to maintain or create openings to promote herbaceous plant communities with vegetation and insects from which turkeys may obtain nutrients and water. Each of these habitat management practices will be discussed in this chapter.

Water

In arid environments, water developments were assumed for many years to benefit both game and nongame species because water scarcity was thought to be a primary limiting factor for wildlife populations (Rosenstock et al. 1999). However, the critical role of water has been questioned by some wildlife biologists (Sanchez and Haderlie 1990). It has been suggested that water developments may not be as beneficial for wildlife as expected and that some adverse impacts may occur, such as increased predation risk, increased competition, and disease transmission risk (Broyles 1995, Brown 1998, Rosenstock et al. 1999). However, a recent literature review on the subject found little evidence that water developments negatively impact wildlife and instead suggests that a wide array of wildlife species benefit from water developments (Krausman et al. 2006). The issue of whether water developments benefit wild turkeys in Texas is probably irrelevant because most water developments are established for livestock and recreation, not wildlife. Therefore, sources of free water that turkeys utilize are most likely stock tanks provided for cattle, reservoirs provided for public recreation, and rivers and creeks. Wild turkeys benefit from these sources of free water even though they were not provided with wild turkeys in mind.

As indicated in chapter 7, turkeys can obtain water in three ways: (1) metabolic water from digested food; (2) preformed water, which is the liquid contained in foods such as succulent leaves or fruits; and (3) free water, which is obtained from sources such as creeks, ponds, or water troughs (Cathey et al. 2007a). All three subspecies of wild turkeys in Texas obtain a substantial portion of their daily water requirements from preformed sources or the food they eat. Cathey et al. (2007a) indicated that turkey females and poults consuming insects and succulent plants may obtain adequate water from the foods they consume. Maintaining herbaceous habitat conditions that provide diverse plant foods also provides good invertebrate habitat, thereby ensuring that wild turkeys meet a significant portion of their water requirements. Consequently, herbaceous openings in forests or brushlands are critical habitats for wild turkeys. Creating or maintaining openings is therefore an important aspect of wild turkey management. This can be accomplished via grazing, prescribed fire, or mechanical or herbicide treatments.

Free water needs of wild turkeys depend on the areas they occupy. For instance, the free water requirements of Eastern wild turkeys are unclear (Healy 1981). In moist environments like hardwood forests, free water may not be important, but in drier environments such as hickory (*Carya* spp.) forests, free water scarcity and foods lacking moisture may reduce habitat quality (Wunz and Pack 1992). For Eastern wild turkeys in oak-pine range where water is generally available, no relationship has been documented between water availability and the distribution of turkey populations (Hurst and Dickson 1992). Nevertheless, rainfall is more abundant in East Texas than in the rangelands of the western half of the state, and there are many stock tanks, ponds, reservoirs, creeks, and rivers. In this context, if Eastern wild turkeys in East Texas require free water, sources are plentiful.

The western half of Texas is drier than East Texas, so it is conceivable that Rio Grande and Merriam's wild turkeys may occasionally require free water, especially during droughts. Collier et al. (2017) reported that during a drought, Rio Grande wild turkeys selected areas close to water. Sources of free water are usually found in riparian habitats in Rio Grande wild turkey range, but it is unclear whether turkeys use these habitats because they need free water or because tall trees are available there for roosting (Beasom and Wilson 1992). Nevertheless, Beasom and Wilson (1992) indicated that water development for livestock probably has a positive influence on Rio Grande wild turkeys. For example, Lehmann (1957) noted that prior to water development on the King Ranch, wild turkeys were rarely observed, but about 10 years after water sources were developed for cattle in 1920, an increase in wild turkey numbers was evident. Additionally, Litton and Harwell (1995) indicated that surface water availability is a characteristic of good turkey range, and the increase in human-made water sources is associated with the expansion of Rio Grande wild turkey distribution in Texas. Nesting females also apparently regard surface water as important; Litton and Harwell (1995) reported that nests are often found within 1,609 m (1 mi) of surface water. Moreover, in South Texas, Currie (2011) reported that in both a dry and a wet year, turkey nests were found less than 1,700 m (about 1 mi) from a permanent water source. Permanent water sources should be spaced no farther than 3.218 km (2 mi) apart, and preferably closer than that if Rio Grande wild turkeys are a management consideration (Litton and Harwell 1995).

For Merriam's wild turkeys in Arizona, permanent water sources seem to be a vital habitat component, because increases in turkey populations have been associated with the construction of water developments (Shaw and Mollohan 1992, Hoffman et al. 1993). Additionally, for Merriam's wild turkeys a

Figure 8.1. Ground level waterer for turkeys with proper escape cover in the background (photo by Dave Hewitt).

water source should be available every 259 ha (640 ac, or 1 mi^2) to ensure that habitat use is equitably distributed (Hoffman et al. 1993, Rosenstock et al. 1999). In habitats occupied by Merriam's wild turkeys, water should be available approximately every 1.5 km (0.914 mi) (Rutherford and Snyder 1983, Hoffman et al. 1993) to 2.6 km (1.615 mi) (Krausman et al. 2006).

A number of recommendations are available relative to the distribution and design of wildlife watering systems for wild turkeys. According to Suarez (2002), sources of water should be spaced no farther than 3 km (1.864 mi) apart on areas managed for wild turkeys, and preferably closer. Beasom and Wilson (1992) recommended that water be provided at ground level where it is easily accessible, especially to young poults that cannot get out if they fall into something like a water trough that requires perching on an edge to obtain water. They also recommend that these ground-level waterers be created by extending a pipe from a windmill 10–20 m (30–50 ft) and locating the water close to escape cover. Furthermore, these waterers should be fenced to exclude livestock, which will trample screening and escape cover. They indicate that barbed wire rather than net wire should be used to allow birds to go through or under fences. Two to three strands of barbed wire with the bottom strand 46 cm (18 in) above the ground will be sufficient. Ranches with rotational grazing systems should have water sources in all pastures, and turkey waterers should be located about 0.4 km (0.25 mi) from the central water source because turkeys avoid water at the center of these grazing systems (Prasad and Guthery 1986). Where subsurface water is limited, precluding the use of windmills, water catchments such as "gallinaceous guzzlers," which capture and store precipitation (fig. 8.1) and make water available to wildlife, can provide water for wild turkeys (Beasom and Wilson 1992).

Grazing

In addition to ensuring that the water requirements of wild turkeys are met, the vegetation communities on a property must also be managed properly to ensure that the food and structural cover requirements for wild turkeys are met. Rangelands and forests can be degraded with excessive use by domestic and wild herbivores. Overgrazing used to be common in many countries, including the United States and Mexico. The negative effects of overgrazing on wild turkeys have been discussed by Blakey (1944). Cattle grazing seems to be more important for Rio Grande and Merriam's wild turkeys than for Eastern wild turkeys because cattle grazing is very common on the rangelands occupied by the Rio Grande and Merriam's subspecies. However, cattle grazing also occurs in East Texas, so it can impact Eastern wild turkeys as well, but not to the same extent as it does Rio Grande and Merriam's wild turkeys. Therefore, for all three subspecies, nesting and brooding habitat are the most negatively affected by overgrazing. Other detrimental impacts associated with cattle grazing include nest trampling, nest abandonment, increased nest predation, reduced food availability, and modified movement patterns (Beasom and Wilson 1992).

Cattle grazing and nesting and brooding cover

Throughout the range of the North American wild turkey, one factor that does not change is that wild turkeys nest on the ground. Therefore, nest sites occur where there is adequate horizontal and lateral screening cover that consists of well-developed herbaceous or woody vegetation, logging slash, or rocks 0.5–1 m (3 ft) tall (Porter 1992, Beasom and Wilson 1992, Wakeling and Shaw 1994, Alldredge et al. 2014). Reduced nesting cover height or reduced cover as a result of overgrazing has a detrimental impact on wild turkey populations (fig. 8.2). Livestock grazing can also have an impact on brooding habitat because wild turkey broods, particularly young broods, rely on herbaceous habitats for screening cover and foraging (Beasom and Wilson 1992, Hoffman et al. 1993, Mollohan et al. 1995, Alldredge et al. 2014). For Rio Grande wild turkeys, which occupy rangeland habitats instead of forests, maintaining sufficient herbaceous cover through proper grazing is an important management consideration (fig. 8.3). Although Eastern and Merriam's wild turkeys often nest in the understories of forests, nests and important brooding habitat also occur in forest glades or other herbaceous openings that are grazed by livestock. Therefore, proper grazing management needs to be considered for Eastern and Merriam's wild turkeys as well (Hoffman et al. 1993, Mollohan et al. 1995, Alldredge et al. 2014).

Very little research has been done on the impacts of grazing management on wild turkeys in East Texas,

Figure 8.2. Overgrazed rangeland in South Texas (photo by J. Alfonso Ortega-S.).

Figure 8.3. Good Rio Grande wild turkey nesting and brooding habitat in South Texas as a result of proper grazing management (photo by Landon Fritz).

probably because livestock production is not viewed as a traditional wild turkey management technique in the same way as timber harvesting, prescribed burning, and farming are. The information available indicates that moderate grazing of forests or woodlands does not appear to be detrimental to turkeys (Dickson et al. 1978). If cattle are part of a land management plan and wild turkeys are also a management consideration, sufficient nesting and brooding cover needs to be maintained during spring and summer months. Many pastures in East Texas today are composed of different varieties of introduced or exotic grasses, such as Bermuda grass and Bahia grass (*Paspalum notatum*), and Eastern wild turkeys often readily use these tame pastures for nesting and brood-rearing purposes, particularly where pastures of native grass species are scarce. Introduced or tame pastures as well as pastures composed of native vegetation should be maintained at a minimum height of 50 cm (20 in), and cattle grazing management should be flexible to maintain this height (Alldredge et al. 2014). Alldredge et al. (2014) also indicated that cattle producers should be flexible relative to cattle stocking rates, adjusting them as necessary depending on land conditions, particularly during droughts, and that rotational grazing systems are one way to maintain herbaceous vegetation at the ideal height for wild turkeys. Furthermore, they recommended that cattle producers consider suspending grazing in nesting and brooding habitats during nesting and brooding seasons. They also stated that an ideal situation for wild turkeys includes grazing cattle in nesting and brooding habitats during late summer and then resting pastures until the following August.

Rio Grande wild turkeys must adapt to livestock grazing throughout their range in Texas because livestock grazing is probably the most common land use on Texas rangelands. Therefore, just as for Eastern wild turkeys, maintaining sufficient herbaceous cover on nesting and brooding habitats is critical for Rio Grande wild turkey production. This is more of a challenge for Rio Grande wild turkeys because the rangelands they occupy are more arid than the areas of East Texas, and soils are typically not as productive. In South Texas, independent of herbaceous biomass availability, over 93.5% of the nests of Rio Grande wild turkeys were found in pastures with no cattle grazing (Currie 2011). Therefore, selection of nest sites by Rio Grande wild turkeys appears to be inversely related to grazing pressure (Beasom and Wilson 1992). Additionally, Hall et al. (2007) reported that nesting females did not use areas grazed by cattle. Moreover, Ransom et al. (1987), in a study conducted at the Welder Wildlife Refuge in South Texas, reported that all the turkey nests found were either in areas with no cattle grazing or in pastures with continuous grazing and light stocking rates. Merrill (1975) found that a four-pasture deferred rotation grazing system in South Texas benefited wild turkeys because adequate nesting cover was maintained. Therefore, on lands where Rio Grande wild turkeys are a management priority, if grazing occurs it should be conducted under light stocking rates. Moreover, important nesting and brooding habitats should be protected if possible by removing cattle from these areas during the fall to ensure that sufficient nesting and brooding cover is available for turkeys during the next spring and early summer.

However, in South Texas during wet years, herbaceous cover may become too tall and dense for nesting females. Merrill (1975) reported that a year after the construction of a grazing exclosure in an area where turkeys apparently nested, nest density was 1 nest/2.8 ha (1 nest/7 ac). Turkey nests were not found in the grazing exclosure five years after it was constructed. Clearly, herbaceous vegetation became too dense for nesting females. Therefore, if wild turkeys are an important consideration relative to grazing management, managers need to closely monitor the forage standing crop of herbaceous vegetation in order to avoid both excessive removal of the forage standing crop and excessive accumulation of herbaceous vegetation.

Merriam's wild turkeys in south-central New Mexico showed no preference for grazed or ungrazed pastures under rotational grazing (Jones 1981). However, Mollohan et al. (1995) and Hoffman et al. (1993) indicated that grazing on Merriam's wild turkey range in Arizona and Colorado, respectively, should not exceed moderate levels, and that rest-rotation grazing systems are better for managing herbaceous cover than continuous grazing. In addition, both stated that grazing should be suspended in turkey habitat until midsummer to protect nesting and brooding cover as well as to provide adequate food and foraging cover. Furthermore, when nesting habitat is grazed, utilization of herbaceous cover should not exceed 50% to ensure that sufficient nesting cover remains (Hoffman et al. 1993). The seed heads of grasses are important winter foods for Merriam's wild turkeys, so grazing should be monitored on winter range to ensure that grass seeds remain to supply this important food (Mollohan et al. 1995).

Cattle grazing and nest depredation and trampling

Excessive cattle grazing can have a negative impact on nest losses to predators because the reduction of herbaceous cover can increase nest exposure to predators. Almost all research on wild turkey nest destruction relative to livestock grazing has been conducted in areas occupied by Rio Grande wild turkeys. Nevertheless, it is reasonable to presume that similar results would occur for Eastern and Merriam's wild turkey nests located in herbaceous vegetation. In South Texas, artificial turkey nest depredation exceeded 90% and was higher on pastures under continuous stocking than on pastures with deferred rotation and high-intensity low-frequency grazing systems (Baker 1978). However, Bareiss et al. (1986) reported no effect of cattle grazing (short-duration grazing and continuous stocking) on artificial nest losses in South Texas. These results agree with the findings of the Texas Hill Country study by Koerth et al. (1983), which reported that trampling losses of simulated turkey nests with short-duration grazing systems (5.3 ha/steer [13 ac/steer]) were no different from those on a continuously grazed pasture (8 ha/steer [20 ac/steer]). Nest losses can occur at very high stocking rates, although Koerth et al. found that only one nest was lost to trampling on a pasture with the highest stocking density (0.4 ha/animal unit [1 ac/animal unit]), and no trampling losses occurred on another pasture with a high stocking density (0.6 ha/animal unit [1.5 ac/animal unit]). Therefore, cattle trampling losses may not be an issue unless stocking density is higher than 0.4 ha per animal unit (Bareiss et al. 1986).

Brush Management

Brush is an important component of wild turkey habitat. Since wild turkeys prefer to use their legs instead of their wings to escape threats, and when they do fly, they typically do not fly long distances, brush represents important escape cover. Woody vegetation also provides roost sites, and mast is an important food for all three wild turkey subspecies. However, too much brush can be a problem for wild turkeys since lack of open areas usually indicates limited herbaceous vegetation for nesting and brooding. The brush-to-opening ratio requirements preferred by wild turkeys are well documented in the scientific literature. It is important to remember that turkeys may perform well under a variety of woody vegetation/opening combinations. However, generally 10% to 25% of a landscape should be clearings for Eastern wild turkeys (Wunz and Pack 1992) and Merriam's wild turkeys (Hoffman et al. 1993), whereas about 50% of a landscape should be clearings for Rio Grande wild turkeys (Beasom and Wilson 1992). The size of openings or clearings also matters relative to wild turkeys. Clearings for Rio Grande wild turkeys should be less than 800 m (875 yd) wide (Beasom and Wilson 1992) (fig. 8.4). Brush clearing is therefore an important management technique to adjust brush-to-opening ratios on a landscape to provide appropriate habitat conditions for wild turkeys, particularly on rangelands. However, brush management operations must be carefully planned so that existing vegetation communities important to wild turkeys are not damaged. Therefore, before such operations are initiated on a property, a plan should be developed.

The first step in developing a brush management plan is to determine which areas of the landscape must remain undisturbed. For example, clearing riparian areas along rivers and creeks should be avoided because these vegetation communities not only provide wild turkeys with important roost sites and escape cover but are valuable movement corridors as well (Fulbright and Ortega-S. 2013). Riparian habitats also accumulate moisture, which helps maintain herbaceous and woody plant communities, especially during drought. In addition to riparian areas, there may be other portions of pastures targeted for management that must remain undisturbed because they support a natural diversity of mast-

Figure 8.4. Appropriately distributed clearings for Rio Grande wild turkeys (photo by J. Alfonso Ortega-S.).

producing plants that provide important wild turkey foods. Usually, when brush management treatments are applied to areas with high plant diversity, the plant community changes and becomes less diverse. In South Texas, when brush treatments are applied to plant communities with a high diversity of brush vegetation, these areas tend to become dominated by mesquite and huisache a few years after initial treatment, which reduces the value for wildlife. After determining which areas will be left undisturbed, it is important to identify which areas will respond best to brush treatment. There may be some areas of poor soils where the response to a treatment will be limited. For example, plant communities of cenizo and guajillo that grow on shallow soils around Benavides and Laredo, Texas, may remain unchanged despite the application of a brush management treatment. In these situations, there would be little reason to devote resources to a plant community that would not improve wildlife habitat.

Different practices may be used in brush management programs, from mechanical treatments, to prescribed fire, to herbicide applications that target specific plant species. One of the most economical and ecologically friendly practices is prescribed fire, which when properly conducted is an excellent tool to create or maintain openings in brush-dominated plant communities.

Prescribed burning

Wild turkeys can benefit from prescribed burning because fire applied in the appropriate manner often results in increased production of seed-producing grasses and forbs as well as an increase in invertebrates (Cathey et al. 2007b, Alldredge et al. 2014). The timing of burns is very important, as it affects the type of vegetation that will grow afterward. For example, in South Texas, late fall and winter burns encourage the germination of forbs and cool-season grasses, while early spring burns will stimulate the growth of warm-season grasses.

Two types of fires can be conducted for vegetation management: controlled burns and prescribed burns. Controlled burns use constructed or natural fire lines to burn a determined area and maintain the fire within this area. Prescribed burns are conducted under a predetermined season, environmental conditions, and fuel loads to accomplish specific objectives. The fire prescription is developed to create a fire intensity that generates the desired effect on the plant community (Fulbright and Ortega-S. 2013). Environmental factors including ambient temperature, fine fuel load, moisture content of fine fuels, relative humidity, soil moisture, and wind speed determine fire intensity (White and Hanselka 1989). It is important to become familiar with the regulations and safety procedures specific to controlled or prescribed burning in a specific state because nearly all states have laws dictating liability and criminality associated with burning (Yoder et al. 2003). Fulbright and Ortega-S. (2013) provide the following objectives for prescribed burning:

- Suppressing woody vegetation
- Increasing the life of other mechanical or chemical treatments
- Clearing openings of woody debris after mechanical or chemical treatments
- Increasing patchiness of landscapes
- Promoting forb cover and production
- Reducing excessive mulch
- Stimulating regrowth of herbaceous vegetation

The first step in planning a prescribed burn is to outline the objectives of the burn and develop an appropriate prescription to achieve those objectives. Objectives will depend on the subspecies of turkey being managed and the plant communities targeted for management. In the eastern half of the state, turkeys prefer to nest in areas that receive prescribed burns on a three-year cycle (Alldredge et al. 2014). The resprouting woody vegetation along with the flush of grasses and forbs stimulated by the fire provides ideal nesting cover. Since most areas in the eastern half of Texas can be burned on a three-year rotation, if not more frequently, this system of fire and regrowth coincides very well with turkey management (fig. 8.5). In fact, turkeys prefer to live, nest, and raise broods in woods managed on a three-year fire rotation. In the Coastal Plains and Piedmont regions of the southeastern United States, prescribed burning to manage habitat for Eastern wild turkeys is usually conducted in January and February, and no later than March 15. Moreover, fires exclude oak and hardwood transition areas between pine upland and gum swamps. Pine forest or mixes of longleaf, shortleaf, loblolly, and slash pine have evolved with fire, so periodic fires using well-distributed 0.40–2 ha (1–5 ac) spot burns that consume one-third to one-half of a burn management unit each year will maintain the open understory needed for turkeys. Prescribed burns may be repeated every two to three years, although some sites may require annual burns (Yarrow 2009a). In longleaf pine savannas, fire is the primary practice used to increase understory richness, diversity, and evenness (Brockway and Lewis 1997). Mature pines, mixed pines and hardwoods, hardwoods, young pines, and shrub-scrub stands are selected by Eastern wild turkeys within longleaf pine–dominated landscapes, and in these landscapes fire cannot occur more frequently than a minimum of every three years (Little et al. 2014).

Prescribed burning on rangelands inhabited by wild turkeys should be conducted during fall and winter to avoid disturbing nesting females, destroying nests, and killing young broods that concentrate activities in grasslands and savannas (Cathey et al. 2007a). Furthermore, burning during fall and winter promotes forb growth, as these are usually the first plants to emerge during the end of winter and beginning of spring (fig. 8.6). Summer and winter fires may be used to manage encroachment of cedar, juniper, and other woody species. Prescribed fire may also be used to remove understory brush in roosting areas to create openings for foraging and brood rearing (Cathey et al. 2007b). Rio Grande wild turkeys inhabit more semiarid and arid regions of the state than the Eastern subspecies. For this reason, it is often difficult to plan prescribed fires on a set rotational schedule. In the western extremes of the Rio Grande wild turkey's range in Texas, consider utilizing prescribed fire opportunistically as fuel loads and weather dictate.

Prescribed fire can also be a useful habitat management tool for Merriam's wild turkeys. Thompson

Figure 8.5. Prescribed burn conducted to improve Rio Grande wild turkey habitat in South Texas (photo by J. Alfonso Ortega-S.).

Figure 8.6. Forb response to a winter prescribed burn in South Texas (photo by J. Alfonso Ortega-S.).

(1993) indicated that, similar to prescribed fire for Eastern wild turkeys, burning in Montana forests inhabited by Merriam's wild turkeys should be conducted on a three-year cycle. He stated that burned areas may not have much utility for turkeys during the first two years after a fire but should be useful in subsequent years because of the flush of herbaceous growth that serves as nesting and brooding habitat and also provides food. Knopp (1959) reported that wildfires can be detrimental to Merriam's wild turkeys because females have been found dead on nests where wildfires have occurred. However, he also indicated that in Arizona, Merriam's wild turkey populations increased in areas of dense fir forest because openings were created by fires, resulting in herbaceous plant communities that were previously absent.

When utilizing prescribed fire to manage wild turkey habitat, it is important to understand how fire intensity affects the plant community. Scifres (1980) indicated that a minimum of 2,802 kg/ha (2,499 lb/ac) of fine fuel properly distributed would fulfill most prescribed burning objectives in South Texas at a wind speed of 8 to 24 km/hour (5–15 mi/hour). Intense, hot fires occur with relative humidity between 25% and 45% (White and Hanselka 1989), and burn uniformity is lower when relative humidity is higher than 60% (Wright and Bailey 1982). Intense prescribed fires can top-kill nearly all woody plants, reducing canopy cover of brush species. Nonsprouting species such as Ashe juniper (*Juniperus ashei*) can be killed with prescribed fire, but mortality of sprouting plants is usually less than 10–15% (Owens et al. 2002). Some mast-producing plant species like tasajillo and desert yaupon (*Schaefferia cuneifolia*) may decline in abundance after burning (Ruthven et al. 2003). For herbaceous vegetation, the season of burning is important. For instance, in tallgrass prairie the season fires were applied resulted in dominance of different plant associations (Howe 1995). In the Gulf Prairies and Marshes, fall burns resulted in a reduction in forb production, while winter burns increased it (Box and White 1969). Detailed burn prescriptions have been published by Fulbright and Ortega-S. (2013).

Mechanical methods

Optimum habitat for wild turkeys consists of a matrix of openings used for feeding and brood rearing, tall trees for roosting, and woody mast-producing vegetation that may also be used as escape and protective cover. The diverse herbaceous vegetation that occurs in these openings produces seeds and attracts insects that represent important wild turkey foods. Prescribed burning can create openings for wild turkeys, but often too much woody canopy in forests or brushlands prevents growth of the fine fuel necessary to carry a fire. Consequently, mechanical methods are often utilized to create openings so that prescribed burning can be used to maintain them. When conducting mechanical brush treatments, managers should remember that wild turkeys often remain close to woody escape cover (Hoffman et al. 1993, Cathey et al. 2007a, Alldredge et al. 2014). Therefore, it is important to avoid creating openings where woody edges (escape cover) are more than 200 m (600 ft) apart (Scott and Boecker 1977). Furthermore, care should be exercised not to remove roost trees or roosting habitat (Beasom and Wilson 1992). In fact, brush treatments should not occur near important roosting habitats because turkeys may abandon roosts. Once treatments are completed and fine fuel loads have responded, periodic prescribed burning will help maintain openings by reducing brush invasion and rejuvenating herbaceous cover by removing thick, decadent, and matted grass.

A variety of mechanical methods may be used to create or maintain the openings required by wild turkeys in the forests of East Texas and the Brush Country of South Texas. Vegetation may be killed by removing tops, severing plants at ground level and leaving crowns and roots intact, or uprooting or severing plants below the crown. Brush species that sprout from the crown, stem, and root usually survive

Figure 8.7. An aerator being used to manage brush to improve wildlife habitat in South Texas (photo by Tim Fulbright).

top removal, and only the aerial part of the plant is killed (Fulbright and Ortega-S. 2013).

Appropriate top removal equipment used to create or maintain openings for wild turkeys includes aerators, mowers, and roller choppers. Top removal treatments are less expensive than plant removal treatments, and the impact on plant diversity is less severe. However, retreatment of resprouting woody plants is necessary every three to five years. For example, granjeno can reach half the height it had prior to mowing within 10 months after treatment (Hamilton et al. 1981). Managers also need to understand that repeated top removal treatments on single-stemmed plants such as mesquite stimulate the production of multiple stems, and multistemmed plants will produce even more stems. Therefore, repeated application of top removal treatments may lead to very dense stands of brush, which are of little use to wild turkeys. When top removal treatments are applied, long-term planning for maintenance treatments must be considered. For example, important wildlife plant species such as Texas kidneywood (*Eysenhardtia texana*) and coma (*Sideroxylon lanuginosum*) may be lost by repeated application of top removal treatments (Fulbright 1987; Schindler and Fulbright 2003).

Mechanical aerators can also be used to create openings for wild turkeys. They are designed to loosen compacted soils and to increase water infiltration on intensively managed pastures (fig. 8.7). Aerators equipped with a series of blades measuring 15 × 15 cm (5.9 × 5.9 in) and mounted on drums are often used for vegetation top removal. The drums are filled with water to increase weight. Two aerators pulled in tandem are generally utilized to open brushy pastures (Fulbright and Ortega-S. 2013). The blades of aerators create pits on the soil surface that facilitate water infiltration (Hanselka et al. 1993), and additional moisture accumulation in these pits promotes herbaceous seed germination and thus more wild turkey food.

Roller choppers are similar to aerators, but roller choppers have blades mounted parallel to the drum axis and the blades extend the entire width of the drum. Roller choppers can be 2.4 to 4.6 m (8 to 15 ft) wide (Wiedemann 1997). Two or three roller choppers may be linked together to increase the width of the treated strips, and drums may be filled with water, sand, or cement to increase weight. Large farm tractors or crawler tractors are used to pull this type of equipment. Roller choppers may be used to crush and sever stems of larger brush on irregular terrain where a mower cannot be used (Fulbright and Ortega-S. 2013). Several brush species in South Texas, such as guajillo and blackbrush acacia, become denser and grow longer and denser thorns, which may persist for years following roller chopping treatment. For instance, in a study conducted by Schindler et al. (2004), thorns of blackbrush acacia remained more numerous nine years after a roller chopping treatment, compared with blackbrush acacia in untreated areas. Similar responses were obtained with granjeno and honey mesquite. Therefore, in order to maintain treated areas in a condition that wild turkeys will use, maintenance treatments, including prescribed fire, herbicide, or repeated roller chopping, should be conducted every two to five years following the initial aerator treatment.

Mowers and shredders can also be used to create openings for wild turkeys. These pieces of equipment can be fork mounted so that the blades are connected to the front of a power source, or drag-type mowers can be mounted to a three-point hitch and pulled behind a tractor (Fulbright and Ortega-S. 2013). Most mowers are 2.1 to 4.6 m (7 to 15 ft) wide and leave stubble that is 7.6–15.2 cm (3–6 in) tall after mowing (Wiedemann 1997). Drag-type mowers may be used in vegetation communities with stems less than 6.4 cm (2.5 in) tall and on smooth terrain where large woody stumps are absent. Mowers can also be used as a maintenance treatment in roller chopped or other brush treatment areas unless large stumps and trunks are present on the soil surface (Fulbright and Ortega-S. 2013).

Bulldozing or blading can also be used to top-kill woody vegetation. A blade mounted on a crawler tractor is pushed along the ground surface and removes the stems of woody plants. The blade can also uproot large woody plants. Compared to aerating, roller chopping, and mowing, bulldozing removes the tops of woody plants closer to the soil surface and causes more soil disturbance. However, topsoil may be lost because bulldozers typically push soil into mounds (Scifres 1980).

Additional mechanical woody vegetation management techniques include disking, grubbing, and root plowing, which all remove plants and therefore increase the life of the treatments. Disking is used

Figure 8.8. Disked strips created to provide forbs for wildlife in South Texas (photo by Landon Fritz).

to remove existing vegetation cover to increase early successional forbs attractive to wild turkeys, as well as other wildlife species (Webb and Guthery 1983, Fulbright 1999) (fig. 8.8). Crawler tractors are used to pull heavy, offset disks to sever roots of shallow-rooted woody plants. Disks are generally 91–107 cm (36–42 in) in diameter. Trunks and stems of deep-rooted plants are severed but usually resprout from lateral and adventitious buds in the crown and stem bases of the plant (Fulbright and Ortega-S. 2013), so follow-up treatment is often necessary to prevent brush from becoming too dense posttreatment and avoided by wild turkeys. Additionally, Fulbright (1999) indicated that disking may increase canopy cover of annual forbs and cause a decline of perennial forbs, which can be an issue because perennial forbs are more important to wildlife than annual forbs, as they constitute a more stable food supply. Disking every four or five years may increase herbaceous plant species richness compared to disking every year, which reduces plant species richness (Fulbright 2004).

Grubbing is a highly selective method to control woody vegetation. Compared to root plowing, grubbing usually results in a high kill of treated plants with much less disturbance to soils and herbaceous vegetation (Fulbright and Ortega-S. 2013). Grubbers with U-shaped blades can be operated with farm tractors, and it is possible to remove 155 honey mesquite plants per hour (McFarland and Ueckert 1982). Grubbers are most effective when there is enough soil moisture to allow the grubber to completely penetrate the soil surface, because roots are more easily extracted from the soil profile and exposed roots desiccate more easily (Fulbright and Ortega-S. 2013). Since grubbing is used to control individual plants, it is extremely useful when removing woody vegetation near turkey roosts because destruction of roost trees can be avoided (Cathey et al. 2007a).

Root plowing is the most aggressive mechanical method of woody plant removal. A root plow is a heavy-duty V-shaped blade 3–5 m (10–16.4 ft) wide pulled by a crawler tractor that excavates to a depth of 30–40 cm (12–16 in) beneath the soil surface. The roots of woody plants are severed, preventing regrowth of most woody species except shallow-rooted plants (Wiedemann 1997). Root plowing is the most effective method of mechanical brush control because canopy cover may be reduced for 20 years posttreatment (Welch et al. 1985). Annual forbs may increase following root plowing of dense stands of woody plants, and the increase of forbs may persist for up to 20 years posttreatment (Fulbright and Ortega-S. 2013). Increases in grass may also be realized. For example, in the eastern South Texas Plains, grass canopy cover was 45% higher 17 to 18 years after the initial treatment on sites that were root plowed and raked compared to undisturbed sites (Ruthven et al. 1993). However, root plowing is the most expensive method of mechanical brush control, and when followed by raking, it destroys herbaceous cover, necessitating reseeding. Unfortunately, exotic grasses like buffelgrass (*Cenchrus ciliaris*) or Kleberg bluestem (*Dichanthium annulatum*) may invade root plowed areas (Fulbright and Ortega-S. 2013), thereby degrading wild turkey habitat because of the loss of native herbaceous foods and reduced insect diversity and abundance (Flanders et al. 2006). In South Texas, Kleberg bluestem was 300% more abundant on root plowed areas 16 to 17 years after the initial treatment (Ruthven et al. 1993).

Herbicides

Like mechanical brush management, herbicide application to dense stands of woody vegetation can also create openings that improve wild turkey nesting and brooding habitat, as well as increase herbaceous food supplies. In East Texas, herbicides are recommended to manage openings created by timber management operations (Alldredge et al. 2014). Dense, woody thickets can begin to dominate these openings at the expense of the herbaceous vegetation communities that Eastern wild turkeys prefer, and application of herbicide can manage these brush invasions. In addition, Beasom and Scifres (1977) found that wild turkeys were not negatively impacted by herbicide treatment of brush in South Texas. After brush defoliation, turkeys frequented adjacent untreated areas more than treated areas, but birds did not completely stop using treated areas and were actually more abundant on the treated areas 27 months posttreatment. The increased abundance could have been a response to increased herbaceous cover and the associated increase in foods two years following treatment.

One advantage of using herbicides to remove brush and create openings is that soil disturbance is minimized, reducing the risk of exotic plant invasions (fig. 8.9). Additionally, it is possible to target specific brush species that may have reduced value for turkeys. Beasom and Scifres (1977) indicated that extensive forb mortality or "forb shock" may result after herbicide treatments of brush for up to two years posttreatment, which may have been why turkeys spent more time in untreated areas following herbicide treatments in their study. Therefore, if feasible, individual plant

Figure 8.9. Herbicide-treated brush in South Texas (photo by J. Alfonso Ortega-S.).

application methods should be considered because individually treating selected woody plants minimally disturbs valuable forbs and grasses that, in addition to producing seeds, also attract insects. Aerial application of herbicides should be avoided in and around roosting habitat in favor of individual plant applications to ensure that active roosts are preserved.

A wide variety of chemicals are available to control different types of vegetation. In general, herbicides may be classified by method of application and by mode of action on the plant. Herbicides may be applied to the soil or to plant foliage. Foliar-applied herbicides can be categorized as downwardly mobile, upwardly mobile, or contact herbicides (Scifres 1980). Downwardly mobile herbicides move from leaves to actively growing parts of the plant. Some examples of this type of herbicide include auxin growth regulators, such as clopyralid (3,6-dichloro-2-pyridinecarboxylic acid); dicamba (3,6-dichloro-2-methoxybenzoic acid); dicamba plus 2,4-D (2,4-dichlorophenoxyacetic acid); picloram (4-amino-3,5,6-trichoro-2-pyridinecarboxylic acid); picloram plus 2,4-D; triclopyr [(3,5,6-trichloro-2-pyridinyl)oxy]acetic acid; triclopyr plus 2,4-D;, and metsulfuron (methyl 2-[3-(4-methoxy-6-methyl-1,3,5-triazin-2-yl)ureidosulfonyl]benzoate) (McGinty 2017). Hexazinone (3-cyclohexyl-6-dimethylamino-1-methyl-1,3,5-triazine-2,4-dione) and tebuthiuron (1-[5-tert-butyl-1,3,4-thiadiazol-2-yl]-1,3-dimethylurea) are upwardly translocated chemicals that inhibit photosynthesis and can be applied to the soil surface (Fulbright and Ortega-S. 2013). As already indicated, herbicide combinations are available for different types of vegetation. For example, triclopyr plus picloram (1%) dissolved in diesel and applied to stems killed 70% of the huisache plants treated (Avila C. and Ortega-S. 1991). In addition, herbicides may be used as a maintenance treatment after roller chopping or other mechanical brush management to maintain openings for wild turkeys.

Helicopters can be used to apply herbicides to create openings of irregular shapes in woody vegetation communities. For example, openings of 4 ha (10 ac), which are the appropriate size for wild turkeys, can be created with picloram, triclopyr, picloram plus triclopyr, and picloram plus 2,4D in South Texas (Stewart et al. 2000). Similar results may be obtained with carpeted rollers mounted on the front or rear of farm tractors. Carpeted rollers are cylindrical drums covered with carpet and the herbicide is wicked onto plant leaves and stems from the drum (Mayeux 1987). Brush may also be treated with backpack sprayers or sprayers mounted on all-terrain vehicles.

Food Plots

Openings created for wild turkeys may be planted with nutritious forage plants that in addition to producing greens and seeds often attract a variety of insects, which are also important foods. Food plots may therefore be used to help fulfill turkey food requirements when the availability and nutritive value of native food plants are limited. For example, Beasom and Wilson (1992) indicated that agricultural fields planted to small grains adjacent to woodlands benefit Rio Grande wild turkeys. In Missouri, Kurzejeski and Lewis (1990) stated that the highest turkey densities are found in landscapes composed of 50% mast-producing woodlands and 50% openings where at least 15% of the openings are planted to corn, soybean, or milo.

Additionally, the Natural Resources Conservation Service (NRCS) (1999) indicates that in certain situations food plots can improve habitat for wild turkeys if planted in small openings adjacent to forest or along woody travel corridors. Similarly, Lewis (1992) advocated establishing openings in a legume-grass mixture to improve wild turkey habitat where forests make up the majority of a landscape. Grass or wheat (*Triticum aestivum*)-legume mixtures need to be renovated every three years. Lehman et al. (2007) reported that Merriam's wild turkeys benefited from visiting farms and consuming waste grain provided to livestock during winters in the Black Hills of South Dakota.

Plants used for food plots may be annuals or perennials. Annual plants need to be reseeded every year, while perennials may produce enough seeds for self-reseeding. Plants available for food plots in different regions of Texas may be legumes, graminoids, or mixtures of both. Legumes have the capacity to fix nitrogen from the atmosphere, and the forage is high in crude protein. Moreover, legumes often attract more insects than graminoids, and as a forage, legumes are very attractive to wild turkeys (McPeake et al. 2010). Cool-season food plots provide forage during late fall and winter. Cool-season plants that represent useful foods for wild turkeys include chufa, oats (*Avena sativa*), wheat, and triticale (*Triticale hexaploide*) planted with legumes such as alfalfa (*Medicago sativa*), Austrian winter peas (*Pisum sativum*), hairy vetch (*Vicia villosa*), and clovers (*Trifolium* spp.) (Beasom and Wilson 1992, Hurst and Dickson 1992). These food plots will provide good-quality forage from September to early summer in the southern Great Plains into North Texas and from November to April or May in South Texas. Cereal grains including oats, wheat, triticale, and rye may also be planted without legumes in the winter in order to provide a source of highly nutritious food for wild turkeys when native foods are less abundant (Fulbright and Ortega-S. 2013). For example, common rye (*Secale cereale*) has a crude protein content of 24% when it is very young and actively growing (Ullrey et al. 1987).

Warm-season food plots provide forage from early spring to fall. Lablab (*Lablab purpureus*) and cowpeas (*Vigna unguiculata*) are good-quality annual legumes and produce more forage than other annual legumes such as soybeans and mung beans (*V. radiata*) (Feather and Fulbright 1995). Other perennial plants that may be used for warm-season food plots include mixes of creeping bundleflower (*Desmanthus virgatus*), which produce abundant hard seeds and attract insects. The Natural Resources Conservation Service (1999) provides numerous herbaceous and woody plant seeding recommendations for the regions of the United States inhabited by Eastern, Rio Grande, and Merriam's wild turkeys. Recommendations on seeding rates for different seed mixes as well as specific plant species to use for food plots have been published by McPeake et al. (2010) and Fulbright and Ortega-S. (2013).

There are some potential risks associated with establishing food plots for wild turkeys. Food plots may concentrate birds and increase the risk of transmissible diseases as well as make turkeys more vulnerable to predators (Hurst and Dickson 1992, Cathey et al. 2007b). To decrease the risk of disease, food plots should be 0.8–2 ha (2–3 ac) in size to spread out feeding birds, and they should be moved frequently so that turkeys are not exposed to potential diseases and parasites for extended periods (Cathey et al. 2007b). Additionally, establishing food plots with plants that are not native to the planting site increases the risk that exotic vegetation will be introduced. Careful consideration should be given to the genuine necessity of food plots before they are established.

Forest Management

Forest management for wild turkeys in Texas is relevant primarily to Eastern wild turkeys, which inhabit the hardwood and pine forests of East Texas, and to a lesser extent to Merriam's wild turkeys, which currently appear to be restricted to the forested rangelands of Guadalupe Mountains National Park in West Texas. However, it is important to recognize that turkey habitat management is rarely the primary goal of forest management. Forest management for Eastern wild turkeys in hardwood and oak-hickory ecosystems is rarely independent of timber management or other economic activities (Wunz and Pack 1992). Nevertheless, if maintaining wild turkey populations is desired, then certain management activities can benefit wild turkeys under the primary forest management umbrella.

Managing forests for wild turkeys requires harvesting and postharvesting maintenance practices that provide vegetation species and structural diversity within and between stands of timber (Hoffman et al. 1993). Moreover, Mollohan et al. (1995) suggest that in addition to managing for within-stand structural diversity, high cover availability and clumps of woody vegetation should be retained. Furthermore, riparian habitats should be left undisturbed, because the vegetation in these habitats often provides important foods and cover (Bidwell et al. 1989, Burk et al. 1990, Hurst and Dickson 1992, Miller at al. 2000). Basically, if turkeys are a management priority of forest management, forests should be managed in a manner that provides diverse habitats across the landscape so that adequate nesting and brooding cover, escape and loafing cover, roosts, and travel corridors are provided.

For the sake of simplicity and as far as wild turkeys are concerned, forest management involves even-aged and uneven-aged timber harvesting. Even-aged forest management is commonly known as clear-cutting and is the preferred method of timber harvesting because it is often more economical and easier to plan and control. Clear-cutting is not necessarily harmful for Eastern wild turkeys in pine forests (Campo et al. 1989), in oak-hickory and northern hardwood ecosystems (Wunz and Pack 1992), or in western forests occupied by Merriam's wild turkeys as long as it is done properly. Clear-cutting of trees or groups of trees of similar age promotes vigorous growth of early-successional herbaceous plants and new brush species, creating a mosaic of cutover stands interspersed through stands of older trees (Yarrow 2009b). Large clear-cuts that cover expansive areas do not benefit wild turkeys (Knopp 1959). Wunz and Pack (1992) indicated that clear-cuts that exceed 12 ha (30 ac) are usually detrimental to Eastern wild turkeys.

Instead, where clear-cutting is used, timber should be harvested so that small openings distributed throughout a landscape are created and maintained. Pine forests in East Texas are now denser than those that occurred historically, so in today's pine forests managed for wild turkeys, providing openings is important. In East Texas, Campo et al. (1989) indicated that in order for pine clear-cuts to be used by nesting females and their broods, they need to be managed so that abundant herbaceous vegetation is maintained. Yarrow (2009a) recommended that clear-cuts not exceed 25 ha (50 ac), and preferably not 10 ha (25 ac), in southeastern hardwood forests, and 40 ha (100 ac) in pine forests. Openings larger than 12 ha (29.7 ac) are generally considered harmful to Eastern turkey populations (Wunz and Pack 1992). Healy and Nenno (1983) indicated that openings from 0.5 to 10 ha (1.25 to 24 ac) served as useful brooding habitats in eastern deciduous forests. Mollohan et al. (1995) stated that where clear-cutting is used in Merriam's wild turkey range, clear-cuts should not exceed 8 ha (20 ac). Hoffman et al. (1993) recommended that 10–25% of a forest should be maintained in natural or created openings for Merriam's wild turkeys and that openings should range from 1 to 2 ha (2 to 5 ac).

Wunz and Pack (1992) provide a chronology of turkey use of clear-cuts. They indicate that during the first 10 years after clear-cutting, the opening created is used largely by nesting females, as well as broods that may frequent the edges. During the next five years as overstory develops, broods start moving into the interior of the clear-cut. However, as shade increases in clear-cuts between years 15 and 25, herbaceous cover begins to recede, rendering clear-cuts less attractive turkey habitats. According to Wunz and Pack (1992), clear-cuts are not useful to turkeys when they are 20 to 40 years old because this pole/sapling stage further reduces herbaceous cover and the young woody plants are not yet producing mast. After 50 years, clear-cuts start producing mast in sufficient quantities and are open enough to attract turkeys again.

Although smaller clear-cuts that are managed to maintain herbaceous cover provide suitable wild turkey habitat, uneven-aged timber management seems to provide better habitat conditions for wild turkeys. Unlike even-aged management or clear-cutting, uneven-aged management results in landscapes with tree stands of different ages often adjacent to one another (Natural Resources Conservation Service 1999), which provides increased plant species and structural diversity within a forest. Uneven-aged management of forests produces stands of varying ages, thereby increasing the structural diversity of the forest and eliminating the 30–40-year period of poor mast production that occurs with clear-cuts (Wunz and Pack 1992). Uneven-aged forest management is recommended for both Eastern wild turkeys (Wunz and Pack 1992) and Merriam's wild turkeys (Hoffman et al. 1993, Mollohan et al. 1995). Forests under uneven-aged management therefore often provide more attractive habitats to wild turkeys.

Uneven-aged management can be accomplished via single tree or group selection. Group tree selection involves cutting all trees in an area from 0.8 ha (1.98 ac) for Eastern wild turkeys in eastern forests (Wunz and Pack 1992) and up to 8 ha (20 ac) for Merriam's wild turkeys, though smaller cuts are better (Mollohan et al. 1995). The obvious advantage of group selection cutting for managing forests for wild turkeys is that group selection can be accomplished for several targeted forest stands each year in successive years, thereby resulting in a mosaic of diverse habitat types that are favored by wild turkeys. Group selection also enables wildlife biologists and forest managers to target specific forest stands for improvement that are not particularly useful to wild turkeys in their current condition. Stands with trees and canopies that are too dense to maintain an herbaceous understory can be harvested, creating an opening that could provide future nesting, feeding, and loafing sites. Properly planned group selection cuts of varying sizes between 1 ha (2 ac) and 8 ha (20 ac), with irregular shapes that increase habitat edge, and accomplished over a 10-year planning horizon will yield a forest composed of the habitat diversity preferred by wild turkeys.

Single tree selection involves harvesting only mature trees, which creates vacancies in the forest that will promote faster growth of trees and undergrowth around the mature trees that are removed (Wittwer et al. 1990). Single tree selection is often used to improve or preserve important wild turkey habitat components such as a forest glade or a spring or seep where it might be necessary to remove a single tree (Wunz and Pack 1992). Single tree removal also tends to favor shade-tolerant trees, as well as those tree species that tolerate competition from other trees, which is not necessarily negative when mast-producing tree species preferred by wild turkeys such as beech are favored (Wunz and Pack 1992). However, as Wunz and Pack (1992) note, not all shade-tolerant species are good for wild turkeys. Furthermore, they indicate that single tree selection tends to remove the best trees like oaks (*Quercus* spp.), black cherry (*Prunus serotina*), and white ash (*Fraxinus americana*), which produce mast consumed by wild turkeys. Mature oaks should always be preserved because the acorn crops produced are very important wild turkey foods. In addition, active roosts like mature ponderosa pines in Merriam's wild turkey habitat should be preserved (Hoffman et al. 1993). If wild turkeys are a management priority and single tree selection is used to harvest timber, time and effort are needed to ensure that tree species beneficial to wild turkeys are preserved and those that are not are targeted for harvest.

Maintaining clear-cuts and group selection cuts is also important in order to encourage wild turkeys to continue using them. Canopies should remain open by thinning them periodically and applying prescribed burns every 3–5 years (Alldredge et al. 2014). In commercial pine stands, thinning should begin at 12 to 15 years of age, with subsequent thinning every 5 to 10 years. Thinning methods include herbicide application or a variety of mechanical techniques such as shredding, bulldozing, or mulching (Alldredge et al. 2014). However, clumps of woody vegetation, such as thickets of young oak or other mast-bearing species, should be maintained in cuts because clumps of shrubs provide not only food but also cover (Mollohan et al. 1995). Hoffman et al. (1993) also recommend that some logging slash that is not raked and piled should be left in openings following timber cutting because slash often provides nest sites and cover.

Literature Cited

Alldredge, B. E., J. B. Hardin, J. Whiteside, J. I. Isabelle, S. Parsons, W. C. Conway, and J. C. Cathey. 2014. Eastern wild turkeys in Texas: biology and management. Texas A&M AgriLife Extension Publication WF-011. Texas A&M University, College Station, USA.

Avila C., J. M., and J. A. Ortega-S. 1991. Aplicación basal de dos herbicidas sobre el control de un complejo de malezas en Aldama, Tamaulipas. Memorias. Séptimo Congreso Nacional de Manejo de Pastizales. Sociedad Mexicana de Manejo de Pastizales, Cd. Victoria, Tamaulipas, Mexico.

Baker, B. W. 1978. Ecological factors affecting wild turkey nest predation on South Texas rangelands. Proceedings of the Annual Conference of the Southeastern Association of Fish and Wildlife Agencies 32:126–136.

Bareiss, L. J., P. Schulz, and F. S. Guthery. 1986. Effects of short-duration and continuous grazing on bobwhite and wild turkey nesting. Journal of Range Management 39:259–260.

Beasom, S. L., and C. J. Scifres. 1977. Population reactions of selected game species to aerial herbicide applications in South Texas. Journal of Range Management 30:138–142.

Beasom, S. L., and D. Wilson. 1992. Rio Grande turkey. Pages 306–330 *in* J. G. Dickson, editor. The wild turkey: biology and management. Stackpole Books, Mechanicsburg, Pennsylvania, USA.

Bidwell, T. G., S. D. Shalaway, O. E. Maughan, and L. G. Talent. 1989. Habitat use by female Eastern wild turkeys in southeastern Oklahoma. Journal of Wildlife Management 53:34–39.

Blakey, H. I. 1944. Wild turkey vs. range management. Texas Game and Fish 2:6–7, 14–15.

Box, T. W., and R. S. White. 1969. Fall and winter burning of South Texas brush ranges. Journal of Range Management 22:373–376.

Brockway, D. G., and C. E. Lewis. 1997. Long-term effects of dormant season prescribed fire on plant community diversity, structure and productivity in a longleaf pine wiregrass ecosystem. Forest Ecology and Management 96 (1/2):167–183.

Brown, D. E. 1998. Water for wildlife: belief before science. Pages 9–16 *in* J. M. Feller and D. S. Strouse, editors. Environmental, economic and legal issues related to rangeland water developments. Arizona State University College of Law, Tempe, USA.

Broyles, B. 1995. Desert wildlife water developments: questioning use in the Southwest. Wildlife Society Bulletin 23:663–675.

Burk, J. D., G. A. Hurst, D. R. Smith, B. D. Leopold, and J. G. Dickson. 1990. Wild turkey use of streamside management zones in loblolly pine plantations. Proceedings of the National Wild Turkey Symposium 6:84–89.

Campo, J. J., W. G. Swank, and C. R. Hopkins. 1989. Brood habitat use by Eastern wild turkeys in eastern Texas. Journal of Wildlife Management 53:479–482.

Cathey, J. C., K. Melton, J. Dreibelbis, B. Cavney, S. L. Locke, S. J. DeMaso, T. W. Schwertner, and B. Collier. 2007a. Rio Grande wild turkey in Texas: biology and management. Texas AgriLife Extension Report B-6198. Texas A&M University, College Station, USA.

Cathey, J. C., S. Locke, D. Ransom Jr., S. J. DeMaso, T. W. Schwertner, and B. Collier. 2007b. Habitat appraisal guide for Rio Grande wild turkey. Texas AgriLife Extension Publication SP-317. Texas A&M University, College Station, USA.

Collier, B. A., J. D. Guthrie, J. B. Hardin, and K. L. Skow. 2017. Movements and habitat selection of male Rio Grande wild turkeys during drought in South Texas. Journal of the Southeastern Association of Fish and Wildlife Agencies 4:94–99.

Currie, C. R. 2011. Development of an appraisal guide for Rio Grande wild turkey habitat in southern Texas. Thesis, Texas A&M University–Kingsville, Kingsville, USA.

Dickson, J. G., C. D. Adams, and H. S. Hanley. 1978. Response of turkey populations to habitat variables in Louisiana. Wildlife Society Bulletin 6:163–166.

Feather, C. L., and T. E. Fulbright. 1995. Nutritional quality and palatability to white-tailed deer of four warm-season forages. Wildlife Society Bulletin 23:238–244.

Flanders, A. A., W. P. Kuvlesky Jr., D. C. Ruthven III, R. E. Zaiglin, R. L. Bingham, T. E. Fulbright, and L. A. Brennan. 2006. Effects of invasive exotic grasses on South Texas rangeland breeding birds. Auk 123: 171–182.

Fulbright, T. E. 1987. Effects of repeated shredding on a guajillo (*Acacia berlandieri*) community. Texas Journal of Agriculture and Natural Resources 1:32–33.

Fulbright, T. E. 1999. Response of white-tailed deer foods to discing in a semiarid habitat. Journal of Range Management 52:346–350.

Fulbright, T. E. 2004. Disturbance effects on species richness of herbaceous plants in a semi-arid habitat. Journal of Arid Environments 58:119–138.

Fulbright, T. E., and J. A. Ortega-S. 2013. White-tailed deer habitat: ecology and management on rangelands. Texas A&M University Press, College Station, USA.

Hall, G. I., M. C. Wallace, W. B. Ballard, D. C. Ruthven, M. J. Butler, R. L. Houchin, R. T. Huffman, R. S. Phillips, and R. Applegate. 2007. Rio Grande wild turkey habitat selection in the southern Great Plains. Journal of Wildlife Management 71:2583–2591.

Hamilton, W. T., L. M. Kitchen, and C. J. Scifres. 1981. Height replacement of selected woody plants following burning or shredding. Texas Agricultural Experiment Station Bulletin B-1361. Texas A&M University, College Station, USA.

Hanselka, C. W., S. D. Livingston, and D. Bade. 1993. Renovation practices to improve rainfall effectiveness on rangeland and pastures. Texas Agricultural Extension Service Publication L-5077. Texas A&M University, College Station, USA.

Healy, W. M. 1981. Habitat requirements and habitat management for the wild turkey in the southeast. Virginia Wild Turkey Foundation, Ellison, USA.

Healy, W. M., and E. S. Nenno. 1983. Minimum maintenance versus intensive management of clearings for wild turkeys. Wildlife Society Bulletin 11:113–120.

Hoffman, R. W., H. G. Shaw, M. A. Rumble, B. F. Wakeling, C. M. Mollohan, S. D. Schemnitz, R. Engel-Wilson, and D. A. Hengel. 1993. Management guidelines for Merriam's wild turkeys. Colorado Division of Wildlife Report 18. Denver, USA.

Howe, H. F. 1995. Succession and fire season in experimental prairie plantings. Ecology 76:1917–1925.

Hurst, G. A., and J. G. Dickson. 1992. Eastern turkey in southern pine-oak forests. Pages 265–285 *in* J. G. Dickson, editor. The wild turkey: biology and management. Stackpole Books, Mechanicsburg, Pennsylvania, USA.

Jones, K. H. 1981. Effects of grazing and timber management on Merriam's turkey habitat in mixed conifer vegetation of southcentral New Mexico. Thesis, New Mexico State University, Las Cruces, USA.

Knopp, T. B. 1959. Factors affecting the abundance and distribution of Merriam's turkey (*Meleagris gallopavo merriami*) in southeastern Arizona. Thesis, University of Arizona, Tucson, USA.

Koerth, B. H., W. M. Webb, F. C. Bryant, and F. S. Guthery. 1983. Cattle trampling of simulated ground nests under short duration and continuous grazing. Journal of Range Management 36:385–386.

Krausman, P. R., S. S. Rosenstock, and J. W. Cain III. 2006. Developed waters for wildlife: science, perception, values and controversy. Wildlife Society Bulletin 34:563–569.

Kurzejeski, E. W., and J. B. Lewis. 1990. Home ranges, movements, and habitat use of wild turkey hens in northern Missouri. Proceedings of the National Wild Turkey Symposium 6:67–71.

Lehman, C. P., M. A. Rumble, and L. D. Flake. 2007. Winter habitat selection patterns of Merriam's wild turkeys in the southern Black Hills, South Dakota. Western North American Naturalist 67:278–291.

Lehmann, V. W. 1957. Conservation and management of game. Pages 761–766 (appendix) *in* Tom Lea, "The King

Ranch," volume 2. Little, Brown, Boston, Massachusetts, USA.

Lewis, J. B. 1992. Eastern turkey in midwestern oak-hickory forests. Pages 298–301 *in* J. G. Dickson, editor. The wild turkey: biology and management. Stackpole Books, Mechanicsburg, Pennsylvania, USA.

Little, A. R., M. J. Chamberlain, L. M. Conner, and R. J. Warren. 2014. Habitat selection of wild turkeys in burned longleaf pine savannas. Journal of Wildlife Management 331:180–187.

Litton, G. W., and F. Harwell. 1995. Rio Grande turkey habitat management. Publication W7100–263. Texas Parks and Wildlife Department, Austin, USA.

Mayeux, H. S., Jr. 1987. Application of herbicides on rangelands with a carpeted roller: timing of treatment in dense stands of honey mesquite. Journal of Range Management 40:348–352.

McFarland, M. L., and D. N. Ueckert. 1982. Mesquite control: use of a three-point hitch mounted, hydraulically assisted grubber. Texas Agricultural Experiment Station Bulletin PR-3981. Texas A&M University, College Station, USA.

McGinty, A. 2017. Reference guide for Texas ranchers. http://texnat.tamu.edu. Accessed October 10, 2016.

McPeake, R., R. Roberg, C. Self, and D. Long. 2010. Establishing wildlife food plots. FSA 9092. University of Arkansas Division of Agriculture, Little Rock, USA.

Merrill, L. B. 1975. Effect of grazing management practices on wild turkey habitat. Pages 108–112 *in* L. K. Halls, editor. Proceedings of the National Wild Turkey Symposium. Texas Chapter of The Wildlife Society, Austin, USA.

Miller, D. A., B. D. Leopold, G. A. Hurst, and P. D. Gerard. 2000. Habitat selection models for Eastern wild turkeys in central Mississippi. Journal of Wildlife Management 64:765–776.

Mollohan, C. M., D. R. Patton, and B. F. Wakeling. 1995. Habitat selection and use by Merriam's wild turkey in northcentral Arizona. Research Branch Technical Report No. 9. Arizona Game and Fish Department, Phoenix, USA.

Natural Resources Conservation Service. 1999. Wild turkey (*Meleagris gallopavo*). Fish and Wildlife Management 12:1–11.

Owens, M. K., J. W. Mackley, and C. J. Carroll. 2002. Vegetation dynamics following seasonal fires in mixed mesquite/acacia savannas. Journal of Range Management 55:509–516.

Porter, W. F. 1992. Habitat requirements. Pages 202–213 *in* J. G. Dickson, editor. The wild turkey: biology and management. Stackpole Books, Mechanicsburg, Pennsylvania, USA.

Prasad, N. L. N. S., and F. S. Guthery. 1986. Wildlife use of water under short duration and continuous grazing. Wildlife Society Bulletin 14:450–454.

Ransom, D., O. Rongstad, and D. Rusch. 1987. Nesting ecology of Rio Grande turkeys. Journal of Wildlife Management 51:435–439.

Rosenstock, S., W. Ballard, and J. C. Devos Jr. 1999. Viewpoint: benefits and impacts of wildlife water developments. Journal of Range Management 52:302–311.

Rutherford, W. H., and W. D. Snyder. 1983. Guidelines for habitat modification to benefit wildlife. Colorado Division of Wildlife, Denver, USA.

Ruthven, D. C., III, T. E. Fulbright, S. L. Beasom, and E. C. Hellgren. 1993. Long-term effects of root plowing on vegetation in the eastern South Texas Plains. Journal of Range Management 41:351–354.

Ruthven, D. C., III, A. W. Braden, H. J. Knutson, J. F. Gallagher, and D. R. Synatzske. 2003. Woody vegetation response to various burning regimes in South Texas. Journal of Range Management 56:159–166.

Sanchez, J. E., and M. K. Haderlie. 1990. Water management on Cabeza Prieta and Kofa National Wildlife Refuges. Pages 73–77 *in* G. K. Tsukamoto and S. J. Stiver, editors. Proceedings of The Wildlife Water Development Symposium, 30 November–1 December 1988, Las Vegas, Nevada. Nevada Chapter of the Wildlife Society, USDI BLM, and Nevada Department of Wildlife.

Schindler, J. R., and T. E. Fulbright. 2003. Roller chopping effects on Tamaulipan scrub community composition. Journal of Range Management 56:585–590.

Schindler, J. R., T. E. Fulbright, and T. D. A. Forbes. 2004. Long-term effects of roller chopping on antiherbivore defenses in three shrub species. Journal of Arid Environments 56:181–192.

Scifres, C. J. 1980. Brush management: principles and practices for Texas and the Southwest. Texas A&M University Press, College Station, USA.

Scott, V. E., and E. L. Boeker. 1977. Responses of Merriam's turkey to pinyon-juniper control. Journal of Range Management 30:220–223.

Shaw, H. G., and C. Mollohan. 1992. Merriam's turkey. Pages 331–349 *in* J. G. Dickson, editor. The wild turkey: biology and management. Stackpole Books, Mechanicsburg, Pennsylvania, USA.

Stewart, K. M., T. E. Fulbright, and D. L. Drawe. 2000. White-tailed deer use of clearings relative to forage availability. Journal of Wildlife Management 64:733–741.

Suarez, R. 2002. Texas turkey talk. Texas Parks and Wildlife Department Report PWD BK W7000–827 (5/02). Texas Parks and Wildlife Department, Austin, USA.

Thogmartin, W. 2001. Home-range size and habitat selection of female wild turkeys (*Meleagris gallopavo*) in Arkansas. American Midland Naturalist 145:247–260.

Thompson, W. L. 1993. Ecology of Merriam's turkeys in relation to burned and logged areas in southeastern Montana. Dissertation, Montana State University, Bozeman, USA.

Ullrey, D. E., J. T. Nellist, J. P. Duvendeck, P. A. Whetter, and L. D. Fay. 1987. Digestibility of vegetative rye for white-tailed deer. Journal of Wildlife Management 51:51–53.

Wakeling, B. F., and H. G. Shaw. 1994. Characteristics of managed forest habitat selected for nesting by Merriam's turkeys. Pages 359–363 *in* W. W. Covington and L. F. DeBano, technical coordinators. Sustainable ecological systems: implementing an ecological approach to land management. US Forest Service General Technical Report RM-247.

Webb, W. M., and F. S. Guthery. 1983. Response of wildlife food plants to spring discing of mesquite rangeland in northwest Texas. Journal of Range Management 36:351–353.

Welch, T. G., R. P. Smith, and G. A. Rasmussen. 1985. Brush management technologies. Pages 15–24 *in* C. J. Scifres, W. T. Hamilton, J. R. Conner, J. M. Inglis, G. A. Rasmussen, R. P. Smith, J. W. Stuth, and T. G. Welch, editors. Integrated brush management systems for South Texas: development and implementation. Texas Agricultural Experiment Station Bulletin 1493. Texas A&M University, College Station, USA.

White, L. D., and C. W. Hanselka. 1989. Prescribed range burning in Texas. Texas Agricultural Extension Service Publication B-1310. Texas A&M University, College Station, USA.

Wiedemann, H. T. 1997. Factors to consider when sculpting brush: mechanical treatment options. Pages 88–95 in D. Rollins, D. N. Ueckert, and C. G. Brown, editors. Brush sculptors: symposium proceedings. Texas Agricultural Extension Service, Texas A&M University, College Station, USA.

Wittwer, R. F., D. W. Marcouiller, and S. Anderson. 1990. Even and uneven-aged forest management. Oklahoma State University Extension Facts No. 5028. Oklahoma Cooperative Extension Service, Oklahoma State University, Stillwater, USA.

Wright, H. A., and A. W. Bailey. 1982. Fire ecology: United States and southern Canada. Wiley, New York, New York, USA.

Wunz, G. A., and X. C. Pack. 1992. Eastern turkey in eastern oak-hickory and northern hardwood forests. Pages 232–264 *in* J. G. Dickson, editor. The wild turkey: biology and management. Stackpole Books, Mechanicsburg, Pennsylvania, USA.

Yarrow, G. 2009a. Biology and management of Eastern wild turkey. Clemson Cooperative Extension Service Fact Sheet 35. Clemson University, Clemson, South Carolina, USA.

Yarrow, G. 2009b. Managing for wildlife diversity in managed forests. Clemson Cooperative Extension Service Fact Sheet 20. Clemson University, Clemson, South Carolina, USA.

Yoder, J., D. M. Engle, M. Tilley, and S. Fuhlendorf. 2003. The economic logic of prescribed burning law and regulation. Journal of Range Management 56:306–313.

9

Diseases and Parasites

Our health relies entirely on the vitality of our fellow species on Earth.

—HARRISON FORD

Wild turkeys in the United States are hosts to a wide range of viral (Akey et al. 1981, Candelora et al. 2010, Allison et al. 2014), bacterial (Hatkins and Phillips 1986, Gerhold and Fischer 2003), and fungal (Davidson et al. 1989, Elsmo et al. 2016) pathogens. Additionally, protozoa (Atkinson and Forrester 1987, Fedynich and Rhodes 1995, Dubey et al. 2000), trematodes (Maxfield et al. 1963, Hon et al. 1975, McJunkin et al. 2003), cestodes (Hon et al. 1975, Amr et al. 1988), nematodes (Hon et al. 1975, Hopkins et al. 1990), ectoparasites (Bishopp and Trembley 1945, Kellogg et al. 1969, Lane et al. 2006), neoplasia (Forrester 1992, Elsmo et al. 2016), and cardiac disease (Frame et al. 2015) have been documented from wild turkeys. Few, if any, studies of wild turkeys have documented a relationship between the presence of pathogens and changes in wild turkey populations (Hayes et al. 1992, Peterson et al. 2002), and other studies have been inconclusive (Alger et al. 2017). The focus of this chapter is on etiologic agents and disease processes that have been isolated from or for which there is serologic evidence of exposure in wild turkeys from Texas. A discussion of diseases and parasites in an ecological context to will be provided, as will a short section covering management of diseases and parasites in turkey populations.

Viruses

Newcastle disease virus

Seventeen of 143 Rio Grande wild turkeys (12%) livetrapped during the winters of 1963–1965 on the Rob and Bessie Welder Wildlife Refuge in Sinton, Texas (San Patricio County), were reported as positive for antibodies to Newcastle disease virus using the microtiter hemagglutination inhibition test. All samples that were initially reactive were tested again, and only turkeys that reacted twice on the hemagglutination inhibition test were considered positive for antibodies (Glazener et al. 1967). However, Trainer et al. (1968) stated that this conclusion was erroneous based on hemagglutination inhibition testing of 513 turkeys livetrapped on the Welder Wildlife Refuge during the winter months of 1966 and 1967 in which there were no reactors. Additionally, Trainer et al. (1968) reported that "subsequent testing has resulted in completely negative serologic findings." It is not clear whether samples from the initial study were retested, or whether their conclusion was based on 100% negative reactivity in their study. Roslien and Haugen (1970) tested serum from 10 male and 29 female Rio Grande wild turkeys livetrapped in Sonora, Texas (Sutton County), and found one turkey (2%) that was suspicious for antibodies to Newcastle disease virus. The testing method was not indicated. Hemagglutination inhibition testing of 77 Rio Grande wild turkeys from Aransas (17), Brooks (37), and San Patricio (23) Counties and 30 Eastern wild turkeys from Smith County yielded no birds that were positive for antibodies to Newcastle disease virus (Hensley and Cain 1979). Hemagglutination inhibition testing of serum to detect antibodies to Newcastle disease virus in 442 Rio Grande wild turkeys from five counties (Donley, Refugio, San Patricio, Willacy, and Zavala) revealed no positive results. Isolation attempts for Newcastle disease virus from 511 cloacal and tracheal swabs from the same study group were uniformly negative (Rocke and Yuill 1987). Sixty-four Rio Grande wild turkeys were livetrapped in Kerr and Bandera Counties and were tested for antibodies via hemagglutination inhibition testing, and all were found to be negative when the positive cutoff was set at a titer of more than 1:10 (Peterson et al. 2002).

Vesicular stomatitis virus

Thirty percent (36/122) of Rio Grande wild turkeys from the Welder Wildlife Refuge that were tested for antibodies to vesicular stomatitis virus using a HeLa cell metabolic inhibition tissue culture system had positive reactions to the New Jersey variant of the vesicular stomatitis virus, but only 7% (8/120) reacted to the Indiana variant of this virus. Six of the positive reactors to the Indiana variant also reacted to the New Jersey variant (Glazener et al. 1967). Trainer et al.'s (1968) coincidental study of Rio Grande wild turkeys from the Welder Wildlife Refuge reported an 18% prevalence (81/445) of the New Jersey variant and a 5% prevalence (24/468) of the Indiana variant of the vesicular stomatitis virus using the same testing system as Glazener et al. (1967).

Arboviruses

Rio Grande wild turkeys livetrapped during the winters of 1963–1965 on the Welder Wildlife Refuge showed little to no evidence of antibodies to Venezuelan encephalitis virus (2/165; 1%), California encephalitis virus (0/202; 0%), Western encephalitis virus (4/202; 2%), and Eastern encephalitis virus (0/202; 0%) in a HeLa cell metabolic inhibition tissue culture system, but 13/202 (6%) were positive for antibodies to St. Louis encephalitis virus. All turkeys with antibodies to St. Louis encephalitis virus were males (Glazener et al. 1967). Eight seasons (1963–1970) of serosurveillance for arbovirus exposure conducted during January and February on the Welder Wildlife Refuge using a metabolic inhibition test on HeLa cells demonstrated little evidence of exposure to the selected etiologic agents, with the exception of St. Louis encephalitis virus. The number and percentage that were positive were as follows: Eastern encephalitis virus (3/963; 0.3%), Western encephalitis virus (50/963; 0.5%), California encephalitis virus (2/9,630; 0.2%), St. Louis encephalitis virus (82/963; 9%), and Venezuelan encephalitis virus (7/963; 0.7%). There was a direct temporal correlation with the positive results of the testing for St. Louis encephalitis virus and an outbreak of St. Louis encephalitis virus infections in people in Corpus Christi, Texas, approximately 48 km (30 mi) from the refuge. In a previous paper by Trainer et al. (1968) that includes data from Trainer (1970), the authors concluded that the high prevalence of St. Louis encephalitis virus exposure did not have a deleterious effect on the turkey population, as a decrease in turkeys on the refuge was not observed (Trainer 1970). Roslien and Haugen (1970) tested serum from nine Rio Grande wild turkeys that were livetrapped in Sonora, Texas (Sutton County), using "standardized tests" for Western encephalitis virus and found all samples to be negative for antibodies.

Encephalomyocarditis virus

Ninety-two Rio Grande wild turkeys livetrapped on the Welder Wildlife Refuge during the winter months of 1963–1965 were negative (0%) for antibodies to encephalomyocarditis virus using the HeLa cell metabolic inhibition tissue culture system (Glazener et al. 1967). These results are consistent with those of Trainer et al. (1968), who reported that 100% of 297 Rio Grande wild turkeys trapped on the Welder Wildlife Refuge during the winter months of 1964–1967 were negative for antibodies to the same virus using the same testing system. There is data overlap between the two studies, but it does not appear that Rio Grande wild turkeys in South Texas were exposed to encephalomyocarditis virus in the 1960s.

Chicken embryo lethal orphan virus

Thirty-nine Rio Grande wild turkeys (10 males and 29 females) that were trapped in Sonora, Texas, were negative for chicken embryo lethal orphan virus via serologic testing. Nine turkeys from the same group were tested for this virus by the saturated serodisc method, and one turkey had a positive titer of 200. The authors were not able to explain this incongruity in results (Roslien and Haugen 1970).

Fowlpox

One of 3 moribund Rio Grande wild turkeys from a group of 330 that were livetrapped in Sutton County, Texas, was diagnosed with fowlpox infection

(*Borreliota* sp.) at the Sonora Sub-Station of the Texas Agricultural Experiment Station (Thomas 1964).

Avian influenza virus

Four-hundred forty serum samples from Rio Grande wild turkeys livetrapped in five counties (Donley, Refugio, San Patricio, Willacy, and Zavala) over a three-year period were negative for antibodies to avian influenza virus when tested with an agar gel precipitation test. Similarly, avian influenza virus was not recovered from a culture of 511 tracheal and cloacal swabs of the same study group (Rocke and Yuill 1987). Seventy Rio Grande wild turkeys from Bandera and Kerr Counties, Texas, were negative for antibodies to avian influenza virus upon testing with agar gel immunodiffusion tests (Peterson et al. 2002).

Reticuloendotheliosis virus

Polymerase chain reaction (PCR) testing showed that the serum of 2/70 (3%) Rio Grande wild turkeys from Kerr and Bandera Counties was positive for proviral DNA of reticuloendotheliosis virus, and both turkeys were females from Kerr County. Reticuloendotheliosis virus was subsequently isolated from whole blood from 1/37 (2.7%) of these females. Both females that were PCR-positive for reticuloendotheliosis virus were also positive on serum plate agglutination screening tests for *Mycoplasma gallisepticum* and *M. synoviae*. Infection with reticuloendotheliosis virus can result in immunosuppression in Attwater's prairie chickens (*Tympanuchus cupido attwateri*) (Barbosa et al. 2007) and domestic fowl (Dunn 2016, Walker et al. 1983), and that may explain the coinfections detected in this study. Additionally, the females from which reticuloendotheliosis virus was isolated were also positive for *M. synoviae* via hemagglutination inhibition testing. The PCR-positive females had significantly lower body weights than the 33 females in this study that were not positive for proviral DNA, and both females were dead within eight months of testing (Peterson et al. 2002). Ley et al. (1989) diagnosed reticuloendotheliosis virus and histomoniasis in a female Eastern wild turkey that died on the day of discovery in Martin County, North Carolina, and Hayes et al. (1992) diagnosed reticuloendotheliosis virus in a female Eastern wild turkey from Ossabaw Island, Georgia. This female was emaciated and demonstrated neurologic deficits that were severe enough to warrant euthanasia. Although the relationship between infection with reticuloendotheliosis virus and population dynamics has yet to be understood, this virus causes high mortality (Witter and Fadley 2003) and immunosuppression (Barbosa et al. 2007) in domestic fowl, and its potential negative effect on wild turkey populations should not be underestimated. See the section on mycoplasmas for additional discussion of potential negative impacts of diseases on wild turkey populations.

Turkey coronavirus

Forty-five Rio Grande wild turkeys trapped in Kerr and Bandera Counties were tested for antibodies to turkey coronavirus via indirect fluorescent antibody testing and were determined to be negative (Peterson et al. 2002).

Adenoviruses

Serum samples from 211 wild turkeys from Texas and Florida were negative for the hemorrhagic enteritis/marble spleen disease adenoviruses using the precipitin antibody test. The results indicate that these adenoviruses are not commonly found in wild turkeys. However, caution may be warranted, as both diseases are omnipresent in pen-reared domestic poultry and there are opportunities for contact between high-density commercial flocks of pheasants or domestic turkeys and wild turkeys (Domeruth et al. 1977).

Bacteria and Bacteria-like Organisms

Mycoplasma spp.

Twenty-nine Rio Grande wild turkeys livetrapped on the Welder Wildlife Refuge during the winter months of 1963–1965 were negative (0/29; 0%) for agglutinating antibodies to *Mycoplasma gallisepticum* (Glazener et al. 1967). In an overlapping study conducted by Trainer et al. (1968) during the winter months of 1964–1967, all turkeys (0/96; 0%) were negative for antibodies to *M. gallisepticum*. According to Hensley and Cain (1979), tube agglutination tests for screening, followed by plate testing for confirmation, yielded 12 Rio Grande wild turkeys from Blanco (1/28; 3.6%), Brooks (8/62; 12.9%), and Motley (3/48; 6.3%) Counties that were positive for antibodies to *M. gallisepticum*. No Rio Grande wild turkeys from Aransas (0/16; 0%), Gray (0/41; 0%), and San Patricio

(0/25; 0%) Counties were antibody-positive, and no Eastern wild turkeys from Smith County (0/30; 0%) were antibody-positive. In a separate study, 70 Rio Grande wild turkeys from Bandera and Kerr Counties, Texas, were screened for antibodies to *M. gallisepticum*, *M. synoviae*, and *M. meleagridis* using serum plate agglutination testing and verified with hemagglutination inhibition testing. Fifty-six (80%) of the serum plate agglutination tests for *M. gallisepticum* agglutinated, but all were negative for specific antibodies for *M. gallisepticum*. The same 56 samples were positive for *M. synoviae* with serum plate agglutination testing, and 10 (18%) were verified to have specific antibodies to *M. synoviae* upon hemagglutination inhibition testing when a positive titer cutoff was set at more than 1:10. No turkeys had positive serum plate agglutination tests for *M. meleagridis* (Peterson et al. 2002). Serum samples from 442 Rio Grande wild turkeys from five counties (Donley, Refugio, San Patricio, Willacy, and Zavala) were screened for antibodies to *M. gallisepticum*, *M. synoviae*, and *M. meleagridis* using rapid plate agglutination testing, with confirmation by microtiter hemagglutination inhibition testing. Although none of the samples were reactive on hemagglutination inhibition testing, the average prevalences of antibodies detectable via rapid plate agglutination testing to *M. gallisepticum*, *M. meleagridis*, and *M. synoviae* were 12%, 51%, and 37%, respectively (Rocke and Yuill 1987). *Mycoplasma* spp. were cultured from 1,090 cloacal and tracheal swabs from 482 turkeys in this study, and direct immunofluorescence testing revealed that no isolates were *M. gallisepticum*, *M. meleagridis*, *M. synoviae*, *M. pullorum*, *M. gallinaceum*, *M. iowae*, or *M. gallinarium*. Ten isolates were also tested via indirect immunofluorescence, and five were determined to be *M. gallopavonis*, serotype F; the remaining five isolates could not be speciated (Rocke and Yuill 1987). Fritz et al. (1992) looked for antibodies to *M. gallisepticum* in Wheeler and Shamrock, Texas (Wheeler County), using rapid plate agglutination as a screening test and hemagglutination inhibition testing for confirmation. The results were 2/14 (14%) and 19/68 (24%), respectively, for the rapid plate agglutination testing and 0/14 (0%) and 3/68 (4%), respectively, for the hemagglutination inhibition testing. Rapid plate agglutination was used as the sole testing modality for antibodies to *M. synoviae* and *M. meleagridis* in this study. Results were 11/14 (79%) for the *M. synoviae* samples from Wheeler, and 2/35 (6%) for the samples from Shamrock. The samples tested for antibodies to *M. meleagridis* were 11/14 (79%; Wheeler) and 0/34 (0%; Shamrock). *Mycoplasma gallisepticum* was isolated from the lung tissue of one of the turkeys trapped in Shamrock and later necropsied (Fritz et al. 1992). Ten male and 29 female Rio Grande wild turkeys trapped near Sonora, Texas (Sutton County), were negative for evidence of exposure to mycoplasmas upon "standardized" testing (Roslien and Haugen 1970).

Chlamydophila (Chlamydia) *psittaci*

Rio Grande wild turkeys from the Welder Wildlife Refuge were positive for antibodies (2/54; 4%) to *Chlamydophila (Chlamydia) psittaci* when tested with an indirect complement fixation test (Glazener et al. 1967). These findings are consistent with those of Trainer et al. (1968), who found that 2/118 (2%) turkeys trapped on the Welder Wildlife Refuge had antibodies to *C. psittaci* when tested with a standard tube hemagglutination test over four winters. It is important to note that there is temporal and author overlap between these studies, and that overlap among study specimens is highly likely. According to Roslien and Haugen (1970), one pooled serum sample from 4 Rio Grande wild turkeys livetrapped in Sutton County had a positive titer of 8. However, 15 turkeys that were individually tested were uniformly negative. Hensley and Cain (1979) discovered that all Rio Grande wild turkeys from Aransas (16), Blanco (28), Brooks (60), Gray (30), Motley (44), and San Patricio (24) Counties were negative for antibodies to *C. psittaci* when tested via direct complement fixation testing, as were all Eastern wild turkeys from Smith County (30). Peterson et al. (2002) reported that 70 Rio Grande wild turkeys from Bandera and Kerr Counties, Texas, were negative for antibodies to *C. psittaci* when tested with an elementary body agglutination test with a positive cutoff value of more than 1:20.

Salmonella pullorum and *S. typhimurium*

Standard tube agglutination testing failed to reveal any turkeys from the Welder Wildlife Refuge with antibodies to *Salmonella pullorum* or *S. typhimurium*

(Glazener et al. 1967). These findings match those of Trainer et al. (1968) in an overlapping study that used the same testing method and found that 0/148 (0%) turkeys were positive for agglutinating antibodies. In a somewhat contrasting study, Roslien and Haugen (1970) found that 15% of 39 Rio Grande wild turkeys that were livetrapped in Sutton County were positive for antibodies to *S. pullorum*, and no turkeys were positive for antibodies to *S. typhimurium* using the same testing modality. Hensley and Cain (1979) found that Rio Grande wild turkeys were positive for antibodies to *S. pullorum* (1/16; 6.3% for Aransas County and 4/48; 8.3% for Motley County) and negative (0/27, 0/62, 0/41, and 0/25 for Blanco, Brooks, Gray, and San Patricio Counties, respectively) via tube agglutination testing. One Eastern wild turkey out of 30 tested (3.3%) from Smith County was positive for *S. pullorum* antibodies via tube agglutination testing. Rio Grande wild turkeys from Brooks County (3/62; 4.8%) were positive for antibodies to *S. typhimurium*, and 82 turkeys from Aransas (16), Gray (41), and San Patricio (25) Counties were negative for antibodies via tube agglutination testing. One of 30 (3.3%) Eastern wild turkeys from Smith County was positive. No turkeys from Blanco or Motley Counties were tested for *S. typhimurium*. Rocke and Yuill (1987) reported that 511 cloacal and tracheal swabs from 442 turkeys from five Texas counties (Donley, San Patricio, Refugio, Willacy, and Zavala) did not grow *Salmonella* spp. in lactose broth. Tube agglutination testing of serum from 70 Rio Grande wild turkeys from Bandera and Kerr Counties was negative for antibodies specific to *S. pullorum* and *S. typhimurium* (Peterson et al. 2002).

Aegyptianella pullorum

The first North American report of the highly pathogenic intraerythrocytic rickettsia (*Aegyptianella pullorum*) was made by Castle and Christensen (1985) when 24/300 (8%) Rio Grande wild turkeys from three noncontiguous locations (Chaparrosa Ranch, Zavala County; Campo Alegre Ranch, Willacy County; and Welder Wildlife Refuge, San Patricio County) in South Texas were positive via isodiagnosis for this organism. Twenty-one out of 142 (15%) turkeys from Chaparrosa Ranch were positive, 3/48 (6%) from Campo Alegre Ranch were positive, and none (0/110; 0%) from the WWR were positive. All positive turkeys were diagnosed via subinoculation and recovery on blood smears; no direct blood smears from the original turkeys demonstrated *A. pullorum*.

Endoparasites

Protozoa

One-hundred thirty-three Rio Grande wild turkeys from Welder Wildlife Refuge were examined via thin blood smear for evidence of hemoparasites during the winters of 1963–1964 and 1964–1965 (Cook et al. 1966). There was 100% (63/63) prevalence of *Haemoproteus meleagridis* in juvenile turkeys less than 1 year old, and 63% (44/70) prevalence in adult turkeys, for an overall prevalence of 80% (107/133). There was no evidence of microfilariae, *Leucocytozoon* sp., *Plasmodium* sp., or *Trypanosoma* sp., although these parasites were part of the search image of the study. In a separate study, 31/39 (79%) peripheral blood smears from Rio Grande wild turkeys trapped in Sutton County were positive for *H. meleagridis* (Roslien and Haugen 1970). No evidence of *Trypanosoma*, *Leucocytozoon*, or *Plasmodium* spp. was noted.

Forty-one percent (123) of Rio Grande wild turkeys from three noncontiguous counties in South Texas (San Patricio, Zavala, and Willacy) were positive for a novel species of *Plasmodium* (subgenus *Novyella*) using isodiagnosis and/or examination of direct blood smears. Three percent of the 123 turkeys (8) that were positive for *Plasmodium* were diagnosed solely upon examination of direct blood smears (Castle et al. 1988). In the same study, 76% (255/350) of the turkeys were positive for *H. meleagridis* using the same diagnostic techniques, and 73% (94/123) of the turkeys that were positive for *Plasmodium* were coinfected with *H. meleagridis*. It was noted in this study that there was no indication of infection with *Leucocytozoon smithi* upon examination of blood smears. One of 330 (0.3%) Rio Grande turkeys that was livetrapped in Sutton County, Texas, was diagnosed with infectious enterohepatitis (blackhead) caused by *Histomonas meleagridis* (Thomas 1964). Fifty years ago it was generally believed that blackhead could seriously decimate wild turkey populations (Markley 1967). Although there are no reports of mortalities from infectious enterohepatitis in Texas, this pathogen has been documented to cause mortality in Eastern wild turkeys in North Carolina (Craig and Barkalow

1950) and in Pennsylvania, where it was considered to be a factor in a population decline (Kozicky 1948).

Cestodes and nematodes

Six male and six female Rio Grande wild turkeys from Concho County were examined for helminth parasites. One hundred percent (12/12) were infected with the cestode *Metroliasthes lucida*, 67% (8/12) contained the cestode *Raillietina williamsi*, and 33% (4/12) contained the cestode *Liga brasiliensis*. Fifty-eight percent (7/12) were infected with the nematode parasite *Heterakis gallinarum*. Although coinfections must have occurred, the data do not indicate which ones were observed. No trematodes were discovered (Pence and Bickel 1977).

Ectoparasites

Lice and mites

A single Rio Grande wild turkey collected in January 1951 in Kleberg County was found to be parasitized with an uncounted number of the following mallophagan lice: *Oxylipeurus polytrapezius*, *O. corpulentus*, *Menacanthus* sp., and *Chelopistes meleagridis* (Hightower et al. 1953). In Sutton County, Texas, one Rio Grande wild turkey of 330 (0.30%) had a clinically significant infestation of scaly leg mites (*Knemidokoptes mutans*) (Thomas 1964).

Aflatoxin

Aflatoxins are toxic fungal metabolites produced by molds that grow on grains and vegetables under favorable environmental conditions and can be harmful to animals and humans (Schweitzer et al. 2001, Moore et al. 2013). Aflatoxins (particularly *Aspergillus flavus* and *A. parasiticus*) are concerns to wildlife managers because these toxic substances often occur in corn (Schweitzer et al. 2001), which is commonly used as a supplemental food in feeders or spread along farm and ranch roads to attract wildlife. Although there is little information in the scientific literature about wild turkey use of corn feeders, it is common knowledge among Texas landowners and hunters that wild turkeys readily consume corn when and where it is offered, sometimes daily. Therefore, corn tainted with aflatoxin could pose a potential threat to wild turkeys.

For example, Quist et al. (2000) reported that four-month-old wild turkey poults provided with diets that contained 100–400 μ of aflatoxin/kg feed for two weeks displayed decreased feed consumption and weight gains, as well as negative physiological responses compared to poults that were not provided food treated with aflatoxin. Furthermore, Quist et al. (2000) found that the most significant effects occurred in poults fed 400 μ aflatoxin/kg feed. Research using domestic turkey poults yielded similar results. Giambrone et al. (1985) reported that aflatoxin was highly toxic to two-week-old domestic turkey poults provided with a capsule containing 500 or 1,000 ppb of aflatoxin daily and that poults were dead 18 days after trials started. Poults provided with capsules containing 200 ppb of aflatoxin suffered mild toxicity. Nevertheless, Giambrone et al. (1985) believed that aflatoxin levels as low as 100 ppb were not safe for turkey poults. Similarly, Rauber et al. (2007) provided domestic turkey poults with aflatoxin dosage ranging from 20 to 1,000 ppb and concluded that turkey poults are very sensitive to aflatoxin poisoning, particularly at doses greater than 200 ppb. To avoid poisoning wild turkeys with aflatoxin, Schweitzer et al. (2001) recommended that grains contaminated with aflatoxin at levels equaling or exceeding 100 ppg not be sold as wildlife feed.

Population and Community Ecology Perspectives

Wildlife managers and wildlife veterinarians should consider diseases and disease processes when making management decisions (Davidson et al. 1982) or assessing potential causes of population declines (Busch and Williams 1970, Forrester et al. 1980, Forrester 1991). However, as noted by Davidson and Wentworth (1992), "Most wild turkeys are infected by several species of parasites at some point during their lives, but these infections usually are not intense enough to produce clinical disease or death." One major exception to this generalization may be the parasite *Histomonas meleagridis*, the causative agent responsible for blackhead, infectious enterohepatitis, or histomoniasis, which can be extremely lethal to turkeys. The vector that transmits histomoniasis is the nematode *Heterakis gallinarum*. This nematode infects the ceca of many galliform species; some groups of galliforms such as grouse, chukars, and peafowl are, like turkeys, highly susceptible, whereas other groups such as pheasants, chickens, and quail are not as susceptible. Today, there are typically barriers between commercial poultry operations and populations of wild turkeys, thus preventing widespread opportunities for transmission of blackhead from chickens and other domestic fowl to turkeys. This kind of ecological perspective probably helped wild turkey restoration by cautioning against the release of carrier species into habitats where wild turkeys were present, and not raising domestic chickens and turkeys in the same place (Reid 1967).

One can argue that parasite and disease ecology is one of the least understood and most challenging aspects of game bird research. To date, the majority of papers on diseases and parasites in wild turkeys and most other game birds are based on samples from observational studies, which often are opportunistic because they are based on samples obtained from hunter check stations or from birds displaying aberrant behavior in the wild, rather than random samples that represent the turkey population. Thus, we often lack a community ecology or population context for interpreting the roles that parasites and diseases play in year-to-year changes in wild turkey abundance. This is precisely why blackhead is so important in the context of wild turkey management; it provides us with an ecological setting in which to gauge potential losses while also knowing the management tactics with potential for success.

In Texas, wild turkey population trends based on Christmas Bird Count data were mostly increasing from 2000 to 2013, a trend driven largely by the relatively high abundance of the Rio Grande subspecies. However, based on data collected beginning in 1995, harvests of both Rio Grande and Eastern wild turkeys peaked around 2005 and have been mostly declining since then (Brennan et al. 2017). What do these trends mean, if anything, with respect to whether diseases and parasites are playing a role? With only survey data based on samples collected opportunistically from hunters, it is impossible to say. We do know, however, that managers attempting to restore populations of the Eastern subspecies in East Texas have faced significant challenges for decades. Might there be some parasite or disease present in the Eastern subspecies that is not present in Rio Grande wild turkeys? In the absence of experimental or comparative data on the parasite and disease profiles of these two subspecies, this will be impossible to determine. Thus far, there is no evidence that parasites or diseases are responsible for inflicting additive mortality in the Eastern subspecies, or that Rio Grande populations can somehow compensate for losses from diseases and parasites. The problem is that there is no evidence because such studies have yet to be conducted.

Disease Management

The disease and parasite review provided in this chapter identifies 10 viral pathogens and 7 bacterial pathogens, as well as a number of endoparasites and ectoparasites that occur, or have occurred, among wild turkeys in Texas. A few additional viruses and bacteria have been identified from wild turkeys in the southeastern United States that have not been identified in turkeys from Texas but could possibly appear. Clearly, wild turkey populations in Texas harbor pathogens and parasites, but these have not yet caused known outbreaks or noticeable population declines. In fact, population declines attributable to pathogens or parasites appear to be rare throughout the geographic range of the wild turkey in North America, with the possible exception of avian pox (Davidson and Wentworth 1992). However, the fact that an epidemic among wild turkeys in Texas has not been observed does not mean that an undocumented event has not occurred in the past, or that it could not occur in the future.

What should landowners or wildlife biologists do who are interested in or concerned about the presence of diseases and parasites in the wild turkey populations they manage? Being vigilant about the outward physical condition of wild turkeys inhabiting a property is certainly important. If moribund turkeys, turkeys in poor condition, or turkey carcasses that have not been scavenged start to appear on a property, then concern is warranted. A Texas Parks and Wildlife Department (TPWD) biologist or game warden can be contacted and invited to the property to collect carcasses or legally euthanize sick birds and then arrange to have them transported to a veterinary diagnostic laboratory for necropsy. Necropsies can reveal the cause of death and possible involvement of pathogens or parasites.

A more proactive approach to monitoring diseases and parasites in wild turkey populations would be to institute a disease management program. A number of review papers outline how disease management programs for free-ranging wildlife should be established, maintained, and conducted (Scott 1988, Gilmartin et al. 1993, Morner et al. 2002). The disease management programs described in these publications represent thoughtful and well-organized plans that emphasize consideration of not only the relationships between specific pathogens and their host animals, but also the important roles that the population dynamics of hosts, the condition of the habitat the hosts occupy, and environmental conditions play in disease/host relationships. Unfortunately, these comprehensive disease management programs would almost certainly be impractical relative to wild turkeys because the expense of implementing and maintaining them would be beyond what most landowners or TPWD would be able to afford or willing to spend (Cathey et al. 2007).

Disease outbreaks that affect wild turkey populations have not been documented in Texas, although outbreaks could have occurred unnoticed. Therefore, it appears that wild turkeys in Texas are exposed to a variety of pathogens and parasites that rarely impact populations. Nevertheless, when wild turkey translocations are contemplated in order to reintroduce birds to unoccupied former ranges, disease surveillance programs should be seriously considered because of the risk of introducing diseases to resident wild turkeys at or near release sites. Castle and Christensen (1985), Fritz et al. (1992), Kock et al. (2010), and Sainsbury and Vaughan-Higgins (2012) highlighted some of the risks that wildlife translocations pose if they are conducted without prior surveillance. Disease surveillance is not inexpensive; having a veterinary diagnostic laboratory develop tests and analyze biological samples can cost thousands of dollars, especially when screening for multiple pathogens. However, disease surveillance is not as expensive as implementing and maintaining a comprehensive disease management program. The importance of disease surveillance prior to translocation of wild turkeys in Texas has been recognized, because several surveillance and reconnaissance studies on wild turkeys have been conducted in South Texas (Hensley and Cain 1979, Rocke and Yuill 1987) and the Edwards Plateau (Peterson et al. 2002). Wild turkey translocations occur almost annually in East Texas, where Eastern wild turkeys are translocated from other states (most recently Iowa and Missouri and potentially West Virginia) to appropriate release sites in the Piney Woods. All the birds are tested for West Nile virus and *Salmonella pullorum* and are examined by a veterinarian prior to release either in their state of origin or when they arrive in Texas (J. Hardin, unpublished data). Wild turkey translocations are also being conducted in South Texas, and surveillance for antibodies to *Salmonella* spp. and *Mycoplasma* spp. has been conducted on turkeys sampled on two capture sites prior to translocation to release sites. Neither of these situations is ideal from a surveillance perspective because screening is restricted to two pathogens. And, relative to the South Texas translocations, all birds are released before surveillance results are obtained. Therefore, it is possible that diseases are being introduced to resident wild turkey populations at release sites. However, in South Texas, results revealed that birds testing positive for the diseases displayed antibodies, indicating exposure. Active *Salmonella* and *Mycoplasma* organisms did not appear to be present in the birds sampled (C. Hilton, unpublished data). There has been no indication that disease outbreaks have occurred at release sites in South Texas or the Piney Woods. In fact, in South Texas, reports from ranch owners and personnel from ranches where turkeys were released suggest that turkey populations are doing well. There is no indication that disease outbreaks have occurred, though this is not certain. A similar situation seems to exist for Eastern wild turkeys translocated to the Piney Woods. However, as indicated earlier in this chapter, it is possible that an undocumented disease carried by translocated birds from other states may be complicating the success of the Eastern wild turkey reintroduction program.

Another important consideration relative to wild turkey translocations involves translocating birds captured near commercial turkey operations. Disease transmission between domestic turkeys and wild turkeys that inhabit areas where domestic turkeys are produced is a possibility that should not be ignored. Markley (1967) warned that during the planning stages of wild turkey reintroduction projects, the proximity of source birds to domestic turkey farms should be critically reviewed. Therefore, it is inadvisable to translocate wild turkeys from areas where commercial domestic turkey operations exist because of the possibility of moving diseases and parasites to release sites. Fortunately, this rarely occurs today because state wildlife agencies are aware of the dangers commercial poultry operations pose to wild turkey populations. Furthermore, biosecurity at commercial poultry operations has improved significantly over the past 50 years so that there is little opportunity for exposure between domestic birds and wild turkeys.

Conclusion

The absence of a report of a particular pathogen or disease in Texas should not be interpreted as proof that a specific pathogen or disease does not occur in wild turkeys in Texas. Mortalities can be overlooked (Thomas et al. 2015), and disease investigations and reports are frequently opportunistic (Davidson et al. 1985, Howerth 1985, Howerth and Rodenworth 1985) or take place in other states (Huggins and Dauman 1961, Hurst 1980, Davidson et al. 1985, Davidson et al. 1988, Lindsay et al. 1994, Hoffman et al. 1997, Mock et al. 2001, Poppenga et al. 2005, Ingram et al. 2015). Caution should be exercised against underestimating the significance of subclinical infections (Fritz et al. 1992, Alger et al. 2017), and research geared toward management decisions is warranted (Jacobson and Hurst 1979, Alger et al. 2015, Thomas et al. 2015). Consideration should also be given to research on pathogens that are documented to have a negative effect on population levels of domestic fowl (Goodwin et al. 1988, Gingerich et al. 2002) or other gallinaceous birds (Castle and Christensen 1984, Drew et al. 1998).

Literature Cited

Akey, B. L., J. K. Nayar, and D. J. Forrester. 1981. Avian pox in Florida wild turkeys: *Culex nigripalpus* and *Wyeomyia vanduzeei* as experimental vectors. Journal of Wildlife Diseases 17:597–599.

Alger, K., E. Bunting, K. Schuler, J. Jagne, and C. M. Whipps. 2015. Diagnosing lymphoproliferative disease virus in live wild turkeys (*Meleagris gallopavo*) using whole blood. Journal of Zoo and Wildlife Medicine 46:806–814.

Alger, K., E. Bunting, K. Schuler, and C. M. Whipps. 2017. Risk factors for and spatial distribution of lymphoproliferative disease virus (LPDV) in wild turkeys (*Meleagris gallopavo*) in New York State, USA. Journal of Wildlife Diseases 53:499–508.

Allison, A. B., M. K. Keel, J. E. Philips, A. N. Cartoceti, B. A. Munk, N. M. Nemeth, T. I. Welsh, et al. 2014. Avian oncogenesis induced by lymphoproliferative disease virus: a neglected or emerging retroviral pathogen? Virology 450–451:2–12.

Amr, Z. S., K. E. Hyland, and J. E. Myers. 1988. *Metroliasthes lucida* in the Eastern wild turkey from Rhode Island. Journal of Wildlife Diseases 24:572–573.

Atkinson, C. T., and D. J. Forrester. 1987. Myopathy associated with megaloschizonts of *Haemoproteus meleagridis* in a wild turkey from Florida. Journal of Wildlife Diseases 23:495–498.

Barbosa, T., G. Zavala, S. Cheng, and P. Villegas. 2007. Full genome sequence and some biological properties of reticuloendotheliosis virus strain APC-566 isolated from endangered Attwater's prairie chickens. Virus Research 124:68–77.

Bishopp, F. C., and H. L. Trembley. 1945. Distribution and hosts of certain North American ticks. Journal of Parasitology 31:1–54.

Brennan, L. A., D. L. Williford, B. M. Ballard, W. P. Kuvlesky Jr., E. D. Grahmann, and S. J. DeMaso. 2017. The upland and webless migratory game birds of Texas. Texas A&M University Press, College Station, USA.

Busch, R. H., and L. E. Williams Jr. 1970. Case report: a Marek's disease-like condition in Florida turkeys. Avian Diseases 14:550–554.

Candelora, K. L., M. G. Spalding, and H. S. Sellers. 2010. Survey for antibodies to infectious bursal disease virus serotype 2 in wild turkeys and sandhill cranes of Florida, USA. Journal of Wildlife Diseases 46:742–752.

Castle, M. D., and B. M. Christensen. 1984. Blood and gastrointestinal parasites of Eastern wild turkeys from Kentucky and Tennessee. Journal of Wildlife Diseases 20:190–196.

Castle, M. D., and B. M. Christensen. 1985. Isolation and identification of *Aegyptianella pullorum* (Rickettsiales, Anaplasmataceae) in wild turkeys from North America. Avian Diseases 29:437–445.

Castle, M. D., B. M. Christensen, and T. E. Rocke. 1988. Hematozoan parasites of Rio Grande wild turkeys from southern Texas. Journal of Wildlife Diseases 24:88–96.

Cathey, J. C., K. Melton, J. Dreibelbis, B. Cavney, S. L. Locke, S. J. DeMaso, T. W. Schwertner, and B. Collier. 2007. Rio Grande wild turkey in Texas: biology and management. Texas AgriLife Extension Report B-6198. Texas A&M University, College Station, USA.

Charlton, K. G. 2000. Antibodies to selected disease agents in translocated wild turkeys in California. Journal of Wildlife Diseases 36:161–164.

Cook, R. S., D. O. Trainer, and W. C. Glazener. 1966. *Haemoproteus* in wild turkeys from the Coastal Bend region of

South Texas. Journal of Protozoology 13:588–590.

Craig, F. R., and F. S. Barkalow Jr. 1950. Blackhead in wild turkeys on free range in North Carolina. Wildlife of North Carolina 14:18–19.

Davidson, W. R., V. F. Nettles, C. E. Couvillion, and H. W. Yoder Jr. 1982. Infectious sinusitis in wild turkeys. Avian Diseases 26:402–405.

Davidson, W. R., V. F. Nettles, C. E. Couvillion, and E. W. Howerth. 1985. Diseases diagnosed in wild turkeys (*Meleagris gallopavo*) of the southeastern United States. Journal of Wildlife Diseases 21:386–390.

Davidson, W. R., H. W. Yoder, M. Brugh, and V. F. Nettles. 1988. Serological monitoring of Eastern wild turkeys for antibodies to *Mycoplasma* spp. and avian influenza viruses. Journal of Wildlife Diseases 24:348–351.

Davidson, W. R., E. B. Shotts, J. Teska, and D. W. Moreland. 1989. Feather damage due to mycotic infections in wild turkeys. Journal of Wildlife Diseases 25:534–539.

Davidson, W. R., and E. J. Wentworth. 1992. Population influences: diseases and parasites. Pages 101–128 *in* J. G. Dickson, editor. The wild turkey: biology and management. Stackpole Books, Mechanicsburg, Pennsylvania, USA.

Domeruth, C. H., D. J. Forrester, D. O. Trainer, and W. J. Bigler. 1977. Serologic examination of wild birds for hemorrhagic enteritis of turkey and marble spleen disease of pheasants. Journal of Wildlife Diseases 13:405–408.

Drew, M. L., W. L. Wigle, D. L. Graham, C. P. Griffin, N. J. Silvy, A. M. Fadly, and R. L. Witter. 1998. Reticuloendotheliosis in captive greater and Attwater's prairie chickens. Journal of Wildlife Diseases 34:783–791.

Dubey, J. P., C. F. Quist, and D. L. Fritz. 2000. Systemic sarcocystosis in a wild turkey from Georgia. Journal of Wildlife Diseases 36:755–760.

Dunn, J. 2016. Reticuloendotheliosis in poultry. Merck veterinary manual online. http://www.merckvetmanual.com/poultry/neoplasms/reticuloendotheliosis-in-poultry. Accessed December 16, 2016.

Elsmo, E. J., A. B. Allison, and J. D. Brown. 2016. A retrospective study of causes of skin lesions in wild turkeys (*Meleagris gallopavo*) in the eastern USA, 1975–2013. Journal of Wildlife Diseases 52:582–591.

Fedynich, A. M., and O. E. Rhodes Jr. 1995. Hemosporid (Apicomplexa, Hematozoea, Hemosporida) community structure and pattern in wintering wild turkeys. Journal of Wildlife Diseases 31:404–409.

Forrester, D. J. 1991. The ecology and epizootiology of avian pox and malaria in wild turkeys. Bulletin of the Society of Vector Ecologists 16:127–148.

Forrester, D. J. 1992. A synopsis of disease conditions found in wild turkeys (*Meleagris gallopavo* L.) from Florida, 1969–1990. Florida Field Naturalist 20:29–56.

Forrester, D. J., P. P. Humphrey, S. R. Telford Jr., and L. E. Williams. 1980. Effects of blood-induced infections of *Plasmodium hermani* on domestic and wild turkey poults. Journal of Wildlife Diseases 16:237–244.

Frame, D. D., E. J. Kelly, and A. Van Wettere. 2015. Dilated cardiomyopathy in a Rio Grande wild turkey (*Meleagris gallopavo intermedia*) in southern Utah, USA. Journal of Wildlife Diseases 51:790–792.

Fritz, B. A., C. B. Thomas, and T. M. Yuill. 1992. Serological and microbial survey of *Mycoplasma gallisepticum* in wild turkeys (*Meleagris gallopavo*) from six western states. Journal of Wildlife Diseases 28:10–20.

Gerhold, R. W., and J. R. Fischer. 2003. Avian tuberculosis in a wild turkey. Journal of Wildlife Diseases 49:164–166.

Giambrone, J. J., U. L. Diener, N. D. Davis, V. S. Panangala, and F. J. Hoerr. 1985. Effect of purified aflatoxin on turkeys. Poultry Science 64:859–865.

Gilmartin, W., E. Jacobson, W. Karesh, and M. Woodford. 1993. Monitoring, investigation and surveillance of disease in free-ranging wildlife. Journal of Zoo and Wildlife Medicine 24:389–393.

Gingerich, E., R. E. Porter, B. Lupiani, and A. M. Fadly. 2002. Diagnosis of myeloid leukosis induced by a recombinant avian leukosis virus in commercial white leghorn egg laying flocks. Avian Diseases 46:745–748.

Glazener, W. C., R. S. Cook, and D. O. Trainer. 1967. A serologic study of diseases in the Rio Grande turkey. Journal of Wildlife Management 31:34–39.

Goodwin, M. A., W. L. Steffens, I. D. Russell, and J. Brown. 1988. Diarrhea associated with intestinal cryptosporidiosis in turkeys. Avian Diseases 32:63–67.

Hatkins, J. M., and W. E. Phillips Jr. 1986. Isolation of *Listeria monocytogenes* from an Eastern wild turkey. Journal of Wildlife Diseases 22:110–112.

Hayes, L. E., K. A. Langheinrich, and R. L. Witter. 1992. Reticuloendotheliosis in a wild turkey (*Meleagris gallopavo*) from coastal Georgia. Journal of Wildlife Diseases 28:154–158.

Hensley, T. S., and J. R. Cain. 1979. Prevalence of certain antibodies to selected disease-causing agents in wild turkeys in Texas. Avian Diseases 23:62–69.

Hightower, B. G., V. W. Lehmann, and R. B. Eads. 1953. Ectoparasites from mammals and birds on a quail preserve. Journal of Mammalogy 34:268–271.

Hoffman, R. W., M. P. Luttrell, W. R. Davidson, and D. H. Ley. 1997. Mycoplasmas in wild turkeys living in association with domestic fowl. Journal of Wildlife Diseases 33:526–535.

Hon, L. T., D. J. Forrester, and L. E. Williams Jr. 1975. Helminths of wild turkeys in Florida. Proceedings of the Helminthological Society of Washington 42:119–127.

Hopkins, B. A., J. K. Skeeles, G. E. Houghten, D. Slagle, and K. Gardner. 1990. A survey of infectious diseases in wild turkeys (*Meleagris gallopavo silvestris*) from Arkansas. Journal of Wildlife Diseases 26:468–472.

Howerth, E. W. 1985. Salmonellosis in a wild turkey. Journal of Wildlife Diseases 21:433–434.

Howerth, E. W., and N. Rodenworth. 1985. Fatal systemic toxoplasmosis in a wild turkey. Journal of Wildlife Diseases 21:446–449.

Huggins, E. J., and C. F. Dauman. 1961. *Mediorhynchus grandis* (Acanthocephala: Gigan-torhynchidae) in a wild turkey of South Dakota. Journal of Parasitology 47:30–31.

Hurst, G. A. 1980. Histomoniasis in wild turkeys in Mississippi. Journal of Wildlife Diseases 16:357–358.

Ingram, D. R., D. L. Miller, C. A. Baldwin, J. Turco, and J. M. Lockhart. 2015. Serologic survey of wild turkeys (*Meleagris gallopavo*) and evidence of exposure to avian encephalomyelitis virus in Georgia and Florida, USA. Journal of Wildlife Diseases 51:374–379.

Jacobson, H. A., and G. A. Hurst. 1979. Prevalence of parasitism by *Amblyomma americanum* on wild turkey poults as influenced by prescribed burning. Journal of Wildlife Diseases 15:43–47.

Kellogg, F. E., A. K. Prestwood, R. R. Gerrish, and G. L. Doster. 1969. Wild turkey ectoparasites collected in the southeastern United States. Journal of Medical Entomology 6:329–330.

Kock, R. A., M. H. Woodford, and P. B. Rossiter. 2010. Disease risks associated with translocated wildlife. Revue scientifique et technique 29:329–350.

Kozicky, E. L. 1948. Some protozoan parasites of the Eastern wild turkey in Pennsylvania. Journal of Wildlife Management 12:263–266.

Lane, R. S., T. F. Kucera, R. H. Barrett, J. Mun, C. Wu, and V. S. Smith. 2006. Wild turkey (*Meleagris gallopavo*) as a host of ixodid ticks, lice and Lyme disease spirochetes (*Borrelia burgdorferi* sensu lato) in California state parks. Journal of Wildlife Diseases 42:759–771.

Ley, D. H., M. D. Ficken, D. T. Cobb, and R. L. Witter. 1989. Histomoniasis and reticuloendotheliosis in a wild turkey (*Meleagris gallopavo*) in North Carolina. Journal of Wildlife Diseases 25:262–265.

Lindsay, D. S., P. C. Smith, and B. L. Blagburn. 1994. Prevalence and isolation of *Toxoplasma gondii* from wild turkeys in Alabama. Journal of the Helminthological Society of Washington 61:115–117.

Markley, M. H. 1967. Limiting factors. Pages 199–244 *in* O. H. Hewitt, editor. The wild turkey and its management. Wildlife Society, Washington, DC, USA.

Maxfield, B. G., W. M. Reid, and F. A. Hayes. 1963. Gastrointestinal helminths from turkeys in southeastern United States. Journal of Wildlife Management 27:261–271.

McJunkin, J. W., R. D. Applegate, and D. A. Zelmer. 2003. Enteric helminths of juvenile and adult wild turkeys (*Meleagris gallopavo*) in eastern Kansas. Avian Diseases 47:1481–1485.

Mock, D. E., R. D. Applegate, and L. B. Fox. 2001. Preliminary survey of ticks (Acari: Ixodidae) parasitizing wild turkeys (Aves: Phasianidae) in eastern Kansas. Journal of Medical Entomology 38:118–121.

Moore, D. L., S. E. Henke, A. M. Fedynich, J. C. Laurenz, and R. Morgan. 2013. Acute effects of aflatoxin on northern bobwhites (*Colinus virginianus*). Journal of Wildlife Diseases 49:568–578.

Morner, T., D. L. Obendorf, M. Artois, and M. H. Woodford. 2002. Surveillance and monitoring of wildlife diseases. Revue scientifique et technique 29:67–76.

Pence, D. B., and S. Bickel. 1977. Helminths of wild turkeys in West Texas. Proceedings of the Helminthological Society of Washington 44:104–105.

Peterson, M. J., R. Aguirre, P. J. Ferro, D. A. Jones, T. A. Lawyer, M. N. Peterson, and N. J. Silvy. 2002. Infectious disease survey of Rio Grande wild turkeys in the Edwards Plateau of Texas. Journal of Wildlife Diseases 38:826–833.

Poppenga, R. H., A. F. Ziegler, P. L. Habecker, D. L. Singletary, M. K. Walter, and P. G. Miller. 2005. Zinc phosphide intoxication of wild turkeys (*Meleagris gallopavo*). Journal of Wildlife Diseases 41:218–223.

Rauber, R. H., P. Dilkin, L. Z. Giacomini, C. A. Araujo de Almeida, and C. A. Mallman. 2007. Performance of turkey poults fed different doses of aflatoxin in the diet. Poultry Science 86:1620–1624.

Reid, W. M. 1967. Etiology and dissemination of the blackhead disease syndrome in turkeys and chickens. Experimental Parasitology 21:249–275.

Quist, C. F., D. I. Bounous, J. V. Kilburn, V. F. Nettles, and R. D. Wyatt. 2000. The effect of dietary aflatoxin on wild turkey poults. Journal of Wildlife Diseases 36:436–444.

Rocke, T. E., and T. M. Yuill. 1987. Microbial infections in a declining turkey population in Texas. Journal of Wildlife Management 51:778–782.

Roslien, D. J., and A. O. Haugen. 1970. Some blood parasite and disease antibody findings in wild Rio Grande turkeys stocked in Iowa. Proceedings of the Iowa Academy of Science 77:93–96.

Sainsbury, A. W., and R. J. Vaughan-Higgins. 2012. Analyzing disease risks associated with translocations. Conservation Biology 26:442–452.

Schweitzer, S. H., C. F. Quist, G. L. Grimes, and D. L. Forster. 2001. Aflatoxin levels in corn available as wild turkey feed in Georgia. Journal of Wildlife Diseases 37:657–659.

Scott, M. E. 1988. The impact of infection and disease on animal populations: implications for conservation biology. Conservation Biology 2:40–56.

Thomas, J. M., A. B. Allison, E. C. Holmes, J. E. Phillips, E. M. Bunting, M. J. Yabsley, and J. D. Brown. 2015. Molecular surveillance for lymphoproliferative disease virus in wild turkeys (*Meleagris gallopavo*) from the eastern United States. PLoS ONE 10(4):e0122644. https://doi.org/10.1371/journal.pone.0122644. Accessed May 19, 2018.

Thomas, J. W. 1964. Diagnosed diseases and parasitism in Rio Grande wild turkeys. Wilson Bulletin 76:292.

Trainer, D. O. 1970. The use of wildlife to monitor zoonoses. Journal of Wildlife Diseases 6:397–401.

Trainer, D. O., W. C. Glazener, R. P. Hanson, and B. D. Nassif. 1968. Infectious disease exposure in a wild turkey population. Avian Diseases 12:208–214.

Veatch, J. K., R. D. Applegate, and S. J. Osborne. 1998. Serologic indices of some diseases in Kansas wild turkeys. Avian Diseases 42:393–396.

Walker, M. H., B. J. Rup, A. S. Rubin, and H. R. Bose Jr. 1983. Specificity in the immunosuppression induced by avian reticuloendotheliosis virus. Infection and Immunity 40:225–235.

Witter, R. L., and A. L. Fadly. 2003. Reticuloendotheliosis. Pages 517–535 *in* Y. M. Saif, J. Barnes, J. Glisson, L. McDougald, and D. Swayne, editors. Diseases of poultry. 11th edition. Iowa State University Press, Ames, USA.

10

Wild Turkey Management

We don't just manage land. We're supposed to be leaders. Conservation leaders. Leaders in protecting and improving the land.

—JACK WARD THOMAS (2004)

The art and science of wild turkey management has taken many forms over the last 150 years. The earliest efforts occurred in the late 1800s with the Texas state legislature's efforts to curtail extensive market hunting (Suarez 2002). However, many early legislative measures were ineffective, so turkey population trends continued to decline during the first half of the twentieth century. In was not until 1919, when the state legislature enacted a reasonable annual bag limit, coupled with the efforts of conservation-minded landowners and the employment of game wardens in the 1920s, that the remaining turkey populations in Texas were effectively protected (Suarez 2002). However, for most wild turkey populations in the state, these efforts came much too late, because by 1939 wild turkeys were restricted to small pockets of their former geographic range in Texas (Goodrum 1939). Aggressive management was deemed necessary to restore the state's wild turkey populations, so the Texas Game, Fish, and Oyster Commission and later the Texas Parks and Wildlife Department (TPWD), in cooperation with many landowners, developed and applied management techniques that have succeeded in providing Texans with the largest wild turkey population in North America, consisting of three subspecies. Success was not achieved overnight, however; it required patience and the realization that developing techniques to manage wild turkey populations is essential to not only the maintenance of sustainable populations, but to wild turkey restoration efforts as well. Therefore, this chapter will discuss the importance of wild turkey management in Texas, followed by discussion of how TPWD manages the state's wild turkey population. Then it will outline how landowners can develop a wild turkey management plan and where they can obtain assistance with developing a plan.

Why Is Wild Turkey Management Important?

Turkey management in the twenty-first century has changed significantly since the early 1900s (Leopold and Cummins 2016). Restoration efforts are generally complete, and attention is now focused primarily on harvest management and habitat management. Declines in turkey populations at the landscape scale can be attributed largely to habitat loss, and in some cases to density-dependent factors (Byrne et al. 2015, Eriksen et al. 2016, Stevens et al. 2017). Rio Grande wild turkey populations in Texas likely reached a saturation point in the 1980s and declined to more sustainable numbers in recent years. However, habitat management is critical to maintaining current population levels and, in some cases, to promoting population growth.

TPWD has made wild turkey management a priority, not only because turkeys are an important component of the state's ecosystems but also because the citizens of Texas value wild turkeys. The 2011 National Survey of Fishing, Hunting, and Wildlife-Associated Recreation showed that 13.7 million US residents over the age of 16 hunted and contributed $33.7 billion in the process. Fifty percent of those expenditures were spent in the pursuit of big game, which includes wild turkeys in this analysis. Texas alone accounts for 1.1 million hunters. So why should these figures matter to landowners, land managers, and the nonhunting public? Texas hunters contributed $1.8 billion to the Texas economy in 2011. Of that, $837 million was trip related. Considering that 59% of hunters live in urban areas, this means that urban dollars are brought into rural Texas economies. These urban hunters spend money on items such as food and lodging, transportation, and other trip expenses. In addition, these dollars do not go just to private landowners. In fact, most of the money goes to local businesses that provide hunters with food and lodging. Most game animals in Texas are found hours away from big cities like Houston and Dallas, resulting in an infusion of cash into many small communities. These hunter dollars often play a significant role in the prosperity of many small Texas towns.

Considering the dollars and cents involved, it makes sense that many Texas ranches today have diversified to cater to the hunting community. With the precarious state of ranch economics today, it simply makes financial sense for landowners to provide sustainable hunting opportunities in order to ensure that satisfied customers return each year to these small-town farms and ranches. The science behind turkey management is strong and can provide the needed answers to most of the harvest and habitat management questions these landowners have. It can also help them provide sustainable populations and the experiences hunters desire. In addition, when landowners and land managers create habitat for wild turkeys, they are benefiting a suite of nongame species that can attract nonconsumptive outdoor enthusiasts such as birders.

Texas Parks and Wildlife Department Statewide Wild Turkey Management

Wild turkey management has been a resounding success for the Rio Grande wild turkey in Texas. As indicated in chapter 3, Texas supports the largest number of wild turkeys in the United States, and 95% of the available Rio Grande wild turkey habitat is currently occupied. Although efforts to restore Eastern wild turkey populations remain ongoing, restoration of the much more abundant Rio Grande subspecies has been suspended. TPWD's current management strategy is to monitor the wild turkey population and develop regulatory frameworks that allow for the sustainable harvest of wild turkeys in Texas.

Texas turkey hunting

Harvest regulations are designed to protect game species while at the same time providing for sustainable recreational hunting opportunities. Seasons are established based on the biology of the species in question and population surveys conducted by TPWD staff. Biologists therefore conduct population monitoring of game species across the state. The surveys are generally designed to monitor game species at the ecoregion scale. However, staff also consult with private landowners on a number of population monitoring techniques designed to capture game species population trends at the ranch scale. These same biologists provide free, nonbinding wildlife and habitat management recommendations.

TPWD manages wild turkey harvest across large landscapes, which are referred to as wild turkey management zones (figs. 10.1 and 10.2). However, individual landowners may impose more restrictive harvests on their properties and often do. These wild turkey management units are delineated based on population densities, population trajectories, and breeding chronology. Information on seasons and bag limits is published annually in TPWD's *Outdoor Annual* and can be viewed online at www.tpwd.texas.gov or on the TPWD Outdoor Annual app.

The spring turkey season in most of Texas's Rio Grande wild turkey range is designed to provide the greatest number of hunting opportunities by capturing the majority of the spring gobbling activity. This liberal framework recognizes both the high Rio Grande turkey densities and low average harvest rates in Texas. Unlike in many southeastern and midwestern states with relatively high harvest rates, in Texas Rio Grande wild turkey harvest rarely exceeds 5% of the population at the ecoregion scale. Alternatively, TPWD institutes a more conservative season on the Eastern wild turkey because of lower densities. Texas

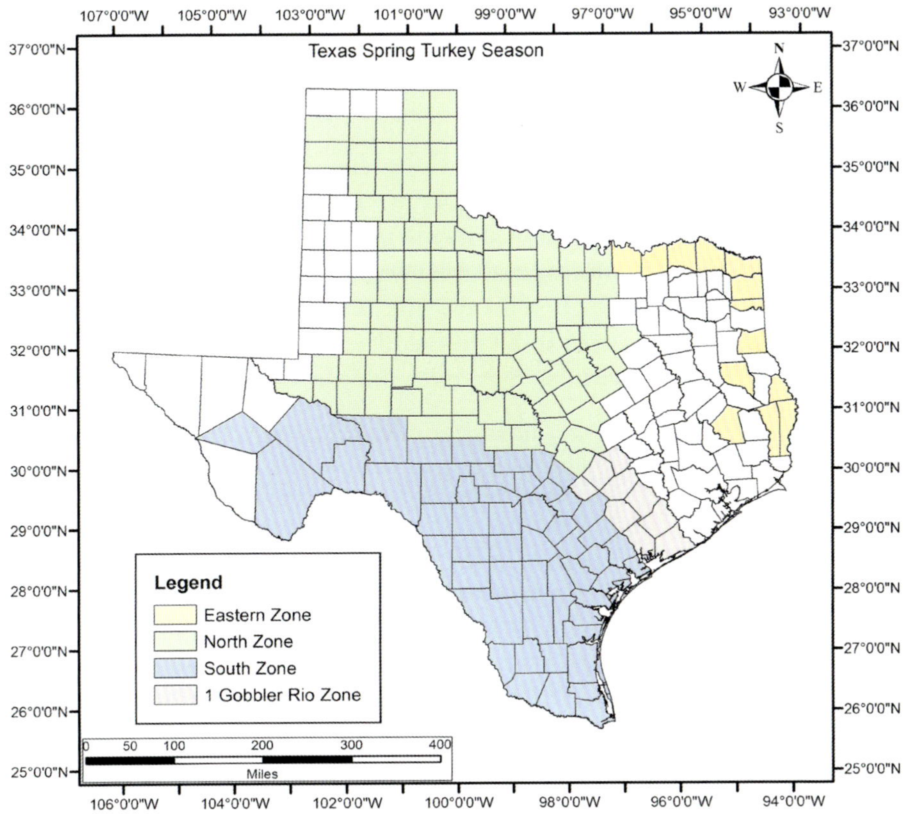

Figure 10.1. Spring wild turkey hunting zones in Texas (Source: Texas Parks and Wildlife Department).

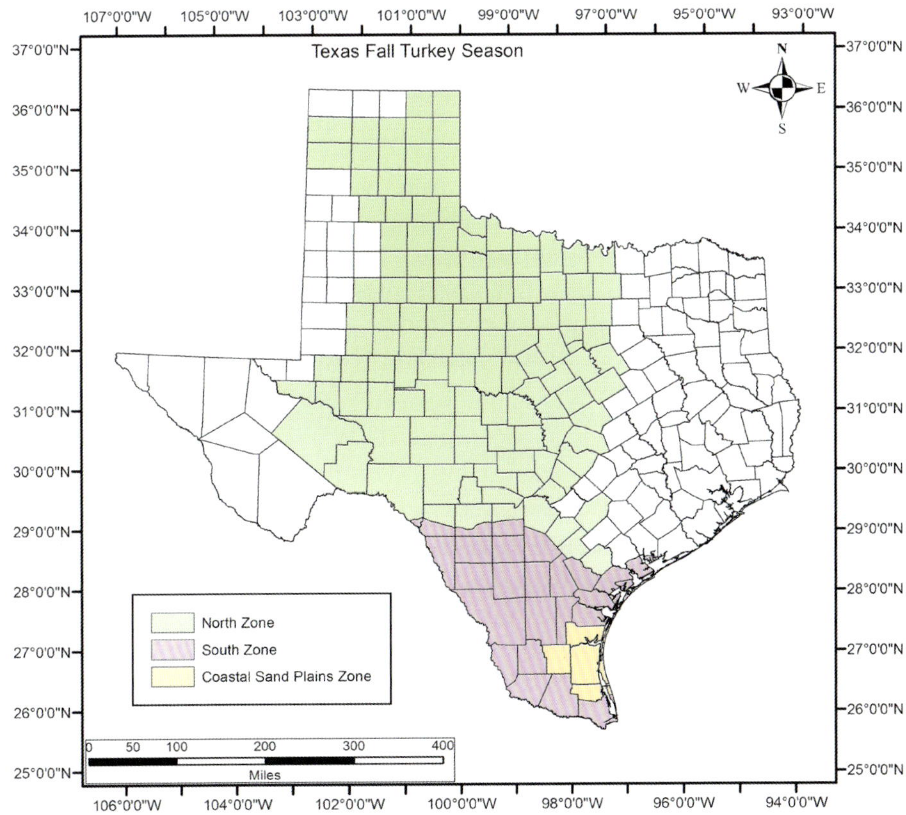

Figure 10.2. Fall wild turkey hunting zones in Texas (Source: Texas Parks and Wildlife Department).

provides a 3-week season on Eastern wild turkeys in 13 counties beginning in late April. The timing of this season ensures that most females have been bred prior to opening day.

Texas also offers a fall wild turkey season in a large portion of the Rio Grande wild turkey range. The fall season mirrors that of the white-tailed deer (*Odocoileus virginanus*), in which both archery and general gun seasons are offered. Youth seasons are provided in both the spring and fall in an effort to recruit new hunters.

Wild turkey hunter numbers and subsequent harvest have declined along with a general decline in overall hunter numbers across game species. During the 1990s, Texas hosted close to 150,000 turkey hunters, who harvested about 60,000 turkeys annually. As of the publishing of this book, Texas hosts approximately 80,000 hunters, who harvest about 38,000 turkeys annually. While turkey hunter numbers have declined, their success rate has increased, from about 40% in the 1990s to just over 45% today. Texas consistently hosts some of the highest numbers of turkey hunters in the country.

TPWD technical guidance program

Texas is a very large and ecologically diverse state, and wild turkeys occupy all of its ecoregions. There are many habitat generalities across ecoregions, such as nesting, brooding, and roosting cover, at least from a structural standpoint. There are also stark differences, such as the availability of roosting cover and vegetation community composition. Therefore, TPWD provides technical guidance to landowners in all the ecoregions of Texas.

TPWD biologists are located throughout the state and conduct censuses on a variety of game species. Because most of Texas is private land, one of the primary functions of TPWD biologists is providing free, nonbinding technical guidance to private landowners. These biologists assist private landowners by developing management plans and strategies, recommending harvest rates, and providing training on the use of a variety of management tools.

TPWD wildlife management areas

TPWD owns or manages over 400,000 ha (1 million ac) of land statewide. These wildlife management areas (WMAs) have a variety of functions, including public hunting, research, and demonstration. Wild turkeys occur on many of these WMAs, and turkey populations are incorporated in the wildlife management plans developed for each WMA. The WMAs are important because research conducted in these areas contributes to our knowledge of Texas wildlife. Moreover, they also serve an important educational function because the public has the opportunity to learn about the wildlife that inhabits WMAs simply by visiting them and talking to staff.

Statewide wild turkey surveys

TPWD assesses wild turkey harvest at both the state and ecoregion scales through TPWD's Small Game Harvest Survey. This survey tracks hunter and harvest trends for 19 species of migratory and upland game birds. It was first conducted after the 1981–1982 hunting season and has been conducted annually since the 1986–1987 hunting season. A survey form is mailed to 20,000 randomly selected hunters each February, with several follow-up mailings sent to nonrespondents. The purpose of the survey is to track hunter and harvest trends for each species at both the statewide and ecoregion levels. When paired with ecoregion harvest rates assessed through statewide banding efforts, the survey can provide a reasonable estimate of density at the ecoregion scale.

Since 1978, TPWD staff have periodically assessed statewide wild turkey distribution. This assessment is based on local biologists' knowledge of the landscape in which they work. TPWD biologists with responsibilities for specific counties map the areas of known turkey distribution, and supervisory staff then outline the current statewide turkey distribution. In 2014, TPWD staff developed a distribution assessment using Google Earth. TPWD field staff were provided a Google Earth file. This file consisted of a 10-minute grid that covered all of Texas. Each 10-minute grid was tied to a Google Docs survey. Once biologists selected a specific grid, they were taken to a survey to report the presence or absence of wild turkeys. These assessments were completed in 2015. These distribution assessments demonstrate the growth and expansion of Texas's wild turkey population over the past few decades, as indicated in the distribution maps in chapter 3.

The Wild Turkey Management Plan

Statewide management of wild turkeys is important because the information obtained from hunters and TPWD field staff is necessary to periodically determine the status of wild turkeys in Texas, which enables TPWD to adjust bag limits and season lengths when necessary. However, except for TPWD wildlife management areas, most active wild turkey management on the ground occurs among private landowners interested in wild turkeys. It is possible, and even likely, that many landowners do not know how to institute a wild turkey management plan on their property. Therefore, because this book provides a wealth of information about wild turkey natural history and ecology, it is appropriate to provide readers with a short discussion about what goes into an effective wild turkey management plan.

Wild turkey management involves numerous activities, including appropriate habitat management, population management, and people management. Every property will probably have unique wild turkey management challenges, and each individual landowner will have his or her own unique management objectives. Therefore, every property will likely require a creative approach to wild turkey management in order to ensure that wild turkey populations are maintained at sustainable levels while satisfying the management objectives of the individual landowner. In cases where a landowner's management objectives are not compatible with maintaining sustainable wild turkey numbers, the landowner's wishes must be respected. However, on properties where a landowner wants to manage for wild turkeys, a management plan can and should be developed for the property. Numerous tools are at the disposal of wildlife biologists and land managers charged with developing a wild turkey management plan. The challenge is to apply methodology that maintains healthy wild turkey populations, while also achieving landowner objectives. So, what important techniques can be employed to develop a management plan that maintains healthy wild turkey populations?

Estimating turkey numbers

One of the first steps in developing a management plan for wild turkeys is to determine whether wild turkeys inhabit a property, and if they do, the size of the local population should be estimated. Determining whether wild turkeys inhabit a farm or ranch is easy because turkeys are noticeably gregarious birds. If they are present, they are usually easy to detect, and it is generally possible to hear them when they fly up to roosts in the evening and leave roosts in the morning. So, driving ranch or farm roads in the early morning and evening and stopping and listening for a few minutes will often reveal the presence of turkeys. Game and trail cameras work well in determining whether wild turkeys are present on a particular property, since turkeys readily utilize bait stations. In addition, visiting likely roosting habitats or ponds or stock tanks and looking for wild turkey tracks and feathers is also a good way to establish whether turkeys are using a property.

Once it has been established that wild turkeys are using a farm or ranch, an effort to estimate turkey abundance on the property should be made. A number of methods can be employed to estimate turkey abundance, and Locke et al. (2011) provide a good summary of these survey techniques. Counts of wild turkeys at roosts during the morning (Cook 1973, Butler et al. 2006), trail camera surveys (Cobb et al. 1996, Cobb et al. 1997), and aerial counts (Caveny 2009) can be used to survey wild turkey populations. In addition, gobble counts, incidental observations while hunting deer or driving ranch roads, and estimating female-to-poult ratios (Butler et al. 2007) during the summer will yield data that can be compared during successive years to monitor turkey population trends. These techniques can be effective at the ranch or landowner-association scale, depending on the location in the state, but they may yield unreliable results at larger scales. Obtaining wild turkey density estimates is a challenge for biologists because of wild turkey behavior and their ability to move considerable distances daily. The most promising methods yet developed involve counting wild turkeys during road surveys. Erxleben et al. (2011) developed a road-based survey method and determined that unbiased density estimates could be obtained if censuses were conducted from December to March in the Rolling

Plains and Edwards Plateau. Unfortunately, unbiased results apparently cannot be obtained in South Texas because the vegetation communities are too dense. A better alternative for Rio Grande wild turkey surveys at large scales may be aerial surveys (Caveny 2009). After it has been determined that wild turkeys are present on a property and some level of abundance has been determined, it is important to decide how abundance will be monitored on at least an annual basis. Any of the aforementioned population monitoring techniques will work to monitor turkey populations as long as proper procedures are followed and a monitoring schedule is adhered to.

Habitat management

If turkeys inhabit a property for which a management plan is being developed, the habitat should be appraised to determine whether any important habitat requirements are limited. Cathey et al. (2007a) developed a useful habitat appraisal guide for Rio Grande wild turkeys for landowners on rangelands throughout Texas, while Curry (2010) published a habitat appraisal guide for turkeys in South Texas. Habitat appraisal guides have not been published for Eastern or Merriam's wild turkeys in Texas. Nevertheless, wild turkeys have basic habitat needs regardless of subspecies, so these basic requirements need to be the primary focus when appraising habitat for wild turkeys. Habitat requirements and management needs are detailed and discussed in chapters 7 and 8 of this book, and habitat appraisal guides are referenced in chapter 8. Therefore, the purpose of this section is to focus on what to do when essential habitat requirements are limited.

Wild turkeys rely on several key habitat factors to sustain local populations. These include roosting cover, nesting cover, brood-rearing habitat, and water within sufficiently large areas of usable space to maintain a viable population. These habitat features must be near one another in order to sustain wild turkeys on a property, but also scattered across the larger landscape in order to sustain a population at the county, watershed, or ecoregion scale. The absence of any one of these features could lead to population declines. The level of decline is often driven by the scale at which one or more of these habitat features are absent. The habitat feature that is most limiting is often driven by the area of the state in which a turkey population lives. The subsections below address each potential limiting factor separately, as well as potential remedies.

Where are my roost trees, and are they limited in distribution?

Regardless of where a farm or ranch is located in turkey range in Texas, and regardless of the subspecies of turkey using the property, roost sites are a basic requirement for maintaining turkey populations (Crockett 1973). Roosting cover is often widely available in the eastern half of Texas and is therefore rarely a management concern. However, roosting cover is often the most limiting factor to the success of Rio Grande wild turkeys in semiarid and arid regions of Texas. These regions include the South Texas Brush Country, Rolling Plains, High Plains, and Trans-Pecos ecoregions. Management practices will vary from roost to roost and may include simple human avoidance, active habitat management such as fencing or direct planting of seedlings, or even development of constructed roosts.

If brush or timber management is a landowner's objective, it is critical to leave sufficient roosting habitat and escape cover associated with roosts on the property to maintain Eastern, Rio Grande, and Merriam's wild turkey populations. In the case of Rio Grande wild turkeys, locating and designating active roost sites for protection should be a priority before clearing operations are initiated because of the scarcity of roosting habitat in some portions of the Rio Grande wild turkey's range (Cathey et al. 2007b). Rio Grande wild turkeys sometimes use different areas for summer and winter roosts. Winter roosts represented either by very large trees with spreading canopies or by groups of large trees are useful because they can accommodate large winter flocks of females and young birds, while a single roost during spring and summer is often sufficient to accommodate a nesting or brooding female and small groups of males. Ideally, designated roosting habitat should cover a minimum of 4–6 ha (10–15 ac), and at least 10–15% of the roosting habitat should consist of woody cover (Swearingin et al. 2010).

Maintaining roosting habitat is important during land-clearing operations (Beasom and Wilson

1992), but brush under roosts needs to be removed too. A wild turkey management plan should address practices that reduce the cover of midstory species (medium-sized trees and shrubs) growing under the canopy of roost trees. This will often enhance and extend the life of traditional roost sites and may also reduce the risk of roost loss to wildfire or even prescribed fire by reducing ladder fuels. Care should be taken when clearing these midstory trees and shrubs because the use of heavy equipment under the canopy of roost trees can disturb root systems and kill the trees. Typically, a lighter approach such as chainsaw removal, mulching, or shearing is preferable.

Another potential limiting factor associated with roosts is a lack of open area adjacent to a roost. Haucke (1975) found clearings adjacent to all actively utilized roost sites in South Texas. Maintaining an opening consisting of grasses and forbs adjacent to a roost is important because wild turkeys prefer to land in an open area when they vacate roosts in the morning and when they approach a roost in the evening. Moreover, an opening adjacent to a roost facilitates detection of approaching predators before turkeys fly up to the roost, as well as when they are roosting and when they leave the roost in the morning (Haucke 1975). However, openings close to or adjacent to a roost should be created or improved when turkeys are not using roosts during midday, because mechanical operations will disturb turkeys and possibly result in roost abandonment (Cathey et al. 2010).

The presence of exotic tree species can also limit natural turkey roosts. Species such as salt cedar (*Tamarix ramosissima*) have invaded some riparian areas of the state, and these areas often provide the best roost sites because of the availability of tall trees along watercourses. These exotic species typically outcompete native roost trees and eventually reduce their abundance along riparian systems. Removing invasive exotic species like salt cedar is often critical for promoting future roost trees. Also, in areas where traditional flooding regimes have changed because of upstream damming, managers may need to do some direct planting (Perotto-Baldivieso 2005). Direct planting of fast-growing species such as cottonwood is an excellent practice to accelerate the reestablishment of native roost trees along riparian systems and provide the next generation of roost sites.

In some extreme situations, such as the drought of 2011 when traditional natural roost sites were lost because of widespread tree mortality on Texas rangelands, a stopgap measure may be needed. Turkeys have often been observed using human-made structures such as active windmills, utility towers, and power lines. In fact, if turkeys are observed using these structures, it indicates that natural roosts are limited in the area. Rio Grande wild turkeys will often readily use a well-designed constructed roost in areas where natural roosts are limited or absent. Constructed roosts can be assembled from a variety of materials. Modifications to active or abandoned windmills can provide a constructed turkey roost. The primary focus should be a well-built structure capable of withstanding the weight of numerous wild turkeys as well as high winds and ice. This structure should try to replicate a wild turkey's preferred roosting structure by providing numerous horizontal perches that allow multiple turkeys to space themselves comfortably (fig. 10.3). A number of designs can be used to build constructed wild turkey roosts. Most important is that the structure is stable and at least 7 m (20 ft) high (Cathey et al. 2007b), and that the roosting platform is as large as possible to accommodate 15–20 birds (Mitchell, unpublished data). Multiple designs can be used to fabricate platforms. Platforms can be constructed from materials such as welded pipes or tubing, 8 cm (3 in) wooden posts, or 0.61 × 1.83 m

Figure 10.3. An active constructed wild turkey roost on a ranch in South Texas (photo by Robert Sanders).

(2 × 6 ft) boards fashioned into an *X* or pentagon placed horizontally near the top of roost structures. Turkeys will often use a design that is very stable and accommodates numerous birds where natural roosts are limited or absent. These structures can even have multiple stories to increase the number of wild turkeys capable of using them. It is often desirable to build several constructed roosts adjacent to one another, or in a cluster, to accommodate a large flock of roosting turkeys. The roosting platform of one constructed roost in South Texas collapsed because the accumulated weight of a large group of turkeys was too heavy for it.

Siting constructed roosts in appropriate locations is critically important for increasing the probability that wild turkeys will use them. There is no point in building a constructed roost in the middle of an open field or in a location far from a water source because it is unlikely turkeys will use it. To better ensure utilization, resourceful managers develop constructed roost sites along riparian areas or near permanent water sources, and if possible close to sites where historic roosts were lost. Constructed roosts can also be incorporated near active roost sites in order to enhance and expand existing roosting cover if it is determined that roosts are becoming a limiting factor.

However, as mentioned previously, constructed roosts are only a stopgap measure. Management should not end with the establishment of constructed roosts but should rather begin with them. Native roost trees should be planted in groups or mottes near constructed roosts as well as active roost sites. As with any natural resource management practice, plan for some failure by planting large numbers of trees. The species used should be based on those that have traditionally occurred in a particular area of the state and those that are available. These may include live oak, pecan, cottonwood, and hackberry. Watering, fencing, and other protective measures, such as tree tubes to protect from herbivory or from white-tailed bucks rubbing antlers on saplings, are often required to ensure the survival of these trees. Other species that can be planted at roost sites include American elm, bald cypress (*Taxodium distichum*), cedar elm, walnut, and soapberry (*Sapindus saponaria*). When developing the roosting portion of a management plan, identify the tree species present on a property that serve as wild turkey roosts in the area before selecting a species to plant if establishment of additional roosting habitat is deemed necessary. If additional roosts are needed, make an effort to establish tree species that are native to the property under management. Visit with your local TPWD or Natural Resources Conservation Service (NRCS) biologist or other wildlife professional to learn about a variety of options for protecting existing roost sites and for planning for the next generation of turkey roost trees.

A final consideration relative to managing for wild turkey roosts concerns disturbance. In regions of the state where roost trees are limited, the shade of tall roost trees is often attractive to people as a site for hunting camps, houses, barns, and various activities. Unfortunately, these activities sometimes cause turkeys to abandon active roost sites, particularly if wild turkeys are unused to humans (Smith 1975). In regions where roosting cover is limited, this could be the difference between having and not having turkeys on the property or management area. To maintain or increase usable space for wild turkeys, development of anthropogenic features should be at least a few hundred yards from active roost sites. There are numerous instances of wild turkeys roosting in the tall trees of a ranch headquarters or hunting camp compounds, particularly when feeders are provided to attract deer and other wildlife species and when turkeys are not harassed. If wild turkeys become habituated to human activities, then the activities associated with a ranch headquarters will not be an issue. Indeed, wild turkeys often roost in large trees near dwellings, barns, and other structures. However, new construction should be avoided around or near active roosts because this could cause turkeys to abandon a traditional roost they have used for generations.

Is enough woody cover (brush or timber) present?

The amount and distribution of woody cover in the form of brush or trees can have a profound impact on just how much of a farm or ranch is usable for wild turkeys. Wild turkeys spend most of their life along the edges of wooded and open habitats. Rarely do they venture too far from these edges. These areas provide rapid escape from predators, loafing cover, and foraging opportunities, as many tree and brush species provide hard and soft mast consumed by wild turkeys.

Forested habitat can make up more than 90% of the cover in the eastern half of the state. However, suitable forest habitat for Eastern wild turkeys should consist of an open herbaceous understory that provides good visibility as well as foraging and nesting habitat. In the western half of the state, areas consisting of as little as 30% woody cover can be adequate for wild turkeys as long as the woody vegetation is distributed adequately throughout a property, thereby maximizing the woody/herbaceous edge. Regardless of the location in Texas, woody cover, often along rivers and smaller drainages, provides the opportunity for exchange of wild turkey genes as well as ingress and egress over very large landscapes by serving as critical travel corridors. Without this habitat connectivity, populations can become isolated and even locally extinct in some extreme cases. Fragmenting features on the landscape such as interstate highways, expansive agricultural fields, and large reservoirs increase the likelihood of fragmented and isolated populations. Therefore, landowners interested in wild turkeys should avoid fragmenting woody cover and should instead manage their properties in a manner that provides corridors linking important habitats, and if possible other wild turkey populations.

Is there enough herbaceous cover to support nesting and brood rearing?

Throughout the range of the North American wild turkey, one factor does not change. Wild turkeys nest on the ground in lateral cover consisting of well-developed herbaceous or woody vegetation less than 1 m (3 ft) tall (Porter 1992). Less prominent but often associated with nesting cover is a canopy layer consisting of trees, shrubs, vines, or woody debris 0.5–1 m (1.5–3 ft) above the nest site. The availability of herbaceous cover is positively correlated with reproductive success. Also, since a wild turkey population is sustainable only with adequate nesting and brooding success and subsequent population recruitment, maintaining adequate and well-dispersed herbaceous cover on a property to serve as brooding habitat is critical.

Wild turkey brooding habitat is consistent across the wild turkey's range in the United States and consists of herbaceous vegetation interspersed with woody cover (Porter 1992). Ideally, this herbaceous cover will be between boot high and knee high. In addition to enhancing nest success, managing for boot-high to knee-high grasses and weeds also provides the necessary structure for quality brood-rearing cover. Brooding cover should be viewed not only from the perspective of the height and density of herbaceous cover, but also from the distribution of openings. Wild turkey females have been known to move miles with day-old poults to find quality openings to serve as brooding cover. However, brood survival has been hypothesized to decline as the distance between nesting and brooding cover increases (Porter 1992).

Managers interested in wild turkeys should consider the timing and location of management practices, as well as how those practices might impact nesting and brooding females during the most critical period of a wild turkey's life cycle. For example, before beginning mowing and haying operations in May and June, recognize that turkeys prefer to nest in herbaceous habitat types, so mowing or haying these areas in May and June would likely destroy nests, thereby impacting recruitment of juvenile birds into the fall population. Turkeys are going to lay eggs somewhere, even if quality nesting cover is not available. The real question is, why mow during the nesting season when there is a genuine risk of disturbing nesting females or destroying nests, not to mention destroying nesting and brooding habitat? If turkey production is a management objective on a property, mowing and similar management activities should be avoided in potential nesting cover during the primary nesting and early brooding period of May and June.

Prescribed fire is an excellent tool to create and improve wild turkey nesting and brooding habitat as well as to increase usable space. Because of high annual rainfall in excess of 100 cm (40 in) across most of the Eastern wild turkey's range in Texas, woody vegetation requires regular disturbance in order to maintain usable space. In this area of the state, usable space consists primarily of forested landscapes with an open understory that provides few visual obstructions. Fire historically provided the primary disturbance in this landscape, maintaining up to 12 million hectares (30 million acres) of usable habitat for the Eastern wild turkey. The absence of fire on the landscape has played a significant role in the failure of numerous wild turkey restoration efforts because of the encroachment of invasive shrubs such as yaupon holly (*Ilex vomitoria*) and eastern red cedar (*Juniperus virginiana*).

In the eastern half of the state, turkeys prefer to nest in areas that have received a prescribed fire within the previous three years (Yeldell et al. 2017). These prescribed fires take tall woody vegetation back to ground level. The resprouting woody vegetation along with the flush of grasses and forbs stimulated by the fire provides ideal nesting cover. Since most areas in the eastern half of Texas can be burned on a three-year rotation, if not more frequently, this system of fire and regrowth coincides very well with turkey management. In fact, turkeys prefer to live, nest, and raise broods in woods managed on a three-year fire rotation. Prescribed burning should be conducted during spring on a 3 year-year rotation to create the open forest under stories wild turkeys prefer. Turkeys will generally not use areas not burned every three years. Furthermore, as indicated in chapter 8, burning during fall and winter promotes forb growth, as forbs are usually the first plants to emerge at the end of winter and beginning of spring.

In the western half of the state, where nesting habitat is limited, the required vegetation conditions can be developed in a number of ways. Prescribed burning is often a less efficient management tool on rangelands with serious brush infestations. These dense brushy areas often lack the fine fuels (grasses and forbs) necessary to carry a prescribed fire capable of reducing woody cover. Under these conditions, developing herbaceous openings through mechanical or chemical treatments often increases the availability of nesting and brooding habitat as well as eventually increasing the fine fuel loads necessary to carry a prescribed fire. Therefore, mechanical and chemical techniques that reduce brush cover, such as roller chopping, aerating, or disking, must often be applied on rangelands infested with dense brush before prescribed burning can provide efficient management.

When conducting mechanical brush treatments, managers should remember that wild turkeys often remain close to woody escape cover. Consequently, it is important to avoid creating large openings that place woody edges (escape cover) more than 200 m (600 ft) apart. Once brush management operations are completed and fuel loads have recovered, periodic prescribed burning will help maintain openings by reducing brush invasion and rejuvenating herbaceous cover by removing thick, decadent, and matted grass. Periodic prescribed fires will help promote the growth of new food-producing grass and forb species, which will in turn attract insects for growing poults. Rio Grande wild turkeys inhabit more semiarid and arid regions of the state relative to the Eastern subspecies, so it is often difficult to plan prescribed fires on a set rotational schedule. In the western extremes of the Rio Grande's range in Texas, consider utilizing prescribed fire opportunistically as fuel loads and weather allow.

A wild turkey management plan should also include prescribed grazing relative to managing and maintaining herbaceous vegetation for nesting and brooding habitat. Typically, livestock grazing is an important land-use practice on most rural rangelands and pastures throughout Texas. Some of the most heavily utilized brooding habitat in East Texas consists of cattle pastures. Farther west across Texas, livestock grazing becomes an increasingly important management concern on the rangelands inhabited by Rio Grande and Merriam's wild turkeys.

Herbaceous conditions compatible with turkey production are regularly attained using livestock grazing in Texas. However, this is often complicated by the weather. Drought is a fact of life in Texas, and dry years are actually more common than years of even average rainfall. Clearly, rainfall is essential to grass and forb growth, so annual rainfall affects the condition of wild turkey nesting and brooding cover, not to mention the overall fitness of wild turkeys. The impact of drought is often more significant farther west across the state. For this reason, Rio Grande and Merriam's wild turkey populations are typically the most significantly impacted by drought. Regardless of where wild turkeys occur in Texas, livestock grazing can impact populations because too much grazing, and in some cases too little grazing, can have a negative impact on nesting and brooding habitat conditions as well as on overall usable space.

While land managers cannot control the weather, they can manage grazing pressure in a manner conducive to maintaining healthy and sustainable wild turkey populations. Like prescribed fire, proper grazing management can be a good habitat management tool for wild turkeys. The priority must be to provide adequate herbaceous vegetation during spring and summer to conceal nesting females and broods from predators.

The key to grazing management is periodic rest and adjustments to grazing pressure in order to accomplish the desired residual herbaceous cover. This is achieved by adjusting stocking rates and rotating livestock as necessary based primarily on annual rainfall. On Texas rangelands, inadequate herbaceous cover resulting from overgrazing can be a primary limiting factor inhibiting turkey production. Inadequate herbaceous cover limits turkey production by reducing quality of nesting cover available for females, thereby increasing the potential detection of nesting females and poults by an assortment of predators. Reduced herbaceous cover also reduces the availability of important plants and insects, which provide critical protein necessary to sustain growing poults. Although wild turkeys will readily utilize heavily grazed and short-grass pastures at certain times, it is necessary to maintain sufficient herbaceous cover throughout the year. Conversely, it is also important to avoid allowing grass in pastures to become so dense that turkeys will not use them.

As part of a wild turkey habitat appraisal, landowners and managers should determine whether the current stocking rates are appropriate to provide adequate nesting and brooding cover across a significant portion of the farm or ranch. If not, stocking rates will need to be adjusted to provide sufficient herbaceous cover to maintain a sustainable wild turkey population. Vegetation conditions of pastures must be carefully monitored on a frequent basis (at least once a week), and livestock stocking rates adjusted or grazing animals rotated to other pastures. A grazing management plan tailored to turkey production should be designed to identify specific stocking rates and a grazing rotation schedule that maintains appropriate wild turkey habitat conditions but has the flexibility to adjust to the erratic climate typical of Texas. Droughts will occur, and typically cattle prices will fluctuate. Managers are advised to plan for these eventualities.

Habitat management for wild turkeys often requires applying several of the vegetation management techniques discussed in this section. For example, on brush-infested rangelands, mechanical and/or chemical treatments will likely be necessary before effective prescribed burning can be implemented, because herbaceous vegetation must be released to supply sufficient fine fuel for a fire. Prescribed burning on a rotation that matches herbaceous production and rates of woody encroachment for a given region of the state might then be implemented together with a grazing management plan that maintains herbaceous habitat conditions for wild turkeys. Maintaining historic roost sites should also be included in a management plan so that open understories are maintained for wild turkeys.

Is there enough water to support a wild turkey population?

This question does not refer to climatic conditions, but rather to the need to provide enough consumable water to sustain individuals as well as populations of wild turkeys. Just as for all animals, water is necessary for wild turkey survival. It has often been assumed that wild turkeys require free or standing water from lakes, stock tanks, seeps, ponds, creeks, and other sources. This has not been proven scientifically (Beasom and Wilson 1992), but it has been proven that wild turkeys fulfill a substantial portion of their daily water requirements from preformed and metabolic water, which they derive from dew and food items they consume (Cathey et al. 2007b). Nevertheless, one cannot conclude that turkeys do not drink, because they readily utilize free water when and where it is available. Dew and moisture-rich food items may at times be limiting, particularly during droughts, so providing sources of free water can help keep wild turkeys on a property during drought and is an important consideration in any wild turkey management plan (Glazener 1967).

So, together with habitat management that provides a diversity of plants and other foods to furnish preformed water, a wild turkey management plan should ensure that sufficient free water is provided as well. Numerous water sources, from creeks and rivers to stock tanks and seeps, are often abundant in East Texas, to the point that free water supplies are generally not a management concern for Eastern wild turkeys. Still, landowners and land managers should determine whether sources of free water are limited in their particular area of management in East Texas, and whether stock tanks or other watering devices need to be provided. On semiarid and arid rangelands of Texas, free water is an even more important requirement of wild turkeys because of extremes in temperatures and evaporation rates, which are typically higher in these regions. Schorger (1966) indicated that many areas in the Southwest are suitable for wild turkeys but lack suitable water sources. Additionally, wild turkey numbers increased on the King Ranch about 100 years ago once windmills were established throughout the ranch and water storage tanks were modified for wildlife (Lehmann 1957).

A number of recommendations are provided in chapter 8 relative to the distribution and design of wildlife watering systems; therefore, a summary of potential considerations is provided here. Water sources should be spaced no farther than 3 km (2 mi) apart in areas managed for wild turkeys (Suarez 2002). Water sources for turkeys should be fenced to exclude livestock if possible and should be at ground level and easily accessible so that poults do not drown in water troughs (Beasom and Wilson 1992). In addition, ranches with multiple pastures should have water in every pasture. Where a central water source exists for livestock, an additional water source should be established for wild turkeys and located at least 0.4 km (0.25 mi) from the central water source (Prasad and Guthery 1986). Water catchments that capture and store precipitation and make water available to wildlife, such as "gallinaceous guzzlers," provide water for wild turkeys in areas where subsurface water is limited (Beasom and Wilson 1992).

How much space is required to sustain a wild turkey population?

Spatial requirements of wild turkeys are discussed in chapter 7, and because wild turkeys have large home ranges that vary in size between seasons, sites, and individuals and according to age and sex, large areas need to be managed to maintain a self-sustaining wild turkey population. Eastern wild turkey home ranges can vary from 405 ha (1,000 ac) to over 1,214 ha (3,000 ac), whereas Rio Grande wild turkey home ranges can vary from as little as 200 ha (500 ac) for nesting females in South Texas to almost 3,237 ha (8,000 ac) for juvenile females in the Texas Panhandle. Merriam's wild turkeys have similarly large home ranges, from about 405 ha (1,000 ac) to 2,000 ha (5,000 ac). So clearly, the availability and abundance of roosting, nesting, and brooding habitats along with water influence the amount of space required to sustain a wild turkey population. Therefore, because a single wild turkey may require several thousand acres to fulfill its annual life cycle, wild turkey management must be considered on a landscape scale, as indicated in chapters 7 and 8.

This may seem impossible to many landowners who do not own or control tens of thousands of acres. However, remember that wild turkeys generally inhabit rural areas where human disturbances are minimal. So, landowners interested in wild turkeys should conduct management operations that provide all the habitat requirements of wild turkeys on their farms and ranches because at the very least, the habitat created could prove essential for wild turkeys that use the property, even if only intermittently. For example, preserving and maintaining a few active roost sites, adequate nesting and brooding habitat, and well-distributed sources of water should encourage wild turkeys to use a property on a regular basis. Groups of landowners can also form "wild turkey cooperatives," where a number of properties adjacent to or near one another are collectively managed for wild turkey production. Such an arrangement between neighbors who are interested in enjoying wild turkeys can result in a landscape that harbors a sustainable wild turkey population. Generally, however, landowners interested in wild turkeys can maintain turkeys on their property by providing the birds with adequate food and water as well as roosting, nesting, and brooding habitat.

Predator control

Many landowners worry that predators are an obstacle to their efforts to manage game populations on their properties. Some ask whether predator control is justifiable and whether it even works. Predator control is controversial, not only among wildlife professionals but also within current society. Predator control was once pervasive throughout the United States, beginning when Europeans colonized America. It was not until the 1970s, when President Nixon banned the use of poisons on federal lands, that perspectives on predators really began to change (Leopold and Chamberlain 2002). When research started to focus on predator control, it quickly became clear that it is a very complex issue and that many concerns need to be considered before predator control is applied.

Leopold and Chamberlain (2002) discuss the complexity of predator control from an unbiased perspective and recommend following a protocol before predator control operations are implemented. One of the most important considerations they highlight is determining whether predator control is necessary to improve populations of desired wildlife. Perhaps habitat limitations are responsible for reduced populations of the preferred wildlife species. Corrective habitat management may then eliminate the need for predator control. Another important recommendation of Leopold and Chamberlain (2002) is identifying the specific predator species responsible for the mortality experienced by the preferred wildlife species. Coyotes are often assumed to be important wild turkey predators, but in Mississippi, Chamberlain and Leopold (1999) indicated that turkey feathers were very rarely found in coyote stomachs. Often raccoons, opossums, armadillos, foxes, snakes, ravens, and crows are more effective wild turkey nest predators than larger predators such as coyotes and bobcats (Dreibelbis et al. 2008, Melville et al. 2014). Furthermore, landowners often believe that raptors are important wild turkey predators, but even if they are on occasion, raptors cannot be harmed because federal law protects them.

Blanket removal of all predators is not desirable and is often impossible. Furthermore, reducing the population of one predator may result in a population increase of another predator, which may cause additional problems. For example, the predator population that increases after a targeted predatory species has been reduced may be more efficient at preying on deer or young livestock. Alternatively, a significant reduction of a specific predator may release rodent and lagomorph (rabbit) populations, which could negatively affect important wildlife habitat. Therefore, it is important to evaluate whether predator control is necessary before deciding to implement it.

Is predator control an effective means of increasing wild turkey populations? Lehmann (1957) indicated that employing several full-time trappers to implement intensive predator removal on the King Ranch during the 1930s and 1940s resulted in increased wild turkey and white-tailed deer populations. Beasom (1974) also reported that intensive short-term removal of almost 500 game bird predators in South Texas resulted in a significant increase in wild turkey populations but cautioned that such efforts are time consuming and expensive. However, Guthery (1995) acknowledged that although coyotes destroy game bird nests and kill nesting females, the removal of coyotes would have little impact on game bird numbers because renesting rates would compensate for female and nest losses from coyotes, and mortality from other sources would likely increase because of the removal of coyotes from the predator-prey system. It is possible that a landowner could remove sufficient numbers of predators to improve a wild turkey population in the short term if the landowner was willing to bear the cost and effort required to do so. However, such an intensive effort is rarely financially sustainable in the long term for most landowners and would probably not be desirable because of the potential negative impacts the constant removal of predators would have on the ecosystem.

So, when would predator removal be justified? The Wildlife Society provided guidance in a position statement supporting predator control under three scenarios, one of which involved efforts to restore a wild animal population (Leopold and Chamberlain 2002). So, if wild turkey population restoration is a management objective, then predator control could be warranted for a short period. In situations where wild turkeys are being translocated to a site where they have been extirpated or where densities are low and habitat conditions are suitable, predator removal could begin a few months before turkey releases occur, which is typically during winter in Texas. Predator control could continue into the summer after turkeys are released to relieve the translocated birds of predation pressure while they are adjusting to a new environment and to reduce predation on nesting females, their nests, and their broods. If an effective wild turkey management plan has been implemented and a wild turkey population becomes established, predator control could be suspended the following fall. Predators do kill turkeys, but this has occurred for as long as wild turkeys and predators have shared the same landscapes. It is important to remember that wild turkeys have evolved numerous adaptations to effectively avoid predators. They are intelligent birds that are very wary, roost in trees, prefer open areas where predators can be easily detected, have a high reproductive potential, and are attentive to their young (Leopold and Chamberlain 2002). If landowners manage their properties to provide the habitat that wild turkeys require, then the presence of predators should not negatively impact a turkey population.

Harvest Management

If wild turkey hunting is a goal of a landowner, then harvest management should be incorporated into a wild turkey management plan. Landowners and their guests must abide by hunting regulations established by TPWD, which were detailed earlier in this chapter. Therefore, turkey hunting on any property cannot start until the day a season begins, hunting must be done during the designated daily time period, and hunters must not exceed the bag limits established for each county. However, landowners can regulate hunting pressure. They can regulate the number of birds harvested on their property by establishing an annual quota, which represents the number of turkeys that can be harvested on their property during a season. They can also designate a specific age group of birds that can be harvested on their property (juveniles and adults, or adults only). In certain areas of the state, the sex of the bird harvested (bearded females and males, or males only) is regulated by TPWD, but landowners can establish their own regulations as long as these do not violate state laws. However, before making harvest management decisions, a landowner should learn the condition of the wild turkey population on the property.

Litton and Harwell (1995) provide a good summary of techniques landowners should consider to illuminate the condition of wild turkey populations. They state that winter roost counts of Rio Grande wild turkeys can provide an estimate of Rio Grande wild turkey numbers. The road survey method described by Erxleben et al. (2011) can be used to estimate Rio Grande wild turkey numbers in the Edwards Plateau and Texas Panhandle. Road surveys conducted during July and August can also be used get female/poult ratios, which represents production, and male/female sex ratios can also be obtained. Litton and Harwell (1995) indicate that a ratio of three poults/female represents excellent production, while ratios of two poults/female and one poult/female represent fair and poor production, respectively. Litton and Harwell also state that a sex ratio of two to three females/male is considered optimal because it fulfills the reproductive needs of a population and provides sufficient numbers of males for hunting.

Landowners can also learn a great deal about the status of wild turkey populations on their farms and ranches by examining birds that have been harvested to determine their age and sex. Females are not as colorful as males, so distinguishing the two is relatively straightforward. Just as males can be distinguished from females based on plumage, juveniles can be distinguished from adults based on the characteristics of specific feathers. Pelham and Dickson (1992) indicated that the molting pattern of retrices (tail feathers) on young turkeys of both sexes permits young birds to be differentiated from adults. Young wild turkeys replace retrices gradually during their first molt, which occurs up to their second fall. Therefore, the central three to five retrices on the tail when it is spread out are noticeably longer on young birds (fig. 10.4) than on adults, whose tail retrices are uniform in length (fig. 10.5). Pelham and Dickson (1992) also indicated that the greater upper secondary coverts (wing bars) of young birds are uneven and irregular in length (fig. 10.6), whereas these feathers are uniform in length on adults (fig. 10.7). Furthermore, they stated that the ninth and tenth primary feathers on the wings of juvenile birds during their first fall are retained and are pointed with dark tips (fig. 10.8). The ninth and tenth primaries on adult birds have been replaced and have round tips as well as white bars that extend to the tip of the feather (fig. 10.9).

The characteristics of the specialized feathers called a beard, which appear on the lower neck of wild turkeys, can also be used to sex and age birds (Pelham and Dickson 1992). Unlike other turkey feathers, beards are not replaced during molts and therefore grow continually. Generally only males have beards (fig. 10.10), and although an estimated 1–5% of females also grow beards, these are shorter and not as dense as those of mature males (Cathey et al. 2007b, Pelham and Dickson 1992). Pelham and Dickson (1992) provided the following beard growth progression for males. The beards on young males, often referred to as jakes, are amber and from 1.3 to 6.4 cm (1.5 to 2.5 in) long during their first fall and increase to 7.6–12.7 cm (3–5 in) during their first spring and are amber tipped. Mature males, including those at or beyond their second spring, will typically have a beard longer than 17.8 cm (7 in).

Figure 10.4. Tail retrices of a juvenile Rio Grande wild turkey. Note that the retrices in the center are longer than the rest of the tail retrices (photo by Bill Kuvlesky).

Figure 10.5. Tail retrices of an adult Rio Grande wild turkey. Note that the tail retrices are all of uniform length (photo by Bill Kuvlesky).

Figure 10.6. Upper secondary coverts (arrow) of a juvenile Rio Grande wild turkey. Note that the row of these feathers is uneven (photo by Bill Kuvlesky).

Figure 10.7. Upper secondary coverts (arrow) of an adult Eastern wild turkey. Note that the row of these feathers is uniform and feathers are all approximately the same length (photo by Jason Hardin).

Figure 10.8. The ninth and tenth primary feathers (arrows) of a juvenile Rio Grande wild turkey. Note that the ends of the ninth and tenth primary feathers are brownish gray and do not have barring (photo by Bill Kuvlesky).

Figure 10.9. The ninth and tenth primary feathers (arrows) of an adult Eastern wild turkey. Note that the ninth and tenth primary feathers have barring along their entire length (photo by Jason Hardin).

Figure 10.10. The beard of a mature Rio Grande wild turkey male (photo by Larry Ditto).

Figure 10.11. The legs of a juvenile Rio Grande wild turkey are characterized by grayish scales (photo by Bill Kuvlesky).

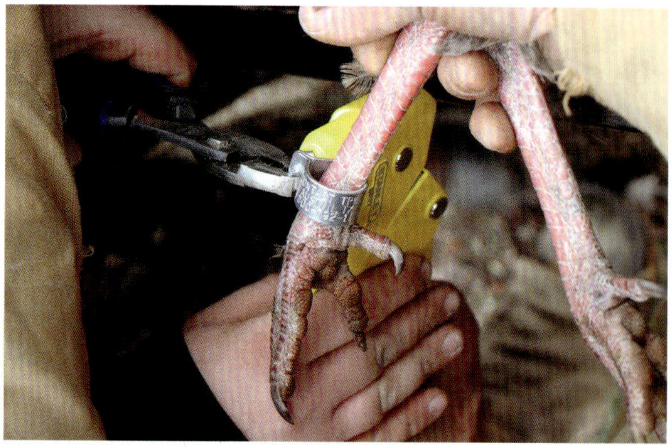

Figure 10.12. The legs of an adult Eastern wild turkey are characterized by pink scales (photo by Jason Hardin).

The appearance of the legs can also be used to differentiate young wild turkeys from mature birds. The scales on the legs of young birds are smoother and more heavily pigmented and so appear darker (fig. 10.11) than the legs of adults (Pelham and Dickson 1992). As a bird ages, pigmentation diminishes, so adult legs become pink (fig. 10.12) compared to the brown to gray of juvenile birds. A leg characteristic that can be used to differentiate males from females is the spur, which is the protuberance that extends from the leg above the foot and continues to grow as a male turkey ages. The length of the spur can also be used to differentiate juvenile and adult males. The spurs of juvenile males are short and blunt during their first year (fig. 10.13), whereas the spur becomes longer and more pointed or sharper (fig. 10.14) in successive years for adults.

Landowners can even examine the shape of turkey dung to determine the sex of wild turkeys. The dung of females when deposited on the ground is circular, whereas it is linear and elongated for males (fig. 10.15). Therefore, examination of dung on the ground in areas frequented by wild turkeys, such as under roosts and around water sources and feeding areas, can provide supplemental information about the sex ratios of wild turkeys on a property under turkey management.

Decisions regarding harvest quotas can be made in a more informed manner once a landowner understands the status of the turkey population. Litton and Harwell (1995) indicated that harvesting 10–20% of the males would be conservative, whereas

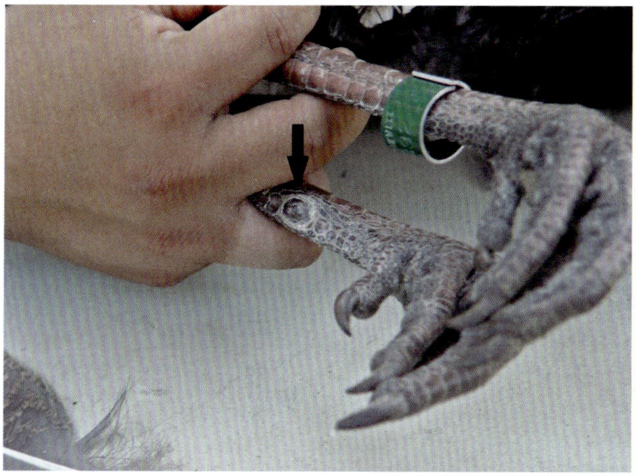

Figure 10.13. The protuberance (arrow) on the leg of a juvenile Rio Grande wild turkey represents the spur (photo by Bill Kuvlesky).

Figure 10.14. The spurs of a mature adult male Eastern wild turkey (photo by Jason Hardin).

Figure 10.15. Dung of a Rio Grande wild turkey male (longer feces) and female (rounder feces) (photo by Bill Kuvlesky).

harvesting 30% would be liberal and should probably be implemented only after two to three years of good production. Harvesting females can have significant negative impacts on local wild turkey populations. If females are hunted, harvest should be conservative and should occur only where and when wild turkeys are abundant and in areas with light hunting pressure. Landowners, managers, and hunters should be cognizant of local regulations regarding the harvest of females, because these vary across Texas. It is not legal to harvest wild turkey females in the eastern half of Texas, and regulations vary in the western half between spring and fall. Landowners should maintain accurate annual records of harvest data in order to establish population trends that, when examined over time, will allow a landowner to learn how a turkey population responds to wet and dry cycles as well as to changes in habitat resulting from weather, management operations, or harvest quotas. Flexibility is also important because a landowner must be able to adjust harvest quotas in response to unpredictable events, such as drought, that affect wild turkey populations.

Other Considerations

Often there are additional considerations when developing a wild turkey management plan. For example, of great interest to many managers is feeding wildlife. A question biologists regularly receive is "What can I feed them?" In general, food is not a limiting factor for wild turkeys. If adequate nesting and brood-rearing cover, sufficient roosting habitat, and adequate water and usable space are provided, then turkeys will be able to find adequate food. Turkeys are dietary generalists that will graze like cattle on green grasses, strip grass seeds off standing grass, select the leaves, buds, and seeds of weedy plants, eat hard and soft mast as available, and ingest essentially any animal matter they can catch and swallow. Insects typically found in turkey crops include grasshoppers, beetles, caterpillars, and other arthropods. However, hunters and researchers have also found crawfish, frogs, lizards, cicadas, and numerous other examples of animal matter. Occasionally, insects can be limiting for the growth of young poults, but favorable climate and good habitat management generally remedy this limitation.

Literature Cited

Alldredge, B. E., J. B. Hardin, J. Whiteside, J. L. Isabelle, S. Parsons, W. C. Conway, and J. C. Cathey. 2014. Eastern wild turkeys in Texas: biology and management. Texas AgriLife Extension Publication WF-011. Texas A&M University, College Station, USA.

Beasom, S. L. 1974. Intensive short-term predator removal as a game management tool. Transactions of the North American Wildlife and Natural Resources Conference 39:230–240.

Beasom, S. L., and D. Wilson. 1992. Rio Grande turkey. Pages 306–330 *in* J. G. Dickson, editor. The wild turkey: biology and management. Stackpole Books, Mechanicsburg, Pennsylvania, USA.

Butler, M. J., W. B. Ballard, M. C. Wallace, S. J. DeMaso, and R. D. Applegate. 2006. Comparing techniques for counting Rio Grande wild turkeys at winter roosts. Pages 112–117 *in* J. W. Cain III and P. R. Krausman, editors. Managing wildlife in the Southwest: new challenges for the 21st century. Southwest Section of The Wildlife Society, Alpine, Texas, USA.

Butler, M. J., G. I. Hall, M. C. Wallace, W. B. Ballard, R. S. Phillips, J. H. Brunjes, and R. D. Applegate. 2007. Utility of poult-hen counts to index productivity of Rio Grande wild turkeys. Proceedings of the National Wild Turkey Symposium 9:159–168.

Byrne, M. E., M. J. Chamberlain, and B. A. Collier. 2015. Potential density dependence in wild turkey productivity in the southeastern United States. Proceedings of the National Wild Turkey Symposium 11:329–351.

Cathey, J. C., S. Locke, D. Ransom Jr., S. J. DeMaso, T. W. Schwertner, and B. Collier. 2007a. Habitat appraisal guide for Rio Grande wild turkey. Texas AgriLife Extension Publication SP-317. Texas A&M University, College Station, USA.

Cathey, J. C., K. Melton, J. Dreibelbis, B. Cavney, S. L. Locke, S. J. DeMaso, T. W. Schwertner, and B. Collier. 2007b. Rio Grande wild turkey in Texas: biology and management. Texas AgriLife Extension Report B-6198. Texas A&M University, College Station, USA.

Cathey, J. C., J. Wimberley, L. Redmon, S. Locke, B. Collier, R. Perez, and J. Hardin. 2010. Managing brush near Rio Grande wild turkey roosts. Texas AgriLife Extension Publication ESP-382. Texas A&M University, College Station, USA.

Caveny, R. J. 2009. Estimating distribution and abundance of Rio Grande wild turkeys in South Texas. Thesis, Texas A&M University, College Station, USA.

Chamberlain, M. J., and B. D. Leopold. 1999. Dietary patterns of sympatric bobcats and coyotes relative to trends in prey abundance in central Mississippi. Proceedings of the Annual Conference of the Southeastern Association of Fish and Wildlife Agencies 53:204–219.

Cobb, D. T., D. L. Francis, and R. W. Etters. 1996. Validating a wild turkey population survey using cameras and infrared sensors. Proceedings of the National Wild Turkey Symposium 7:213–218.

Cobb, D. T., R. S. Fuller, D. L. Francis, and G. L. Sprandel. 1997. Research priorities for monitoring wild turkeys using cameras and infrared sensors. Proceedings of the Annual Conference of the Southeastern Association of Fish and Wildlife Agencies 51:362–372.

Cook, R. L. 1973. A census technique for the Rio Grande turkey. Pages 279–283 *in* G. C. Sanderson and H. C. Schultz, editors. Wild turkey management: current problems and programs. University of Missouri Press, Columbia, USA.

Crockett, B. C. 1973. Quantitative evaluation of winter roost sites of the Rio Grande turkey in northcentral Oklahoma. Pages 211–218 *in* G. C. Sanderson and H. C. Schultz, editors. Wild turkey management: current problems and programs. University of Missouri Press, Columbia, USA.

Curry, C. 2010. Development of a habitat appraisal guide for Rio Grande wild turkeys in South Texas. Dissertation, Texas A&M University–Kingsville, Kingsville, USA.

Dreibelbis, J. Z., K. B. Melton, R. Aguirre, B. A. Collier, J. Hardin, N. J. Silvy, and M. J. Peterson. 2008. Predation of Rio Grande wild turkey nests on the Edwards Plateau, Texas. Wilson Journal of Ornithology 120:906–910.

Eriksen, R. E., T. A. Brown, K. B. Scott, T. W. Hughes, M. D. Akridge, and C. S. Penner. 2016. Status and distribution of wild turkey in the United States: 2014 status. Proceedings of the National Wild Turkey Symposium 11:7–18.

Erxleben, D. R., M. J. Butler, W. B. Ballard, M. C. Wallace, M. J. Peterson, N. J. Silvy, W. P. Kuvlesky Jr., et al. 2011. Wild turkey (*Meleagris gallopavo*) association to roads: implications for distance sampling. European Journal of Wildlife Research 57:57–65.

Glazener, W. C. 1967. Management of the Rio Grande wild turkey. Pages 453–492 *in* O. H. Hewitt, editor. The wild turkey and its management. The Wildlife Society, Washington, DC, USA.

Goodrum, P. D. 1939. Annual report of the Game, Fish, and Oyster Commission—Game Management. Pittman-Robertson Report. Texas Game, Fish, and Oyster Commission, Austin, USA.

Guthery, F. S. 1995. Coyotes and upland gamebirds. Pages 104–107 *in* D. Rollins, C. Richardson, T. Blankenship, K. Canon, and S. Henke, editors. Coyotes in the southwest. Texas Parks and Wildlife Department, Austin, USA.

Haucke, H. H. 1975. Winter roost characteristics of Rio Grande turkeys in South Texas. Proceedings of the National Wild Turkey Symposium 3:164–169.

Lehmann, V. W. 1957. Conservation and management of game. Pages 761–766 (appendix) *in* Tom Lea, "The King Ranch," volume 2. Little, Brown, Boston, Massachusetts, USA.

Leopold, B. D., and M. Chamberlain. 2002. Predator control: here we go again. Proceedings of the Annual Conference of the Southeastern Association of Fish and Wildlife Agencies 56:239–254.

Leopold, B. D., and J. L. Cummins. 2016. Integrating science into the policy-making process. Proceedings of the National Wild Turkey Symposium 11:25–38.

Litton, G. W., and F. Harwell. 1995. Rio Grande turkey habitat management. Texas Parks and Wildlife Department Federal Aid Project W-129-M. Texas Parks and Wildlife Department, Austin, USA.

Locke, S. L., J. C. Cathey, B. A. Collier, and J. B. Hardin. 2011. Guide to abundance estimation techniques for Rio Grande wild turkey. Texas AgriLife Extension Bulletin WF-050. Texas A&M University, College Station, USA.

Melville, H. I., W. C. Conway, M. L. Morrison, C. E. Comer, and J. B. Hardin. 2014. Artificial nests identify possible nest predators of Eastern wild turkeys. Southeastern Naturalist 13:80–91.

Pelham, P. H., and J. G. Dickson. 1992. Physical characteristics. Pages 32–45 *in* J. G. Dickson, editor. The wild turkey: biology and management. Stackpole Books, Mechanicsburg, Pennsylvania, USA.

Perotto-Baldivieso, H. L. 2005. GIS-based multiple scale study of Rio Grande wild turkey habitat in the Edwards Plateau of Texas. Dissertation, Texas A&M University, College Station, USA.

Porter, W. F. 1992. Habitat requirements. Pages 202–213 *in* J. G. Dickson, editor. The wild turkey: biology and management. Stackpole Books, Mechanicsburg, Pennsylvania, USA.

Prasad, N. L. N. S., and F. S. Guthery. 1986. Wildlife use of livestock water under short duration and continuous grazing systems. Wildlife Society Bulletin 14:450–454.

Schorger, A. W. 1966. The wild turkey: its history and domestication. University of Oklahoma Press, Norman, USA.

Smith, D. M. 1975. Behavioral factors influencing variability of roost counts for Rio Grande turkeys. Proceedings of the National Wild Turkey Symposium 3:170–175.

Stevens, B. S., J. R. Bence, W. F. Porter, and C. J. Parent. 2017. Structural uncertainty limits generality of fall harvest strategies for wild turkeys. Journal of Wildlife Management 81:617–628.

Suarez, R. 2002. Texas turkey talk. Texas Parks and Wildlife Department Report PWD BK W7000–827 (5/02). Texas Parks and Wildlife Department, Austin, USA.

Swearingin, R. M., W. B. Ballard, R. S. Phillips, S. McKenzie-Damron, M. J. Butler, M. C. Wallace, R. N. Walker, and D. C. Ruthven III. 2010. Winter roost characteristics of Rio Grande wild turkeys in the Rolling Plains of Texas. Proceedings of the National Wild Turkey Symposium 10:251–263.

Yeldell, N. A., B. S. Cohen, A. R. Little, B. A. Collier, and M. J. Chamberlain. 2017. Nest site selection and nest survival of Eastern wild turkeys in a pyric landscape. Journal of Wildlife Management 81:1073–1083.

11

Establishing and Maintaining Relationships with Private Landowners

Learning to work with private landowners is the art behind application "on the ground." Just remember. Your reputation (good or bad) will quickly spread throughout the landowner network.

—JIMMY RUTLEDGE

Most wild turkeys in Texas occupy private lands. Therefore, effectively managing wild turkeys in Texas requires working with private landowners. Few wildlife biologists or other turkey enthusiasts receive any formal training in working with landowners. Fortunately, working with a private landowner usually requires the common-sense approach of behaving like an appreciative guest. However, there are intricacies associated with effectively establishing a productive relationship with a private landowner that not only benefit wild turkeys, but also result in a productive, long-standing relationship that yields positive results for both the landowner and the natural resources on the property.

This chapter summarizes the necessary and helpful elements for effectively working with private landowners or land managers. The goal is to share some of the things we wished we had realized or known earlier in our careers. Some of it may be obvious, some of it may be insightful, but most of all, we hope it inspires you to view your role as a voice for conservation as you work with private landowners and land managers.

Part I—Building a Relationship

As a conservation professional, one of the first things to understand is that you are in the people business. Your technical expertise may be in range management, agronomy, forestry, watershed management, or wildlife management, but make no mistake—you are in the people business as much as or more than you are in the conservation business. Before any meaningful long-term conservation assistance takes place on private lands, a relationship of trust must be established. Trust and confidence are the cornerstones of developing relationships with landowners.

Earning their trust

Landowners in general are not impressed by your title, your degree, or where you went to school. You will have to work hard to earn their trust. Landowners are impressed by professionals who know what they are talking about and who demonstrate that they want to help. Starting out on the right foot and making a positive first impression are important.

Earning the trust of landowners is not always easy and is usually a slow process. If you work for a government agency, you must understand that many landowners have a built-in distrust or skepticism regarding the government and its employees. They may have had a negative experience with your agency or another agency. You will have to work hard to prove that you are there to help them and not just carry out the mandates of your agency.

"Good things on the land happen over time and are seldom the result of a single encounter" (J. R. Bell, personal communication). Since earning the trust of a landowner is a slow and gradual process, patience and persistence become key elements for success. You must have a long-term outlook if you really want to be effective in working with landowners. In German, we would say, "If it doesn't take much time, it's not worth much" (D. Mertz, personal communication).

Understand your responsibility and privilege

When you are invited out to a farm or ranch, it is important that you understand the magnitude of your responsibility. In many cases, the property is worth several million dollars, in some cases many millions of dollars. It is an extremely valuable asset. The advice you provide will affect the value of the property—not only the economic value, but also the ecological value. Apart from the economic and ecological value, the land has a great deal of personal value to the landowner and the family, especially if it has been in the family for several generations. Never forget: their land is sacred to them. It is not just a piece of land. It is a great responsibility to know that your input has the capacity to either increase or decrease the value of their land.

Management decisions regarding wild turkeys may have impacts on neighboring properties, and even on towns and cities downstream. In effect, these decisions affect many people besides the landowner.

It is also important to acknowledge that it is a privilege to be invited onto someone's land. In addition to seeing the land, you will often get to know the family, share meals with them, and over time, perhaps become a trusted adviser. You will be rewarded by seeing things that most people never see. Some natural resource professionals get it backward—they think it is a privilege for landowners to have them come out to their land. Landowners will be able to sense whether you appreciate the opportunity and privilege of being asked to be of service, and if they sense that you do, it will help build the relationship.

Whom do you really work for?

Another way to earn trust and build a relationship with landowners is to make sure they know that you are really working for them. Your paycheck may come from a conservation organization, an agency, or a private company, but landowners must know that your priority is working with *them*. Yes, you owe allegiance to your employer, your boss, and your organization, but in order to gain the trust and confidence of landowners, it is important to have the mind-set that working for them is your job. They will know the difference.

Learn to listen

Listening is a skill that must be learned. For most of us, the ability to listen carefully does not happen naturally. When we gain some expertise or knowledge in some area, we tend to talk too much and try to impress people with our knowledge. We have much we want to say that we think will help landowners, but too often we say too much too soon.

We cannot possibly overemphasize the importance of listening as a key to working effectively with landowners. "Critical listening" is a skill that requires your full and undivided attention. Each landowner is different, and each farm or ranch is different; therefore, each approach for assisting will be unique. Only by listening attentively and asking thoughtful questions will you be able to gain the proper insights and information. Before you can be of any real help to landowners, you must invest the time and energy to listen to their story, their goals, their problems, their situation, and their ideas, and you will probably have to ask some probing questions to get the information you need. Listening is a prerequisite for providing assistance and is essential for building a lasting relationship with landowners. Listening well is hard work.

In the words of Clay County rancher Deborah Clark, "Having a conservation professional come out on our land is a lot like dating. At first I ask them a few questions, then they ask me a few questions, then based on those answers, we decide if we want to continue the relationship. If the relationship continues, then trust develops and I invite them to our ranch and enjoy spending time with them learning more about conservation opportunities on our land."

It is their land; honor their objectives

When assisting landowners, it is tempting to tell them what you would do if it was your land. Don't make that mistake, for the simple reason that it is not your land—it is *their land* and they have their own objectives. When landowners invite you for assistance, work hard to determine what *their land management goals and objectives* are and then honor those objectives.

You may or may not agree with their objectives, but understand that your job is to help them achieve their objectives in a way that is consistent with conservation and sustainability. If they do not come right out and state their objectives, then you will need to work with them to help them define and develop what they really want for long-range and short-range objectives.

When goals and options are discussed, it is important for landowners to understand both the long-term and short-term effects and consequences of the practices involved. A common mistake advisers make is to impose their own preferences, opinions, and favorite practices onto their land management assistance. Some of this is natural and unavoidable, but work diligently to help landowners achieve their objectives (not yours) in the best way possible. Your job is to help facilitate the process, not determine the outcome.

Stan Reinke, a former range conservationist for the Soil Conservation Service (SCS) and Natural Resources Conservation Service (NRCS), tells the following story: "I was working with a landowner in the Coastal Prairie. We were discussing brush control on his land and he stated that he wanted to restore the land back to it true original prairie condition. I questioned this since the ranch had a very viable hunting operation for deer, quail and turkey. I knew that the removal of the brush would severely impact these hunting enterprises. When I asked him why he wanted to do this, his answer was, 'Because I want it that way.' Even though I thought the decision was wrong, it was his land and he makes the decision and has to live with the consequences."

Everyone who has worked with landowners has had similar experiences, and we might not always agree with the direction a landowner wants to go or the means to get there. But our job is not to set their objectives for them—it is to discern and then help them achieve their goals for their land and to help them do so in a way that is consistent with long-term sustainability and conservation.

Learn to read people

In addition to your technical and ecological skills, you will need to learn the skill of reading people if you are to be successful in working with landowners. There is no single approach that works well for all landowners; you will have to be flexible enough to work with all kinds of different people and to understand how best to communicate with them and gain their trust. As mentioned previously, learning to read people does require the skill of critical listening, but it also requires the ability to discern what is unspoken. Poncho Ortega, a wildlife scientist with the Caesar Kleberg Wildlife Research Institute and a grazing/wildlife specialist, says, "The most difficult part of working with landowners is to be able to get a clear idea of what they want in terms of stewardship, productivity, economics and the time and resources they want to devote to accomplish it. In many cases you need to be able to read between the lines in order to discern what they want."

Kent Mills, a range nutritionist with Hi-Pro Feeds and formerly with Ezell-Key Feeds, as well as a rancher and educator, states, "The most important element for working with landowners is to listen to them and be able to determine their goals, motivations, abilities, potential, desire, dedication and their financial capability." Landowners will usually not come right out and tell you these things directly, and you will probably not want to come right out and ask, but your success in working with them will depend on your ability to discern these things. Learn to ask appropriate probing questions, but be mindful not to cross the line and get nosy or probe too deeply before you have gained their trust. Reading people is an art that needs to be cultivated if you are going to be successful and effective.

Don't tell people what they should do

Bill Eikenhorst, a Brenham veterinarian and multigeneration rancher in Washington County, provided a good general characterization of private landowners in Texas when he said, "Landowners by nature are most often contrarians, who pride themselves on independent actions and self-reliance." Private landowners do not usually appreciate being told what they should do, especially by an outsider or a government agent. People want to make their own decisions. Our job as their adviser is not to tell them what they should do, but rather to clearly present them with all the information and options necessary for them to make good decisions. We may think we know what they should do, but the best and most lasting adoption of ideas involves the ability to lead, guide, motivate, and inspire people to consider all options so they can make the best choices based on their unique circumstances. Avoid the mistake of being the big expert and telling landowners what they should do with their land. This approach does not work.

Part II—Personal Character Qualities

As you begin to build working relationships with landowners and land managers, certain character qualities will help you be effective and gain their trust and confidence. These character traits are like a catalyst in a chemical reaction—they make the process happen much faster and lead to a better outcome. If these traits are weak or missing, it will hinder or prevent you from being effective.

Humility

Genuine humility will take you a long way with most landowners. Landowners usually do not appreciate arrogant people who think they know everything. They do appreciate someone who is knowledgeable yet humble. Humility involves the realization that you do not have all the answers and that you are always still learning. Humility acknowledges that other people often know a lot more than you do and have better insights.

Everyone has an ego, but the humble person has learned to suppress it. For some of us, it takes constant reminders that we are not nearly as smart or as good as we think we are. If you come across as a big-shot expert on everything, landowners will usually take offense and you will most likely not be invited back. Even when you are very good at what you do, a humble attitude will help people accept your ideas and input.

Integrity and trustworthiness

Those who work most effectively with landowners tend to be people of high personal integrity and are completely trustworthy. Most landowners possess these traits, and they expect and appreciate them in others, especially their advisers. You may live in the same small community as some of the landowners, and your behavior and values away from work will become known in the community. Integrity and trustworthiness involve who you are 24 hours a day, seven days a week.

Work ethic

Landowners and land managers are usually hardworking people. You will gain a great deal of respect if they see that you have a great work ethic and if you work hard to help them. Too many people today believe that a job involves only 40 hours a week. Seldom will a successful person put in only 40 hours. In working with landowners, you must be willing to work long days when necessary, often 12–14 hours, and some long weeks. If you are in the 40-hour rut, your effectiveness will be reduced.

A prime example of a great work ethic comes from George Nelle. When George had worked for his employer for 40 years, the boss recognized him for his exceptional service with a big dinner. During the dinner, the boss told the crowd, "If George were to get run over by a truck, we would have to hire three men to replace him." Few people will ever match that level of performance and service, but having a great work ethic will help make you irreplaceable with landowners and your employer. George went on to work nine more years and greatly helped the company become successful and profitable. One of the core purposes of a work ethic in our profession is to *help others* to become as successful as possible.

Respect and empathy

Always show genuine respect for landowners, their family, employees, land, animals, and ideas. Even if you disagree with them on some things, showing respect will be noticed and will help you gain their respect. Learn to empathize with landowners by putting yourself in their boots. Being a landowner is not as glamorous as some people think; there are many hardships and difficulties to endure. Be especially mindful when people are going through calamities such as drought, wildfire, health problems, loss of loved ones, or other difficult times. Russell Stevens, a wildlife and range consultant with the Noble Research Institute in Ardmore, Oklahoma, says, "They need to know that you care about them, and can understand their needs. Showing them you care is paramount to building their trust."

Handling disagreement

In 1948, Aldo Leopold said that "conservationists are notorious for their dissentions," and this is still true today. There are many opinions and perspectives regarding the best land management practices, and you will frequently be faced with disagreements from both landowners and fellow professionals. There is not just one right way to do things, so be prepared for differences of opinion.

It is sometimes tempting to simply go with the most popular viewpoint and avoid disagreement. Renowned range ecologist E. J. Dyksterhuis offers these words of wisdom: "The professional conservationist must often make an independent and even unpopular stand. The non-professional is content with promotion of that which is currently acceptable or popular."

In some cases, you will have to be thick skinned and endure criticism but stick with your convictions. In other cases, you will need to accommodate other viewpoints. In all cases, be gracious, professional, and always willing to reevaluate your position.

Do not improvise; be honest

On many occasions, you will not have an adequate answer or solution. Landowners appreciate honesty and the admission that you do not know the answer to all their questions. Do not improvise or "wing it" when you are unsure of the best response to a difficult question, and do not speak beyond your level of knowledge. Landowners can generally spot a phony, and it will immediately harm your credibility. Be quick to admit when you don't know something and be sure to research the question and get back to them promptly.

At other times you may inadvertently give landowners bad information. Sometimes in our zeal to be helpful, we speak prematurely and give bad advice. As soon as you discover you have given bad information, be quick to fess up and tell the landowner of your mistake. Don't rationalize or make excuses; simply admit it and then work to find the right answer. Landowners are usually very forgiving when you demonstrate this kind of honesty, and it can help build trust and credibility.

Learn from mistakes

Each of us who contributed to this chapter has enjoyed some success in working with landowners, but we have also made plenty of mistakes. In fact, much of the advice presented here can be traced to our mistakes and their consequences. Mistakes can be very good teachers and character builders if you learn from them. Just remember the adage "A person who makes no mistakes is a person who is not doing anything." You will make mistakes if you are actively involved with landowners. The right response to mistakes is to acknowledge them and figure out how to avoid repeating them. By discovering our flaws, we can learn how to overcome our weaknesses and turn them into opportunities for improvement.

Continual self-improvement

Professional conservationists are always aware of the need for continual self-improvement. Never get to the point where you think you have all the right answers—this is arrogant and foolhardy. Nature and natural resources are far too complex for anyone to think they have it figured out. Dan Caudle, a retired NRCS range conservationist and natural resource management consultant/adviser, offers these words of truth regarding complacency: "Anyone who is completely satisfied with himself either has an enormous ego, a short memory or very low standards."

Self-improvement should include improvement in technical skills as well as people skills, especially communication (listening, speaking, and writing). Make self-improvement a priority, even if you have to do it on your own time and at your own expense.

Confidence and assertiveness

As you strive for excellence and self-improvement, and as your skills and abilities develop, you will naturally gain a degree of confidence. The proper degree of confidence and convictions will help your message be taken more seriously. Confidence is a positive quality when correctly expressed. However, false confidence and overconfidence are negative qualities, so be mindful of the fine line between confidence and arrogance.

After you have earned the trust of landowners and gained some confidence and credibility, on some occasions you may have to be more forceful in expressing your message. According to Russell Stevens, "There are times and places where we need to be assertive in order to protect a resource or to ensure that the landowner is able to continue operating."

Character matters

Landowners are usually good judges of character. They can tell whether you are a person of sincerity, honesty, integrity, and humility who is respectful and will work hard to help them. It is not enough to have excellent ecological and natural resource skills—effective work with landowners requires many character qualities in addition to technical ability.

Part III—Professionalism and Exceptional Service

We are not just in the conservation business and the people business—we are also in the service business. The highest standards of professionalism and service will help you achieve your goal of being able to work effectively with landowners.

Go out of your way

In all facets of assistance, go beyond what is required; go out of your way to provide the very best service and assistance. This requires an intentional focus on excellence. Some organizations and agencies seem content with average, mediocre performance, but when working with landowners, the standard should be one of exceptional service. Landowners will take note of the extra effort you put forth, and this will help build trust and confidence. The excellent advice of Bill Eikenhorst, a veterinarian and rancher in Brenham, is straightforward: "Under promise and over deliver—Always."

Give a genuine compliment

During your visits to the property, be observant and look for things that owners or managers are doing well. Compliment them when you notice something praiseworthy. Landowners like to know that you have noticed the good things they are doing. However, don't go too far and gush with false or insincere compliments. Landowners can tell the difference between flattery and genuine compliments.

Written reports

When your day on the property has ended, your work is only half done. The professional will find the time to promptly develop a written report summarizing the discussions of the day. Landowners usually appreciate this kind of extra effort, and it helps reinforce and document major issues. The report also allows you to follow up on things that may need more research or investigation. Do not wait too long to develop the report—do it while everything is fresh in your mind. Take the time to write thoughtful, thorough, practical, and informative reports after each visit. The value of these reports is often greater than we think, for both landowners and ourselves.

Always thank them; always be gracious

At the end of the day, always thank the landowner for the privilege of spending time with them on their property. Although this is just common courtesy, it will also help reinforce your good character and build the relationship. Likewise, always be gracious, not just to those who are kind and considerate, but also to the old belligerent hardhead. Being gracious means treating people better than they might deserve and going out of your way to be helpful, even to those who are ungrateful.

Professional etiquette

Several other items fall under the category of normal professional etiquette. These are the expected norms for a professional relationship, and failure in any of these will hinder effectiveness: (1) always be on time and be well prepared; (2) promptly return all phone calls and messages; (3) do not check phone messages, texts, or email while out with a landowner because doing so is a sign of disrespect. Be careful of your mannerisms and how you dress and speak. You are trying to fit into the landowners' culture, not stick out like a sore thumb. Dress should be similar to the norm for landowners of the region and should generally be conservative and not draw attention. Speak slowly and distinctly (many older landowners, like older professional conservationists, are hard of hearing). Men, leave your earrings at home; men and women, cover your tattoos; don't wear a "Save the Wolves" T-shirt or anything that might be offensive to their way of life. Do not invite yourself hunting or fishing, or even drop hints of such. If you do a good job with landowners, you will get plenty of invitations. Do not hunt for arrowheads, and ask permission before you take photos on their land.

Part IV—Technical Expertise

Parts I, II, and III of this chapter concern primarily honing people skills, providing service, and building effective working relationships. These are vitally important. However, developing technical expertise in your field is equally important and is the primary reason you have been invited to a farm, ranch, or rural property. Your job is to have the necessary natural resource skills, knowledge, and ability to help landowners set a course for their land management, conservation, and stewardship.

In the digital age, natural resource workers have instant access to immense volumes of technical information that was not available a decade ago. This information can help us do our jobs better; however, Dan Caudle advises, "Don't mistake access to information as an acceptable alternative for knowledge, understanding, or experience. Information is a supplement, not a substitute." Nature and natural resources are one of the most complex disciplines, and those who provide assistance need to have the appropriate technical skills and practical knowledge and be able to communicate it.

Become well rounded in natural resources

You may consider yourself a specialist in one field or another (agronomy, native plants, forestry, grazing management, wildlife, watersheds, prescribed fire, etc.), but in order to work effectively with landowners, you need to have a broad level of natural resource knowledge relevant for your region. Landowners often need and want assistance that involves more than your knowledge of wild turkeys and their habitat. You cannot be an expert in everything, but you need to have a basic working knowledge of the natural and agricultural resources of your area. Donnie Frels, retired project leader for the Texas Parks and Wildlife Department's Edwards Plateau Ecosystems Management Project, says, "Be a good field biologist—plants, animals, livestock, soils, insects, birds and how they interact. Good field biologists, really good, are rare and always coveted by landowners, often resulting in successful programs." Your title may not be "biologist," but in the world of agriculture and natural resources we must all have excellent biological and ecological skills. When a landowner asks you, "What flower or plant is that?" knowing the answer will gain you more than you will ever know. Study and know your plant life.

Learn to read the land

The ability to read the land is both an art and a science. It takes time to learn the ecological dynamics of a certain region; take the time to study and observe the interactions of plants, animals, soil, and water and how they are affected by management. Rory Burroughs, manager of the Hackberry Creek Ranch in Kent and Fisher Counties and owner of Comprehensive Land Management, notes, "The ability of reading the land will tell you a lot about the past management and the history of the property."

Learning to read the land starts with keen observation. Try to spend plenty of time alone, without distractions, observing what has happened and what is happening with the land. At the beginning in a new geographic area, it will be important to spend time with someone who has this ability to read the land. Reading the land starts with observation but goes much deeper. Dan Caudle says, "Don't just observe, but learn to evaluate, investigate, analyze, and ask why." Natural curiosity and the desire to understand how the land works are important elements for successful natural resource professionals.

Learn plants

As noted above, one of the most fundamental aspects of reading the land and providing landowner assistance is knowledge of plants. The "language" of the land is written with plants. The person who knows the plant life of a region will be in high demand—this is a skill that is highly respected and sought after among landowners. According to Rory Burroughs, "Sharing your knowledge of plants is almost always a great icebreaker experience with landowners." Plant knowledge begins by learning to identify and name plants and deepens as you learn their ecological value and function, where they tend to grow, and how they respond to management. No single skill is more important than a working knowledge of the plants of your area.

Tools of the trade

Imperative for being effective with landowners is a good working knowledge of the land management techniques and practices used in your region. These tools will vary from region to region and by land use. For forest, rangeland, and wildlife habitat purposes, the tools will include the familiar ax, plow, cow, fire, and gun espoused by Aldo Leopold (1949) along with all their variations.

A common mistake of land management advisers is to promote only a few favorite practices, or in some cases to overemphasize only one tool (such as prescribed burning or brush control) while ignoring other essential practices. By analogy, each tool in a woodworker's toolbox is needed and appropriate for certain jobs. No one tool does everything; hence, the craftsperson needs to be adept at choosing and using the right tools in the right situation.

Another mistake to avoid is bad-mouthing certain tools you may have a personal bias against (such as root plowing, herbicides, summer burning, or high fences). All tools have their proper place and should be considered when they fit the need. Remember that the choice of tools is up to the landowner. We may advise, but it is not our place to decide.

Appreciate economic realities

Those who provide assistance to landowners are often removed from the economic realities of owning and managing land. Poncho Ortega advises, "The ability to relate recommended practices to economic investment and return is very important; we must remember that many of these ranchers are making a living from their operations, even though they love to have turkeys on their land." Many of the things we discuss with a landowner are expensive and often will not result in an economic return. We must be aware of the initial up-front costs of all practices used in the area in addition to ongoing management and maintenance costs. Some landowners have outside income they are willing to invest in the land without a direct economic return. Others, including most bona fide agricultural producers, are on a tight budget and always carefully consider the financial ramifications of their plans. Economic constraints often trump even the very best conservation intentions.

No simple solutions

Nature and natural resources are complex. On top of that, land management and landowners are complex. H. L. Mencken once said, "For every complex problem, there is a solution that is simple, neat, and wrong." We agree. Simple solutions to complex problems will not work most of the time, no matter how promising they seem. Practices and techniques that seem too good to be true usually fail and often backfire, actually making things worse. Instead of searching for and endorsing simple solutions, dig deeper to consider the ripple effects and unintended consequences of quick-fix solutions. If a landowner is willing to risk trying new and unproven techniques, a small-scale test can help determine whether the new practice merits further consideration.

Flexibility, innovation, and creativity

Things do not always turn out as planned. Murphy's Law seems to be the norm for natural resource management and agriculture. Being flexible will help accommodate the unexpected. Whether you are helping landowners develop a wild turkey management plan, a grazing plan, or a timber harvest plan, realize that such plans may change the moment the ink dries. Landowners are often not in a position to make final, absolute decisions and stick with them no matter what. Changes in the weather, the markets, a family situation, the economy, their goals, and a dozen other factors will alter plans. Landowners and their advisers must be flexible and creative to accommodate unforeseen changes. Conservation planning is an always-changing, never-ending process.

Cultivate your gifts

Nearly everyone who ends up in this line of work has some special talents and abilities that have inspired the decision to work in natural resources. Whatever your innate interests and gifts may be, focus on these to develop your special abilities and expertise. Cultivate what comes naturally in the areas in which you have a high ability and interest. These will often be the areas in which you make the biggest impact and contribution.

As you cultivate and improve your abilities in these areas, make certain that you become a good steward of your gifts. Pass along your expertise to others, both landowners and fellow professionals, with humility, generosity, and enthusiasm. Learn to communicate your passion and ability in these areas of special interest.

Become an expert—but don't get tunnel vision

Although you will need to develop a broad range of knowledge about the natural resources of your region, most professionals also develop an area of expertise. Strive to become the recognized authority in your region in some aspect of your work. Developing this expertise and your reputation will take time and diligent effort, but it will pay off. As you become well known in your area for some special skill or ability, you will be in high demand, since landowners often seek out experts. Your expertise can be a great foot in the door, and then you can use your other natural resource skills to provide well-rounded assistance.

The downside to having expertise in some area is the danger of getting tunnel vision and thinking only of your specialty and ignoring other important aspects. Landowners seldom think in only one dimension—they are thinking about many things simultaneously and usually need multifaceted assistance.

Don't try to be a soloist—work with others

With time, commitment, and hard work you are likely to become well known in your region for your abilities, and your reputation may grow. However, no matter how good you become, don't think that you can be a one-person show. There will always be areas outside your skill set where you need the input and expertise of others. Acknowledge your limitations, be willing to call on others for help, and recognize them in the process. Work to develop a network of fellow professionals with a wide range of skills in all facets of land management. Get to know them and avail yourself of them. Be willing to refer landowners to other specialists or call on them for advice and other perspectives. Gene Miller, a retired technical guidance biologist with TPWD who now works for the National Wild Turkey Federation, has been assisting private landowners for 41 years and says, "We must be willing to stifle our territorial tendencies for the greater good of serving private landowners."

Seek mentors

Most longtime successful natural resource workers give a great deal of credit to the mentors who have helped them during their career. Seeking mentors and spending time with them will be an important part of both your professional development and self-improvement. In every area, there are people who are anxious to share what they have learned. Seek them out. Your mentors should include a combination of successful landowners and experienced natural resource professionals. From these mentors, you can gain wisdom, inspiration, and enthusiasm and benefit from their experience. According to Jimmy Rutledge, a wildlife biologist with 37 years of experience working with private landowners for the SCS, TPWD, and now a large private ranching concern, "A few key individuals will make a huge difference in your career and your effectiveness." When they see that you are anxious to listen and learn, they will often take you under their wing and help you excel. When you have gained some degree of expertise and wisdom, then it will be your turn to be a mentor to the next generation.

Develop critical thinking skills

Developing critical thinking skills is one of the most important things that will help you be effective with landowners. It is easy to recycle the same old solutions, answers, and perspectives of the past; it is much harder to think independently without common professional biases. Critical thinking forces you to separate your emotions, opinions, paradigms, wishes, and traditions from what is factually true. It involves thinking things through carefully, logically, and without preconceived ideas of outcomes. Too often in natural resource management, we see what we want to see, or we see what we have been programmed to see, rather than the true picture. Critical thinking can help separate good science from bad science and can help you develop sound interpretations, conclusions, and applications from scientific studies.

Speaking and writing

As you gain experience and expertise in your profession, you will want to develop the ability to speak in public and to write well. Although most of us would rather spend time individually with landowners, our efforts can be greatly multiplied through speaking and writing. You will be able to reach people you would otherwise never meet. At first, your public speaking may start with helping at field days and local landowner events, speaking to small groups informally. As you gain skill and confidence, you will probably be asked to speak at larger events. Start writing by submitting articles to the local newspaper or various newsletters. Get the advice of a good editor to help you in your writing and do not get offended when they suggest improvements. Learning to speak and write concisely, clearly, and convincingly will bear a great deal of fruit and will help many landowners. Photography will greatly enhance your ability to communicate; take your camera with you and use it often. A good picture is indeed worth a thousand words, and photos will help landowners visualize and relate to your message of conservation and natural resource management.

Become a great teacher

Our profession requires understanding complex ecological relationships. Science-based knowledge of nature, agriculture, and natural resource management is what we deliver to landowners. The way in which we deliver this information is crucial and requires that we learn the skill of being a great teacher. A great teacher does more than transfer knowledge.

Dalton Merz, a retired state range conservationist for the NRCS in Texas who has a reputation as a great teacher, says, "I am a 'show and tell' teacher. Landowners seem to learn well by this 'show and tell' process." Besides the important role of professional assistance, Merz has learned that "landowners learn best from other landowners; it is always best to see it on the land and have the landowners tell their success or failure stories." Therefore, another facet of assisting landowners with wild turkeys is to facilitate landowner-to-landowner learning through field days, informal ranch visits, or other opportunities for landowners to learn from each other.

Our work with landowners and managers must go beyond telling, explaining, and demonstrating natural resource information and ecological principles. We must also find ways to inspire and motivate landowners to incorporate the information we share into their everyday farming, ranching, and land management activities. William Ward said, "The mediocre teacher tells. The good teacher explains. The superior teacher demonstrates. The great teacher inspires." We must find ways to instill and encourage genuine and practical land stewardship ethics without being preachy or idealistic. When landowners observe your skill, enthusiasm, professionalism, and dedication to their cause and to the well-being of their land, they will value your assistance and will listen. As they gain confidence in and appreciation of your abilities and expertise, they will be more likely to consider your message and adopt some of the ideas you have inspired.

Conclusion

As two professionals who love the land and appreciate the vital role of private landowners and private land stewardship, we have presented ideals that represent our best efforts to communicate the principles we have found important for working with landowners. This material, when properly understood and diligently applied, will help you become a more successful conservationist, specialist, adviser, or consultant. The information will help you assist landowners and their managers as they endeavor to produce crops, livestock, timber, wildlife, water, and other natural resource values on their land in a practical and sustainable manner.

Your work with landowners lies at the intersection of agriculture, ecology, natural sciences, sustainability, human nature, and social dimensions. Your work is important to individual landowners and their families and is likewise important to society, which benefits from well-managed private land. Give your utmost to this profession and strive for excellence each day. If you do, you will find it to be a rewarding and stimulating vocation, providing an important service to present and future generations and to your community, state, and country.

Literature Cited

Leopold, A. 1949. A Sand County almanac. Oxford University Press, New York, New York, USA.

Chapter Appendix

In preparing this chapter, we relied on input from several experienced natural resource specialists across Texas, including Deborah Clark; J. R. Bell; Rory Burroughs; Larry Butler, PhD; Dan Caudle; Bill Eikenhorst, DVM; Kent Ferguson; Donnie Frels; Dee Ann Littlefield; Dalton Merz; Gene Miller; Kent Mills; Poncho Ortega, PhD; Stan Reinke; Jimmy Rutledge; and Russell Stevens. Their brief biographies follow.

DEBORAH CLARK has been ranching in Clay County, Texas, for many years. She is the consummate conservationist.

JAMES R. BELL has 48 years of experience working with landowners. He is currently a rangeland management consultant in the private sector. From 2001 to 2010 he worked for DuPont as a consultant on rangeland brush and weed control. He began his career with the SCS and NRCS in 1969 and retired in 2000, having served as a rangeland management specialist working with private ranchers and training field office personnel in Texas.

RORY BURROUGHS is owner of Comprehensive Land Management, a private company specializing in mechanical brush treatments and other range improvement practices. He also provides real estate and wildlife management assistance to landowners and is manager of Hackberry Creek Ranch in Kent and Fisher Counties, Texas.

DR. LARRY BUTLER was the executive producer and host of *Out on the Land*, a weekly half-hour television show dedicated to stewardship and conservation. He retired in 2007 from the NRCS after over 32 years of assisting private landowners in numerous technical positions, serving throughout the United States and as state conservationist in Texas.

DAN CAUDLE is a rangeland management specialist and natural resource management consultant/adviser with more than 48 years of experience in providing technical assistance to ranchers, natural resource managers, agencies, and organizations on all aspects of range and pasture management. He has extensive work experience throughout Texas and the Gulf Coast Prairies and Marshes of Louisiana.

BILL EIKENHORST, DVM, owns a large, successful veterinary practice in Brenham, Texas, and is a multigenerational landowner in Washington Country. He uses his extraordinary knowledge of animal ecology to teach people about the relationship of people and animals to the land. He has been instrumental in helping Texas Brigades become an effective youth conservation movement and has served in leadership positions in several conservation organizations, including the Texas Wildlife Association and Quality Deer Management Association. Dr. Eikenhorst has also become well known for his skill in restoring native prairie habitat across several regions in Texas.

KENT FERGUSON is a retired Texas state rangeland management specialist for the NRCS. He invested his 36-year public service range management career in working with private landowners and is currently involved in full-time ranching and consulting.

DONNIE FRELS was employed as a wildlife biologist with TPWD for over 30 years. He was the project leader for the Edwards Plateau Ecosystems Management Project, where he supervised daily operations, management, and research on three wildlife management areas in Central Texas. He and his staff interacted with and assisted thousands of landowners annually to encourage sustainable conservation and land stewardship.

DEE ANN LITTLEFIELD grew up being very involved on large, multigenerational family ranches in Arizona, an experience that led her to an occupation in agriculture communications. In 2003 she began a career with the NRCS as a public affairs specialist, serving at the state level in Texas and Oklahoma, where she has helped provide environmental stewardship information to landowners and millions of others through various media outlets. With her diverse background in ranching, the private sector, and the NRCS, she has over 20 years of business, professional, and personal agricultural and conservation experience.

DALTON MERZ is actively involved in ranching, consulting, and teaching after his retirement from SCS and NRCS. For 35 years, he served as a range conservationist at various levels, including Texas state range conservationist. He is well known for his special skills in communicating with landowners and his practical knowledge of livestock and range practices.

GENE T. MILLER is a certified wildlife biologist with 41 years of professional experience. He served as a technical guidance biologist with TPWD, assisting private landowners. Currently, he is a regional biologist with the National Wild Turkey Federation, working in West Texas and Oklahoma.

KENT MILLS is a range nutritionist with Hi-Pro Feeds and was formerly with Ezell-Key Feeds. He has extensive practical knowledge and experience in rangeland forages and ruminant nutrition in Texas and the Southwest. His unique forage sampling service has helped hundreds of ranchers make informed decisions about stocking rates, forage availability, supplemental feeding, and livestock performance. Mills began his career in 1972 working on the Fuller Ranch near Snyder, Texas, and then teaching ranch management courses at Western Texas College until 1982, when he began his work in the feed business.

STEVE NELLE began his career in 1976 and worked for the SCS and NRCS for 35 years as a range conservationist and wildlife biologist, assisting landowners across Texas. Since 2011, he has been involved in private range, wildlife, and watershed consulting and assistance.

DR. PONCHO ORTEGA has been involved in ranching since he was a young boy growing up in Mexico. Following his formal education, Dr. Ortega directed agricultural and land management research at 82 experiment stations across Mexico. He is currently a professor and research scientist at the Caesar Kleberg Wildlife Research Institute, Texas A&M University–Kingsville. His research interests include livestock-wildlife interactions and habitat management on private ranches. He has been actively involved in ranching as well as consulting for cattle and wildlife operations in Mexico and Texas for the past 23 years.

STAN REINKE worked with private landowners in the natural resources business for 48 years. He previously served as a range conservationist for the USDA/SCS and NRCS and as a range specialist for environmental defense.

JIMMY RUTLEDGE has 37 years of experience working with landowners in natural resource management. He began his career as a range conservationist with the SCS and then worked for 22 years as a wildlife biologist for TPWD. He currently serves as a wildlife habitat specialist and wildlife biologist for a large private organization. His work has focused on directly assisting landowners in developing plans to reach their land management and stewardship goals.

RUSSELL STEVENS is a wildlife and range consultant with the Noble Research Institute in Ardmore, Oklahoma. His work with landowners and managers includes wildlife and range management issues such as habitat improvement, prescribed fire, grazing management, plant identification, and feral hog impacts on agriculture. Stevens joined the Noble Foundation in 1989.

This chapter has been adapted with permission from the USDA Natural Resources Conservation Service bulletin authored by Steve Nelle, *Working Effectively with Private Landowners: A Guide for Conservationists*, Temple, Texas. It contains general principles that are applicable to nearly every situation; however, it is not a cookbook approach since each landowner and each piece of land is unique.

12

Conservation

Without hunting there would be no conservation, without conservation there would be no wildlife.

—ROB KECK

The *Merriam-Webster Dictionary* defines conservation in two parts: the protection of animals, plants, and natural resources; the careful use of natural resources to prevent them from being lost or wasted. This two-part definition of conservation is directly applicable to our stewardship of nearly all wildlife species, including the wild turkey. Note that the terms "protection" and "careful use" are at the core of this definition.

There are numerous ways that conservationists can protect and make careful use of wild turkey populations. It was the absence of protection and careful use that nearly drove wild turkey numbers to oblivion a century ago. Early protective measures, including state legislation during the late nineteenth and early twentieth centuries, fell well short of the mark. It was not until 1919 that a reasonable annual bag limit of three males per season, coupled with the efforts of conservation-minded landowners and the employment of game wardens in the 1920s, started the effective protection of the remaining turkey populations in Texas (Suarez 2002). Fortunately, factors related to protection and careful use have resulted in the widespread recovery of wild turkey populations that we enjoy today.

The Lacey Act of 1900, which prohibited the interstate sale of wildlife, was arguably the first legislation to lay the groundwork for wild turkey conservation. The Lacey Act, along with state prohibitions on hunting, protected the remaining wild turkey flocks. The 1937 Pittman-Robertson Act, which generated an excise tax on sporting arms and ammunition, along with state-generated matching funds, provided state wildlife agencies with critical funding to implement wild turkey conservation and restoration of populations. Meaningful restoration efforts began in the 1940s. Through these efforts, the Texas Game and Fish Commission and later the Texas Parks and Wildlife Department (TPWD) captured and moved over 33,000 Rio Grande wild turkeys across Texas. Today, thanks to these efforts, Texas hosts some of the highest densities of wild turkeys in the country.

Habitat, Education, and Hunting

Habitat, education, and hunting are often considered the conceptual "three-legged stool" with respect to wildlife conservation, especially for game species such as the wild turkey. Take away one of these three legs and the stool topples over. Keep all three legs in place and the stool is a practical device to sit on or to keep things off the floor.

Habitat

Land-use practices favorable to wild turkey habitat recovery began in the 1920s and 1930s as small tenant farms were abandoned and forests that were once overharvested began to recover via succession. Forest cover in the eastern United States was about 30% or less during 1900 and had recovered to more than 60% by the 1960s. Many forested areas that were cleared for agriculture were marginal for growing crops. Such areas eventually reverted to vegetation dominated by mature trees by way of natural plant succession, although many deforested areas were also replanted by people. The accidental by-product of these changing land uses was that in about a half century or less, wild turkey habitat was restored on a grand scale throughout most of the bird's original geographic range. To use a theater analogy, by the 1950s or so, the habitat stage was constructed, but the script had yet to be written for the play that would tell the story of wild turkey restoration.

These changing land-use practices provided an accidental increase in overall wild turkey habitat. However, sustaining wild turkey habitat does not happen by accident. Purposeful management can be implemented in a variety of landscapes to maintain, improve, and even increase habitat for wild turkeys. Practices such as prescribed fire, timber thinning, brush control, and protection of roosting habitat are all purposeful management practices beneficial to wild turkeys (see chapter 8).

Education

As it turned out, people had a lot to learn when it came to wild turkey population restoration. Early efforts to use game-farm birds for population restoration were met with repeated and dismal failures. Kennamer et al. (1992) indicated that more than 330,000 birds released on over 800 sites had a 95% failure rate. Diseases, poor genetic quality, and most importantly the loss of "wildness" as the result of raising multiple generations in captivity were thought to be the primary causes of the failure of farm-raised stock to recover wild turkey populations (Leopold 1944, Kennamer et al. 1992). It was only after people learned how to trap and transplant wild turkeys in the 1950s that restoration efforts really began to pay off. By the early 1990s, a total of more than 2.5 million Eastern wild turkeys occupied 37 states. There were an estimated 75,000 Florida wild turkeys, more than 630,000 Rio Grande wild turkeys, and more than 100,000 Merriam's wild turkeys, respectively (Kennamer et al. 1992). Habitat recovery set the stage, and learning how to trap and translocate wild turkeys resulted in the award-winning play that we know today as "Wild Turkey Restoration."

Continuing education remains critical in Texas as new science and subsequent habitat management practices become available. TPWD and other conservation organizations periodically offer educational events for landowners, hunters, and other members of the public interested in wild turkey conservation (fig. 12.1). Many of these events are hosted on wildlife management areas where wildlife biologists speak about wild turkey natural history and habitat man-

Figure 12.1. An educational public field day (photo by Jason Hardin).

agement in an outdoor setting and answer questions from the audience. Texas has played a key role in developing new GPS technology that is changing how biologists and researchers view the ways wild turkeys use their landscape. Organizations such as Texas A&M AgriLife Extension, Texas Wildlife Association, and the National Wild Turkey Federation partner with universities and TPWD to educate landowners and hunters in the science of wildlife and habitat management.

Hunting

Although conservation efforts can be effective in the absence of hunting, hunting is most successful when implemented in the context of conservation. The wild turkey is a classic example of this philosophy. As noted earlier, the cessation of hunting was an essential first step in wild turkey conservation. In many cases, hunting was largely inconsequential because wild turkeys had been extirpated over entire states and ecological regions during the nineteenth century.

As wild turkey numbers recovered, it became apparent that hunting seasons could be implemented without harming populations. For example, Keck and Langston (1992) noted that in the mid-1960s fewer than 20 states had spring wild turkey hunting seasons; by 1991, wild turkeys were hunted in all 48 contiguous states, as well as Hawaii. Conservation, or in this case "careful use," is a common theme that runs across all aspects of hunting wild turkeys. All states have strict regulations that limit the total number of hunting days as well as the total number of birds a hunter can take. These regulations are developed from recommendations by state agency wildlife biologists along with advisory groups and are based on a number of biological and sociological considerations (Kurzejeski and Vangilder 1992). In certain counties of East Texas where the recovery of the Eastern subspecies remains a conservation challenge, hunting is severely restricted or even prohibited. In areas of the state where wild turkeys are most numerous, TPWD provides more liberal seasons.

Wild turkey hunting generates conservation opportunities because hunters value these birds in ecological, recreational, aesthetic, economic, and sometimes even spiritual contexts. The hunting community, through the Federal Aid in Wildlife Restoration Act or Pittman-Robertson Act of 1937, contributes to the restoration and management of game species through the purchase of firearms, ammunition, hunting equipment, and hunting licenses. It is these funds, and therefore the hunting community, that has most significantly contributed to the restoration and management of game species and the habitats in which they reside. Therefore, the cycle of hunters begetting game animal restoration and management begets more hunters.

Wild Turkey Conservation Today

The contemporary landscape of wild turkey conservation, especially in Texas, represents a bright spot in wildlife management. Stakeholders in the world of wild turkey conservation include nongovernmental organizations such as the National Wild Turkey Federation and Las Huellas; state agencies such as TPWD; federal agencies such as the US Forest Service, Natural Resources Conservation Service, and US Fish and Wildlife Service; and academic institutions such as universities that conduct research on wild turkeys as well as train and educate students to become wildlife biologists. Each of these stakeholder organizations, as well as wild turkey hunters themselves, has played, and continues to play, important roles in developing the critical mass of success that the world of wild turkey conservation has enjoyed for the past four decades or more.

Wild turkey conservation has taken many forms over the past 150 years. Early efforts were focused primarily on protection of remaining populations. These efforts eventually included restoration, a practice that evolved from the unfortunate releases of thousands of game-farm turkeys to the exclusive use of wild-trapped turkeys. Today, conservation efforts are entering a stage of habitat management and restoration. Today's issues are numerous. Habitat fragmentation caused by a growing human population is rampant. Fragmenting features include the expansion of urban and suburban areas into once-remote landscapes and the development of reservoirs that flood critical bottomland hardwood forests. A changing climate has led to the loss of critical roosting cover in semiarid regions of the state through drought and changing flood regimes. The loss of historical management practices such as prescribed fire has allowed brush to encroach into forest understories in East Texas, and on rangelands throughout Texas resulting in degraded habitat. These and numerous other factors must continue to be addressed in order to sustain current densities of wild turkeys.

Literature Cited

Keck, B., and J. Langston. 1992. Recreational use. Pages 388–407 *in* J. G. Dickson, editor. The wild turkey: biology and management. Stackpole Books, Mechanicsburg, Pennsylvania, USA.

Kennamer, J. E., M. Kennamer, and R. Brenneman. 1992. History. Pages 6–17 *in* J. G. Dickson, editor. The wild turkey: biology and management. Stackpole Books, Mechanicsburg, Pennsylvania, USA.

Kurzejeski, E. W., and L. D. Vangilder. 1992. Population management. Pages 165–185 *in* J. G. Dickson, editor. The wild turkey: biology and management. Stackpole Books, Mechanicsburg, Pennsylvania, USA.

Leopold, A. S. 1944. The nature of heritable wildness in turkeys. Condor 46:133–197.

Suarez, R. 2002. Texas turkey talk. Texas Parks and Wildlife Department Report PWD BK W7000–827. Texas Parks and Wildlife Department, Austin, USA.

13

Research Priorities

Research is creating new knowledge.

—NEIL ARMSTRONG

Many wildlife scientists have devoted time and effort to learning about the specific needs of wild turkeys in Texas and have also identified limiting factors that, if addressed, have the potential to enhance wild turkey populations in the state. The goal of these scientists is to formulate and test hypotheses that will yield information that will not only further science by developing new questions but will also perhaps provide solutions to challenges and solve problems. However, all too often in wildlife management, tens of thousands of dollars are devoted to researching a problem, and then when a reasonable solution is found it is not implemented, often because of a lack of funds.

There are many research projects in Texas that could improve our understanding of wild turkey ecology, management, and restoration. A substantial portion of wild turkey research funding has been provided by TPWD; it has funded wild turkey research in Texas for decades and continues to fund it today. TPWD's research priorities are driven by the goal of improving how the department and landowners manage wild turkey populations. Although there are many unknowns in the wild turkey world, the department must prioritize needs and fund research projects that have the potential to significantly change how TPWD manages wild turkeys or influences populations. The recommendations provided here represent some of TPWD's current priority research needs, and several are ongoing research projects. Other research needs may arise as dictated by the availability of research funding and population and landscape changes. So, what are the current wild turkey research priorities in Texas?

Wild Turkey Evolution and Taxonomy

A range-wide phylogeographic study based on DNA sequences of multiple mitochondrial and nuclear genes is needed that includes the five wild subspecies and domestic representatives of the South Mexican turkey to better assess the evolutionary relationships among the wild turkey subspecies, determine historical population structure, and estimate long-term effective population sizes and divergence times of intraspecific lineages. Another research need is applying ecological niche models to examine how the geographic range of the wild turkey has changed in response to past climate changes, which also provides an independent way to test inferences about biogeography and demography based on the results of phylogeographic studies. A range-wide study of adaptive genetic variation using SNPs is needed that incorporates representatives of all subspecies, including domestic lineages, to identify loci under selection and relate signatures of selection to environmental variables. Additional research should include a multivariate analysis of geographic variation in plumage and other phenotypic traits on which the five wild turkey subspecies are based to determine the extent of clinal variation and how differences in physical traits relate to climate and other environmental variables. Finally, a thorough review of the original subspecies descriptions is needed as part of a thorough taxonomic review based on the results of multilocus genetic studies and analysis of geographic variation to determine the validity of each subspecies and suggest possible taxonomic revisions.

Population Ecology

It is difficult to improve wild turkey management and monitor restoration efforts without the ability to estimate wild turkey demography. Wild turkey biologists and land managers are currently hamstrung in efforts to effectively manage wild turkey populations because a reliable survey method does not exist to estimate wild turkey densities. Developing a survey method that yields reliable density estimates needs to be a priority in order to better monitor restoration efforts and recognize where management emphasis should be placed. This is particularly relevant to current Eastern wild turkey restoration efforts and will also be important should decisions be made to restore Merriam's wild turkey populations in West Texas. Annual recruitment of young individuals into a population is critical to sustaining populations year after year. Therefore, obtaining a better understanding of wild turkey poult movements, survival, and sources of mortality for all three subspecies of wild turkeys in Texas is critical to identifying management decisions that could mitigate declines and improve wild turkey populations. Similarly, since females produce poults, a better understanding of female survival at the ranch, landscape, and ecoregion scales is needed. Furthermore, information about wild turkey productivity at various levels of abundance will also improve management of all three subspecies of wild turkeys in Texas.

Harvest Management

Several research priorities exist regarding harvest management of wild turkeys in Texas. First, TPWD recognizes the lack of reliable information about wild turkey harvest rates throughout Texas. Therefore, an assessment of harvest rates through a statewide banding study is needed. Another valuable statewide research project would be an evaluation of wild turkey nesting and gobbling chronology as it relates to spring hunting season frameworks.

Habitat

From a habitat perspective, much work has been accomplished over the past 20 years, and as a result, our knowledge about Rio Grande and Eastern wild turkey habitat requirements in Texas has improved. Nevertheless, there is little information on wild turkey habitat use at multiple scales of resolution. For example, we need to learn more about wild turkey habitat needs at the individual bird, population, and metapopulation levels. A multiscale habitat perspective is critical now because habitat fragmentation has become a genuine issue for wild turkeys in Texas. A lack of purposeful management on a landscape scale in East Texas is fragmenting landscapes where Eastern wild turkey restoration is under way, and to some extent, it is likely undermining restoration efforts by isolating wild turkey populations in the Piney Woods into habitat islands. Fragmentation also threatens Rio Grande wild turkeys near urban areas that have recently exhibited explosive growth such as the San Antonio/San Marcos/Austin Corridor as well as the Lower Rio Grande Valley and Laredo. In addition to this urban growth, the explosion of small hobby ranches and farms in the Hill Country within an hour's drive of Austin and San Antonio has further fragmented Rio Grande wild turkey populations. A thorough examination of current wild turkey use of landscapes in the ecoregions occupied by wild turkeys in Texas is needed to determine the extent of fragmentation that currently exists and, if necessary, how to restore habitat to establish corridors linking wild turkey populations. We also need to know how fragmentation is impacting nesting and brooding habitats. Another important research need is evaluating the importance of maintaining riparian corridors statewide, because riparian vegetation communities are important wild turkey habitat features within a landscape. Riparian corridors provide roost sites, foraging and loafing habitats, escape cover, often water, and travel corridors.

Habitat Management

Identifying ways to better manage wild turkey habitat is also important. For example, we need to manage livestock grazing in a manner that benefits wild turkeys. Clearly, limiting grazing or excluding livestock from important nesting and brooding habitats during the fall preceding the spring nesting and summer brooding seasons is important. However, grazing management recommendations that address wild turkey herbaceous cover needs on a seasonal basis need to be developed for specific vegetation communities in each ecoregion of Texas. Managing livestock grazing in the Piney Woods is just as important for Eastern wild turkeys as managing Hill Country and Cross Timbers rangelands is for Rio Grande wild turkeys. The impacts of exotic vegetation on wild turkey populations is also a concern in Texas. It has already been demonstrated that exotic grass invasions impact grassland and shrubland bird communities in South Texas; pastures dominated by exotic grasses have lower plant species diversity than native grasslands. Although wild turkeys will utilize exotic grass communities, these communities may not represent quality habitat. Exotic grass communities provide fewer plant foods and are poorer habitats for invertebrates, which are important wild turkey food items. Therefore, we need to determine how invasions of Old World bluestems, Guinea grass, Lehmann lovegrass, buffelgrass, coastal Bermuda grass, and Bahia grass impact wild turkey populations.

Climate Change

It is also important to confront the issue of climate change and what can be done to mitigate its effects on wild turkey populations. In South Texas, wild turkeys are highly sensitive to drought and shut down reproductive efforts during spring months with low rainfall. Thus, research on the impacts of climate change on wild turkey population dynamics should be a priority. Furthermore, the severe drought in South Texas from 2012 to 2015 apparently resulted in considerable mortality among mature live oaks and hackberry trees, which often line riparian corridors and are critical natural Rio Grande wild turkey roosts. Continuing loss of such an important habitat component because of climate change would certainly have a negative impact on wild turkey populations. Therefore, since we know that wild turkeys will use manmade roosts, it is important to determine where on a landscape to provide these roosts so that wild turkeys will use them, and to identify a roost design that turkeys prefer.

Merriam's Wild Turkey

Merriam's wild turkeys have been largely ignored in Texas. It appears that the only population occurs in Guadalupe Mountains National Park in West Texas, but a reliable estimate of wild turkeys in the park does not exist. Moreover, almost nothing is known about this population and the potential factors that may limit its growth. Therefore, a thorough study of Merriam's wild turkey ecology in Guadalupe Mountains National Park should be conducted. Included within this study should be an assessment of habitat use and availability to determine whether current habitat is sufficient to meet the needs of a sustainable wild turkey population. Additionally, if restorations are being considered in the Davis Mountains, daily habitat use patterns of both Merriam's and Rio Grande wild turkeys should be assessed using GPS transmitters to evaluate habitat suitability for both subspecies and to evaluate hybridization risks. It may be possible to identify a Merriam's wild turkey restoration site that Rio Grande wild turkeys are unlikely to colonize.

Predator Control

Predator control is a sensitive issue today, even in Texas. Therefore, the decision to initiate predator control research should be carefully considered. There should be solid justification to do so. For example, predator control research might be justifiable where efforts to restore Eastern wild turkey populations are ongoing and if Merriam's wild turkey restoration is initiated. Identifying major predators and removing those that can be legally harvested prior to and after turkey translocations could facilitate restoration of populations by potentially enhancing production during the nesting and brooding season following wild turkey releases. So research designed to evaluate the impacts of predators and predator control on wild turkey populations at multiple scales (ranch, county, ecoregion) might be warranted.

Diseases and Parasites

A number of diseases and parasites have been identified in wild turkeys in Texas. Newcastle disease, salmonella, and mycoplasma are some of the diseases that are commonly identified in wild turkey populations, not only in Texas but also throughout the geographic distribution of wild turkeys in North America. However, reticuloendotheliosis virus and the highly pathogenic intraerythrocytic rickettsia bacteria are disease organisms that have been identified more recently. In addition to diseases, endoparasites such as cestodes and nematodes as well as a variety of lice appear to commonly infest wild turkeys in Texas. There does not appear to be any risk to wild turkey populations from exposure to disease infections or parasite infestations. Nevertheless, disease surveillance studies have been restricted to a few locations in select areas of Texas, and most of these studies were done over 40 years ago. There is a genuine need to initiate broader, more comprehensive disease and parasite studies that cover each ecoregion of Texas. Specifically, each ecoregion should be adequately sampled for diseases and parasites deemed to be of potential concern where wild turkey populations occur. TPWD is the obvious agency to organize and direct a comprehensive statewide disease study.

Human Dimensions

Involving Texans interested in wild turkey management and conservation would be worthwhile because the public would not only become stakeholders in these efforts but would also be an important source of data that would be valuable in making policy and management decisions. For example, citizen scientists might serve as an effective means for assessing changes in wild turkey populations at the ecoregion scale. Surveys of avid bow hunters, birders, and other outdoor enthusiasts might be a way to assess abundance of wild turkeys and could even be conducted by TPWD cooperators. Another worthy research project would be a survey of the public to determine whether and how the conservation community should address wild turkey restoration in unoccupied habitat along the 97th meridian between Interstates 35 and 45. As part of this survey, it would be possible to get public opinion on the hybridization of Eastern and Rio Grande wild turkeys that would likely occur in portions of this corridor. Would the public care that a pure genetic strain would not exist, or would people care only that wild turkey populations are restored, even if they are hybrids? The number of hunters who pursue wild turkeys and the number of wild turkeys harvested annually in Texas have both declined by almost 50% since the 1990s. Despite an increase in hunter success, this decline in hunters is a source of concern for TPWD officials because it is possible that hunters are finding it increasingly difficult to locate wild turkeys. Therefore, a survey of hunters who purchase upland game bird endorsements could help determine whether wild turkeys are harder to locate than they were 20 years ago or if finding a place to hunt is harder than it was 20 years ago. TPWD has also identified a need to conduct hunter and landowner attitude surveys to evaluate and potentially improve the wild turkey regulatory process.

Conclusions

Texas has arguably been at the forefront of wild turkey research in the United States over the past 25 years. TPWD has responded to the concerns of wild turkey enthusiasts and has funded numerous projects that have yielded abundant useful information that has improved wild turkey conservation and management throughout the state. Nevertheless, as this chapter indicates, numerous challenges remain. This should not be surprising, because the essence of good research is to provide results that stimulate new questions to be addressed through additional research. Therefore, research is and should be a process without end. Clearly, important wild turkey research needs continue in Texas. However, just as clearly, enough interest in wild turkey conservation and management exists among Texans to justify support for additional research. Many talented wildlife scientists in Texas have the enthusiasm and interest to conduct much of the needed wild turkey research suggested in this chapter. Moreover, even more future wildlife scientists are being educated in the state's public school and university systems who can continue this research tradition. There is therefore little doubt that if the will to do wild turkey research is there and remains, we will continue to learn about wild turkeys and apply what we learn to move wild turkey conservation and management forward in Texas.

14

The Future

The future depends on what we do in the present.

—MAHATMA GANDHI (1869–1948)

Throughout this book we have identified what we currently know about wild turkeys in Texas. Many aspects of wild turkey life history are shared by all three subspecies (Eastern, Rio Grande, and Merriam's) discussed in this book, and for the most part, we have sufficient knowledge of wild turkey life history to manage and conserve wild turkey populations, as well as to restore populations where necessary in Texas. However, this book specifically identifies the many things we need to learn in order to further wild turkey management and conservation, and especially to increase the success of restoration efforts. Therefore, we believe that Mahatma Gandhi's quote about the future depending on what we do in the present is particularly relevant to ensuring the future of wild turkeys in Texas.

The Current Status of Wild Turkeys in Texas

The future of the Rio Grande wild turkey in Texas is bright. Rio Grande wild turkeys currently occupy almost 90% of their historic geographic range in Texas thanks to the efforts of many dedicated TPWD officials, private landowners, university scientists, nongovernmental organizations such as the National Wild Turkey Federation and Las Huellas, and, most importantly, the many rank-and-file members of the public interested in wild turkeys in Texas. Indeed, as indicated earlier in this book, Texas continues to harbor more wild turkeys than any other state in the United States, the majority of which are Rio Grande wild turkeys. The decades of long effort to restore Rio Grande wild turkeys in Texas have been so successful that TPWD has largely suspended efforts to restore Rio Grande wild turkey populations in Texas because it does not appear to be necessary.

Eastern wild turkey populations are also more abundant now than they were 40 years ago thanks to determined efforts to restore them to their former range in the Piney Woods. However, challenges remain because populations have evidently declined in some counties, forcing TPWD officials to suspend hunting seasons there. We hope that recently developed release techniques will increase the success of restoration efforts in East Texas.

Despite the restoration successes evident for the Rio Grande and Eastern subspecies, Merriam's wild turkey populations may be in jeopardy in Texas. It is possible that the only Merriam's wild turkey population remaining in Texas is in Guadalupe Mountains National Park. Efforts to restore Merriam's wild turkeys to the Davis Mountains over 30 years ago evidently failed because of hybridization with Rio Grande wild turkeys that have been expanding their range into the mountains of West Texas. As of the publication of this book, we are not aware of any plans to resume attempts to restore Merriam's wild turkeys to their historic range in West Texas.

Overall wild turkey numbers in Texas are higher than they were at the end of the 1990s. However, the state's wild turkey population may have declined over the past five years. Therefore, although Texas currently has millions of wild turkeys, concerns do exist about maintaining these populations and restoring and increasing them where necessary. The remainder of this chapter will be devoted to some of these major concerns and ways to address them in a manner that benefits wild turkey conservation and management in Texas.

Population Dynamics

Wildlife biologists responsible for the management of wild turkeys in Texas are currently hamstrung because a technique that provides reliable estimates of wild turkey densities does not yet exist. Some road and aerial survey techniques hold promise, but there is not yet a technique that provides precise estimates in every ecoregion of the state. In addition, better information about female and poult survival, sources of mortality, and movements is needed in almost every ecoregion. We have learned a lot about wild turkeys in Texas over the past 30 years, but in order to move wild turkey conservation and management forward, we must develop a reliable survey technique that works statewide as well as learn more about important aspects of female and poult ecology.

Land-Use Practices

Although overall populations in the state are stable, land-use practices have the potential to negatively impact future turkey populations. Texas is unique in that most of the land is privately owned and therefore subject to management practices based on individual landowners' beliefs and the land-use practices they have traditionally desired. Although Texas landowners realize that significant economic incentives exist for managing their properties for wildlife, livestock production has long been and will continue to be a significant land use in Texas. Consequently, improper grazing by livestock as well as native and exotic herbivores that are not managed properly has the potential to degrade turkey habitat to the point of unsuitability by reducing critical vegetative cover. Lack of herbaceous cover will negatively impact wild turkey population dynamics by limiting productivity because fewer females will nest, and those that do will be more exposed to predators. Fewer broods will be produced, and those that are will be subjected to higher mortality rates. Therefore, poor grazing management has the potential to negatively impact wild turkey populations at multiple scales (ranch, county, and ecoregion), particularly if overgrazing is pervasive at large scales in a region. The threat of overgrazing is particularly relevant to Rio Grande and Merriam's wild turkeys because they occupy semiarid to arid rangelands where herbaceous production depends on rainfall. Even though annual average precipitation is higher in East Texas, excessive livestock overgrazing of important nesting and brooding habitats in the Piney Woods can also limit Eastern wild turkey annual production. In order to effectively address grazing management issues, we must learn more about how grazing impacts wild turkey populations and then provide landowners with grazing management recommendations that benefit wild turkey populations.

For the Eastern wild turkey, interspersion of forested areas and open grasslands provides the annual habitat requirements needed to maintain self-sustaining populations. In many areas of East Texas, the forest understory has become too dense to provide the proper habitat for the Eastern subspecies. Proper forest management practices are important for the future of this subspecies in Texas. Typically, openings in forests such as clearings or food plots provide adequate vegetative cover for nesting and brood rearing, while densely forested areas fail to produce enough herbaceous biomass to meet these cover requirements. Low nest success coupled with high brood mortality is limiting Eastern wild turkey populations. Prescribed fires, forest thinning, and appropriately scheduled grazing by domestic livestock at proper stocking rates, or combinations of these activities, should be utilized to restore habitat to a usable condition.

Another threat to wild turkey populations in Texas is habitat fragmentation. Poor forest structure is clearly limiting restoration of Eastern wild turkeys in the Piney Woods because commercial pine plantations are unsuitable vegetation communities that will not be occupied by wild turkeys. Many plantations also separate existing turkey populations and, because they are unsuitable vegetation communities, do not serve as corridors that are needed to facilitate exchange between populations. Oil and gas exploration and production is another factor that could be fragmenting Rio Grande wild turkey habitat. With the discovery and recent activity associated with the "Eagle Ford Shale," fracking has emerged in Texas as an important industry. This large-scale energy exploration has fragmented formerly contiguous habitat, resulting in Rio Grande wild turkey habitat loss. Furthermore, the recent discovery of the "Wolfcamp Shale" geologic formation in West Texas and the fracking associated with oil and natural gas production will likely result in fragmentation of habitats potentially important to Merriam's wild turkey restoration. An assessment of current habitat use and resource availibility should be done on an ecoregion scale to determine how fragmentation is affecting wild turkey populations. This type of work is currently ongoing for Eastern wild turkeys in the Piney Woods but should be extended to unoccupied areas in the corridor between Interstates 35 and 45 where wild turkey restoration is being contemplated, as well as to the ecoregions occupied by Rio Grande wild turkeys.

The Merriam's wild turkey is often overlooked by many Texas landowners and outdoor enthusiasts. The Merriam's subspecies is not as well known as the more numerous and popular Rio Grande and Eastern subspecies. In fact, most Texans are probably unaware that Merriam's wild turkeys even occur in Texas. The primary limiting factor for this subspecies is quite simply ignorance. In addition to knowing almost nothing about their ecology, we do not even know how many currently exist in Guadalupe Mountains National Park. Moreover, because their native habitat is the higher mountain ranges in West Texas where grasslands and forests still exist, potential habitat exists as islands within the sea of the Chihuahuan Desert, and we do not know whether habitat conditions are suitable or even whether enough suitable habitat currently exists to support sustainable Merriam's wild turkey populations. Therefore, decisions need to be made regarding the efficacy of restoring Merriam's wild turkey populations in Texas. Are Texans interested in pursuing this, and if they are, is restoration beyond Guadalupe Mountains National Park even possible? If adequate habitat does exist, is there enough interest among the public and those who own these lands to conserve and maintain the habitat for Merriam's wild turkeys? These important questions need to be addressed soon if Merriam's wild turkeys are to be preserved and recovered.

Involving Public Stakeholders

The successful restoration of wild turkeys to Texas would not have been possible without the interest and support of public stakeholders. The millions of dollars that TPWD has invested in wild turkey restoration over the past 70–80 years is a tribute to the interest and concern that private landowners, hunters, and other outdoor enthusiasts have exhibited toward wild turkeys in Texas. Clearly, Texans remain proud enough of the successful history of wild turkey conservation and management in the state to continue to support ongoing restoration activities, as well as efforts to learn more about wild turkey ecology in order to move conservation and management forward. Therefore, a concerted effort should be made to continue and even expand public engagement in wild turkey restoration, conservation, and management in Texas.

A good start would be conducting a statewide public survey targeting private landowners, hunters, and other outdoor enthusiasts to obtain opinions about current TPWD wild turkey regulations and management policy. TPWD could also survey the public to determine opinions about wild turkey restoration in the Interstate 35–Interstate 45 corridor and whether the public cares about the Eastern/Rio Grande hybridization issue. Similarly, a public survey could determine whether there is interest in resuming Merriam's wild turkey restoration efforts in West Texas.

In addition to surveys, additional efforts could be made to expand public involvement in wild turkey conservation and management through citizen science. Implementing and organizing a statewide wild turkey survey program utilizing hunters, birders, and landowners who spend considerable time outdoors would not only yield trend data on wild turkey abundance in each of the state's ecoregions where turkeys occur, but would also stimulate or increase interest among the public in wild turkey conservation and management in Texas. Additionally, simply providing interested members of the public with opportunities to participate in active wild turkey management and research activities would accomplish a great deal in elevating public interest in wild turkeys. This has already been successfully accomplished with Eastern wild turkey restoration, as volunteers have enthusiastically participated in translocating and releasing Eastern wild turkeys at restoration sites. Cooperative efforts between TPWD and the Texas Chapter of the National Wild Turkey Federation have yielded many chapter members who have dedicated their free time to Eastern wild turkey restoration. Similar efforts to engage the public in other ecoregions where active wild turkey work is ongoing should be encouraged.

Education

TPWD offers occasional educational opportunities regarding wild turkeys in Texas, generally on one of the wildlife management areas (WMAs) the agency administers. Texas A&M AgriLife Extension also offers similar educational opportunities and often cooperates with TPWD biologists to do so. Moreover, TPWD and AgriLife personnel have written educational bulletins about wild turkeys that are available online. Members of the public interested in wild turkey conservation and management can visit WMAs that harbor wild turkeys and talk to staff about wild turkey ecology and management. Although educational opportunities are available, more could be accomplished to broaden public education. For example, more could be done to educate youth beyond those who are hunters. TPWD and AgriLife personnel almost certainly provide youth education, but more could be accomplished by visiting public schools more frequently, particularly in the larger cities in Texas. Most Texas high schools have agriculture programs, and today most of them teach a class or two in wildlife management. So most high school agriculture teachers would welcome visits by wildlife biologists to teach their students about wild turkeys. It is likely that similar visits could be extended to elementary and middle school students.

Another facet of wildlife education in Texas that has been largely ignored is establishing positive working relationships with private landowners. Wildlife management students at universities in Texas get very basic information about wildlife management and ecology through the curricula they complete for their degrees. A few even get the opportunity to work on wildlife research projects conducted on private lands by their professors. These students are exposed to how their professors and graduate student supervisors work with private landowners. However, like their peers who do not get these field experiences, they do not receive any formal instruction about how to work effectively with private landowners. Moreover, most hunters and other outdoor enthusiasts who either have or desire access to private lands are forced to learn on their own how to relate to private landowners. Common sense dictates that one should behave as a considerate guest and do what private landowners ask when visiting their property. This is clearly important. For young wildlife biologists just starting their careers in Texas, working on private lands is going to be a reality, yet few if any of them receive any training on how to work with private landowners. Chapter 11 of this book gives budding wildlife professionals and anyone else with a desire to access private lands insights from professionals with decades of experience about how to establish and maintain positive relationships with private landowners. This chapter is a good starting point, but additional educational opportunities should be provided. Incorporating relevant material into ongoing wildlife curricula at the university and even high school level would help accomplish this for students. In addition, workshops or seminars hosted by TPWD or AgriLife personnel would be an effective way of educating the public about working with private landowners. Finding ways to improve public awareness about wild turkeys in Texas will go a long way toward increasing public support for the issues highlighted in this chapter and will move wild turkey conservation and management forward.

Conclusions

Texas is blessed with citizens who care about wild turkeys and take pride in the state's long effort to successfully restore wild turkey populations to much of their former geographic range. We are also fortunate to have a state wildlife agency that is a proven leader in the field of wild turkey research, conservation, and management. TPWD has invested tens of millions of dollars to ensure that Texans can enjoy the long tradition of wild turkey recreation that currently exists in the state. Much has been accomplished to make Texas the state with the highest number of wild turkeys in North America. However, more can be accomplished in the future to continue to move wild turkey conservation and management in Texas forward. We have identified a number of priorities in this chapter that should be addressed to improve wild turkey conservation and management, but these are by no means the only priorities. The citizens of Texas will ultimately dictate what future wild turkey priorities are, and to a significant degree TPWD will be charged with seeing that these priorities are addressed. Perhaps most important in securing the future of wild turkeys in Texas is that landowners, state and federal wildlife biologists, wild turkey NGOs, university scientists, and, most importantly, Texans interested in wild turkeys continue to work together to benefit wild turkey populations in Texas. We have a very good tradition in this regard, one that we hope will continue.

Appendix 1

Additional Resources

This book focuses on Texas, although we believe it has value beyond the state anywhere Rio Grande, Eastern, and Merriam's wild turkeys exist. Nevertheless, we hope that interested readers will make use of the numerous available published and online resources. These materials range from short missives and articles on the internet that are written expressly for nonprofessionals to technical bulletins and scientific articles written by and for wildlife biologists. One very important resource for nonprofessional wild turkey enthusiasts is the National Wild Turkey Federation (NWTF), a nongovernmental organization that was established decades ago for the express purpose of wild turkey conservation. The NWTF has numerous articles and bulletins available online about the five subspecies of wild turkeys that inhabit North America (National Wild Turkey Federation 2015). Moreover, the NWTF employs at least one professional wildlife biologist to represent almost every state in the United States that has wild turkeys. Texas alone has two wildlife biologists who are available to assist anyone interested in wild turkeys.

In addition, almost every state in North America that supports wild turkey populations has at least one wild turkey bulletin available online to anyone wanting to learn about basic wild turkey biology and management. Many states also provide information for turkey hunters, including suggestions on how to hunt wild turkeys as well as the laws associated with wild turkey hunting. For example, the Texas Parks and Wildlife Department (TPWD) (2015) has numerous publications available online that provide information about the three subspecies of wild turkeys in Texas (Cook and Gore 1984, Campo and Dickson 1990, Suarez 2002). TPWD wildlife biologists are also stationed in almost every county in Texas, and these individuals, as well as TPWD technical guidance biologists stationed regionally throughout the state, are available to help wild turkey enthusiasts.

Furthermore, the Texas A&M AgriLife Extension (2018) can assist landowners interested in wild turkeys. Texas AgriLife has extension wildlife biologists who are available for assistance, as are many of the county agents stationed in every Texas county. Texas AgriLife also has a number of recently published online extension articles that provide life history and management information about Rio Grande (Cathey et al. 2007a, b) and Eastern wild turkeys (Conway et al. 2010, Alldredge et al. 2014).

Additionally, several federal agencies provide wild turkey expertise to the public. The USDA Natural Resources Conservation Service (NRCS) has field offices in almost every county in Texas, and field office staff can often be helpful regarding wild turkey management. The NRCS (1999) provides a good general information bulletin for wild turkeys. The US Forest Service (2018) also provides a great deal of information online about wild turkeys. Other federal agencies that provide general information on wild turkeys are the National Park Service (2018) and the US Fish and Wildlife Service (2017), particularly relative to the national wildlife refuges that feature wild turkeys as an important wildlife species.

The online material provided by the NWTF, TPWD, Texas AgriLife, and federal agencies is useful for anyone interested in wild turkeys in Texas, but it consists mainly of short summaries that provide basic information. More comprehensive information exists, including several books about wild turkeys that have been written by wildlife professionals over the past 70 years. For example, Mosby and Handley (1943) published the first book about wild turkeys, which detailed the status and life history of wild turkeys in Virginia. Schorger (1966) provided a very thorough book detailing wild turkey history in the Americas. It includes details about turkey domestication in Mexico, taxonomic and physical descriptions of the extinct and current North American subspecies, a description of current geographic ranges, a history of population trends and abundance, detailed life history information, the history of population restoration, and information on wild turkey management. Hewitt (1967) edited the first comprehensive book about wild turkeys, which includes 18 chapters contributed by wild turkey biologists specializing in various aspects of wild turkey life history and management. Hewitt's book was considered the most definitive source of wild turkey life history and management information until Dickson (1992) published his book 25 years later. One of the clear intentions of Dickson's book was to provide updated information about wild turkeys, and like Hewitt's book, it consists of chapters contributed by wild turkey biologists who were either experts on one of the five North American subspecies or specialists in various aspects of wild turkey life history, management, and conservation. Dickson's book has been a particularly valuable resource because it provides detailed information about each of the five subspecies of wild turkeys in North America. Perhaps the most recent, comprehensive source of information on wild turkeys is the life history account (McRoberts et al. 2014) provided by the Birds of North America Online program of the Cornell Laboratory of Ornithology (2018).

Direct assistance from wildlife scientists at some of the various agricultural universities in Texas is also available. Wildlife faculty at the Caesar Kleberg Wildlife Research Institute at Texas A&M University–Kingsville, Texas A&M University, Texas Tech University, Stephen F. Austin State University, Tarleton State University, and the Borderlands Research Institute at Sul Ross State University have conducted research on wild turkeys in Texas and can be of service to landowners seeking assistance with wild turkey management.

Literature Cited

Alldredge, B. E., J. B. Hardin, J. Whiteside, J. L. Isabelle, S. Parsons, W. C. Conway, and J. C. Cathey. 2014. Eastern wild turkeys in Texas: biology and management. Texas AgriLife Extension Publication WF-011. Texas A&M University, College Station, USA.

Campo, J. J., and J. G. Dickson. 1990. The Eastern wild turkey in Texas. Texas Parks and Wildlife Department Report PWD-8R-7100–137B-2/90. Texas Parks and Wildlife Department, Austin, USA.

Cathey, J. C., S. Locke, D. Ransom Jr., S. J. DeMaso, T. W. Schwertner, and B. Collier. 2007a. Habitat appraisal guide for Rio Grande wild turkey. Texas AgriLife Extension Publication SP-317. Texas A&M University, College Station, USA.

Cathey, J. C., K. Melton, J. Dreibelbis, B. Cavney, S. L. Locke, S. J. DeMaso, T. W. Schwertner, and B. Collier. 2007b. Rio Grande wild turkey in Texas: biology and management. Texas AgriLife Extension Report B-6198. Texas A&M University, College Station, USA.

Conway, W. C., C. E. Comer, G. H. Calkins, and J. Isabelle. 2010. Restoring wild turkey to East Texas: past and present. Faculty Publications Paper 376. Stephen F. Austin State University, Nacogdoches, Texas, USA.

Cook, R. L., and H. G. Gore. 1984. Learn about turkey. Pittman-Robertson Project FW-14-C. Texas Parks and Wildlife Department, Austin, USA.

Cornell Laboratory of Ornithology. 2018. https://birdsna.org/Species-Account/bna/home. Accessed July 31, 2018.

Dickson, J. G. 1992. The wild turkey: biology and management. Stackpole Books, Mechanicsburg, Pennsylvania, USA.

Hewitt, O. H., editor. 1967. The wild turkey and its management. The Wildlife Society, Washington, DC, USA.

McRoberts, J. T., M. C. Wallace, and S. W. Eaton. 2014. Wild turkey (*Meleagris gallopavo*). Account 22 in A. Poole, editor. The birds of North America online. Cornell Laboratory of Ornithology, Ithaca, New York. USA. http://bna.birds.cornell.edu/bna/species/022. Accessed July 29, 2016.

Mosby, H. S., and C. O. Handley. 1943. The wild turkey in Virginia: its status, life history and management. Pittman-Robertson Projects. Virginia Division of Game, Commission of Game and Inland Fisheries, Richmond, USA.

National Park Service. 2018. Wild turkey. https://www.nps.gov/blue/learn/nature/wild-turkey.htm. Accessed July 31, 2018.

National Wild Turkey Federation. 2015. http://www.nwtf.org. Accessed July 29, 2016.

Natural Resources Conservation Service. 1999. Wild turkey (*Meleagris gallopavo*). Fish and Wildlife Habitat Management Leaflet Number 12. https://www.nrcs.usda.gov/Internet/FSE_DOCUMENTS/nrcs143_009939.pdf. Accessed August 14, 2018.

Schorger, A. W. 1966. The wild turkey: its history and domestication. University of Oklahoma Press, Norman, USA.

Suarez, R. 2002. Texas turkey talk. Texas Parks and Wildlife Department Report PWD BK W700–827. Texas Parks and Wildlife Department, Austin, USA.

Texas A&M AgriLife Extension. 2018. Wildlife and fisheries sciences. https://agrilifeextension.tamu.edu/programs/wildlife-fisheries-sciences. Accessed August 14, 2018.

Texas Parks and Wildlife Department. 2015. Turkey in Texas. https://tpwd.texas.gov/huntwild/wild/game_management/turkey/index.phtml. Accessed July 28, 2016.

US Fish and Wildlife Service. 2017. Wild facts about that Thanksgiving bird. https://www.fws.gov/news/ShowNews.cfm?_ID=36179&ref=wild-facts-about-that-thanksgiving-bird-. Accessed July 31, 2018.

US Forest Service. 2018. Rocky Mountain Research Station publication series. https://www.fs.fed.us/rmrs/publications/series?field_citation_value_op=word&field_citation_value=turkey&field_abstract_value_op=word&field_abstract_value=. Accessed July 31, 2018.

Appendix 2

Scientific Names

Plants

Common name	Scientific name
Alfalfa	*Medicago sativa*
American beautyberry	*Callicarpa americana*
American elm	*Ulmus americana*
Anacua	*Ehretia anacua*
Annual ryegrass	*Lolium multiflorum*
Ashe juniper	*Juniperus ashei*
Austrian winter pea	*Pisum sativum*
Bahia grass	*Paspalum notatum*
Bald cypress	*Taxodium distichum*
Beggarweed	*Desmodium* spp.
Big bluestem	*Andropogon gerardii*
Blackberry	*Rubus fruticosus*
Blackbrush	*Coleogyne ramosissima*
Black cherry	*Prunus serotina*
Blackjack oak	*Quercus marilandica*
Black willow	*Salix nigra*
Bladderpod	*Lesquerella* spp.
Blueberry	*Vaccinium crassifolium*
Blue grama	*Bouteloua gracilis*
Bluewood	*Condalia hookeri*
Box elder	*Acer negundo*
Bristlegrass	*Setaria* spp.
Brownseed paspalum	*Paspalum plicatulum*
Buffalograss	*Bouteloua dactyloides*
Buffelgrass	*Cenchrus ciliare*
Burr oak	*Quercus macrocarpa*
Buttonbush	*Cephalanthus occidentalis*
Canada wildrye	*Elymus canadensis*
Cedar elm	*Ulmus crassifolia*

Common name	Scientific name
Cenizo	*Leucophyllum frutescens*
Chufa	*Cyperus esculentus*
Clover	*Trifolium* spp.
Coastal Bermuda grass	*Cynodon dactylon*
Coma	*Sideroxylon lanuginosum*
Common rye	*Secale cereale*
Corn	*Zea mays*
Cowpea	*Vigna unguiculata*
Crabgrass	*Digitaria* spp.
Creeping bundleflower	*Desmanthus virgatus*
Curly mesquite	*Hilaria belangeri*
Desert yaupon	*Schaefferia cuneifolia*
Douglas-fir	*Pseudotsuga menziesii*
Doveweed	*Croton texensis*
Dropseed	*Sporobolus* spp.
Eastern red cedar	*Juniperus virginiana*
Elm	*Ulmus* spp.
Euphorbia	*Euphorbia* spp.
False dandelion	*Pyrrhopappus* spp.
Filaree	*Erodium* spp.
Flat sedge	*Cyperus* spp.
Flowering dogwood	*Cornus florida*
Granjeno	*Celtis pallida*
Ground cherry	*Physalis viscosa*
Guajillo	*Senegalia berlandieri*
Guayacan	*Guaiacum angustifolium*
Gum bumelia	*Sideroxylon lanuginosum*
Hairy grama	*Bouteloua hirsuta*
Hairy vetch	*Vicia villosa*
Hickory	*Carya* spp.
Honey mesquite	*Prosopis glandulosa*
Huisache	*Vachellia farnesiana*
Indiangrass	*Sorghastrum nutans*
Indigo bush	*Amorpha fruticosa*
Kentucky bluegrass	*Poa pratensis*
Kidneywood	*Eysenhardtia texana*
Kinnikinnick	*Arctostaphylos uva-ursi*
Kleberg bluestem	*Dichanthium annulatum*
Lablab	*Lablab purpureus*

Common name	Scientific name
Limber pine	*Pinus flexilis*
Lime prickly ash	*Zanthoxylum fagara*
Little barley	*Hordeum pusillum*
Little bluestem	*Schizachyrium scoparium*
Live oak	*Quercus virginiana*
Loblolly pine	*Pinus taeda*
Longleaf pine	*Pinus palustris*
Milk pea	*Galactia* spp.
Milk vetch	*Astragalus* spp.
Mung bean	*Vigna radiata*
Mustang grape	*Vitis mustangensis*
Netleaf hackberry	*Celtis laevigata* var. *reticulata*
Oats	*Avena sativa*
Panic grass	*Panicum* spp.
Partridge pea	*Chamaecrista fasciculata*
Paspalum	*Paspalum* spp.
Pecan	*Carya illinoinensis*
Persimmon	*Diospyros* spp.
Pinyon pine	*Pinus edulis*
Plains cottonwood	*Populus deltoides*
Plum	*Prunus* spp.
Poison ivy	*Toxicodendron radicans*
Ponderosa pine	*Pinus ponderosa*
Post oak	*Quercus stellata*
Prickly pear	*Opuntia* spp.
Ragweed	*Ambrosia psilostachya*
Redberry juniper	*Juniperus pinchotii*
Rescue grass	*Bromus unioloides*
Ryegrass	*Lolium multiflorum*
Sage	*Artemisia* spp.
Salt cedar	*Tamarix ramosissima*
Shin oak	*Quercus havardii*
Shortleaf pine	*Pinus echinata*
Sideoats grama	*Bouteloua curtipendula*
Signal grass	*Brachiaria* spp.
Silverleaf nightshade	*Solanum elaeagnifolium*
Silver maple	*Acer saccharinum*
Skunkbush sumac	*Rhus trilobata*
Slash pine	*Pinus elliottii*

Common name	Scientific name
Slippery elm	*Ulmus rubra*
Southern magnolia	*Magnolia grandiflora*
Soybean	*Glycine max*
Spanish dagger	*Yucca faxoniana*
Spiny hackberry	*Celtis ehrenbergiana*
Sugar hackberry	*Celtis laevigata*
Sweetgum	*Liquidambar* spp.
Switchgrass	*Panicum virgatum*
Tasajillo	*Cylindropuntia leptocaulis*
Texas bluegrass	*Poa arachnifera*
Texas cupgrass	*Eriochloa sericea*
Texas mountain laurel	*Sophora secundiflora*
Texas persimmon	*Diospyros texana*
Texas red oak	*Quercus buckleyi*
Triticale	*Triticale hexaploide*
Watercress	*Nasturtium officinale*
Western soapberry	*Sapindus saponaria*
Wheat	*Triticum aestivum*
White ash	*Fraxinus americana*
White fir	*Abies concolor*
White oak	*Quercus alba*
White tridens	*Tridens albescens*
Wild cherry	*Prunus avium*
Wild grape	*Vitis* spp.
Wild onion	*Allium* spp.
Wild tobacco	*Nicotiana repanda*
Windmill grass	*Chloris* spp.
Wood sorrel	*Oxalis* spp.
Yaupon	*Ilex vomitoria*

Birds

Common Name	Scientific Name
American crow	*Corvus brachyrhynchos*
Attwater's prairie chicken	*Tympanuchus cupido attwateri*
Blue jay	*Cyanocitta cristata*
Common raven	*Corvus corax*
Eastern wild turkey	*Meleagris gallopavo silvestris*
Florida wild turkey	*Meleagris gallopavo osceola*

Common Name	Scientific Name
Golden eagle	*Aquila chrysaetos*
Gould's wild turkey	*Meleagris gallopavo mexicana*
Graylag goose	*Anser anser*
Great horned owl	*Bubo virginianus*
Merriam's wild turkey	*Meleagris gallopavo merriami*
Northern bobwhite	*Colinus virginianus*
Ocellated turkey	*Meleagris ocellata*
Red-cockaded woodpecker	*Picoides borealis*
Red-tailed hawk	*Buteo jamaicensis*
Rio Grande wild turkey	*Meleagris gallopavo intermedia*
South Mexican turkey	*Meleagris gallopavo gallopavo*

Mammals

Common name	Scientific name
Armadillo	*Dasypus novemcinctus*
Bobcat	*Lynx rufus*
Coyote	*Canis latrans*
Deer mouse	*Peromyscus leucopus*
Feral hog	*Sus scrofa*
Gray fox	*Urocyon cinereoargenteus*
Mountain lion	*Felis concolor*
Opossum	*Didelphis virginiana*
Raccoon	*Procyon lotor*
Red fox	*Vulpes vulpes*
Striped skunk	*Mephitis mephitis*
White-tailed deer	*Odocoileus virginianus*

Reptiles

Common Name	Scientific Name
Texas rat snake	*Elaphe obsoleta lindheimeri*

Contributors

WILLIAM P. KUVLESKY JR. is a professor and assistant dean of the Dick & Mary Lewis Kleberg College of Agriculture and Natural Resources at Texas A&M University–Kingsville and a research scientist at the Caesar Kleberg Wildlife Research Institute. He is coauthor of *The Upland and Migratory Webless Game Birds of Texas*, a chapter contributor to *Texas Quails: Ecology and Management*, and a coeditor of *Quail V: Proceedings of the Fifth National Quail Symposium*.

LEONARD A. BRENNAN is a professor and C. C. Winn Endowed Chair for Quail Research at the Caesar Kleberg Wildlife Research Institute. He is the senior coauthor of *The Upland and Migratory Webless Game Birds of Texas*, coeditor of *Quantitative Analyses in Wildlife Science and Texas Bobwhites*, and coeditor of *Wildlife Science: Connecting Research and Management* and editor of *Texas Quails: Ecology and Management*. He is also a former editor of the *Journal of Wildlife Management*, *Wildlife Society Bulletin*, and a fellow of the Wildlife Society and American Ornithological Society.

J. ALFONSO ORTEGA-S. is a research scientist at the Caesar Kleberg Wildlife Research Institute. He is coauthor of *White-tailed Deer Habitat: Ecology and Management on Rangelands* and coeditor of *Wildlife Ecology and Management in Mexico, both also published in Spanish.*

DAMON L. WILLIFORD is a natural resource specialist III at the Texas Parks and Wildlife Department, Perry R. Bass Marine Fisheries Research Station. He is coauthor of *The Upland and Migratory Webless Game Birds of Texas* and a chapter contributor to *Quantitative Analysis in Wildlife Science*.

JASON B. HARDIN is the Turkey Program leader for the Texas Parks and Wildlife Department. He is a chapter contributor to *Texas Quails.*

HUMBERTO L. PEROTTO-BALDIVIESO is an assistant professor and research scientist at the Caesar Kleberg Wildlife Research Institute.

LANDON C. FRITZ is a wildlife biologist for a private South Texas ranch.

CLAYTON D. HILTON is the Jo and Bruce Gunn endowed director of veterinary technology at Texas A&M University–Kingsville and a wildlife veterinarian for the Caesar Kleberg Wildlife Research Institute.

FRED C. BRYANT is the development director at the Caesar Kleberg Wildlife Research Institute. He is a coauthor of *White-tailed Deer: Their Foods and Management in the Cross Timbers*; *Wildlife Habitat Management on Forestlands, Rangelands, and Farmlands*; *Ranch Management: Integrating Cattle, Wildlife and Range*; and *Texas Bobwhites.*

STEVE A. NELLE, a retired range conservationist and wildlife biologist, spent 35 years with the Soil Conservation Service and Natural Resources Conservation Service.

BRANDON M. MITCHELL is a private lands biologist working on the Texas Gulf Coast.

NOVA J. SILVY is a regents professor and senior faculty fellow in the Department of Wildlife and Fisheries Sciences at Texas A&M University. He is coeditor of *Kansas Upland Game Birds* and editor of the seventh and eighth editions of *The Wildlife Techniques Manual*. He contributed a chapter to *Whitetailed Deer: Ecology and Management*, two chapters to *Ecology and Management of the Mourning Dove*, two chapters to *Research and Management Techniques for Wildlife and Habitats*, a chapter to *Wildlife Research in Texas*, a chapter to the *Handbook of Texas*, a chapter to *Texas Master Naturalist Statewide Curriculum*, a chapter to *Managing Wildlife in the Southwest: New Challenges for the 21st Century*, two chapters to *Texas Quails: Ecology and Management*, a chapter to *Ecology, Conservation, and Management of Grouse*, two chapters to *The Wildlife Techniques Manual*, two chapters to *Wildlife of Mexico*, a chapter to *Becoming a Wildlife Professional*, and two chapters to *Wildlife Ecology and Management in Mexico*. He is also coeditor of *The Greater Prairie Chicken: A National Look*, and senior editor of *Dove Biology, Research, and Management in Texas*.

Index

Other Books in the Perspectives on South Texas Series

Racial Borders: Black Soldiers along the Rio Grande
James N. Leiker

Nesting Birds of a Tropical Frontier: The Lower Rio Grande Valley of Texas
Timothy Brush

White-Tailed Deer Habitat: Ecology and Management on Rangelands
Timothy E. Fulbright and J. Alfonso Ortega-S.

Texas Quails: Ecology and Management
Leonard A. Brennan

Ecología y Manejo de Venado Cola Blanca
Timothy E. Fulbright and J. Alfonso Ortega-S.

Petra's Legacy: The South Texas Ranching Empire of Petra Vela and Mifflin Kenedy
Jane Clements Monday and Francis Brannen Vick

Plants of Deep South Texas: A Field Guide to the Woody and Flowering Species
Alfred Richardson

African Americans in South Texas History
Bruce A. Glasrud

Beef, Brush, and Bobwhites: Quail Management in Cattle Country
Fidel Hernández and Fred S. Guthery

Upland and Webless Migratory Game Birds of Texas
Leonard A. Brennan

Wildlife Ecology and Management in Mexico
Edited by Raul Valdez and J. Alfonso Ortega-S

Photographic Guide to the Vegetation of the South Texas Sand Sheet
Dexter Peacock and Forrest S. Smith